Fundraising M

Analysis, planning and practice

Second edition

This comprehensive introduction to fundraising management provides a thorough grounding in the principles underpinning professional practice. Much more than a 'how-to' guide, the book critically examines the key issues in fundraising policy, planning and implementation, and introduces the most important management tools available to the modern fundraiser.

Fully revized and updated, this new edition is packed with examples and case studies from around the world. It covers every important aspect of the fundraising process, including:

- Planning
- Donor recruitment and development
- Community fundraising
- Corporate fundraising
- Legacy fundraising
- Trust and foundation fundraising
- Legal and ethical frameworks for fundraising

Fundraising Management includes new material on managing fundraising teams, the use of electronic media in fundraising and group dynamics and leadership. This groundbreaking text has been designed primarily to complement the course offered by the Institute of Fundraising, but is a useful text for all fundraising students and professionals.

Adrian Sargeant is the Robert F. Hartsook Professor of Fundraising at Indiana University – Purdue University, USA. He also hold positions at Bristol Business School, UK and Queensland University of Technology, Australia.

Elaine Jay is a specialist in individual fundraising with over 18 years of experience. She has worked with a number of UK charities, including the RSPCA, as well as with Amherst Direct Marketing, WWAV Rapp Collins and Personal Fundraising Partnership. She has worked as a consultant for the past six years.

Fundraising Management

Analysis, planning and practice

Adrian Sargeant and
Elaine Jay

Second edition

Routledge
Taylor & Francis Group

LONDON AND NEW YORK

Second edition published 2010
by Routledge
2 Park Square, Milton Park, Abingdon, Oxon OX14 4RN

Simultaneously published in the USA and Canada
by Routledge
711 Third Avenue, New York, NY 10017

*Routledge is an imprint of the Taylor & Francis Group,
an Informa business*

First published 2010
© 2004, 2009 Adrian Sargeant and Elaine Jay

Typeset in Perpetua and Bell Gothic by Keyword Group Ltd.
Printed and bound in Great Britain by TJ International, Padstow

All rights reserved. No part of this book may be reprinted or reproduced or
utilized in any form or by any electronic, mechanical, or other means, now
known or hereafter invented, including photocopying and recording, or in any
information storage or retrieval system, without permission in writing from the
publishers.

British Library Cataloguing in Publication Data
A catalogue record for this book is available from the British Library

Library of Congress Cataloguing in Publication Data
Sargeant, Adrian.
Fundraising management: analysis, planning and practice / Adrian Sargeant and
Elaine Jay.
p. cm.
Includes bibliographical references and index.
1. Fund raising–Management. I. Jay, Elaine. II. Title.
HV41.2.S27 2009
658.15'224–dc22

2009018684

ISBN 13: 978-0-415-45153-6 (hbk)
ISBN 13: 978-0-415-45154-3 (pbk)
ISBN 13: 978-0-203-86635-1 (ebk)

ISBN 10: 0-415-45153-1 (hbk)
ISBN 10: 0-415-45154-x (pbk)
ISBN 10: 0-203-86635-5 (ebk)

Institute of
Fundraising

Contents

CONTENTS

Plates

Figures

Tables

Exhibits

Chapter 1

The history and development of fundraising practice

'I would leave this work immediately if I thought I were merely raising money. It is raising men that appeals to me.'

Charles Sumner Ward (1905)

OBJECTIVES

By the end of this chapter you should be able to:

■ Describe how the practice of fundraising evolved in the USA and UK.

■ Trace the history of modern fundraising techniques.

■ Describe the key changes that took place in fundraising practice in the twentieth century.

■ Describe the influence of Charles Sumner Ward on modern fundraising practice.

INTRODUCTION

In this text it is our intention to provide a comprehensive guide to modern fundraising practice, examining commonly used techniques such as the solicitation of major gifts and other less personal forms of communication such as direct mail and direct response television. We will also explore the use of emerging new media such as the Internet, digital broadcasting and SMS (short message service) text messaging.

It is our intention to draw on the best of professional experience and academic research on both sides of the Atlantic. The rationale for this is simple. The USA and the UK share a common history and the roots of fundraising are very similar from one country to another – a point that will be developed throughout this first chapter. Importantly, however, the twentieth century has seen a series of contrasting developments in both countries, where the focus has been strongly differentiated and where as a consequence each country can have much to learn from the other. In the USA the practice of major gift fundraising has been greatly refined and in the latter half of the twentieth century a succession of changes to tax legislation led to the creation of a number of distinctive products for this market and a creative approach to the stewardship of individual donors as a consequence. In the UK, the approach to fundraising has tended to focus on the solicitation of high numbers of lower value gifts, typically through the use of direct marketing techniques. It thus makes sense to pool this wealth of knowledge and experience and to add it to a rapidly emerging body of academic research focusing on donor behaviour, public perceptions of the voluntary sector and the use and abuse of specific fundraising tools. It is thus not our intention to provide yet another 'how-to' guide based solely on our professional experience. Rather, we blend theory with practice to provide a solid framework against which the organization and fundraising performance of specific nonprofits might be assessed.

The result we hope is a text that will for the first time provide fundraisers and students of fundraising alike access to an accumulated body of knowledge about how best to manage and operationalize all the key forms of modern fundraising. It is important to begin, however, by recognizing that the roots of such fundraising lay not in the recent past, but rather through an accumulation of practice over many centuries. Indeed, as will become clear in this first chapter, many ideas which seem modern at first glance have actually been around for a very long time indeed.

EARLY PHILANTHROPY AND CHARITY

The word philanthropy comes originally from the Greek and means 'love of mankind'. Robert L. Payton (1984:2) defined it as:

> voluntary giving, voluntary service and voluntary association, primarily for the benefit of others; it is also the 'prudent sister' of charity, since the two have been intertwined throughout most of the past 3500 years of western civilization.

Philanthropy is thus viewed as quite dispassionate and impersonal and concentrates on the resolution of the root causes of human issues. It is concerned with improving the quality of life for all members of a society, by 'promoting their welfare, happiness and culture' (Gurin and Van Til 1990:4).

Charity, by contrast is focused on the poor and is a term drawn from the religious tradition of altruism, compassion and empathy (Ylvisaker 1987). Over the years it has come to be defined somewhat differently from one country to another. In many countries, such as the UK, a charity is a distinctive legal form of organization that has a series of tax advantages enshrined in law. In the USA the term has a wider application and has come to mean simply serving the poor and needy (Gurin and Van Til 1990).

The concept of charity has been around since antiquity and nonprofit organizations of one form or another appear to have been with us since civilization began. References to voluntary giving can be traced back to the beginning of recorded history. The Pharaohs, for example, established some of the earliest charitable trusts, albeit in their case for the somewhat selfish purpose of ensuring the security and perpetuity of their final resting places. Of course, such early arrangements could hardly be described as philanthropic in nature, since the giving in question served only to ensure the deceased's footprint in history and hopefully a glorious afterlife. It was certainly not the intention of these early trusts to enrich the quality of life for others.

Early references to giving of a rather more 'charitable' nature can be found in the Old Testament. Religious sacrifices were commonly offered and the Old Testament of the Bible notes that the patriarch Jacob promised to give a tenth of all that God gave him. Indeed, we read that what is now known as the tithe was well established and organized. The Hebrews believed in sharing what they had with the poor who were traditionally, for example, the recipients of the harvest every seventh year.

Other forms of donation from this time include the vast treasures dedicated to the Delphic Oracle (first recorded as early as the fifth century BC) and the earliest recorded school endowments of Plato in Athens and Pliny at Como. Giving in its various forms has thus been around for many centuries.

FUNDRAISING AND THE RELIGIOUS TRADITION

The earliest recorded instances of formal fundraising activity are frequently linked to the activities of religious faiths. Mullin (1995), in particular, charts the significance of organized fundraising activity to early Jewish charity. In this tradition individual volunteers were clearly assigned within each community to take responsibility for specific fundraising tasks. This reflects the positive moral view of the volunteer fundraiser in the Jewish faith; to quote Rabbi Akiba: 'It is a greater virtue to cause another to give than to give yourself.'

In the Christian tradition the now common practice of the weekly church collection dates from the Dark Ages and in medieval times the Church commonly sent out professional fundraisers (*Quaestores*) to solicit gifts from the wealthy in order that the Church could both support itself and minister to the poor. Indeed, grand fundraising campaigns were often designed and initiated to support the creation of the great cathedrals across Northern Europe, from the Middle Ages onwards. Frequently, professional fundraisers were employed to ensure success. Detailed analytical planning and market segmentation accompanied much of the fundraising that supported these appeals and, as Mullin (1995) demonstrates, a rich variety of forms of fundraising were undertaken. As an example, Table 1.1 depicts the table of gift allocation associated with the fundraising for Troyes Cathedral; monies that were generated by a volunteer committee supported by professional fundraisers.

Fundraising was not only directed at the rich and powerful in society. Bishop (1898) identifies gifts from fundraising in schools, house-to-house and street collections, community fundraising events and even jumble sales, as significant in the generation of income for Milan's cathedral (see Plate 1.1) in 1386.

Over the centuries the Church developed many effective forms of fundraising practice, including the use of the now infamous 'indulgences'. Until Martin Luther publicly rebelled against the practice in 1517, the Church had for 500 years allowed individuals to pay for their sins by making a worldly donation to the Church. The system was simple. After confessing their sins to a priest, an individual would be set an appropriate penance. Ideally this would be dealt with in life, thereby expunging the sin. However, if the individual died before the penance had been paid, it still had to be dealt with before entry to heaven would be permitted. The solution

Table 1.1 *Troyes Cathedral fundraising (£s)*

	1389–90	1390–91	1412–13	1422–23
Appeals	176 (17 per cent)	186 (13 per cent)	160 (15 per cent)	34 (6 per cent)
Legacies	44 (4 per cent)	5 (4 per cent)	54 (5 per cent)	22 (4 per cent)
Citizens	29 (3 per cent)	386 (28 per cent)	40 (4 per cent)	70 (7 per cent)
Big gifts	440 (43 per cent)	250 (18 per cent)	100 (9 per cent)	100 (17 per cent)
Other	331 (32 per cent)	572 (41 per cent)	695 (66 per cent)	380 (66 per cent)
Total	1,020	1,399	1,049	606

Source: Mullin (1995:6, adapted from Murray 1987).

Plate 1.1
*Milan
Cathedral*

Source: © Mary Ann
Sullivan. Reproduced
with kind permission.

was simple. Having been furnished with an appropriate penance, individuals could buy an 'indulgence' to clear their 'debt'. This would reduce the years of punishment that could otherwise ensue and guarantee a speedy entrance to heaven. Indulgences could be purchased for a variety of good works including churches, hospitals and bridges, and were available from professional fundraisers as well as priests. As Mullin (2002:15) notes these indulgences 'exploited very private self interest, or harnessed the vulnerabilities of the poor to such self interest'. The Church has long since abandoned the practice.

THE DEVELOPMENT OF FUNDRAISING IN ENGLAND

Early fundraising in England was conducted against a backdrop of a suspicious state. Social, moral and religious upheavals regularly tore through British society and charities were inevitably bound up therein. One of the oldest surviving charities in England is Week's charity, an organization originally set up in the fifteenth century to provide faggots (bundles of sticks) for burning heretics, an activity supported by the government of the day. The state has therefore long had a vested interest in controlling what should, or should not, be considered charitable in nature. In Tudor times, those seeking to raise funds were well advised to stay within the law or risk fines, flogging, or worse. Even the donors themselves had to be mindful of this legislation, at one stage risking the punishment of having their ears forcibly pierced for giving to the unworthy.

Barbaric though this might sound, Tudor England was much concerned with public order and vagrancy, two concepts which governments of this time saw as inextricably linked. It was thus felt that giving should be strictly controlled to encourage the channelling of alms only to those who were referred to as the impotent poor (i.e. those who, by their age, health or other circumstances, were prevented from earning their own living). The able-bodied poor were to be encouraged to take responsibility for the amelioration of their own condition. In short they should be compelled to find work or starve. Such a preoccupation would, it was felt, preclude the possibility of their finding time to pose a threat to the state. As a consequence all legitimate beggars were licensed and private persons were forbidden to give to anyone not in possession of such a document.

Aside from giving of this very individual and personal nature, there were many great 'general' causes that donors could support at this time. Indeed, many of these are very similar to those we are encouraged to support today. In probably the earliest reference to 'appropriate' charitable causes,

William Langland's fourteenth-century work, the 'Vision of Piers Plowman', exalts rich and troubled merchants to gain full remission of their sins and thus a happy death by the fruitful use of their fortunes:

And therewith repair hospitals,
help sick people,
mend bad roads,
build up bridges that had been broken down,
help maidens to marry or to make them nuns,
find food for prisoners and poor people,
put scholars to school or to some other craft,
help religious orders and
ameliorate rents or taxes.

It was not until 1601, however, that English law officially recognized those causes that might be considered as charitable for the first time. The preamble to the Elizabethan Charitable Uses Act of that year appears to have much in common with the fourteenth-century work alluded to above, delineating as it did the legitimate objects of charity:

Some for the Relief of aged, impotent and poore people, some for Maintenance of sicke and maymed Souldiers and Marriners, Schooles of Learninge, Free Schooles and Schollers in Universities, some for Repair or Bridges, Ports, Havens, Causewaies, Churches, Seabanks and Highwaies, some for Educacion and prefermente of Orphans, some for or towards Reliefe Stocke or Maintenance of Howses of Correccion, some for Mariages of poore Maides, some for Supportacion, Ayde and Help of younge tradesmen, Handicraftesmen and persons decayed, and others for releife or redemption of Prisoners or Captives, and for the aide or ease of any poore inhabitants concerninge payment of Fifteens, setting out of Souldiers and other Taxes.

The Act was significant, not only because it outlined these objects, but also because it acknowledged that trustees and officials of charitable institutions sometimes misused the assets under their care and hence created a means by which they would be made accountable to the public. The law empowered the Lord Chancellor to appoint Charity Commissioners whose responsibility it was to investigate abuses of these charitable uses and to thereby protect the interests of those who had chosen to endow charitable organizations. It perhaps bears testimony to the quality of work undertaken by these early charity legislators that this Elizabethan Act was only repealed in the latter half of the twentieth century. Even today its influence is felt, as the preamble to the Act is still influential in determining those causes that might properly be regarded as being charitable in nature.

Of course, wealth in Elizabethan times was concentrated in the hands of a very small number of individuals, with the vast majority of English society being desperately poor. The wealthy, as now, elected to give by a variety of means. Gifts were made through the Church, directly to other individuals, or perhaps posthumously through the mechanism of a will. Indeed, the significance of this latter source of charitable donation should not be underestimated. Early records suggest that in the period 1480–1660 a variety of causes were supported by this means (see Table 1.2), with the rather low figure donated to religious causes reflecting the increasingly secular nature of the age. Average bequests varied substantially from region to region with the mean bequest to charity from Londoners an almost unbelievably high £255. 12s. 2d.

Table 1.2 Bequests to charity (1480–1660)

Nature of the cause	Per cent of bequests
Relief of the poor	36
Education (enlarging opportunity)	27
Religious causes	21
Social experiments	10
Fabric of communities	5

Source: Jordan (1964).

In other parts of the country the figure was somewhat lower; in Yorkshire, for example, a mere £28. 4s. 6d.

It is interesting to note that this pattern of giving remained relatively static right up until the late nineteenth century which saw a mushrooming in the number of registered charities created. Between 1837 and 1880 there were 9,154 new charities known to the Charity Commissioners and between 1880 and 1900 the number rose sharply to 22,607 (Williams 1989). This proliferation of charities brought with it many problems, notably the increasing number of requests made of the wealthier elements of society for support. It was perhaps time to broaden the appeal of charities.

THE DEVELOPMENT OF FUNDRAISING IN THE USA

The spirit of private philanthropy in the USA evolved from the attitude of the first settlers who came to America from England and Holland. These individuals continued the pattern of support common in Europe at that time and offered substantial sums of their own monies to build churches, schools and colleges. It is important to note, however, that the spirit and practice of American philanthropy is quite distinctive. While in Europe the state often elected to fund such initiatives through taxation, in the USA public needs often existed before government had been established to cater for them (Boorstin 1963). As a consequence voluntary organizations were formed to provide for basic human needs.

The revolution of 1777 led to the creation of many nonprofits as the public was 'swept up in waves of civic enthusiasm and religious fervor' (Hammack 1998:116), with many churches, clinics, schools, orphanages, libraries, colleges and hospitals being built as a consequence. Indeed, the founding fathers had been careful in drafting the constitution to make it difficult for their governments to levy taxes, take vigorous action or grant wealth and power to a privileged few. In the absence of strong taxation religion, education, healthcare and social services had to be funded by alternative means. State legislators responded by making it easier to create nonprofit organizations and began shaping them to the needs of society in a variety of ways, notably excluding them from property tax which at the time was the most significant source of government revenue. States also granted nonprofits land and began regulating their ability to create endowments.

It is important to note that this tradition of private philanthropy has continued and become what Marts (1966) regards as one of the most durable factors of American life. When Alexis de Tocqueville wrote in 1835 of his travels in America he was impressed by the willingness of the people to give freely of their own funds for social improvements (Probst 1962). He observed that when a community of citizens recognized a need for a church, school or hospital, they came together to form a committee, appoint leaders and donate funds to support it.

Today the Internal Revenue Code permits 20 categories of organization to be exempt from federal income tax and the majority of those that are able to receive tax-deductible contributions also fall into one specific category of the code: Section 501(c)(3). To qualify for this additional benefit organizations must operate to fulfil one of the following broad purposes: charitable, religious, scientific, literary or educational. A number of narrower purposes are also included: testing for public safety and prevention of cruelty to children or animals. The code also requires that no substantial part of an organization's activity should be focused on attempts to influence government, either directly or through participation in political campaigns.

Amongst the earliest major fundraising campaigns to take place in the USA were those designed to establish the famous colleges of Harvard in Massachusetts and William and Mary in Virginia. Americans gave generously to create these opportunities for their children, but additional support was often sought from overseas. Since the colleges of that era existed to educate both laymen and the clergy, ministers were frequently employed to fundraise on behalf of these great endeavours. The first example of this is credited as taking place in the early 1600s when three ministers were despatched from America to England to raise money for Harvard College. One such minister came back with £150 – a pretty good sum at the time. A second stayed in England as a minister, while the third met his death on the gallows, a fact which perhaps illustrates that fundraising has always been a somewhat perilous profession!

Other early fundraisers included Benjamin Franklin who undertook a number of campaigns and was known for the careful manner in which he planned them. When asked for his advice he was said to have remarked:

> In the first place, I advise you to apply to all those whom you will know will give something; next, to those whom you are uncertain whether they will give anything or not, and show them the list of those who have given; and lastly, do not neglect those whom you are sure will give nothing, for in some of them you may be mistaken.
>
> (Quoted in Gurin and Van Til 1990:14)

Indeed, much of the fundraising of the day and throughout the nineteenth century was conducted through the medium of personal solicitation, in some cases by paid solicitors. Church collections and the writing of begging letters were also common. It was not until 1829 that the first instance of committed or regular giving is reported. In that year a fundraiser by the name of Matthew Carey sought annual subscriptions of $2 or $3 to support a number of local institutions. Unfortunately only small sums were raised in total and the drive was eventually abandoned.

THE ROOTS OF RAISING MONEY BY MAIL

While direct forms of fundraising from individuals were common in both the UK and the USA prior to and right through the twentieth century, individual solicitations were not the only technique employed by fundraisers. The use of the mail for the purposes of fundraising also has a surprisingly long history. Indeed, there is evidence that professional coaching in the development of fundraising letters has existed since the Middle Ages. A fourteenth-century 'fundraising' handbook developed by monks at a Cistercian monastery in Austria, for example, advocated that an applicant's letter must consist of:

- a honeyed salutation
- a tactful Exordium (an introduction to the purpose of the application)
- a Narration (to set the scene with a description of the present situation or problem)

- a Petition (the detailed presentation of the application)
- a Conclusion (a graceful peroration).

The monks even went so far as to supply 22 model letters to illustrate the application of this approach, each of which was framed to offer a different justification for the merit of philanthropy. These included 'generosity to avoid ridicule'; 'the wealthy's obligation to give'; 'do as you would be done by'; 'to be kind is better than being an animal'.

The practice of developing 'model' letters appears to have been consistently adopted throughout the centuries that followed. In 1874 a set of 34 directories of such letters were found to be in use in London by a gang of begging letter impostors. The criminal fraternity of the time apparently found it remarkably easy to divest the wealthy of a significant share of their income by using these carefully crafted letters. So widespread was the problem that the London weekly newspaper *Truth* felt compelled to publish a regular gallery so as to issue warnings about such rogues.

THE ROOTS OF MODERN FUNDRAISING AND GIVING

Although individuals have been engaged in fundraising for centuries, fundraising as a serious profession did not really emerge until the mid-eighteenth century. It was common practice at this time to raise funds by assembling a list of suitable wealthy persons and inviting them to a special function or, more usually, dinner. In addition to potential benefactors, early fundraising manuals typically suggested that the guests for dinner should include a smattering of 'pretty young ladies' which was seen as essential if high-value gifts were to be solicited. It appears that male donors have always been keen to impress with the size of their charitable wallets.

Fundraising in this form, primarily as a series of dinners and special events, continued throughout the nineteenth century. Given that wealth remained concentrated in the hands of comparatively few individuals there was little motivation for charities to broaden the nature of the charitable appeal.

By the early twentieth century, however, the structure of society and the pattern of wealth distribution was beginning to change. There are many important influences on philanthropy and the fundraising profession that date from the turn of the century, including:

- the activity of a number of very wealthy philanthropists;
- one particularly innovative individual – Charles Sumner Ward;
- the intervention of the Great War.

We will now consider each in turn.

The great philanthropists

The influence of a number of great philanthropists was felt on both sides of the Atlantic around the turn of the century. Multimillionaires such as Andrew Carnegie, and J.D. Rockerfeller in the USA and Joseph Rowntree in the UK in the period 1885–1915, sought innovative ways of disposing of their surplus wealth. This was no easy task, since a way had to be found of diverting resources to those that were most in need and not squandered on those who would not draw benefit from the gift. To quote Carnegie, 'the worst thing a millionaire could do would be to give all his money to the unreclaimably poor'. A mechanism was thus sought to distribute private wealth with 'greater intelligence and vision than the individual donors themselves could have hoped to possess' (Gurin and Van Til 1990:15). It is thus in this period that a number of extraordinarily wealthy charitable trusts or foundations were established for the purpose of distributing the wealth of these great philanthropists. Fundraisers were therefore able to look to this new class of organization for support and the genre of the trust/foundation fundraiser was born.

The three charitable trusts set up by Joseph Rowntree in the UK in 1904 were charged with supporting religious, political and social causes. Like their sister organizations endowed by the likes of Carnegie in the USA, these organizations differed from those established in earlier centuries because:

- Their objectives were primarily to achieve some public purpose defined in the deed that established the organization. Such objectives were usually drafted so as to be broad and multiple in nature. The goal of a reorganized Rockerfeller Foundation in 1929, for example, became simply 'the advancement of knowledge throughout the world'.
- They departed from giving to individuals as a means to alleviate suffering, to address the more fundamental and controlling processes (Karl and Katz 1981). Joseph Rowntree wrote into his original trust deeds that much current philanthropic effort was 'directed to remedying the more superficial manifestations of weakness or evil, while little thought is directed to search out their underlying causes' (Rowntree 1904). He criticized the alleviation of Indian famines without examining their causes and directed that none of this three trusts should support hospitals, almshouses or similar institutions.
- They were legally incorporated bodies whose charitable and public purposes were duly recognized.

Much of the established wealth today has been created over the past 100 to 150 years. Indeed, great wealth has been accumulated by families and individuals over the past few decades alone. In the twentieth century a proliferation of famous philanthropists have emerged such as Clore, Getty, Gates, Hamlyn, Laing, Sainsbury, Weston and Wolfson, all of whom have different motivations for giving.

Some undoubtedly chose to support charity out of their own vanity, perhaps to secure their place in history or to excite a degree of timely public recognition for their works, giving out of a desire for self-aggrandizement, or in the search for some personal advantage or honour. Undoubtedly the majority, however, gave because they felt that it was the moral, religious and socially responsible thing to do with their wealth. As Carnegie famously remarked to Gladstone, 'he who dies rich dies disgraced'.

The rich give by many means. They can of course elect to give cash, but most would typically choose to avail themselves of a tax-efficient form of giving, enjoying the fact that the government must then direct substantial funds to their chosen interest, rather than to those of the government of the day. Those with considerable personal wealth may also elect to follow Carnegie and Rowntree's example and establish their own charitable trust for this purpose. Not only does this simplify the administration of tax matters (which need then only be dealt with once a year), it also means that the arduous decision of how much to give to charity need only be taken once a year too. The decision of what to support can then be satisfactorily left to administrators (Hurd and Lattimer 1994).

Other wealthy donors elect to give not only cash, but also the rights to one or more of their services. In the modern era Elton John is particularly well known for his generosity in donating all the proceeds of many of his public performances to charity and the novelist Catherine Cookson signed away the royalties from the novel *Bill Bailey's Lot* to charities.

Charles Sumner Ward

Charles Sumner Ward is credited with revolutionizing the practice of fundraising in both the UK and the USA. Indeed he is regarded by many as the father of modern fundraising. At the turn of the century he was the General Secretary of the YMCA in Grand Rapids, Michigan, USA, and spent most of his time raising funds to keep the doors of that organization open. He engaged in the traditional forms of major gift fundraising described above and in an endless round of dinners and public engagements. He was to radically change this approach with the creation of what he later referred to as the first ever 'intensive' campaign in history.

In 1905 he was charged with the task of raising $90,000 for a new YMCA building in Washington DC. Rather than dilute the campaign over a period of many months he reasoned that if plans were made well in advance it should prove possible to limit the fundraising to a single week. In reality Ward met his target well before the week was up, and he went on to administer many other successful campaigns, notably to help the War effort in 1916.

Ward's 'intensive' or 'whirlwind' campaigns were based on four general principles:

1 *Concentration of time* Ward believed that businessmen were willing to work for a worthy cause if only they could find the time. By telescoping an appeal for funds into the space of one or two weeks (depending on the size of a city) he was able to secure the active help of those business leaders who were needed to spearhead the drive. Shortening the campaign had the further advantage of keeping it, for its duration, front-page news in the community. Even when, in later years, Ward directed national campaigns for hundreds of millions and the appeal had to last longer, he always set the shortest feasible time. As he was fond of noting 'one can raise more money in six days than in six years'.

2 *Organization* Before the appeal for funds began, the groundwork of a campaign had to be laid with military precision. A large force of the most influential people in a city had to be built up and each individual was carefully informed of exactly what they would be responsible for. Above all, Ward saw the generation of a number of pace-setting gifts as essential. The day the pioneering campaign began the newspapers carried two front-page pictures, one of J.D. Rockerfeller who contributed $100,000 and one of a local newsboy who had contributed a humble single dollar. The inference was obvious, this was a big-money campaign, but it was also a campaign that concerned the humblest individual in society.

3 *Sacrifice* In soliciting workers one got nowhere by minimizing the time and effort required. To do that was to cut the ground from under a campaign. Far better to say that the job was a big job and then convince people that the cause was worth it.

4 *Education* The public must be made to see why it had a stake in the success of the appeal. First of all, the cause must be sound; then it must be brought to the public through all available media of publicity.

In respect of this latter element Ward ensured that in the months before a campaign news articles slowly built up the need. Civic pride was skilfully manipulated, 'What other cities have done Baltimore can do'. A notable facet of each campaign was the clock that he set up in conspicuous locations. He would set the hour hand at the Roman numeral XII under which would be written the amount of the goal. As the campaign moved forward the minute hand advanced ever closer to the hour to show how much nearer the goal had become. The clocks generated a substantial amount of public interest and excitement, which Ward complemented with a series of news stories. He was the first to employ publicity directors whose role was to keep all the newspapers supplied with material to keep the campaign on the front page.

Ward was also the first to recognize the significance of arranging a pace-setting gift in advance of a campaign. Such a gift would usually be from a tenth to a third of the total and would be conditional on the full amount being raised in the allotted time.

Such was his success that in 1912 Ward was asked to come to England to raise £300,000 for the central YMCA. Needless to say there was some considerable scepticism amongst conservative London that Ward's methods would curry favour with a British public not used to such brazen 'hard sell' techniques.

The Times editorial, however, was surprisingly supportive:

> It is scarcely necessary to say that this American scheme is no happy-go-lucky attempt, relying for its results on its novelty. Its fame as a new thing, undoubtedly helps it, but the success is really due to a knowledge of human nature and an extremely shrewd application of business principles in securing the advantage at the psychological moment.

Conservative London yielded and sponsors of the campaign were ultimately to include the Prime Minister, the Lord Mayor and Lord Northcliffe, publisher of The Times.

The profession of individual fundraising was changed forever.

The Great War

The advent of the First World War not only stimulated growth in charities registered to address the needs of victims, it also served to accelerate greater prosperity throughout society, further broadening the potential giving constituency to include all but the poorest elements of society. It was also at this time that 'modern' corporate philanthropy was born and for the first time wealthy corporations began to support need in society.

In the UK charitable appeals linked to the war proliferated, with over 15,000 war charities registered between 1916 and 1918 and significant innovation in fundraising practice occurred as a consequence. Fowler (1999) notes that by the end of the Great War, most of the techniques we are familiar with today had been invented and had reached peaks of varying efficiency.

> During the War itself there were at least three such innovations: flag days, spreading collections to communities overseas, and lotteries. In each case the idea was pioneered by one or more charities, then a host of other bodies copied it.
>
> (Fowler 1999:1)

At the outset of the War contributions to charity from the populace at large surged. As an example in the UK, the National Relief Fund, established in August 1914, achieved over £2 million within two weeks of its foundation. Seizing an entrepreneurial opportunity, fundraisers quickly developed 'Flower Days' (the then established medium by which cash collections were undertaken) into the more nationalistic Flag Day theme often characterized by the use of ribbons and other symbols of support. It is interesting to note how immediately recognisable this innovation is against the current vogue for charity ribbons and lapel badges. Their success was considerable and the organization behind them not inconsequential.

Donor motivation took on a prescient form. Early appeals for Belgian refugees offered the first real opportunity for ordinary members of the public to contribute to the war effort: 'most people in the movement were motivated at first not by an overwhelming compassion for the refugees – though of course, pity played its part – but by a simple desire to *do*, to be involved in the war effort' (Cahalan 1982:56).

11

WIDENING THE GIVING CONSTITUENCY

The proliferation of the number of charities around the turn of the century coincided with generally increasing levels of prosperity, a fact which provided the charities of the time with a unique opportunity to begin to expand what had traditionally been very low levels of participation in giving.

Advances in print technology played an important part in promoting the emergence of off-the-page advertising campaigns in newspapers supporting a wide range of appeals from the suffragette movement to the maintenance of private hospitals. Nonprofit communications became more generalist in nature and appeal advertisements became commonplace in the popular press. Advertising was generally becoming more sophisticated at this time as the nineteenth-century advertising agencies that had traditionally done little more than sell space on behalf of their patrons reacted to a sharp increase in competition. Agencies found themselves providing an ever wider range of services to their clients in order to secure business and hence their commission from the media owners. Nonprofits were initially slow to avail themselves of this service (although Dr Barnardo had already established concerted direct-marketing appeals in the UK before the turn of the nineteenth century), but by the advent of the First World War, with the help of their agencies, nonprofits were creating some of the most innovative and exciting advertising of the day. This learning was later developed and integrated with direct marketing by Quaker-inspired commercial philanthropists such as Cecil Jackson-Cole and Harold Sumption (Sumption1995).

The YMCA ad in Plate 1.2 dates from 1916, yet contains so much of what we would still consider today as 'best practice'. The proposition is a simple one: that everyone can give to help the cause. The ad is written in an informal style and engages the reader with a variety of different typefaces. It also presents bundles of need, illustrating what a donation at each level will achieve, together with a cut-out coupon which the donor can send in noting the amount of their gift. The coupon even carries a 'code' at the bottom so that fundraisers could ultimately assess the efficacy of advertising in many different magazines/newspapers.

The Barnado's ad in Plate1.3 was placed in the *Illustrated London News* in the same time period and prompts prospective donors to select the Easter Egg they can most afford to send. The range of prompted donations is quite wide; again suggesting that any sum will make a real difference to the children Dr Barnardo's was there to help. In the period 1910–1950 advertisements for three categories of charitable cause were particularly commonplace and it seemed as though these were the causes most indelibly printed on the British psyche. As Beveridge noted 'Britains favour sailors, animals and children – and in that order'.

Advertisements for good causes were also very common in the United States. Indeed it is interesting to note that the language and style of the early 1900s have many modern parallels. Plate 1.4 depicts a famous ad for the Red Cross which dates from the time of the First World War. The period also saw many other advances in individual fundraising with sales of donated goods, collection boxes and, following a post-regulation slump, charity flag days all proliferating.

In the early 1950s and throughout the 1960s a further revolution in giving behaviour was prompted by concern for famine and poverty abroad made graphically compelling through national newspaper advertisements and the development of structured direct marketing activity. Particularly noteworthy was a series of charity telefons conducted with great success on television channels on both sides of the Atlantic (Seymour 1966; Sumption 1995).

Common throughout these advances was the importance placed on the identification of need and the donors' effective response to it, stewarded in positive fashion by the professional fundraiser. Yet as direct marketing technology grew cheaper and more accessible to the nonprofit

Plate 1.2
Early YMCA advertisement

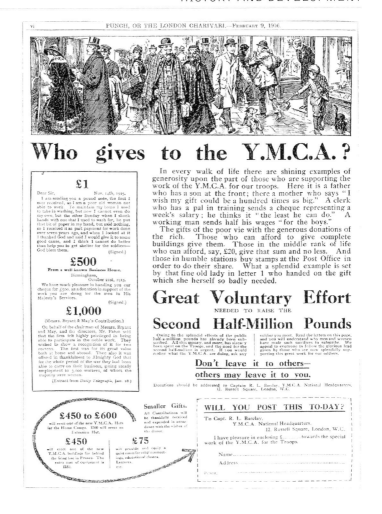

sector and as the early fundraising consultant pioneers were joined by others – notably, converts from commercial advertising agency practices (Harold Sumption, Redmond Mullin and George Smith to name but three) – volume of activity increased and with it public and media scepticism of the methods employed.

It was not until the 1980s, however, that perhaps the greatest changes began to take place in the manner that funds were raised from individuals. Advances in computer technology and the miniaturization thereof now made it possible for nonprofits to invest in a database for the very first time. The first to come on to the market were quite simple affairs that did little more than allow the organization to record the names, addresses and gifts made by their donors. More recent developments have allowed nonprofits to segment their donor base and target a wide variety of communications at an even wider variety of donor segments.

Fundraisers initially slow to adopt modern marketing concepts, strategies and personality in their own view of their role, embraced the methods of the commercial marketplace whole-heartedly from the early 1970s onwards. Professional institutes were established promoting the distinctive and positive role of the professional fundraiser in both the UK and the USA (Institute of Charity Fundraising Managers UK, 1983; National Society of Fundraising Executives USA, 1960). Academic research, textbooks and teaching of nonprofit fundraising and marketing were

13

Plate 1.3 *Early Barnardo's advertisement*   **Plate 1.4** *Early US advertisement*

're-invented' in relation to the new-found skills and disciplines associated with the development of marketing theory (Drucker 1990; Kotler and Andreasen 1991; Clarke and Norton 1992).

In the age of the relational database nonprofits can now establish almost one-to-one dialogues with their donors, ensuring that every communication they receive meets the expectation that a donor might have of the organization. For their part professional fundraisers are now 'relationship fundraisers' stewarding and supporting the lifetime value of prospective donors from first gift to, in the case of legacy fundraising, beyond the grave (Burnett 1992; Wilberforce 2001). In essence, contemporary nonprofits can develop a *silicon simulacrum* of the relationships that individuals might once have had with their butcher or baker. They can be addressed as individuals at a time that suits them with the products/services and 'asks' which experience tells the nonprofit they will find most appropriate.

CONCLUSION

The history of fundraising is much longer than many people believe. While corporate and trust fundraising are comparatively recent phenomena, nonprofits and fundraisers have been around since the start of recorded history. For centuries, the task of fundraising from individuals was largely conducted by the Church, the ministers of which employed many of the same methods of solicitation still commonly in use today. Even techniques such as the use of fundraising letters have been known and employed to good effect since the Middle Ages with copies of 'model' requests dating back over 500 years. While there may therefore be little new in individual fundraising, the twentieth century has certainly seen a number of innovations in the way in which these techniques have been deployed. Charles Sumner Ward's carefully integrated 'intensive' campaigns are certainly worthy of note, as are the advances in computer technology that in a way have brought fundraisers full circle. Until Ward's time all fundraising would undoubtedly have consisted of a series of one-to-one requests. The opening up of mass advertising media in the early part of the twentieth century allowed charities to move away from this to a 'one-to-many' approach. While in its simplest form much individual fundraising still falls into this latter category, the evolution of database technology is making it increasingly possible to return to a 'one-to-one' message. Exactly how this might be accomplished and the benefits thereof will form the focus of much of the rest of this book.

REFERENCES

Bishop Edmund (1898) 'How a Cathedral was Built in the Fourteenth Century – Milan Cathedral', cited in Bishop Edmund (1918) *Liturgica Historica*, Oxford University Press, Oxford.

Boorstin, D.J. (1963) *The Decline of Radicalism: Reflections on America Today*, Random House, New York.

Burnett, K. (1992) *Relationship Fundraising*, White Lion Press, London.

Cahalan, P. (1982) *Belgium Refugee Relief in England during the Great War*, Macmillan, London.

Clarke, S. and Norton, M. (1992) *The Complete Fundraising Handbook*, Directory of Social Change, London.

Drucker, P.F. (1990) *Managing the Non-profit Organization*, Butterworth-Heinemann, London.

Fowler, S. (1999) 'Voluntarism and Victory: Charity, the State and the British War Effort, 1914–1918'. Paper presented to the History of Charity Conference, University of Wales, Bangor, September 1999, p. 2.

Gurin, M.G. and Van Til, J. (1990) 'Philanthropy in its Historical Context', in Jon van Til and Associates (eds), *Critical Issues in American Philanthropy*, Jossey Bass, San Francisco, CA, pp.3–18.

Hammack, D.C. (1998) *Making of the Nonprofit Sector in the United States*, Indiana University Press, Indianapolis.

Hurd, H. and Lattimer, M. (1994) *The Millionaire Givers*, Directory of Social Change, London.

Jordan, W.K. (1964) *Philanthropy in England 1480–1660* George Allen and Unwin, London.

Karl, B.D. and Katz, S.N. (1981) 'The American Private Philanthropic Foundation and the Public Sphere 1890–1930', *Minerva*, XIX: 236–270.

Kotler, P. and Andreasen, A. (1991) *Strategic Marketing for Nonprofit Organizations*, Prentice Hall, New Jersey.

Marts, A.C. (1966) *The Generosity of Americans: Its Source, Its Achievements*, Prentice Hall, Englewood Cliffs, NJ.

Mullin, R. (1995) *Foundations for Fundraising*, ICSA, London.

Mullin, R. (2002) 'The Evolution of Charitable Giving', in C. Walker and C. Pharoah (eds), *A Lot of Give*, Hodder and Stoughton, London.

Payton, R.L. (1984) 'Major Challenges to Philanthropy'. Discussion Paper for Independent Sector, August.

Probst, G.E. (1962) 'The Happy Republic: A Reader', in de Tocqueville's *America*, Harper and Brothers, New York.

Rowntree, J. (1904) 'The Founders Memorandum', reprinted in L.E. Waddilove (1983), *Private Philanthropy and Public Welfare: The Joseph Rowntree Memorial Trust 1954–1979*, Allen and Unwin, London.

Seymour, H.J. (1966) *Designs for Fundraising*, McGraw-Hill, New York.

Sumption, H. (1995) *Yesterday's Trail-blazing and Pointers for Tomorrow*, Brainstorm Publishing, Hertford.

Wilberforce, S. (Ed.) (2001) *Legacy Fundraising*, 2nd edn, Directory of Social Change, London.

Williams, I. (1989) *The Alms Trade*: *Charities, Past Present and Future*, Unwin Hyman, London.

Ylvisaker, P.N. (1987) 'Is Philanthropy Losing Its Soul?', *Foundation News*, May/June, p. 3.

Part I

The fundraising planning process

Chapter 2

Fundraising planning
The fundraising audit

OBJECTIVES

By the end of this chapter you should be able to:

- Outline a process for developing a fundraising plan.
- Explain the purpose of a fundraising audit as the first part of such a process.
- Discuss the key information requirements of a fundraising audit.
- Understand the categories of information gathered in the audit, why these data are important and how such data can be used in planning.
- Utilize key tools commonly employed in the audit process such as PEST, SWOT and portfolio analyses.

INTRODUCTION

In this chapter it is our intention to outline a process that may be employed by nonprofits in planning the fundraising activities they will undertake. While the format may differ slightly from one organization to another, at its core a fundraising plan has three common dimensions.

1   *Where are we now?*   A complete review of the organization's environment and the past performance of the fundraising function. Only when the fundraising department has a detailed understanding of the organization's current strategic position in each of the donor markets it serves can it hope to develop meaningful objectives for the future.

2   *Where do we want to be?*   In this section of the plan the organization will map out what the fundraising department is expected to achieve over the duration of the plan. Typically there will be income-generation targets for the department as a whole and a series of 'sub-objectives' for each category of fundraising (e.g. individual, trust/foundation and corporate).

3   *How are we going to get there?*   This stage of the plan contains the strategy and tactics that the organization will adopt to achieve its targets. The strategy as we shall see in Chapter 4 specifies in general terms what the broad approach to fundraising will be, while the tactics supply the minutia of exactly how each form of fundraising will be undertaken.

In this chapter we will provide a generic framework for fundraising planning and concentrate our attention on the first of these three components of a fundraising plan. We will consider the information requirements an organization will have when it commences the planning process, the sources from which this information can be gathered and a range of analytical tools that can be used to help fundraisers interpret this information.

A PLANNING FRAMEWORK

Figure 2.1 contains a generic fundraising planning framework. Many organizations find it helpful to begin the development of the fundraising plan by restating their vision, mission and the objectives that the organization as a whole has set. A vision is a clear statement of the world that the nonprofit wants to see, while a mission statement maps out how they intend to make that world a reality. As an example, the vision of the National Society for the Prevention of Cruelty to Children (NSPCC) is: *'of a society where all children are loved, valued and able to fulfil their potential'*. Its role in achieving this (the organization's mission) is *'to end cruelty to children'*.

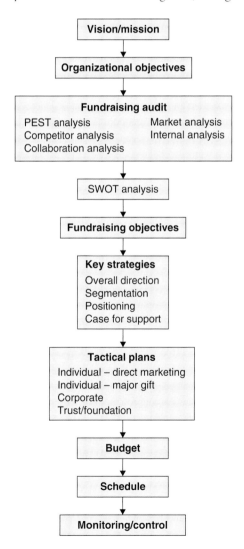

Figure 2.1 *Generic planning framework*

Organizational objectives provide more of the detail of how this will be achieved. They can be couched in terms of service delivery targets to beneficiaries, changes in societal attitudes towards the cause and so on.

Restating the mission and organizational objectives serves to focus the minds of fundraisers on what income is likely to be required and why this is necessary. In short it reminds the fundraising team of the reason for their existence and the impact that will be achieved if they are successful in raising the requisite funds. While it may sound a little trite to say this, the nature of the cause is often a strong motivating factor for all members of staff and fundraisers are no exception. Understanding why funds are needed is thus the fundamental starting point in fundraising planning.

Of course, it is important to recognize that while the director of fundraising may have had some input into the vision, mission and organizational objectives, it is unlikely that he/she will have actually written them. They are simply restated here as an overall guide to the fundraising plan that will follow.

A glance through a selection of nonprofit publicity material reveals that many nonprofits have been intuitively writing vision/mission statements for years, even if they prefer to use alternative terminology such as 'aims', 'purpose' or 'philosophy'. In truth the terminology is unimportant. What matters is that the organization can summarize in a few words its *raison d'être*. Not only does this aid planners in the manner described above, but it can become a remarkably useful reference point for potential donors. Supporters can see at a glance what the organization is trying to achieve and confidently initiate some form of relationship if they feel it will be appropriate.

A selection of other 'missions' is given in Exhibit 2.1

EXHIBIT 2.1 MISSIONS

The European Blues Association is a nonprofit organization and educational institute. Our aim is to be 'the resource' for our members and the general public who are interested in the historical past and the modern progression of the blues. We are dedicated to the appreciation and understanding of all aspects of the music and the African American culture from which it evolved.

The mission of Sue Ryder Care is to be first choice in both neurological and palliative care.

The British Lung Foundation raises funds for research into all lung diseases including asthma, cystic fibrosis and emphysema. We provide information on lung conditions and run a national support network for adults and children living with lung disease.

The mission of the World Wildlife Fund (WWF) is the conservation of nature. Using the best available scientific knowledge and advancing that knowledge where we can, we work to preserve the diversity and abundance of life on Earth and the health of ecological systems by

- protecting natural areas and wild populations of plants and animals, including endangered species;
- promoting sustainable approaches to the use of renewable natural resources; and
- promoting more efficient use of resources and energy and the maximum reduction of pollution. We are committed to reversing the degradation of our planet's natural environment and to building a future in which human needs are met in harmony with nature. We recognize the critical relevance of human numbers, poverty and consumption patterns to meeting these goals.

The reader will appreciate that in all these examples there is a noticeable absence of figures. Mission statements should address what the organization wishes to achieve, but in such a way that the mission can be adopted consistently for a reasonable period of time. It should not be necessary to readdress the mission on an annual basis, since it should serve only to provide the most general of signposts.

Indeed the specific detail of what an organization seeks to accomplish within each planning period would normally form part of the content of the organizational objectives. Drucker (1955) isolated what he believed to be eight aspects of operations where organizational objectives could be developed and maintained. These have been modified slightly below to relate them more specifically to the context of nonprofit organizations:

1   Market standing
2   Innovation
3   Productivity
4   Financial and physical resources
5   Manager performance and development
6   Employee/volunteer performance and attitude
7   Societal needs to be served
8   Public/social responsibility.

Clearly each of these areas has some relevance for fundraisers, even if many of them do not relate specifically to the fundraising function. It is important to realize that these objectives are stated for the organization as a whole to work towards. Their achievement will require a coordination of effort across all divisions/departments within the organization. Managers with responsibility for finance, human resources, service delivery and so on, will all have their part to play in ensuring that the organization delivers what it says it is going to deliver. It is for this reason that it is usual to restate the organizational objectives at the beginning of the fundraising plan. Fundraisers should then be able to isolate what they as individuals need to be able to achieve over the planning period to facilitate the achievement of these wider objectives. There would be little point, for example, in the fundraising department concentrating on raising funds for aspects of the organization's work that are not perceived as congruent with the organization's current goals and failing to raise money for those that are.

THE FUNDRAISING AUDIT

As we noted above, the fundraising planning process can be conceptualized as having three key components

1   Where are we now?
2   Where do we want to be?
3   How will we get there?

The fundraising audit specifically addresses the first of these elements. As such it is arguably the most crucial stage of the whole planning process since without a thorough understanding of the organization's current position it will be impossible for planners to develop any kind of sense of what they can expect to accomplish in the future. The fundraising audit is essentially a detailed review of any factors that are likely to impinge on the organization, taking into account both those generated internally and those emanating from the external environment. The fundraising audit is thus a systematic attempt to gather as much information as possible about the organization and its environment and, importantly, how these might both be expected to change and develop in the medium and longer term futures. A typical framework for a fundraising audit is included in Figure 2.1.

Macro factors

It is usual to begin the process by examining the wider or 'macro' environmental influences that might impact on the organization. Often these may be factors over which the organization itself has little control, but which will nevertheless affect the organization at some stage during the period of the plan. The framework utilized for this analysis is typically referred to as a PEST analysis and comprises the following elements:

- *Political factors* Political factors impacting on fundraising might include government attitudes to the nonprofit sector and recent or forthcoming legislative or regulatory changes that might affect the fundraising environment or fundraising performance, e.g. privacy legislation, changes in inheritance tax or additional fiscal incentives to increase giving.
- *Economic factors* Economic trends are relevant primarily as predictors of future donor behaviour. Trends in wealth, employment, tax, consumption and disposable income impact on all categories of funders from corporate givers and foundations through to individuals.
- *Socio/cultural factors* Key data here will include data on demographics and social attitudes, plus evidence of likely behavioural changes or significant shifts in societal values that might occur over the duration of the plan. For example, trends in levels of civic participation, changes in the formation of families, in levels of trust and confidence in the nonprofit sector and in patterns of working would be considered here.
- *Technological factors* Critical here will be factors such as the likely impact of developments in technology on the nonprofit sector and on fundraising techniques. Developments in web communications, mobile phone technology, automated bank payments and interactive TV would all, for example, fall under this category.

In each case the aim is to accumulate a list of all the pertinent factors and how these are expected to change over the planning period. It is best at this point in the process not to spend too much time deliberating over the impact that these factors might have on the organization, but rather to note them, detail how they might change and move on. The danger of precipitating a discussion at this stage is that other clues as to the impact these PEST factors might have will tend to emerge as the audit process progresses. It is therefore better to consider potential impacts *en masse* when the audit itself is complete. A sample PEST analysis for an environmental charity is provided in Exhibit 2.2

In researching these 'macro' trends the main challenge lies in the selection of accurate and pertinent information. As we are concerned here with writing a fundraising plan, all the points listed should have the potential to impact on the organization's ability to fundraise. They should also be based on careful research, not the gut feelings of the author. For this reason it would be usual to provide details of the reference that was used as the source for the data. The reader can then see which of the items are the opinions of the author and which were based on reported research or the opinions of others.

Data for PEST analyses are typically gathered through secondary sources via desk research, i.e. information is found through existing publications rather than being sourced through the

23

EXHIBIT 2.2 PEST ANALYSIS FOR A UK ENVIRONMENTAL CHARITY

Political

- Implications of Data Protection legislation.
- Introduction of Fund Raising Standards Board.
- Imposition of recycling targets both nationally and locally, raising awareness of the issue.[1]
- Implications of recent budgetary changes to levels of taxation and hence Gift Aid income.

Economic

- Pessimistic economic outlook, UK on the brink of a recession.[2]
- Potential rise in interest rates.[3]
- Falling levels of disposable income.[4]
- Rising unemployment.[5]

Socio-cultural

- Fall in the percentage of younger people in society (our traditional supporter base).[6]

- Greater awareness and concern on the part of the public about environmental issues.[7]
- Increased news coverage of environmental issues.
- Increased levels of activism on environmental issues.

Technological

- Digital television with multi-channels now the norm in UK households.
- Growth in time spent online, particularly in the time spent in online shopping.
- Rapid increase in popularity of social networking sites.[8]
- Rapid increase in the use of SMS text messaging for fundraising.
- Rapid growth in the use of e-mail for campaigning and fundraising.
- Increasing use of viral technologies.[9]
- Increasing use of search engine optimization.[10]

Note 1–10 indicate where details would be supplied of the reference sources for the data.

commissioning of new (or primary) research. In gathering information for a PEST analysis one would look at practitioner and academic journals, books and reports, often via online information databases such as ProQuest available through libraries and academic institutions or by searching the web more generally. Even a simple Google search can generate a lot of helpful data. Reports and publications published by trade bodies such as the Institute of Fundraising and the National Council for Voluntary Organizations (NCVO) could also be utilized. Many nonprofits find that much of the necessary information for the production of PEST analyses is already held internally in the form of publications and reports, or that staff have knowledge of where such information can be sourced. The role of the 'auditor' is often therefore to interview staff, find out what information they have on file or can help with, and manage the gathering of that data. In this scenario the auditor would then seek to update the data where appropriate, and fill in any gaps through further research.

It is important to note that simply identifying the key factors, however, is not enough, and that it is vital that as much data as possible are gathered against each factor to ensure that decision- makers are fully informed. For example, most nonprofits would identify 'increasing use of the Internet' as a key technological trend. Having identified this, the auditor would need to relate this factor to the context of the specific organization. They might hence collate information on the likely growth in users over the duration of the plan, on new features and developments, and on the current use of the Internet in fundraising.

Analysis of competitors

Accurate and full information on the activities, size and market position of competitor organizations is of vital importance to any nonprofit putting together a fundraising plan. The nonprofit marketplace is complex and crowded, with many organizations competing for a limited pool of support. In seeking to successfully raise funds it is therefore essential that an organization conduct a detailed analysis of the activities of key competitors and use this information to inform their own subsequent fundraising strategy.

Of course the starting point in conducting an analysis of the competition is to decide which competitors the organization should profile. There are a number of options:

- *Industry leaders*   The fundraising team will undoubtedly be aware of those competitor organizations that they regard as particularly outstanding in their fundraising activity. From these industry leaders it may be possible to learn a great deal about successful fundraising practice and to borrow exciting new and innovative ideas in respect of the best ways to solicit funds. These nonprofits may be working in the same field, but could equally be working elsewhere in the sector serving entirely different needs. They are thus selected purely on the basis of the quality/originality of the fundraising they undertake.
- *Other nonprofits serving the same cause*   Some nonprofits will assess the strategy and performance of those charities that they perceive to be in direct competition with themselves since they serve the same broad category of cause (e.g. children, animal welfare, environmental defence). The goal here is to gather sufficient data to benchmark the activities of the focal nonprofit against those of its key competitors. The nature of the activities undertaken, the quality of the promotional materials produced and the estimated or actual cost-effectiveness of the fundraising undertaken will all be of interest.
- *Nonprofits of a similar size*   A further strategy employed by some nonprofits is to look at organizations of a similar size to themselves irrespective of the category of cause served. This is a strategy particularly favoured by larger nonprofits who want to ensure that their performance is comparable with organizations of similar size and stature. Once again, organizations will look at the forms of fundraising undertaken, the promotional materials produced and the performance achieved. This can all be used to assist in benchmarking the performance of the focal organization and in highlighting areas of weakness.

Irrespective of the approach adopted there are a number of common categories of information that are typically gathered.

- *Financial performance*   It will generally be instructive to look at how key competitors are performing. This might include the levels of various categories of income they are able to generate and the investment they have made to secure this. This will give the auditor a sense of the returns that might be expected from various forms of fundraising and how the performance of the focal nonprofit might compare with this. It will also be useful to scrutinize those organizations that seem to be achieving significant growth, or doing particularly well at certain forms of fundraising. The reasons for this performance can be ascertained and the data used to inform an organization's own fundraising strategy. If only a few competitors are to be scrutinized it may be possible to obtain copies of their annual reports. If a larger number are to be analysed it would probably be preferable to use an online information source such as www.guidestar.org.uk. More detailed benchmarking data is available in the UK from the Institute of Fundraising, the public information website www.charityfacts.org and the Centre for Inter-Firm Comparisons (which produces a study entitled *Fundratios*). Benchmarking is a subject we address in detail in Chapter 15.

■ *Competitor objectives and ambitions*   Unfortunately while published accounts provide a reasonably reliable picture of the past performance of nonprofit competitors, what is typically of greater interest is how these competitors might behave in the future. It is thus of immense value to research what the objectives and ambitions of those key competitors might be. Clearly if a nonprofit involved in related work has plans for greatly expanding their work, they could prove to be a particularly aggressive competitor for funds in the months and years ahead. It is essential to be aware of changes such as these and to prepare a strategic response.

■ *Past, present and future strategies*   Finally it will also be useful to obtain data about the fundraising strategies/tactics of key competitors. The fundraiser will want to ask questions such as: What kinds of fundraising have they been engaged with in the past? How successful were these? Why was this performance achieved? Which audiences were addressed? What fundraising is being conducted now? How might this change in the future? What is unusual or distinctive about this fundraising? How does it differ from our own? The answers to all these questions have the capacity to inform how an organization can defend itself against competition and improve the quality of its own fundraising activity. Of course, tracking down this kind of information is not easy, but the sector press or local/national media can often contain a lot of information about aspects of fundraising strategy.

One of the most useful ways to gather information on the fundraising activity of competitor organizations is through 'mystery shopping' (i.e. sending in a donation to the organization, and then monitoring the subsequent communications received). Many nonprofits run an ongoing programme of 'mystery shopping' across a range of competitors to track strategies, tactics and creative approaches.

When information has been gathered the auditor will need to present and summarize it in a suitable format. This might involve a comparative study, or an exercise plotting the position of competitors against various axes. One useful tool is to run an analysis of the apparent strengths and weaknesses of each competitor, and an assessment of how their activities might impact on the focal organization in the future.

Potential collaborators

Of course there may be many instances where instead of viewing other nonprofits as competitors, it makes more sense to partner with them to the advantage of all concerned. Such partnerships may open up access to new sources of funds, new markets or simply allow the partner organizations to take advantage of economies of scale and thus lower their costs of fundraising. It may not be economic, for example, for smaller nonprofits to undertake corporate fundraising on their own. Forging an alliance with other 'complementary' or related nonprofits can create a pool of shared resources that would facilitate fundraising from this potential new audience.

Many forms of community fundraising are also conducted collaboratively, where smaller non-profits get together to run a joint campaign for the benefit of a local community and share the costs associated with promoting the campaign.

Nonprofits can also collaborate by sharing lists of donors. This is a practice common in the UK although it tends to be limited to lower value supporters. Nonprofits tend not to share the details of their highest value givers!

Thus in conducting a fundraising audit it will be instructive to consider examples of where organizations have collaborated successfully in the past and the factors that led to that success. The nonprofit should look to see what it could learn from these collaborations and whether there might be any way in which it could work in partnership with others. If this is felt to be desirable it will be instructive to conduct background research into potential partners and to explore how such relationships might develop. An approach to one or more partners could then be included in the fundraising strategy/tactics.

Market factors

The next stage of the audit concerns the gathering of data in respect of the various donor markets the organization is addressing. It may therefore be sensible to structure this section by considering each donor market (e.g. Individuals, Corporates, Trusts, Foundations, Community) in turn. Each of these sections should then be further subdivided into identifiable segments or groups of donors, with current performance and likely future developments considered for each group.

Typically a nonprofit needs to understand:

■ *Who donates to their organization?* Are there certain types of people, corporates or foundations that have elected to offer their support? In the case of individuals, do these individuals have distinctive demographic or lifestyle characteristics that help the organization to understand more about the nature of their target audience?

■ *Donor motivations* Why do each group of donors elect to support the organization? What if anything do they expect to gain in return for their gift? How can the organization best reflect these motives in their fundraising communications?

■ *Donor needs/preferences* What kinds of communications do donors find appropriate? How do they view the communications they currently receive? Could these be improved in some way?

■ *Donor behaviour* Organizations need to understand how donors behave when they give to the organization. How much does each group or segment of donors give? Do higher value donors have any distinctive characteristics or needs? Are certain types of donor more likely to terminate their support than others? What are the primary reasons why donors terminate their support? Is there anything that may be done to address this?

In gathering this information it would again be wise to start with the material that is already available within the organization. Many nonprofits (especially those that use cold list mailings in donor recruitment) commission lifestyle profiling on their donor base and on segments of that base, and generate reports from the donor database which detail the demographics and giving history of supporters. Likewise, fundraisers dealing with major givers, corporates, trusts and foundations and community groups are likely to have reports on file which provide considerable insight into the nature and distinguishing characteristics of the people or organizations they receive income from.

These data should then be supplemented through desk research, looking at the most recent published sources on the key segments and looking to provide data on the size, growth and trends within each identified customer group. Using internal documents, database analysis and key secondary sources on lifestyle, demographic and charity-giving trends, current audiences can be compared against identified market potential to elicit information on each segment. This process will identify opportunities to gather further support from some audiences, attract new groups of donors, or may in some cases identify audiences which are saturated or shrinking, and where the nonprofit might therefore need to consider whether further investment is wise.

Key sources of fundraising data are described in Chapter 3. In some cases it may also be necessary to conduct additional new or 'primary' research. This will also be developed in detail in Chapter 3.

The internal environment

Having now summarized the key external influences on the organization it is possible to move on to consider an audit of the organization's own fundraising activity. The aim here is to scrutinize past fundraising performance and to carefully appraise what has worked well in the past and what has not. Current fundraising activities, trends in performance and the current structure and support systems that underpin fundraising activity will all be considered.

It is impossible to be prescriptive about the exact information requirements but it is likely that the auditor will wish to research

- The past performance of each form of fundraising undertaken, trends in this performance and whether this might vary by the region in which the fundraising is undertaken. The auditor will wish to examine the revenues that are generated, the costs incurred and the returns generated.
- These data should also be examined by the group or segment of donors addressed. What success has the organization had in addressing discrete donor segments? Have some segments proved more responsive than others? If so, why has this been the case? All these data can be valuable in selecting future donors for contact and suggest the optimal ways in which funds could be solicited.
- *Organizational processes* A review of the processes that support fundraising is also warranted. In particular the auditor will want to examine whether these processes are optimal and whether any problems have arisen in caring for donors over the period of the last plan. These processes will include donation processing and handling, mechanisms for dealing with donor communications and queries, internal coordination of strategy with departments such as press/public relations/campaigning, mechanisms for dealing with data protection/privacy issues (see Chapter 18).
- *Organizational structure* The auditor will also want to look at the manner in which the fundraising function is organized and to explore whether this is optimal. In particular the split between the use of paid staff and volunteers will warrant investigation as will the management reporting structures for each fundraising function. Does it make sense to organize the fundraising department in this particular way, or would it be valuable to explore making changes to these reporting structures? If the organization is involved in regional fundraising and managing a network of fundraisers working from home it may also wish to explore whether the definition of these regions is optimal and whether the number of managers is appropriate given the number and spread of employees/volunteers in the regions.

Data for the internal audit are usually gathered through a mixture of desk research and meetings and interviews with staff. Directors and senior staff will be able to provide information on past strategy, tactics and performance, and will also provide the necessary data on financial performance, human resource strategy and issues concerning governance and the general direction of the organization. It is often necessary to interview non-fundraising senior staff at this stage, such as the finance director and the Chief Executive Officer (CEO), to paint the full background picture of the nonprofit and to establish the positioning and importance of fundraising within the organization.

It is then necessary to talk to individual fundraising staff to establish an understanding of the current fundraising work undertaken, to understand what has happened in the past and how the organization has come to have a particular fundraising mix, and to gather information on perceived opportunities and barriers. The auditor undertaking such interviews should also prompt for records and data at these interviews to illustrate, add to and verify the information provided by the interviewee. It is good practice to record the interviews, write them up and then to check the written version with the interviewee for accuracy and to ensure that they have not been misunderstood or their views misrepresented. Again, it often proves necessary to interview non-fundraising staff where areas of work overlap, or where other work areas can impact on fundraising (e.g. within the communications or trading functions and in IT resourcing). If external agencies are retained, especially where those agencies give strategic or planning support, it will also be necessary to interview their staff to get a full picture of the fundraising effort.

As with the external audit, the internal data gathering should be an iterative process, with checks being performed throughout to ensure that full and accurate information is being gathered and expressed. The financial, structural and performance information gathered can be used to provide benchmarking data for comparison against other organizations.

ANALYTICAL TOOLS

The audit of internal factors allows the auditor to capture a wealth of data on the performance of existing fundraising products or services. In essence each form of fundraising that the organization undertakes can be scrutinized to see whether it is worth continuing, what future performance might look like and how it compares with other similar forms of fundraising undertaken by other organizations. While it may be perfectly plausible to draw out a series of such conclusions from raw audit data, it may be preferable to use one of a number of analytical models which can assist the auditor in interpreting the mass of data accumulated.

Product/service life cycle

One of the most fundamental concepts in marketing is the idea that a product or service will pass through several distinctive stages from the moment it is first introduced until it is ultimately withdrawn from the market. An understanding of these stages can greatly aid a fundraiser as the appropriate tactics for the successful management of the product/service will often vary greatly between each stage of its life cycle. Wilson et al. (1994:274) summarize the implications of the lifecycle concept as follows:

1 products/services have a finite life;
2 during this life they pass through a series of different stages, each of which poses different challenges to the organization;
3 virtually all elements of an organization's strategy/tactics need to change as the product/ service moves from one stage to another;

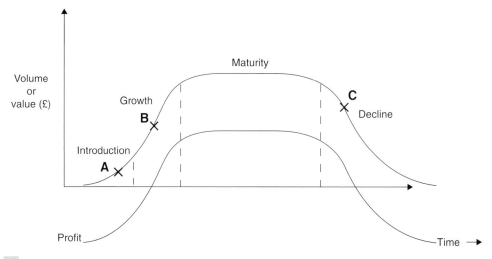

Figure 2.2 *Lifecycle concept*

4   the profit potential of products/services varies considerably from one stage to another;
5   the demands upon management and the appropriateness of managerial styles will also vary from stage to stage.

This idea is illustrated in Figure 2.2. During the introductory stage of the life cycle the product/service will take time to gain acceptability in the market and take-up will hence be relatively low. At this stage the organization will be unlikely to have recouped its initial set-up and development costs and profitability remains negative. Over time as the product begins to gain acceptability in the market, take-up will experience a period of sustained growth and provision of the product should at this stage become profitable. With the passage of time the volume/value of donations will eventually begin to level off as the market becomes saturated, until ultimately the product/service becomes obsolete and take-up begins to decline. At this stage the organization may wish to consider discontinuing the service as with the lower volume of transactions the costs of provision may prove prohibitive. In employing the concept the organization can model either the volume of fundraising transactions generated, or the value of such transactions. Either approach is acceptable.

   Of course, to use this model the fundraiser has to define what he/she means by a product/service. This is trickier than would be the case in for-profit organizations where products/services are typically well defined. In fundraising it may make sense to examine forms of fundraising (i.e. individual, corporate, trust/foundation) or it may make sense to examine specific offers, which may be either bundles of need, or ways in which each category of donor might give (e.g. adopt a dog, charity of the year, challenge events, payroll giving, badger conservation). There is no one right way to use the lifecycle model, it simply depends on which is the best way of looking at the fundraising activities the organization undertakes.

   The lifecycle concept has been much criticized over the years but it can still offer fundraisers considerable utility in that it can help shape the fundraising mix that can be adopted at each stage. As an illustration of this point, consider the role of promotion in supporting a fundraising product. At point (A) in Figure 2.2 the role of promotional support would almost certainly be to inform the potential market that the product exists and the potential benefits it might offer. Raising awareness would be a key task at this stage. As the product moves to point (B) in the life cycle,

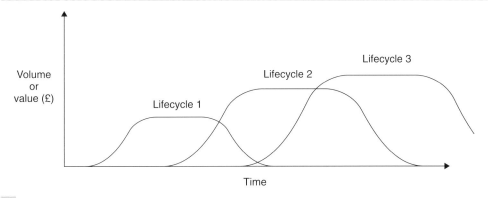

Figure 2.3 *Using the lifecycle for planning*

however, the nature of the market has changed. If the product was new and innovative, other nonprofits will have started to copy the idea and the focus of promotion will need to change. A continual emphasis on awareness would be inappropriate since it would only serve to increase the overall level of demand in the market and thus benefit all competitor nonprofits too. Instead a more useful strategy would be to differentiate the product from that provided by the competition. The emphasis would change to providing a clear positioning in the minds of target consumers/donors. By the time the product moves to point (C) in its life cycle, promotional support may be withdrawn altogether to reduce costs, or additional monies may be spent in an attempt to 'prop up' ailing demand in the market.

The lifecycle model can also be used to plan the introduction of new fundraising products. As an organization realizes that one product is soon to decline it can plan the introduction of new products. This idea is illustrated in Figure 2.3. In this case the organization is attempting to time new product introductions to ensure that the volume/value of donations from this particular source remains relatively constant, or ideally increasing, over time.

It should be noted, however, that nonprofits normally have more than one fundraising product available at any one time and the lifecycle concept has the significant drawback that it tends to focus management attention on each product individually without viewing the organization's portfolio as a coherent whole. Indeed a fundraising department may be viewed as a set of activities or projects to which new ones are intermittently added and from which older ones may be withdrawn. These activities and projects will make differential demands on, and contributions to, the organization as a whole. Hence some form of 'portfolio' analysis might prove a useful tool in deciding how the product mix might be improved, given the resource constraints that are valid at any one time.

Portfolio analysis

While there are a variety of portfolio models that have been employed over the years, these have largely been developed in the business context and are thus difficult to apply to the context of fundraising. In particular fundraisers should studiously avoid any portfolio model that has as its base the concept of market share, since this concept cannot be meaningfully applied to the realm of fundraising. This is the case for two reasons:

1   The sheer scale of the nonprofit sector and the fact that fundraising performance is reported in aggregate terms only means that it would be impossible to meaningfully quantify market share for particular products/services.

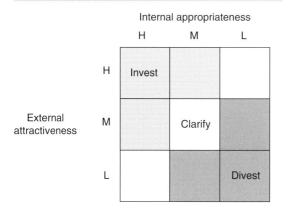

Figure 2.4 *Portfolio analysis*

2   Portfolio models employing market share assume that the performance of a product is related to market share (i.e. that there are economies of scale). This is simply not the case with many forms of fundraising.

However, the model depicted in Figure 2.4 can offer considerable help to fundraisers in appraising the current health of their portfolio of products/services. To utilize the model it is necessary to begin by examining in detail the components of the two axes, namely external attractiveness and internal appropriateness. If we consider first the question of external attractiveness, not all of an organization's fundraising products will be equally attractive to potential funders. Some fundraising products will be more appealing than others and thus more worthy of investment. While the specific factors that drive how attractive a product might be to funders will vary from one organization to another, external attractiveness might typically depend on:

- the level of general public concern about the 'content' of the product
- the number of potential donors, i.e. the potential/actual size of the market
- the perceived impact on the beneficiary group
- the uniqueness or novelty offered by the product
- ease of participation in the product.

It is important to recognize that this list is not exhaustive and the beauty of this model is that organizations can utilize whatever factors they perceive as being relevant to their own environment and circumstances.

Turning now to the question of internal appropriateness, this relates to the extent to which the product fits the profile of the organization providing it. In other words, is it appropriate to provide this product given the skills, expertise, organizational structure and resources available? Relevant factors here might include:

- the extent to which the organization has relevant staff expertise
- the extent to which the organization has past experience of this product
- the fundraising returns generated by the product
- the availability of volunteers.

Once again this list can be expected to vary from context to context and an organization should look to identify those factors which are most pertinent to its particular circumstances.

Having now defined the components of both internal appropriateness and external attractiveness the reader will appreciate that not all the factors identified could be seen as having equal importance to a given organization. For this reason it is important to weight the factors according to their relative importance. Beginning first with external attractiveness this is illustrated in Table 2.1. The reader will note that the weights for the components of each axis should all add up to 1. In the example given, the key factor driving external attractiveness is the perceived impact on the beneficiary group. This therefore receives a relatively high weighting. The issues of novelty and ease of participation are less important and therefore warrant only a low weighting.

The next step is to take each activity in which the organization is engaged and give it a score from 1 (very poor) to 10 (excellent) in terms of how it measures up against each of the components listed. To make this process clear a fictional example (let us call it Activity A – for the sake of argument, a child sponsorship product) has been worked through in Tables 2.1 and 2.2. Considering first the issue of external attractiveness, Table 2.1 makes it clear that this product offers a very clear benefit on the beneficiary group and we thus rate this a 10 out of 10. The product also scores highly against the level of public concern. Unfortunately the product is also available from many other nonprofits and cannot be considered unique. The rating against this dimension is thus only 2 out of 10. The product also offers only average performance in terms of the size of the market and ease of participation in the product. The product thus rates only 5 out of 10 against these dimensions.

Multiplying the weights by the ratings assigned, produces a value for each factor. Summing these values gives an overall score for (in this case) the external attractiveness axis of Activity A of 7.3.

Table 2.1 *External attractiveness*

Factor	Weight	Rating	Value
The level of general public concern about the 'content' of the product	0.2	8	1.6
The number of potential donors	0.2	5	1.0
The perceived impact on the beneficiary group	0.4	10	4.0
The uniqueness or novelty offered by the product	0.1	2	0.2
Ease of participation in the product	0.1	5	0.5
Total	1.0		7.3

Table 2.2 *Internal appropriateness*

Factor	Weight	Rating	Value
The extent to which the organization has relevant staff/volunteer expertise	0.4	8	3.2
The extent to which the organization has past experience of this product	0.1	5	0.5
The fundraising returns generated by the product	0.4	10	4.0
The availability of volunteers	0.1	7	0.7
Total	1.0		8.4

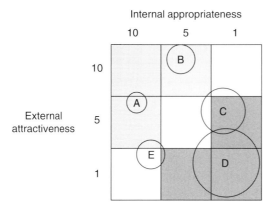

Figure 2.5 *Example portfolio analysis*

The process is identical for internal appropriateness. Each pertinent factor is assigned a weight and each activity in which the organization engages is given a rating according to its performance in respect of each factor. Once again 1 = very poor, 10 = excellent. Returning to our analysis of Activity A we can see that internal appropriateness for this organization is largely driven by staff/volunteer expertise and the returns generated by the product. These factors have relatively high weightings. The returns from our child sponsorship product (Activity A) are obviously excellent and the level of staff/volunteer expertise is also good. Multiplying the weights by the ratings gives us a value for each item and summing these generates an overall score for Activity A of 8.4 on the internal appropriateness axis.

These figures can then be plotted on the matrix on Figure 2.5 where the position of Activity A has been clearly indicated. If it is conceptually useful some organizations choose to take the analysis one stage further and draw a circle around the plotted position, the diameter of which is directly proportional to the percentage of fundraising income it generates. In this way managers can see at a glance the relative significance and position of each of the products in their portfolio. Of course for this to happen all the products that a particular organization provides would have to plotted in this way, just as in Figure 2.5. Only then could an analysis be undertaken of the health and balance of the portfolio as a whole. Depending on the location of each activity within the matrix, the organization can then either look to invest further in its development, divest the activity and use the resources elsewhere, or subject the activity to further evaluation if the position still remains unclear.

Activities in the top left-hand corner of the matrix are clearly those that are highly attractive to their respective market and which the organization is well placed to deliver. These are clear candidates for continuing development.

Activities in the bottom right-hand corner, however, are clearly activities that could be causing an unnecessary drain on resources. They are not seen as attractive by the target funders and the organization has no particular skill in delivering the products. Activities in this area of the matrix should be scrutinized with a view to termination or divestment. After all if these products are not attractive and the organization is not good at providing them, what could be the possible rationale for continuing? Of course this is only a model and the activity would have to be scrutinized very carefully before a divestment decision was taken, but the analysis has at least yielded considerable insight into the potential for valuable resources to be conserved and perhaps put to other, more appropriate, uses.

This leaves the question of activities falling within the central diagonal. These should be carefully evaluated as they are only moderately appropriate for the organization to provide and they have only limited external attractiveness.

The life cycle matrix

In examining the health of a portfolio it is also possible to employ an adapted version of a matrix originally developed by consultants at Arthur D. Little Inc. (see Hofer and Schendel 1978). The matrix is illustrated in Figure 2.6. In this matrix the user plots competitive position against lifecycle stages. The diameters of the circles around each activity are once again proportional to the fundraising revenue that they generate. The goal of using this matrix, as with that detailed above, is to guide investment decisions in fundraising products. In Figure 2.6 Activity A could be labelled a developing winner, Activity B a potential loser, Activity C an established winner and Activity D a loser. The power of this particular matrix is that it illustrates graphically how the products are positioned in respect of various stages of evolution. This may well be important in deciding when to create new products and divest those at the end of their life cycle which lack a clear rationale for their continuing existence.

The decision over where to place an activity on the competitive position axis depends on how that activity rates against a variety of factors. These typically include:

- how well the organization's strengths match the success factors in the particular fundraising market;
- the profitability associated with an activity;
- the extent to which the organization has the requisite fundraising skills;
- the extent to which the organization has developed a reputation in delivering that activity;
- the perceived costs/benefits to the donor of engaging with the activity.

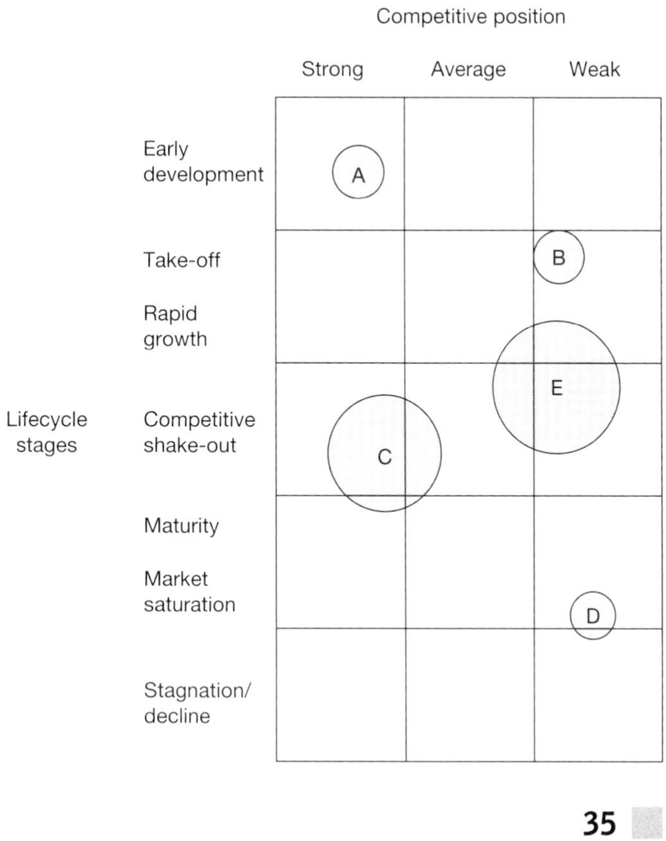

Figure 2.6 *Lifecycle matrix*

Source: Hofer and Schendel (1978).

It is a combination of these factors that will determine how strongly positioned a particular fundraising product might be in its market. In employing the matrix, nonprofits can either take an entirely subjective view of the 'score', or they may construct a weighted axis just as with the previous matrix to impose a little more rigour on the analytical process.

In interpreting this matrix, it is possible to infer a number of conclusions in respect of how the performance of particular products might change over the duration of the plan. Similarly, the matrix can be used to guide investment decisions and in particular to highlight those products that should simply be divested. Those products towards the end of their life cycle where the organization does not have a strong competitive position are clear candidates for this.

Drawbacks of portfolio models

In electing to employ a portfolio model it is essential that the user be aware of some of the disadvantages of such models.

- *Definition of market*   It is not always clear how the market should be defined when drawing conclusions about the position of a product on a given axis. When examining corporate fundraising products, for example, is the market: the whole corporate marketplace, only those corporations that give presently to nonprofits, only those companies in particular sectors, or only those companies of a particular size? It is essential in using a portfolio model that the market is clearly defined and that the implications of this definition are fully understood.
- *Innovation*   The difficulty with some models is that they can understate the significance of an innovative new product. When such products first appear on a matrix they are characterized by low profitability/revenues and a weak market position as they fight to get established. Thus a cursory glance at a portfolio model might suggest that such products are struggling and that divestment is warranted. This is clearly not the case and care is required in interpretation.
- *Divesting unwanted products*   It should be recognized that while a number of fundraising products may be highlighted as candidates for divestment, this may frequently not be desirable. While it makes little financial sense to continue with a particular product, there may be a number of good human reasons why it should be continued. Perhaps volunteers have a long and proud tradition of managing the product and there are strong emotional attachments to its continuation. It may also be the case that some products gain the organization very welcome publicity that assists in the fulfilment of the mission, even though the performance of the activity itself is poor. Nonprofits thus need to subject the recommendations that emerge from a portfolio analysis to greater scrutiny before divestment decisions are actually taken.
- *The desirability of growth*   Finally, most portfolio models assume that an organization is looking to achieve growth in fundraising income and the prescriptions offered by such models may therefore not be appropriate to the circumstances facing every organization.

CONDUCTING AN AUDIT IN A SMALL CHARITY

The framework we offer above is of equal relevance to all organizations irrespective of their size. Even small organizations will be impacted by changes in the macro environment and face the challenges posed by competitors for funds. Small charities will also have an equal if not greater need to exploit opportunities for collaboration and they will certainly need to audit their own internal strengths and weaknesses before they will be in a position to fundraise effectively. All that said there will of course be differences in the approach that will be adopted.

Although a PEST will still be worth considering there are likely, for example, to be fewer macro environmental factors impacting a small day-care centre in Bristol than on a major national charity such as Cancer Research UK. Fundraisers should still take the time to look around at the wider environment to ensure they don't miss any significant changes, but the auditor should not allocate too much time to this section of the audit and/or worry that they have only identified a few points.

It is also true that smaller organizations will find it less useful to look at broad trends in individual or corporate giving taking place at the national level. Published sources will therefore be less helpful than conversations with fellow fundraisers, or the local branches of employer organizations or bodies within the arts and business communities. Talking with professional colleagues already working in the area will be likely to give the auditor more of a sense of the picture locally and offer a regional perspective on the reported national statistics.

THE SWOT ANALYSIS

Clearly at this stage the output from the fundraising audit may be regarded as little more than a collection of data, and in this format it is as yet of limited value for planning purposes. What is required is a form of analysis, that allows the fundraiser to examine the opportunities and threats presented by the environment in a relatively structured way. Indeed, it should at this point be recognized that opportunities and threats are seldom absolute. An opportunity may only be regarded as an opportunity, for example, if the organization has the necessary strengths to support its development. For this reason it is usual to conduct a SWOT analysis (Strengths, Weaknesses, Opportunities and Threats) on the data gathered during the fundraising audit. This is simply a matter of selecting key information from the audit, analysing its implications and presenting it under one of the four headings. The important word here is 'key'. It is important that some filtering of the data gathered at this stage is undertaken so that the analysis is ultimately limited to the factors of most relevance for the subsequent development of strategy. The SWOT addresses the following issues.

■ What are the strengths of the organization? What is the organization good at? Is it at the forefront of particular fundraising developments? Does it have access to a donor segment that is not reached by competitors? Does it have a strong database system/great support agencies/high local awareness?
■ What are its weaknesses? In what ways do competitors typically outperform the organization? Are there weaknesses in terms of internal support or structures? Are there barriers to future development in some areas?
■ What are the main opportunities facing the organization over the duration of the plan? Are there new fundraising techniques to test, new audiences to attract? Are new developments within the organization likely to present extra opportunities for fundraising?
■ What are the major threats facing the organization? Is a major competitor likely to launch a new capital appeal? Will economic changes impact on certain core funders and leave them with less to give? Are planned changes to legislation likely to curtail fundraising activity?

Good SWOT analyses have a number of distinctive characteristics

■ They are relatively concise summaries of the audit data and are typically no more than four to five pages of commentary focusing on key factors only.

- They recognize that strengths and weaknesses are differential in nature. This means that a strength is only a strength if the organization is better at this particular activity or dimension than its competitors. Similarly weaknesses should be examined from the perspective of where the organization lags behind the competition.
- They are clear and easy to read. Quality suffers if items are over-abbreviated and the writer concentrates on micro rather than macro issues. As MacDonald (1995:406) notes: 'if a SWOT analysis is well done, someone else should be able to draft the objectives which logically flow from it. The SWOT should contain clear indicators as to the key determinants of success in the department.'
- A separate SWOT should be completed for each segment of donors critical to the organization's future. What may be perceived as a strength in relation to individual donors may well be a weakness when approaching corporate donors. Thus, the global SWOT analyses that are so frequently conducted by fundraising departments can often tend towards the meaningless. For all but the smallest and simplest organizations a series of highly focused SWOTs will be warranted.

SUMMARY

In this chapter we have introduced the fundraising audit as the first key component of the fundraising plan. We established that it provided an organization with the 'Where are we now?' component of a plan. We have also outlined the information requirements that a nonprofit will have at the commencement of the planning process and suggested why this information is important. In Chapter 3 we shall explore in further detail where a nonprofit can source much of this material and, in cases where existing sources prove unhelpful, the tools and techniques of marketing research that can be used to plug the gaps.

We have also examined a range of product and portfolio models that can be used to assist in the manipulation and interpretation of audit data. The use of such models can greatly enhance the quality of insight gained through the audit process, although it is important for the auditor to understand the underlying assumptions made by these models and the implications for the derivation of subsequent fundraising strategy.

Finally, we have introduced the SWOT analysis as a tool to summarize audit data. This is also essential since it draws out the key factors driving, or likely to drive fundraising perform-ance in the future. A good SWOT analysis should not only summarize the audit data, but also suggest to planners what might be realistic objectives to achieve over the planning period. The SWOT analysis will also suggest the strategy/tactics that can best be employed to achieve these objectives. These are subjects that we return to in Chapter 4 when we examine the final two components of the fundraising plan, namely 'Where do we want to be?' and 'How are we going to get there?'

DISCUSSION QUESTIONS

1   Fundraising audits can be undertaken by external suppliers (agency staff or consultants), or the task can be allocated to internal staff. What do you think would be the advantages and drawbacks associated with each of these routes?

2   List four political, economic, socio-cultural and technological factors likely to impact over the next three years on a USA-based animal welfare nonprofit.

3   Explain the strengths and weaknesses of portfolio modelling for nonprofits.
4   You are fundraising director of a medium-sized UK nonprofit where no formal fundraising planning has been undertaken over the past five years. Prepare a set of notes to be used in a presentation to your trustees on the advisability of investment on a fundraising planning process.

REFERENCES

Drucker, P.F. (1955) *The Practice of Management*, Heinemann, London.
Hofer, C.W. and Schendel, D. (1978) *Strategy Formulation*: *Analytical Concepts*, West Publishing, St Paul, MN.
MacDonald, M. (1995) *Marketing Plans*: *How to Prepare Them, How to Use Them*, Butterworth Heinemann, Oxford.
Wilson, R.M.S., Gilligan, C. and Pearson, D.J. (1994) *Strategic Marketing Management*, Butterworth Heinemann, Oxford.

Chapter 3

Marketing research for fundraising

OBJECTIVES

By the end of this chapter you should be able to:

- Explain the relevance of market research to fundraising planning.
- Distinguish between primary and secondary research.
- Distinguish between qualitative and quantitative data.
- Utilize a wide range of secondary sources of data.
- Identify and employ relevant primary research methods.
- Present marketing research data.
- Brief and monitor the work undertaken by external research agencies.

INTRODUCTION

In the previous chapter we explored a range of information needs typically encountered by a nonprofit in writing a strategic marketing or fundraising plan. While this list seems extensive it must be remembered that good information can be used to great effect in guiding the decisions and policies an organization might adopt and is therefore invaluable.

The sheer number of nonprofit organizations presents donors and other supporters with a vast array of choice. Donors often have multiple opportunities to support very similar (if not identical) causes and programmes. Given this, to compete successfully for funds organizations need to understand their position in the market, the activities of key competitors and also the behaviour of the donors themselves. In respect of this latter category, issues such as why people give, the value they place on the exchange, how they select between competing demands on their resources and so on are all of relevance. If these were all rational 'objective' decisions on the part of the donor there would be little need for marketing research. Fundraisers could take an educated guess about how individuals might think and behave and be right some 90 per cent of the time. Sadly, human beings frequently do not behave rationally and base their decisions on a range of subjective and emotional factors. These are not immediately obvious even to those with considerable experience of a sector and thus research is necessary to identify donor perceptions of each of these dimensions. It is important to stress from the outset that conducting such research need not be an expensive exercise. As we shall shortly see, much can be learned for comparatively little time, effort and expenditure.

Of course market research should not be seen as a substitute for good managerial decision-making. The role of market research is not to usurp executive experience or judgement. Rather market research provides the basic data that managers can utilize to help *inform* the decision-making process. It thus reinforces good decision-making rather than replacing it.

It is also important to note that there is an element of risk associated with every management decision and that decision-making in the absence of research data simply exposes an organization to unnecessary additional risk. In the nonprofit sector this risk is all the more acute because of the agency role that nonprofits play in stewarding the resources supplied by donors. If, for example, a fundraising campaign goes badly wrong and loses the organization money, it will effectively be wasting the resources donated by previous donors to the organization and will put the organization in breach of their trust. Nonprofit managers are thus under a considerable obligation to ensure that the risk inherent in decision-making is held to a minimum.

There are thus a number of advantages to an organization in conducting thorough research in relation to each of the issues highlighted in Chapter 2. Given the plethora of information needs and the equal plethora of potential information sources, there is no shortage of data to be had about the fundraising function or the environment in which it operates. Sadly this is frequently irrelevant, incompatible with the specific information need or excessive in terms of volume. Problems can also arise when managers fail to understand the nature of the information presented and then, even in the presence of high-quality data, the wrong decisions can be taken.

In this chapter we will navigate some of the pitfalls associated with conducting marketing research, outline a process that may be used to manage the activity, explain the research tools and techniques available and, finally, explore how to brief and manage external agencies that might be employed to assist an organization capture data.

DEFINITION

Before beginning with this process it is important to clarify exactly what we mean by marketing research. Over the years there has been considerable confusion between the terms marketing and market research. Although market research has tended to be used as a synonym for marketing research there was originally a distinction drawn between these two terms by virtue of their scope. Market research was regarded as research into markets (e.g. in the case of fundraising: individual donors, corporate supporters and foundations) whereas marketing research applies more broadly to every aspect of marketing. This would thus include researching the activities of competitors, trends in the external environment, the performance of an organization's own fundraising activity and so on.

The American Marketing Association (1961) defined marketing research as 'the systematic gathering, recording and analyzing of data about problems relating to the marketing of goods and services'.

More recently Kotler (1967) prefers to emphasize the goals of marketing research and defines it as: 'systematic problem analysis, model building and fact finding for the purposes of improved decision-making and control in the marketing of goods and services'. Thus marketing research is concerned with the disciplined collection and evaluation of data in order to aid managers in understanding the needs of their target audiences more fully. It can be used to reduce risk in decision-making and to control (to some extent) the risk surrounding each aspect of fundraising.

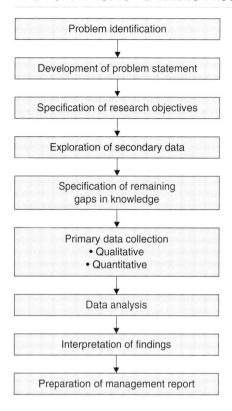

Figure 3.1 *The marketing research process*

While perspectives on the research process frequently differ from one organization to another, the approach adopted will always share a number of common features, as outlined in Figure 3.1. The marketing research process is typically initiated by an organization realizing that it has a problem or issue to resolve. To operationalize this for the purposes of research it must first be expressed as a series of specific research objectives. These are then addressed through initial desk research of existing data. In some cases this may yield all the answers an organization needs, in which case an appropriate analysis of this material can result in the preparation of the requisite report for management. It is frequently the case, however, that not all of the information needs can be met in this way and that new or *primary* data may have to be collected and analysed for this purpose.

In the sections below we will now discuss each element of this process beginning with the specification of the research problem

STATING THE RESEARCH PROBLEM AND RESEARCH OBJECTIVES

The first stage of the research process involves a clear specification of the fundraising problem on which the research is expected to focus. This is essential if the organization is to achieve a satisfactory outcome from the research process, particularly if external agencies are to be employed for the purposes of data collection

Where it is intended that the organization will work with an agency it is important that both management and the research team should work closely together in this crucial task of developing a problem statement. Unless the agency thoroughly understands the issues facing the client it is quite possible that the research objectives designed to provide information to resolve these problems will be irrelevant or possibly even counterproductive.

Having defined the problem, it is then possible to design the research objectives. This requires the organization and/or agency to turn the problem into a series of information needs. Thus, for example, if the problem facing the organization is a fall in bequest income, the research objectives could be written to explore why this might be the case and offer insight into what might be done about it.

In this example the research objectives might appear as follows:

- to quantify and establish trends in the decline in bequest giving;
- to explore the extent to which this decline is unique to the organization in question or shared by the sector as a whole;
- to assess the motives of bequest givers for offering a bequest;
- to assess donor perceptions of the bequest solicitation process;
- to explore the utility of (and donor perceptions of) the various communication channels that may be used to solicit bequests;
- to explore the role of intermediaries in facilitating bequests;
- to identify the barriers to bequest giving.

This list is by no means exhaustive and, depending on the circumstances facing a particular organization, the actual content of this list will vary considerably. The point is that the problem must be broken down into a series of research objectives that will address each of the likely causes for the decline, providing enough information for managers to take remedial action. Again, if an agency is to be employed for the purposes of data collection it must also be involved in selecting research objectives since they may well have insight into the issues which could help shape these objectives, and also because they need to understand the rationale underlying each information need and how it pertains to the problem as a whole.

SECONDARY VERSUS PRIMARY DATA

The next stage in the research process is typically to conduct a desk research of existing information sources. Typically, many of the organization's information needs can be adequately and cheaply met by simply reading through the trade press, research reports or specialist journals. Collectively, these are known as secondary data.

Secondary data are data that have already been collected for some purpose in the past. The data have thus *not* been collected specifically to address the issues at hand. Such data can typically be found within the nonprofit organization in management/consultancy reports or in an analysis of database records, but more frequently they will be found outside the organization in government publications, syndicated research, trade/professional reports, electronic databases, professional/academic journals and so on. A summary of key secondary sources of data is supplied in Exhibit 3.1.

Secondary data are always the starting point in seeking to satisfy research objectives since they have the advantage of being cheap to collect (typically representing only a fraction of the cost of the collection of new fundraising research such as surveys, focus groups, etc.). There are, however, a number of distinct disadvantages in that:

- Data may have been collected for another purpose that may not meet the exact information needs of the organization.

43

EXHIBIT 3.1 SOURCES OF SECONDARY DATA

The Institute of Fundraising (www.institute-of-fundraising.org.uk)

> The Institute is the professional body that represents the interests of UK fundraisers to the media, government and other interested parties. It provides a range of training courses, information about fundraising and a series of 'Codes of Practice' with specialized advice about the implementation of many forms of fundraising.

National Council for Voluntary Organizations (www.ncvo-vol.org.uk)

> Provides an excellent range of publications covering many aspects of nonprofit management. The research department also provides statistics on giving and general trends within the sector. The *UK Civil Society Almanac* and series of 'Foresight' reports are particularly valuable for fundraisers.

Directory of Social Change (www.dsc.org.uk)

> Provides a wide range of publications covering every aspect of nonprofit management. Particularly good at providing information for the smaller nonprofit. Also has an interest in the cost of fundraising and has published work in this field.

Charity Commission (www.charity-commission.gov.uk)

> The body responsible for regulating registered charities in the UK. Provides a range of publications offering guidance to charities and also has a database of charity accounts which must be logged with the commission each year.

Guidestar (http://guidestar.org.uk/)

> A searchable online database currently containing details of the registered 'main' charities in England and Wales. The base information about each charity is provided from the records of the Charity Commission – and details are subsequently maintained and updated by the charities themselves.

Fundraising UK (www.fundraising.co.uk)

> Provides news and information about all aspects of fundraising. It also offers a range of links to other fundraising sites.

Charityfacts (www.charityfacts.org)

> The aim of this public information website is to provide high quality and impartial information about how fundraising works and the costs associated with each category of activity. It provides information for the public, fundraisers and journalists researching the sector.

Third Sector (http://thirdsector.co.uk)

> Offers the latest news and opinion pieces on the state of the third sector in the UK. It carries a high degree of fundraising-related content and many of the latest job advertisements. The website has a useful search facility and also offers the opportunity to sign up to a free e-mail newsletter.

Professional Fundraising (http://www.professionalfundraising.co.uk)

> The UK's only specialized magazine for fundraisers. It provides thought pieces covering new development in fundraising, sector news and commentary. The website offers much 'free to air' material and a facility to sign up to a free newsletter.

Indiana University Center on Philanthropy (http://www.philanthropy.iupui.edu/)

> The Center at IU conducts, coordinates and supports research, building a broad base of knowledge about the causes and consequences of philanthropic behaviour involving individuals,

communities and institutions. It offers a range of research data and publications, together with an annual symposium allowing practitioners to access the latest research.

The Australian Centre for Philanthropy and Nonprofit Studies (www.bus.qut.edu.au/research/cpns/)

The Centre offers a first-rate website that can act as a hub for anyone wishing to research the third sector worldwide. The 'useful links' section is easy to navigate and is easily the most comprehensive gateway on the Web. The Centre's own research is also worth checking out periodically as a good deal of their work is relevant to an international audience.

Social Welfare Research Institute at Boston College (www.bc.edu/research/swri)

The Institute publishes a range of research papers and reports of interest to the fundraising profession. It has tended to focus (although not exclusively) on wealth transfers and major gift fundraising. Many resources may be downloaded free of charge and they produce an excellent electronic newsletter.

International Journal of Nonprofit and Voluntary Sector Marketing (http://www3.interscience.wiley.com/journal/110481870/home)

The *International Journal of Nonprofit and Voluntary Sector Marketing* provides an international forum for peer-reviewed papers and case studies on the latest techniques, thinking and best practice in marketing for the not-for-profit sector. The website has a search facility, so that users can identify relevant material. Some material is available free-to-air while other articles can be purchased online.

HM Government (http://www.hm-treasury.gov.uk/) and (http://www.homeoffice.gov.uk/)

Key government departments such as the Treasury or the Home Office have an active interest in the voluntary sector and their websites often feature pertinent reports, policy papers and statistics.

- Data are often out of date, having been collected a year or more prior to the current investigation.
- Data can be of dubious quality, and thus a careful consideration of the source and the methodology adopted will be warranted to ensure that the data offer appropriate validity and reliability.

Having exhausted the sources of secondary data the organization may then return to the research objectives and determine those that have not been fully addressed with this extant data. Where information gaps remain, it will be necessary to commission primary research to supply the missing information. Primary research involves collecting new data specifically for the purpose of answering the questions posed by the current research objectives. This is typically an expensive exercise and will not be undertaken lightly by the commissioning organization. Primary research may be either qualitative or quantitative.

QUALITATIVE RESEARCH

Fundraisers are frequently concerned with issues such as how donors view the organization, what motivates them to support it, what they like and don't like about the communications they receive and so on. If the organization lacks an understanding of the factors likely to be at work in each case, it would be advised to begin by conducting what is known as *qualitative* research. This form of research is designed to provide such insights and is a good way of gathering data about people's attitudes, feelings and motives. It is impressionistic in style rather than conclusive and it probes for data rather than counting responses. The most common qualitative research methods include detailed 'depth' interviews, focus groups (group discussions) and projective techniques.

Depth interviews

The use of this technique involves the researcher in a free-flowing discussion with members of the group whose opinions are being sought. They are conducted on a one-to-one basis, so that there is no need for the interviewee to feel under any pressure to respond in a socially acceptable way, or to worry what other participants in the research process might think of their views. It is thus a very open and non-threatening research setting and interviewers are trained to put their subjects at ease. Such interviews can be either unstructured or semi-structured, depending on the level of knowledge the researcher has about the factors likely to be of interest. Where a detailed knowledge is lacking the interviewer will find an unstructured approach of most value and facilitate a general discussion of the research question and allow the conversation to focus on whatever factors emerge.

Focus groups/group discussions

This technique requires the researcher to assemble a group of six to ten respondents who agree to take part in (typically) a one- to two-hour discussion that addresses the research objective(s). This discussion may be held at the organization's premises or at a centrally located venue that is easy for the respondents to access. The researcher carefully facilitates a discussion of the topic and ensures that the views of each member of the group are elicited. He/she may also have to deal with 'difficult' personalities that attempt to either dominate the discussion, or fail to express a point of view. It is important that the views of every participant are considered equally and the process of facilitation is thus a highly skilled task. Focus group proceedings are typically either audio or video taped, so that they can subsequently be analysed by the research team.

The biggest drawback of this technique is the cost, with a typical focus group costing between £1,000 and £1,200 and a range of six to eight groups typically being necessary to address a given research task. Basing decisions on a smaller number of groups can be risky since focus group participants may prove to be highly unrepresentative of the donor (or other) population. The insights gained from focus groups can be of considerable value, but this is frequently gained at substantial cost.

Projective techniques

The use of projective techniques has moved in and out of fashion over the past 50 years. They are said to generate considerable insight into feelings, beliefs and attitudes that individuals find it difficult to articulate by other means. A number of techniques are in existence, where research subjects can express their views by 'projecting' those views on to objects, pictures or third parties.

An organization interested in the perception of its brand might thus provide a group of eight to ten individuals with a set of cards and crayons and ask them to create an image that for them embodies the brand. This can also be achieved through the use of clay, where subjects create a physical representation of the brand. The shapes and pictures created can then be subject to expert analysis to identify the common themes that emerge.

Figure 3.2 *Projective techniques*

A further common technique would involve asking subjects to create a personality for an organization or brand. Thus 'if this organization were a well known celebrity – who would it be?' The description and subsequent rationale can then form the basis for discussion.

Projective techniques have also been used in the context of cartoons, where research subjects are presented with a cartoon illustration of a social situation embodying the research objective(s). Blank dialogue boxes (or speech bubbles) will be provided and the subject asked to supply appropriate speech An example is provided in Figure 3.2. The technique works because subjects may find it easier to address some topics by projecting their own values and beliefs on to these cartoon characters, thereby expressing views they would feel uncomfortable expressing in a traditional interview. Again, this speech can be subject to a content analysis at the end of the research process and common themes elicited.

A caveat

It should be noted that qualitative techniques themselves do not constitute valid market research. The samples are inadequate, the method of questioning inconsistent and the means of interpretation subjective. Two or three people (or agencies) doing the same piece of qualitative research can often come up with very different results. This is simply because the use of eight to ten individuals in a focus group is rarely representative of the 'population' as a whole and the results will therefore always have a high degree of bias. To take a fundraising example, one might commission a series of focus groups to determine the reasons why donors support the organization. Such a group would likely generate an excellent list of reasons, but it could never tell you what proportion of the donor base might be motivated by each rationale for support. It is thus only half a story. The real strength of the technique lies in its ability to generate *hypotheses* about how the donor population as a whole *might* feel or *might* behave. These hypotheses should then be tested with quantitative techniques amongst a larger, more representative sample of the population.

47

QUANTITATIVE RESEARCH TECHNIQUES

Quantitative research typically involves the gathering of numerical information about the market or particular audience with which the researcher is concerned. Unlike qualitative research the goal is to quantify the number of members of a particular group who hold certain views, donate in particular ways, are motivated by particular factors and so on.

Quantitative research techniques include:

- *Personal interviews*   These may be conducted by a trained researcher in the home, office or a central location/street. Both qualitative and quantitative data could be gathered, although cost and time restraints frequently confine data collection to quantitative data. The interviewer follows a set script and simply poses a range of questions, noting down the replies he/she receives for subsequent analysis.
- *Telephone interviews*   Increasingly marketing research is being conducted by phone. Researchers from the organization or agency ring a sample of individuals and again follow a set script, posing each question in turn. Modern technology now facilitates a process known as CATI (Computer Assisted Telephone Interviewing) where the questions appear on a screen in front of the interviewer and each response is typed into the database (or the appropriate box clicked through). Depending on the nature of the response the interviewer is then prompted by the system to ask the next appropriate question.
- *Postal questionnaires*   Here the contact with the research sample is impersonal. A series of questions are developed, printed on to a questionnaire and dispatched to members of the target audience whose opinion is sought. Often the response is incentivized in some way and facilitated through the inclusion of a reply-paid or freepost envelope.
- *E-mail questionnaires*   The rise in computer ownership and access to the Internet has made the acquisition of market research data much more affordable. Sudman and Blair (1999) argue that electronic surveys will replace telephone surveys over the next quarter-century as more and more individuals become comfortable with the medium. Surveys can easily be e-mailed to donors or other categories of supporter. Alternatively if the questionnaire is lengthy, it is possible to post the questionnaire on a website and then e-mail respondents asking them to visit the site and complete it. Sudman and Blair (1999) recommend locating the questionnaire in a password-protected part of the site, so that responses from members of the sample do not become confused with those of other site users who decide to complete the questionnaire during their visit.

TAKING A SAMPLE

In undertaking quantitative research it may be possible to solicit the opinions of everyone in the whole group or *population* of interest. Under these circumstances the researcher is effectively conducting a *census* since everyone of interest can be contacted and asked for their views.

More frequently, however, it is not practical to pose questions of everyone in a target population, by virtue of the sheer number of contacts involved, the costs of soliciting their views, or the difficulty of contacting them, perhaps because of their geographic spread. In such circumstances researchers take a sample of the members of the population and calculate statistics about that sample, which allow them to make statements and estimates about the population as a whole, without the need to contact everyone.

There are four main methods for sampling of relevance to fundraisers, namely random sampling, systematic random sampling, stratified random sampling and quota sampling. Random sampling is referred to as *probability sampling*, while quota sampling is referred to as *non-probability sampling*. This difference matters because it impacts on the way we may interpret the results of the research undertaken.

Under random sampling each member of a population has an equal chance of being selected in the sample. Because of this it is possible to calculate a *level of confidence* and limit of accuracy from the results of such a sample. A level of confidence is a statement about how confident we can be about the results from the sample holding good across the population as a whole. At the 95 per cent level of confidence, for example, there is only a 5 per cent (or 1 in 20) chance that the sample results do not hold good for the whole population. Confidence levels can be set higher than this to offer greater accuracy, but this would add substantially to the cost since it would require the extraction of a larger sample.

It is important to note that we are not saying that probability samples are necessarily more representative than non-probability samples. Indeed, the converse can often be true. The point is that probability samples allow for the calculation of *sample error* or the extent to which errors in the results occur because a sample was used rather than asking the whole population for their views. You cannot do this with non-probability samples since no objective method is used in the first place to gather the sample.

We now consider each form of sampling in turn.

Random sampling

To generate a random sample, as noted above, every member of the population must have an equal chance of selection. To take a random sample it is thus necessary to begin by defining or assembling a *sampling frame*. This is simply a complete list of all the individuals in the target population. This may, for example, be a list of names on a database, a directory of organizations or a list of contacts. Each name on this list would then be assigned a number and all the numbers entered into a hat. If a 10 per cent sample of individuals is required, 10 per cent of those numbers and associated names would then be drawn at random out of the hat.

Of course, modern technology now makes this process much less cumbersome and many modern software programmes generate numbers at random which can be used to generate a random sample for the researcher. Indeed, in many cases the researcher will be oblivious to the process since it is necessary only to request this kind of sample from the database software.

Systematic sampling

There are occasions, however, when a truly random sample is not practical, perhaps because the sampling frame is supplied in a list format and where the number of contacts on that list is large. Assigning numbers and then selecting numbers at random from the list would then be time-consuming and potentially costly. Under these circumstances it may be more practical to take a *systematic random sample*. Suppose we wish to take a 10 per cent sample from a list of 1,000 names. We could then proceed by selecting a random start point and thus selecting at random a number between 1 and 10. Suppose we select the number 4. We would then work down through our list taking the 4th name, the 14th name, the 24th name, the 34th name and so on until we had completed the list and extracted the 10 per cent of contacts required. This is a systematic random sample.

Stratified random sampling

To illustrate the need for this form of sampling let's consider the example of a nonprofit wishing to explore the reasons why its donors stop giving, or lapse their support of the organization.

49

Table 3.1 *Age profile of donors*

Age category	Percentage of lapsed file
Under 20	10
21–40	20
41–60	30
61–80	20
80+	10

To investigate this issue it has been proposed that a 10 per cent sample of the lapsed portion of the database be sent a questionnaire to ascertain their views. Intuitively the fundraising team feel that these reasons might vary by the age of the individual. Now suppose that the age profile of lapsed donors is as depicted in Table 3.1

By taking a purely random sample of 10 per cent of these individuals it is possible, however unlikely, that a sample could be generated where all the individuals contacted are over 80. This could greatly bias the results. Instead researchers would better proceed by deciding in advance that of their sample 10 per cent will be under 20, 20 per cent will be aged 21–40, 20 per cent will be aged 41–60, 20 per cent will be aged 61–80 and 10 per cent will be aged over 80. In other words, the composition of the sample mirrors that of the population to ensure that each category or *strata* is properly represented.

Non-probability sampling

With non-probability sampling the chances of selection are not known; therefore the ability to generalize about a population based on the results of a sample are much reduced. Indeed Kumar et al. (1999) argue that the results of non-probability sampling may contain biases and uncertainties that make them worse than no information at all. Not all writers are as pessimistic however and the decision of whether or not to use probability-based sampling will be a function of the degree of accuracy required, the likely costs of error, the population variability and the type of information needed (Tull and Hawkins 1996).

Non-probability sampling does not require the use of a sampling frame and thus the project's costs might be reduced. The sample is chosen at the convenience of the researcher to fit the needs of the particular project. Samples can be created by convenience sampling (simply selecting individuals convenient to the research project), purposive sampling (where individuals are selected who are felt appropriate to the project objectives) or quota sampling.

In quota sampling the researcher makes a clear effort to ensure that the sample they construct mirrors the characteristics of the sample as a whole. Thus if a nonprofit were looking to assess the awareness of their organization/brand among members of the local population, the researchers could proceed by identifying the demographic profile of that population. They might do this by age and gender, for example. They would then create a quota such as that depicted in Table 3.2 to ensure that the balance of people whose opinions they solicit reflects that of the population as a whole

It is important not to confuse quota sampling with stratified sampling. The major difference is that in the former the interviewer/researcher selects the individual respondent, in the latter the selection process is carried out by random selection.

Table 3.2 *Derivation of quota sample*

	Percentage of population	Quota sample (50 individuals)
Male (aged 20–40)	10	5
Male (aged 41–60)	16	8
Male (aged 60+)	26	13
Female (aged 20–40)	14	7
Female (aged 41–60)	10	5
Female (aged 60+)	24	12
Total	100	50

Sample size

The question of how big a sample to use for research is not an easy one to answer as it depends on a number of factors. Much depends on the type of sample, the statistics that will be calculated, the homogeneity of the population and the resources (time, people and money) that are available. It is impossible in this chapter to cover all the pertinent factors, but it is worth noting that there are now a number of tables, calculator functions and software programs that will prompt the user with the relevant questions and generate an appropriate sample size. There are also many websites hosted by research agencies that have sponsored online tools to help the inexperienced researcher.

A surprising point to consider when calculating the sample size is that it has nothing to do with the size of the population. The reason for this is quite straightforward. Rather than the size of the population being the key, it is the extent to which all the members of the population have the same value or response. If you had 20,000 people in a population who all responded in exactly the same way to a direct marketing solicitation, then obviously you would only need a sample of one of them to ascertain the behaviour of the others. However, this is not a very likely scenario. Typically not everyone mailed will give and individuals will give different amounts. Thus what affects the sample size that will be necessary is the variability of the population. Obviously the greater the variability, the larger will be the sample required to estimate aggregate behaviour with any precision.

QUESTIONNAIRE DESIGN

General advice

In designing a research questionnaire there are a number of points to bear in mind.

Overall length

People quickly get bored with completing surveys, particularly in face-to-face or telephone situations. In these circumstances the length of the questionnaire should be held to an absolute minimum with the questions posed tightly integrated with the overall research problem. Postal questionnaires can be somewhat longer since respondents may complete them at their leisure, but researchers employing questionnaires of over four pages will note a sharp drop-off rate in the achieved response rate.

Questions should be clear and unambiguous

Questions should be written in the language of the target audience. It should be remembered that while a fundraiser may be highly conversant with the language employed by the cause, members of the public may not understand much of the specialist terminology and even fewer of the acronyms. These must be studiously avoided or explained.

Each question should also be written and checked for clarity. The question should also avoid ambiguity and the notorious 'and' word. Consider the example in the box. If this question seems appropriate at first glance, consider how a donor might answer if donating to the organization gives them a sense of pride, but they hate the communications they receive. Each question in a questionnaire should address one dimension only.

Please indicate the extent to which you agree with the following statement employing the following scale:

1 = Strongly Disagree
2 = Disagree
3 = No opinion
4 = Agree
5 = Strongly agree

Donating money to this charity gives me a sense of real pride and I enjoy receiving the communications they send me.

1	*2*	*3*	*4*	*5*

Use closed questions wherever possible

It is important when designing a questionnaire to consider how the data will be analysed. Closed questions are much easier to analyse since they only allow respondents a range of options in respect of their response. The example of age category is thus a closed question.

Open questions by contrast invite the respondent to offer an answer which then has to be coded into categories (or interpreted) *post hoc* by the researcher (e.g. Please tell us what you think of our donor communications). It is this latter dimension that makes the inclusion of open

---

Please indicate your age category:

☐ Under 20
☐ 21–40
☐ 41–60
☐ 61–80
☐ 81+

---

questions undesirable since they can substantially slow down the speed of the analysis undertaken and greatly increase the costs of analysis as a consequence. It should be noted however that the use of closed questions requires the researcher to have a firm grasp of the subject area in advance, since they must ensure that the options available to respondents are comprehensive. Where doubt remains, some researchers add a final category, namely 'other – please specify'.

Classifications should be carefully designed

Where closed questions are employed, researchers should take great care to design the categories appropriately. Each option should be discrete, unlike the example here where it is possible to tick two boxes if one is aged, 20, 40, 60 or 80.

Please indicate your age category:

☐ Under 20

☐ 20–40

☐ 40–60

☐ 60–80

☐ 80+

Similarly confusions can arise about the meaning of some categories. Asking for occupation can be a particular problem – for example in one instance an individual chose to describe his occupation as 'bank director' when in reality his role involved greeting customers at the door and directing them to the correct counter!

Avoid leading questions

Leading questions are those that direct the respondent to give a specific answer, thus 'Did the recent financial scandal affect your giving?' is doomed to failure from the outset. Less obviously asking a donor whether they have read a particular magazine or communication may simply prompt them to say 'Yes'. If a researcher is interested in recall of specific communications or the media exposure of a particular individual s/he will be advised to generate a list of communications and to ask the respondent which of them he/she can recall or has read, respectively. Respondents are then less likely to answer in an 'ego-defensive' manner.

Order questions in a logical sequence

In designing a questionnaire it is also important to group together questions that pertain to a particular issue so as not to confuse the respondent as to what specifically is being asked. Similarly it is appropriate to seek to 'funnel' responses from general questions about the issue as a whole down to the specifics of exactly what data are being sought. In other words, questionnaires should be constructed in a logical order that guides the respondent in an orderly manner through the topic.

Keep personal questions until the end

If it is necessary to ask any sensitive questions of respondents, perhaps their ethnic background, income level, religion, or attitudes to tough social issues, it is better to ask these at the end of the questionnaire rather than at the beginning. Asking these questions up front is likely to put off the respondent from completing the questionnaire as he/she is likely to assume that all of the questionnaire will probe for such personal data. Asking for this at the end of a questionnaire, when a respondent has already invested considerable time in the process, and when some form of relationship has been established, is far less likely to result in non-completion.

Pilot test

It is absolutely essential that any questionnaire be piloted before rolling it out to a particular audience. While all the questions posed might seem entirely logical and appropriate to the researcher, there are inevitably a few that create confusion, fail to be understood, or attract answers that the research team were not expecting. A pilot test can be undertaken at low cost with a small percentage of the sample and any necessary changes can be made before the time and expense of the full survey roll-out are incurred.

Scaling techniques for surveys

There are two important scaling techniques that are typically used by researchers in surveys, Likert scales and Semantic Differential scales. There are others, but these are the most commonly employed.

Likert scales

A Likert scale is a list of statements with five (or sometimes seven) possible choices such as 'Strongly agree, Agree, Neutral (or no opinion), Disagree and Strongly disagree'. The scale is used against a battery of questions that are given to respondents. The researcher is then able to measure the attitudes of respondents. Typically the items included in the battery will have been generated from prior qualitative research, or secondary sources. An example battery of questions for Arthritis care is provided here.

---

1 Thinking back to the first time you supported Arthritis Care, how important were the following factors in influencing your decision to start giving? Please circle the appropriate point on the scale.

FACTORS	*Very unimportant*				*Very important*
I believed Arthritis Care's management to be professional	1	2	3	4	5
I felt it was expected of me	1	2	3	4	5
I felt pressured into giving	1	2	3	4	5
I felt that someone I know might benefit from my support	1	2	3	4	5
I felt that Arthritis Care had a good reputation	1	2	3	4	5
I found Arthritis Care's original approach to me professional	1	2	3	4	5
I thought my family/friends would expect me to give	1	2	3	4	5
I wanted to give in memory of a loved one	1	2	3	4	5
My family had a strong link to this charity	1	2	3	4	5

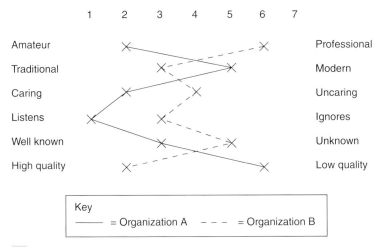

Figure 3.3 *Brand profile of two nonprofits*

In presenting the results from questions designed in this format it is now common practice to present the mean and/or median scores calculated from all the respondents who answered each question. Thus the higher the average score, the greater the degree of agreement with each of the statements listed.

Semantic differential scales

These scales are designed to measure differences between words. As previously, qualitative work may have identified a series of constructs or ways in which people think about the organization and its services. An attitude battery consisting of bipolar constructs can then be developed. A five- or seven-point rating scale is frequently used. As an example the name of a particular organization could appear at the top of a page on a questionnaire. Respondents could then be asked to rate this organization using each of the scales in the battery. Computed results could then allow the researcher to compile an attitude profile, perhaps comparing perceptions of their own organization with those of a key competitor.

In this example the bipolar constructs could include:

Amateur	Professional
Traditional	Modern
Caring	Uncaring
Listens	Ignores
Well known	Unknown
High quality	Low quality

The profile of two organizations could then be compared as indicated in Figure 3.3

DATA ANALYSIS

Qualitative data

The process of data analysis differs greatly between qualitative and quantitative data. Qualitative data from interviews and focus groups is typically transcribed from recordings of the original research.

The resultant text is then input into a software package such as NUD*IST or NVIVO which allows the researcher to examine and code each aspect of the content.

The majority of qualitative software packages operate in a similar way and allow a researcher to highlight a line or lines of text that contain a particular idea. This idea is then assigned a code. Subsequent text containing similar ideas will also be assigned this particular code. In a typical analysis of focus group data there may be 100 or more codes that reflect different facets of the discussion and the response thereto. Text can also be coded according to who is speaking and reflect gender, income, age and so on.

In writing up the results researchers can then request that the software groups the text of the discussions by code – and thus the themes to emerge from each facet of the discussion can easily be written up and peppered with direct quotations from respondents to illustrate why a particular conclusion has been drawn. One might also explore, again using the codes, whether the views of participants varied by categories such as age, gender, income and so on.

An example of this form of analysis and how it is written up is provided in Exhibit 3.2. In this example the researchers were interested to explore the impact of a merger between two or more nonprofits on their subsequent fundraising activity. A series of depth interviews were conducted with senior fundraisers who had experienced the merger process and its outcomes. In the brief abstract reproduced here the researchers report their findings in respect of the critical success factors that drive success in post-merger fundraising. Notice how each idea expressed in the interviews is expressed in turn, described and where appropriate illustrated with a direct quotation. This is typical of the format of many qualitative research reports.

EXHIBIT 3.2   RESULTS OF ANALYSIS

Critical success factors

The interviews began by exploring the facets of the merger process that respondents believed could contribute to successful post-merger fundraising activity. All respondents agreed that a primary factor here was the quality of communication that had been undertaken with donors and other stakeholder groups.

> It is absolutely essential that the reasons for merger are clear and laudable and those reasons are communicated effectively to all stakeholders in such a way that they feel a part of the process.

The notion of involvement was addressed by several respondents who clearly felt that all potential funders should be kept appraised of developments and where appropriate consulted over the action that should be taken. While this is clearly easier in the case of nonprofits who have a few, perhaps institutional, funders, it was still felt to be practical even with direct mail donors.

> We felt it was important to involve all our donor groups in the decision-making, but since we have a database of over 500,000 individuals it was clearly not going to be practicable to consult everyone. We settled on a survey which actually gave us a very useful insight into the issues and concerns that these individuals had.

Aside from the desire that had been expressed to be as inclusive as possible in the decision-making processes, there were often more pragmatic reasons for keeping organizational funders 'in the loop'. In the case of one particularly large merger, for example, the resultant organization would have had 'embarrassingly' high levels of reserves. Indeed some informants were also of the view that the accounting SORP (Statement of Recommended Practice) had highlighted reserves as a particular issue, drawing the attention of potential donors specifically toward this facet of the organization.

> We spent a lot of time thinking about what a merged organization might look like. We thought about each aspect of the organization, its services, structures and financial profile. We recognized that in the case of the latter, the nature of the case we make for support might require change and also that issues such as fundraising ratios and reserves could potentially trip us up in the future.

Other key financial matters of relevance and concern to fundraising management were restricted income funds and endowments, where income/capital can be spent only on specific objects due to limitations applied by previous donors to the charity.

> It is important to look carefully at the nature of the restrictions in order to ensure that the funds can be transferred into the new organization, and/or that the restrictions can be preserved. With funds that are not technically restricted, they can be 'earmarked' or designated in order to respect the wishes of donors if this is thought advisable.

It was noted that consent is required from funders to transfer a restricted fund, and this can be a complex procedure. It therefore proves important to educate funders so that they are aware of the distinction between restricted and unrestricted funds and do not pull out under the impression that the charity has access to more funds than it does in practice.

A further key issue was felt to be the treatment of volunteers. Without exception all respondents felt volunteers should be treated in the same way as paid fundraising staff during the merger and should thus be consulted and kept fully informed throughout. A number of informants had established within their organization a merger committee whose role was to work with key stakeholders such as volunteers, but also service users, charity workers, subscribers, members, patrons and funders to ensure that these key stakeholders are carried along with the merger plans and do not block change. Three respondents had even decided on a joint retreat for key staff from the parties to a merger, the purpose of which was to address questions or concerns and to increase productivity and morale during the merger period. It was felt essential, however, that merger negotiations were not protracted and that agreement be reached as soon as was practicable.

Consequences of merger

Over two-thirds of informants had recorded a decline in fundraising income at the time of the merger and immediately thereafter. There were felt to be a number of key reasons for this phenomenon. First, the level of reserves of the newly merged body (as noted above) was felt to deter many institutional funders. Second, in the case of some of the mergers investigated it was the case that a significant percentage of the database of individual and corporate supporters was shared between the two parties to the merger. Following merger these individuals/organizations tended to offer just one gift where previously there had been two.

> Despite a big push, promoting the efficiencies the new organization had to offer and the enhancements to service provision it could supply, we were disappointed that individuals who appeared on both of the original databases were now largely giving just one gift to the new charity at the same level they would have supported both previously.

Informants also felt that despite the publicity accruing to the merger, many of the individual donors were confused about the identity of the organization and did not recognize the campaign materials from the new organization as being of relevance to them.

> Many of our donors are elderly and we found that many did not recognize the materials we had sent were from us. With hindsight we should probably have made better use of the facets of our brand such individuals would have recognized. The new corporate livery was very different and that was a mistake.

Indeed, the informants agreed the consequences of merger activity would vary by category of funder, and that a strategy that recognized the needs of each group, before, during and after the merger was therefore essential.

Quantitative data

Software packages are also available to analyse quantitative data and these vary in terms of sophistication and cost. Among the most commonly employed are SNAP (which also aids in questionnaire design) and SPSS (Statistical Package for the Social Sciences). There are then a range of statistics that may be calculated to assist the researcher in summarizing and interpreting the results they have achieved. Such analysis is beyond the scope of this text, but interested readers may wish to consult Hair et al. (1995).

The most common forms of summary that are used to represent this form of data include tables, bar charts, histograms and simple numerical summaries such as the mean, median and standard deviation.

Charts

Bar charts or frequency diagrams are probably the most common forms of graphical representation of statistical data. They consist of a series of bars, the height of which is either proportional to the frequency with which a particular outcome occurs, or to the probability that this outcome will occur.

A simple bar chart is presented in Figure 3.4. In this example the total donations to a range of fundraising products are presented for the period shown. While the same information could be presented in tabular form the reader will appreciate the greater degree of impact that can be achieved with a graphic presentation. It is immediately obvious to the eye which of the fundraising products has performed the best.

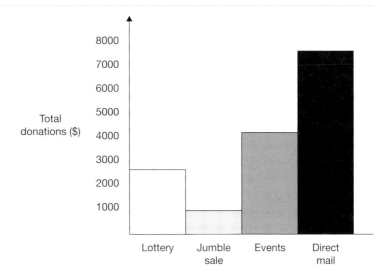

Figure 3.4
*Fundraising
product
performance*

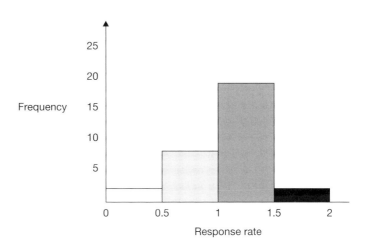

Figure 3.5
*Dolphin Sanctuary
mailing response
rates*

A second type of chart commonly employed for the presentation of data is the histogram (see Figure 3.5). In this case it is not only the height of the bars that is significant, but also the dimensions of the base. In this example the Dolphin Sanctuary has plotted the response rates that it has historically received to one of its most popular recruitment mailings. It seems clear that a common outcome for this particular mailing would be to achieve a response rate of *circa* 1 to 1.5 per cent.

Descriptive statistics

MEAN

One of the most commonly encountered descriptive statistics is the mean – denoted by $\bar{x}$. It is also one of the simplest to calculate. You simply add up the results of a given set of measurements and then divide by the number of measurements. This is shown in the following mathematical notation:

$$\bar{x} = \frac{\sum_{i=1} x_i}{n}$$

In this case the formula simply indicates that to calculate the mean one has to calculate the sum of the values of x from the first observation to the last and then divide by the number of observations (denoted by n).

MEDIAN

A second commonly used descriptor is the median. This is simply the measurement that falls in the middle of a given set of observations or 'distribution'. There are many occasions when it is preferable to quote the median rather than the mean. Specifically the median is preferable where there are a number of outliers in the distribution that would bias the mean and thus give a misleading picture of the nature of the distribution. Suppose, for example, we were interested in reporting the 'average' salaries earned by donors. We take a small sample of the salaries earned for five individuals and obtain $20K, $22K, $23K, $24K and $70K. In this case the median value would be $23K while the mean distorted by the outlier would be $31.8K. The median would thus be a more reasonable representation of this distribution than the mean.

STANDARD DEVIATION

Both the mean and the median give the researcher some idea of where the centre of a distribution is located. While this is clearly useful information researchers are usually also interested to know how spread around this distribution might be. One possible way that this measure might be derived would be to take the difference between each measurement and the mean and then to calculate the average of this deviation. The problem with this approach however is that the deviations will be both positive and negative. Consider a distribution containing the measurements 1, 2 and 3. In this case the mean would be 2 and the deviation −1, 0 and +1. The mean deviation in this case would be zero and we would therefore be no further forward in attempting to find a measure of spread. The way around this difficulty is to calculate the deviations from the mean as previously and then to square these numbers (which removes any negative signs), add these squared numbers together, divide by the number of measurements and then take the square root of the answer. In our previous example the square deviations would be 1, 0 and 1 and their sum would be 2. If we then divide this by 3 to get the mean of the squared deviations and take the square root of the answer we obtain a result of *circa* 0.8. This somewhat wordy description is represented in mathematical notation as follows:

$$s = \sqrt{\frac{\sum_{i=1}(x - \bar{x})^2}{n}}$$

The more spread out a given distribution might be, the greater will be its standard deviation.

RANGE

In cases where the median has been used to describe the 'average' point on a distribution a good measure of spread to accompany this value is the range. The range is simply the highest value observed minus the lowest value. While this is a useful figure it is helpful to recognize that this too can be strongly influenced by outliers. For this reason some researchers prefer to quote the inter-quartile range. This is simply the difference between two points. The lower of these corresponds to a point below which one-quarter of the observations lie (the lower quartile) and the second to the point above which one-quarter of the points lie (the upper quartile).

In the example provided in Exhibit 3.3 we reproduce an extract from a quantitative research report. Here the researchers have chosen to present the data in tabular form and to cite many of the statistics listed above. The objective of this research was to compare the demographic profile

EXHIBIT 3.3 RESULTS OF ANALYSIS: PROFILE OF RESPONDENTS

Tables 3.3 to 3.8 present the details of the demographic profile of respondents. The results are presented for both legacy pledgers and supporters. The results in Table 3.3 illustrate the slight female bias present on many charity databases. There is no significant difference however in the balance of gender between the supporter and pledger groups.

The occupation of each group is depicted in Table 3.4. It may be noted that both the supporter and pledger groups have a high concentration of office/clerical and professional individuals, reflecting the bias towards socio-economic groups B and C1 in giving. The high concentration of teachers/lecturers is also noteworthy and again typical of the profile of many charitable databases. No significant diffeences between pledgers and supporters could be identified.

The income profile of respondents is reported in Table 3.5. In this case it can be seen that pledgers report a significantly lower annual income than supporters (X^2 = 46.98, Significance level 0.000).

Significant differences between the two groups were also reported when examining the marital status of respondents. Pledgers are significantly more likely to be living alone, either because they are single or because they have been widowed (Goodman and Kuskal Tau value 0.061, Significance level 0.000). This difference is also supported in Table 3.7 where it

Table 3.3 Gender of respondents

Gender	Supporter (%)	Pledger (%)
Male	40.2	35.1
Female	59.8	64.9

Table 3.4 Past/present occupation of respondents

Occupation	Supporter (%)	Pledger (%)
Director	5.4	4.2
Housewife/husband	8.5	6.4
Manager	6.9	7.8
Manual/factory	0.9	1.4
Office/clerical	12.6	16.9
Professional	27.0	23.7
Self-employed	6.6	8.0
Shop assistant	0.9	0.8
Skilled tradesman	2.1	2.0
Supervisor	0.7	1.6
Teacher/lecturer	17.0	18.1
Other	11.4	9.0

can be seen that pledgers are significantly less likely to have children (X^2 = 107.55, Significance level 0.000).

Table 3.8 presents the remaining demographic data captured in the survey and in addition presents the total amount donated by each group to the charity sector in the past year. As the results indicate the mean age at which both pledgers and supporters completed their full-time education is very similar, suggesting that many individuals were educated to degree level. No significant difference between the two groups was reported. It can however be seen that pledgers are significantly older than supporters, having a mean age of 68.4 years.

No differences could be discerned between the two groups in relation to the total amount given to charity each year, with supporters offering £601 per annum and pledgers £701. It should be noted that the distributions in each case were highly skewed and that as a consequence a better measure of the typical amount given per annum is the median. The median amount donated per annum by both supporters and pledgers was found to be £300.

Table 3.5 Current income profile of respondents

Category	Supporter (%)	Pledger (%)
Up to £4,999	3.6	4.6
£5,000–£9,999	8.4	17.5
£10,000–£14,999	13.8	17.3
£15,000–£19,999	11.1	14.2
£20,000–£24,999	12.1	14.4
£25,000–£29,999	8.4	7.0
£30,000–£39,999	13.6	10.1
£40,000 +	29.0	14.9

Table 3.6 Marital status

Status	Supporter (%)	Pledger (%)
Single	18.7	34.9
Married	55.1	33.3
Separated	0.3	1.8
Divorced	5.4	5.7
Living with partner	6.2	5.0
Widowed	14.3	19.4

Table 3.7 Presence of children

Children	Supporter (%)	Pledger (%)
No	31.1	61.3
Yes	68.9	38.7

Table 3.8 Demographic and behavioural characteristics

Variable	Supporter mean	Pledger mean	F	Sig
Age at which full-time education completed	20.9	19.0	1.27	0.26
Age	59.2	68.4	53.06	0.00
Amount given to charity each year	£600.64	£701.26	2.41	0.12

and attitudes of individuals who have pledged a bequest to a nonprofit with members of the standard (i.e. non-pledger) supporter base. In this extract the researchers provide the details of their demographic comparison. It is interesting to note that alongside their comparison they have also performed a number of statistical tests to determine whether differences they note between pledgers and supporters are 'significant' differences, represented in the population as a whole, or not significant since they might well be due to sampling errors and the operation of random chance. Comparisons of this type are common in market research and the exact statistical tests that may be employed are a function of the categories of data being examined. This is beyond the scope of this text, but the illustration shows just how useful this additional form of analysis can be.

USING EXTERNAL RESEARCH AGENCIES

At the beginning of the chapter we stressed the need, where external agencies are to be employed in the capturing of data, for senior agency personnel to be involved in defining both the research problem and the research objectives. When an agency is involved in this way it will be necessary to construct a research brief which would include the agreed problem definition and research objectives. If a relationship already exists with a particular agency this can simply be handed over to the respective organization to progress. More usually, however, the brief is used as the basis for competitive tendering, so that the nonprofit can ensure that it is getting the best value for money possible from its agency.

In the case of this latter scenario, the agencies invited to pitch should be asked to respond to the brief with a research proposal document that interprets the research objectives, specifies the data requirements and indicates what methods will be employed to gather the requisite data. This document will also provide details of the proposed costs, and in the case of quantitative research some sense of the level of accuracy of the findings that will be delivered.

The nonprofit is then in a position to select between the competing bids. Partly this will be based on the quality, originality and cost of the proposal. It will also be based on past experience with the organization concerned, their track record with the specific techniques being proposed and the extent to which they have worked with competing organizations – which could be either an advantage or disadvantage depending on the task in hand. Most organizations will want to employ an agency experienced in dealing with the sector, but may not want to work with an agency also assisting a competitor as there could be conflicts of interest and concerns over the confidentiality afforded the project.

In assessing research proposals the following points are relevant.

Methodology

Do the proposed research methods look appropriate given the objectives of the organization? Remember that qualitative and quantitative techniques have their own set of strengths and weaknesses and are better suited to certain kinds of objectives. The nonprofit must therefore ensure that the agency appears to have selected an appropriate methodology.

The nature of the sample

In the case of quantitative research, is the sample proposed representative of the population? It would be usual for researchers to identify the key variables of interest from the outset (perhaps age and gender) and to ensure that the sample comprises an appropriate mix of both. The balance in the sample should reflect the balance in the population.

The size of the sample

Again, in the case of quantitative research, the size of the sample may be an issue. As was noted above, bigger isn't always better! An appropriate sample size is a function of the variability of the population, the number of variables of interest, the analytical techniques it is intended to use and the desired degree of accuracy that is required. Nonprofits should tend to be suspicious of samples, however, where the population is known to be large and variable and the agency is proposing a sample size of less than a couple of hundred individuals. It is surprising how many studies based on very small and potentially very unrepresentative samples are commissioned.

Response rate/non-response bias

Many management reports talk about a survey of X individuals. Let us say for the sake of argument that a researcher claims to have surveyed 2,000 individuals. Often this is the only fact reported. It is only later that one realizes that the response rate obtained was only (let us say) 10 per cent. Their results would thus be based on the views of only 200 individuals. We would have concerns about this since it would put the survey towards the lower end of achievable response rates, but it would not necessarily invalidate the results. The real test is whether the individuals that responded are still representative of the population. There are various ways of testing this. One could look at the characteristics of these individuals, perhaps by age, gender, income, and compare the profile of the respondents with the profile of the population as a whole. If they are broadly similar we might place more faith in the results. We could also take the further step of comparing the responses of the individuals who responded first, with those who responded last and again test for differences. The argument goes that, for example, in the case of postal surveys, those individuals who respond last are likely to be the most like non-responders who by definition never got around to responding at all. Thus if there are differences between these groups we may conclude that there is a strong risk of the views/characteristics of non-responders being quite different from those that responded and thus invalidating the results of the survey. Of course there are many ways of dealing with non-response and from a managerial perspective it is just worth asking an agency how they intend to deal with this dimension.

The degree of accuracy

Reputable agencies and researchers should be able to provide an estimate of the likely accuracy of their research. There is always a likelihood that the findings of a study could have occurred purely by chance. Before basing a strategy on the findings of a given piece of work it is useful to clarify how confident one might be in the findings.

Variables versus constructs

Simple variables such as age, gender, income, height and weight may be measured by a single question. It is necessary to beware of surveys that claim to be able to measure complex social phenomena such as, for example, trust and confidence, by also asking a single question of respondents. Such things are best regarded as 'constructs' and should be measured in a variety of different ways to ensure that the researcher is actually measuring the real phenomena of interest. Thus, rather than asking an individual whether or not they trust charities, which could mean pretty much anything, it is better to ask them the extent to which they trust charities to use donated funds appropriately, not to exploit their donors and so on (as shown in the following example). A single and much more robust measure of trust can then be constructed from the responses to this battery of questions. It is thus worth asking an agency how it would propose to measure key constructs of interest to the organization.

To what extent would you trust voluntary organizations to undertake each of the activities listed?

	Low degree of trust			High degree of trust		
To always act in the best interest of the cause	1	2	3	4	5	6	7
To conduct their operations ethically	1	2	3	4	5	6	7
To use donated funds appropriately	1	2	3	4	5	6	7
Not to exploit their donors	1	2	3	4	5	6	7
To use fundraising techniques that are appropriate and sensitive	1	2	3	4	5	6	7

Having selected a particular agency on the basis of the brief, it will then be necessary to monitor their progress as they begin to develop the project. Most agencies will allocate a client director who will keep the nonprofit appraised of progress. If the organization has commissioned a two-stage project, perhaps beginning with qualitative research, it would be worthwhile asking the agency to report at the end of the first stage before it begins work on a second, perhaps quantitative, phase. This allows the organization to appraise the quality of the work undertaken and to conduct a 'reality' check of the preliminary research findings. There would be little point in progressing with an expensive quantitative study if it were based on an obviously flawed understanding of the particular research issue.

SUMMARY

There will always be a role for high-quality research to aid decision-making in our sector. In this chapter we have proposed a process that organizations can adopt to assist them in managing the research process. We have stressed the need for a clear statement of the research problem and the derivation of specific research objectives. Typically the process then comprises an examination of secondary data sources to see whether the requisite information already exists and may be acquired cost-effectively. In cases where this is not possible it will be necessary to conduct primary research that may be either qualitative or quantitative depending on the nature of the research objectives. We have also outlined in this chapter how both categories of data can be analyzed and written up for the purposes of informing managerial decision-making. In the next chapter we move on to consider how this research may be used to inform the development of fundraising strategy.

DISCUSSION QUESTIONS

1   Distinguish, with examples, between qualitative and quantitative marketing research.
2   As the fundraising manager of a small children's charity looking to explore the motives for legacy giving, explain and justify a programme of marketing research you would propose to adopt to explore this issue.

3   In your role as the fundraising director of a medium-sized arts charity you have been asked by your CEO to commission a piece of donor research. Explain to her the criteria you would use to select between the agencies likely to compete for this business.
4   Prepare a marketing research plan to explore why donors stop giving to an organization of your choice (i.e. why they lapse their support).

REFERENCES

American Marketing Association (AMA) (1961) *Report of the Definitions Committee*, American Marketing Association, Chicago.

Hair, J.F., Anderson, R.E., Tatham, T. and Black, W.C. (1995) *Multivariate Data Analysis with Readings*, Prentice Hall, Englewood Cliffs, NJ.

Kotler, P. (1967) *Marketing Management: Analysis, Planning and Control*, Prentice Hall, Englewood Cliffs, NJ.

Kumar, V., Aaker, D.A. and Day, C.S. (1999) *Essentials of Marketing Research*, John Wiley, New York.

Sudman, S. and Blair, E. (1999) 'Sampling in the Twenty First Century', *Journal of the Academy of Marketing Science*, 27(2): 269–277.

Tull, D.S. and Hawkins, D.I. (1996) *Marketing Research: Measurement and Method*, 6th Edn, Macmillan, New York.

Chapter 4

Strategic planning
The fundraising plan

OBJECTIVES

By the end of this chapter you should be able to:
- Develop SMART fundraising objectives.
- Develop appropriate strategic direction.
- Segment a range of individual and organizational markets.
- Develop a positioning strategy.
- Develop a case for support.
- Integrate plans for specific forms of fundraising into the aggregate fundraising plan for the organization.

INTRODUCTION

The generic format for a fundraising plan identified in Chapter 2 is reproduced in Figure 4.1. In Chapter 2 we dealt with the early stages of the plan, highlighting the significance of the fundraising audit and suggesting categories of data that the fundraising department should look to assemble before writing the operational sections of the plan. The significance of this material lay in developing a detailed picture of where the organization stood presently in relation to its donor markets, competitors and so on. We also reviewed the role and contribution of the SWOT analysis in summarizing this data and suggested that in most cases it would be appropriate to conduct a SWOT analysis on the organization from the perspective of each major category of donors. These, we argued, would provide a good working summary of 'where the organization is now.'

In this chapter we will move on to consider the remaining two components of the plan, namely 'Where do we want to be?' and 'How will we get there?' We will consider the role and derivation of fundraising objectives, the characteristics of good objectives and the role that they play in control. We will also consider aspects of fundraising strategy, including overall direction, segmentation and positioning.

As you read this chapter it is important to bear in mind that nonprofits vary widely in terms of size, available resources and structure. There is therefore no 'one correct' structure for a fundraising plan and no one 'right way' of organizing fundraising activity. The outline we present in

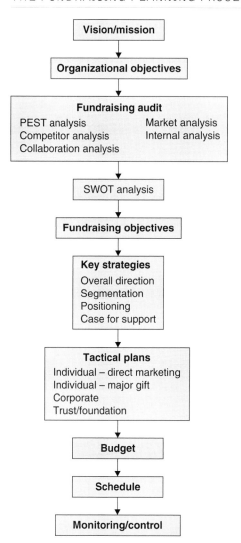

Figure 4.1 *Generic planning framework*

Figure 4.1 is an aggregate fundraising plan, which contains the detail of all the fundraising that the organization will conduct over the planning period (one year, three years, five years, etc.). It contains objectives, generic fundraising strategy and an overview of the tactics the organization will adopt in relation to each form of fundraising undertaken. While this is a common format, some organizations prefer to generate separate documents for each specific form of fundraising and a plan will thus be generated for corporate fundraising, trust/foundation fundraising and individual fundraising. Other organizations prefer a hybrid, where an aggregate fundraising plan exists, typically for use by senior management and the Board of Trustees, with more detailed sub-plans being created at the departmental level for each form of fundraising.

Thus in seeking to provide an overview of fundraising planning we have chosen to structure our debate around one of these alternatives and to focus on a holistic fundraising plan. The detail of planning for distinct forms of fundraising such as corporate, trust/foundation, individual and major gift will be dealt with in subsequent chapters.

SETTING FUNDRAISING OBJECTIVES

Once the organization has identified its current position in the donor market and reviewed what has been accomplished to date it is in a position to decide what might realistically be achieved in the future. As Drucker (1990:107) notes, objectives have a particular significance for nonprofit organizations:

> In a nonprofit organization there is no such (thing as a) bottom line. But there is also a temptation to downplay results. There is the temptation to say: We are serving a good cause. We are doing the Lord's work. Or we are doing something to make life a little better for people and that's a result in itself. That is not enough. If a business wastes its resources on non-results, by and large it loses its own money. In a nonprofit institution though, it's somebody else's money – the donors' money. Service organizations are accountable to donors, accountable for putting the money where the results are and for performance. So, this is an area that needs special emphasis for non-profit executives. Good intentions only pave the way to hell!

In Drucker's view nonprofits should thus be accountable for how they choose to spend their income and that includes what they spend on fundraising. Fundraising objectives ensure that the organization gives adequate consideration to exactly what will be achieved and at exactly what cost.

Objectives are also an important part of the plan as they are the only mechanism by which its success can be measured. If a plan achieves its stated objectives we might reasonably conclude that it has been a success. Without them, one can only speculate as to the planner's original intent and the effectiveness of the activities undertaken. Valuable donated resources could be being wasted, but the organization would have no mechanism for identifying that this was in fact the case.

As a minimum, therefore, fundraising objectives should address the following three issues:

1   The amount of funds that will be raised.
2   The categories of donors that will supply these funds (i.e. individual, corporate, foundation/trust).
3   The acceptable costs of raising these funds.

They can also address more specific issues such as the donor attrition rate (i.e. the percentage of donors lost each year), changes in the lifetime value of donors (see Chapter 6), donor perceptions of service quality and metrics such as average gift, response rate (to postal appeals), return on investment and so on.

For many organizations it may be appropriate to split these objectives out and to consider writing separate objectives for restricted and unrestricted funds, for committed (regular)/uncommitted givers and/or for capital campaigns as against the annual fund. This is frequently appropriate since these forms of fundraising differ greatly. The terms are explained in the following:

■   *Restricted/unrestricted funds*   This terminology simply reflects the fact that donors can offer two distinct types of funds to an organization. Restricted funds are funds donated for a specific purpose and may not be used for general purposes. Thus if a donor donates £1 million to support the extension of a university library, the organization may not use these restricted funds to support teaching costs or management overheads. Unrestricted funds, by contrast, are funds that are donated to support the work of the charity and are not designated to be spent on a particular project or programme. Since many nonprofits desire the maximum possible flexibility the emphasis within fundraising appeals is frequently on unrestricted funds. As the reader will appreciate it makes sense to write objectives for both categories of funds, since the degree of flexibility associated with each category is very different.

■ *Capital campaigns/annual fund*   These terms are more frequently encountered in the United States and refer to two classic forms of fundraising that may be undertaken. The capital campaign is designed as the title suggests to raise 'capital' for a specific and often major project. Thus if a nonprofit needs a new building to house its operations, create a resource centre for adults with disabilities or build a sensory garden for visually impaired children, it will run a capital campaign to raise the requisite funds. The annual fund, by contrast, is the term given to fundraising designed to fund the ongoing running costs of the organization. Nonprofits would typically write a separate plan for each form of fundraising – but in some cases the plan is merged to ensure the maximum possible synergy from the two appeals and in that case it is standard practice to specify objectives for each set of activities.

■ *Uncommited/committed givers*   This terminology is widely employed in the UK to distinguish between donors who have signed up to a regular payment to a charity deducted monthly, quarterly or annually direct from their bank account or credit card. These donors are frequently distinguished separately in fundraising objectives since separate appeals would typically be conducted to recruit committed givers and they tend to receive a tailored programme of communication once they have been recruited which reflects their enhanced value to the organization. The term 'uncommitted' donors is often used to denote donors who prefer to send a series of occasional donations, perhaps writing a cheque in response to ongoing appeals. Since the term can sound derisory of donors who are often very loyal and generous to the organization, some nonprofits prefer to use the terms 'cash' or 'one-off' donors instead.

It is important to realize that the style in which the objectives are written is also a significant issue. Objectives are only of value if it is possible to use them as an aid to managing the organization's resources and hence vague terms and needless ambiguity should be studiously avoided.

> vague objectives, however emotionally appealing are counter-productive to sensible planning and are usually the result of the human propensity for wishful thinking which often smacks more of cheerleading than serious marketing leadership. What this means is that while it is arguable whether directional terms such as decrease, optimize, minimize, should be used as objectives, it seems logical that unless there is some measure, or yardstick, against which to measure a sense of locomotion towards achieving them, they do not serve any useful purpose.
>
> (MacDonald 1984:88)

Hence to be managerially useful, good objectives should exhibit the following characteristics. They should be:

1   *Specific*   Related to one particular aspect of fundraising activity and/or one particular category of donors. Objectives that relate simultaneously to diverse aspects of fundraising are difficult to assess since they may require the organization to use different techniques of measurement and to look across different planning horizons. Attempting to combine activities might therefore lead to confusion, or at best a lack of focus.

2   *Measurable*   Words such as 'maximize' or 'increase' are not particularly helpful when it later becomes necessary to assess the effectiveness of fundraising activity. To be useful, objectives should avoid these terms and be capable of measurement. They should therefore

specify quantifiable values whenever possible, e.g. to achieve a 10 per cent increase in legacy/bequest income.

3   *Achievable*   Fundraising objectives should be derived from a thorough analysis of the content of the fundraising audit, not from creative thinking on the part of managers. Objectives which have no possibility of accomplishment will only serve to demoralize those responsible for their achievement and serve to deplete resources that could have had a greater potential impact elsewhere.

4   *Relevant*   Fundraising objectives should be consistent with the objectives of the organization as a whole. They should merely supply a greater level of detail, identifying specifically what the fundraising function will have to achieve to provide the nonprofit organization with the resources it needs to continue to offer the desired level of service provision.

5   *Time-scaled*   Good objectives should clearly specify the duration over which they are to be achieved. Not only does this help to plan the strategies and tactics by which they will be accomplished but it also assists in permitting the organization to set in place control procedures to ensure that the stated targets will indeed be met. Thus monthly 'sub-targets' for each form of fundraising could be set and corrective action initiated early in the duration of a plan as soon as a variance is detected.

Thus good fundraising objectives should be SMART! (Specific, Measurable, Achievable, Relevant, Time-scaled).

Having now outlined the rules, it might be helpful to actually demonstrate what typical fundraising objectives might include.

■   To attract £250,000 in voluntary income from individual donors by the end of the financial year.
■   To attract £150,000 of (cash) corporate support by the end of November 2009.
■   To attract 100,000 new committed givers by the end of December 2010.
■   To lower the annual attrition rate of individual cash givers to 15 per cent per annum by the end of December 2009.

KEY STRATEGIES

Having specified the objectives it is intended that the plan will achieve, it is now possible to address the means by which these will be accomplished. The broad approach to be adopted is termed 'fundraising strategy' and it is useful to consider this in relation to the following four categories:

1   Overall direction
2   Segmentation strategy
3   Positioning strategy
4   Case for support.

Each will now be considered in turn.

OVERALL DIRECTION

Overall direction pertains to the selection of fundraising methods that will be used to raise funds. Where the organization requires additional funds to those raised in the previous year there are four key strategic directions that it can follow if growth is required (Ansoff 1968). These are

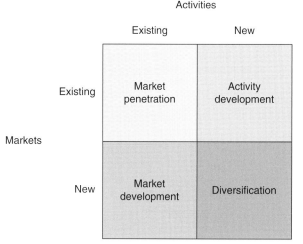

Figure 4.2 *Ansoff matrix*
Source: Adapted from Ansoff, *Corporate Strategy* (1968) Penguin Books: London.

illustrated in Figure 4.2. All the options involve making decisions about the range of fundraising activities that will be conducted and the markets into which they will be delivered. Each strategic option is outlined below.

- *Market penetration*   The first strategic option that may be adopted to achieve growth is market penetration. As Figure 4.2 indicates this involves the fundraiser in attempting to raise more funds from existing donor markets. Existing fundraising activities are continued, but the organization seeks to solicit greater levels of participation from the target donor group. Thus if an organization is utilizing direct marketing to attract new donors it may elect to follow a strategy of market penetration and solicit funds from an ever greater number of these individuals. Similarly if a nonprofit is soliciting funds from major donors in a particular city, it could follow a strategy of market penetration and attempt to find other individuals living in this area who are sufficiently wealthy and have sufficient interest in the cause to offer a major gift.

  It is important to recognize that this strategy involves the least risk of any of the four options. This is simply because the organization utilizes only those fundraising activities it is already familiar with and contacts only those categories of donor it has direct experience of dealing with. By definition it will therefore have a firm grasp of what to expect and the likelihood of the strategy failing because of serious errors on the organization's part is greatly diminished.

- *Activity development*   This option engenders a higher degree of risk, because here the organization achieves growth by developing new forms of fundraising that it will attempt to utilize to solicit funds from existing donor groups. Charities employing direct mail to raise funds might create new products such as 'Adopt a Child' or 'Sponsor a dog' that can be used to generate greater commitment and loyalty from the donor base. Equally, those charities working in the realm of community or local group fundraising could introduce raffles, competitions, jumble sales, for example, to bolster the range of products they can offer to solicit funds.

- *Market development*   Market development involves the organization in seeking new markets for its existing fundraising products or activities. Thus it will look to target new groups of donors who have not previously been addressed by the organization. Nonprofits could seek to enter new counties, cities or geographical regions of the country. They could also decide to target different types of people or organizations than have previously been approached.

This strategy also contains a degree of risk, since while the organization is familiar with the techniques that will be used, it has no prior experience in dealing with these donors and therefore no direct knowledge of how they might react.

■ *Diversification*   This constitutes the highest risk strategy of all. It involves targeting new donors with new products and thus the organization has no experience on which it can rely. Nonprofits, for example, may take a decision to enter the retail or mail order market for the first time and to raise funds by selling products. Others might choose to establish a website to target younger categories of donors. Similarly, in the USA a nonprofit might decide to explore 'planned giving' for the first time (see Chapter 7). These are all examples of diversification.

All attempts to raise additional funds can be classified under one of these four headings and while in itself this may not appear a useful exercise, the real utility of the model lies in providing a structured way for organizations to actively consider *all* of the alternatives available to them, before they decide on those they will actually pursue. In using the model nonprofits should be prepared to brainstorm every possible strategic alternative and then to begin a process of deciding which of the available alternatives is the most appealing and balances the degree of risk to which the organization is exposed. In practice nonprofits will therefore tend to opt for a mix of a number of the four available options.

Table 4.1 contains a summary of the key fundraising activities that are presently conducted in the UK, USA and Australia. In employing the Ansoff model fundraisers can decide which of these

Table 4.1 *Fundraising activities/products*

Individual fundraising	Corporate fundraising
Personal solicitation	Personal solicitation
Direct mail	Charity of the year
Press advertising	Payroll giving
Press/magazine inserts	Staff fundraising events
Direct response television advertising	Sponsored events (e.g. walks)
Radio advertising	Special events / dinners / galas
Face to face or direct dialogue	Cause related marketing
Door to door (soliciting gifts on the doorstep)	Challenge events
Street collections	
Telephone fundraising	
Trading (charity shops / mail order catalogues	
Flag days	
Sale of lottery/raffle tickets	
Jumble sales	
Special events / dinners / galas	
Sponsored events (e.g. walks)	
SMS text messaging	
Internet fundraising	
Challenge events	

could potentially be employed and site them appropriately in the matrix. A more detailed analysis of how appropriate each might be can then be undertaken and decisions taken about the activities that will be taken forward. Organizations often do this by looking at what activities will be adopted in the short, medium and long term, since commencing a completely new form of fundraising is likely to take time to accomplish.

Of course there may be a number of circumstances when the nonprofit does not wish to raise additional funds, or to continue with a particular form of fundraising. Thus two additional strategies warrant consideration

- *Consolidation*   There may be circumstances when the nonprofit has had a particularly good year, or where it has rapidly grown a new fundraising activity to the point where existing volunteer and staff resources are stretched. In either of these two scenarios the nonprofit could look to consolidate its position and rather than grow voluntary income from these sources it could merely look to sustain it.
- *Withdrawal*   This strategy may be appropriate where the levels of voluntary income an activity is generating have fallen significantly, or where the cost of conducting a particular activity can no longer be justified. In these circumstances it can be appropriate to follow a strategy of withdrawal and to terminate the activity altogether.

MARKET SEGMENTATION: SEGMENTING INDIVIDUAL DONOR MARKETS

This process of identifying suitable groups of donors to target is known as 'market segmentation'. Kotler (1991:66) defines it as 'the task of breaking down the total market (which is typically too large to serve) into segments that share common properties'. In a similar vein Wilson et al. (1992:91) define it as 'the process of dividing a varied and differing group of (donors) or potential (donors) into smaller groups within which broadly similar patterns of needs exist'.

Segmentation thus allows the fundraiser to develop a specific offer likely to appeal to the needs/interests of certain groups of donors. Segmentation is only worthwhile where different groups of donors have different needs, or must be approached in a different way from others. The rationale for segmentation is simply that by focusing on a distinctive set of needs or interests, the nonprofit can develop a fundraising programme that uniquely addresses these issues. The fact that this adaptation has taken place makes it more attractive for these donors to give to the organization and enhanced response rates and donations are likely to result.

There are a variety of criteria that can be used to segment both individual and organizational markets. These are outlined as follows.

Demographic segmentation

It may be possible to segment a market on the basis of variables such as age, gender, socio-economic group, family size, family life cycle, income, religion, race, occupation or education. Collectively, these are referred to as demographic variables. In most cases a combination of some or all of these demographic variables will be used in building a profile of existing and prospective donors. Demographic data have been collected over many years and a great deal is known about the behaviour of each grouping in terms of the likely needs, wants, sympathies and preferences of each.

Age, gender, family lifecycle stage, income/occupation and race/ethnicity are possibly the most frequently cited demographic variables used in nonprofit profiling and prospect segmentation.

- *Age* A huge proportion of giving to nonprofits stems from the older sections of the population. Analysis of the Family Expenditure Survey in the UK indicated that for every increase of ten years in the age of the head of the household there is an increased likelihood of giving of 3 per cent, and an increase in the value of donations of 30 per cent (Banks and Tanner 1997). Age tends to be a reliable indicator of the sources of information an individual is likely to use, and to the social influences they are likely to be susceptible to (Philips and Sternthal 1977).
- *Gender* Many studies of giving have demonstrated that women and men give differently. It appears that women tend to spread their giving amongst a greater number of charities, and so tend to give smaller amounts to each one (Sargeant 2004). Most nonprofit donor databases are weighted markedly towards females. Studies in for-profit marketing have shown that the sexes respond very differently, for example, to direct marketing communications. Some nonprofits as a consequence develop 'male' or 'female' copy in their recruitment appeals depending on the target audience.
- *Family life cycle* The concept of a family life cycle was first put forward by Rowntree over a century ago. The version now used was that developed by Wells and Gubar in 1966, which is illustrated in Table 4.2. As a composite model made up of age, number of years married,

Table 4.2 Family lifecycle

Stages in the family lifecycle	Buying patterns
1 Bachelor stage: Young single people living at home	Few financial commitments – recreation and fashion orientated
2 Newly married couples: Young no children	High purchase rate of consumer durables – buy white goods, cars, furniture
3 Full nest 1: Youngest child under 6	House buying is at a peak. Liquid assets are low – buy medicines, toys, baby food, white goods
4 Full nest 2: Youngest child 6 or over	Financial position is improving – buy a wider variety of foods, bicycles and pianos
5 Full nest 3: Older married couples with dependent children	Financial position is improving still further. Some children now have jobs and wives are working. Increasing purchase of desirables – buy furniture and luxury goods
6 Empty nest 1: Older married couples, no children, head of household still in workforce	Home ownership is at peak – savings have increased and financial position improved. Interested in travel, recreation and self-education. Not interested in new products – buy luxuries and home improvements
7 Empty nest 2: Older married, no children living at home, head of household retired	Substantial reduction in income. Buy medical products and appliances that aid health, sleep and digestion
8 Solitary survivor in the workforce	Income still high, but may sell home
9 Solitary survivor retired	Same medical and product needs as group 7. Substantial cut in income. Need for attention and security

Source: Wilson *et al.* (1994). Reproduced with kind permission of Elsevier Ltd.

ages of children and working status, the concept of the family life cycle has proved more useful in many cases than simple segmentation based on age alone. However, it is based on the traditional concept of the nuclear family, and is obviously no longer completely valid as such when one views the current and changing patterns of family life and women's employment. Despite these criticisms, the model remains widely used, and a helpful indicator of propensity to donate.

■ *Income/occupation*   Income has also been proved to be a useful base for segmentation and, despite difficulties in identifying a true picture of income for any particular group, has been shown to be a powerful indicator of propensity to give, and of likely donation levels. Some segmentation systems combine information on income levels and occupation into a single model. In both the USA and the UK this has led to the development of socio-economic groups. Table 4.3 illustrates the categories of occupation that are included in each group. It is interesting to note that the higher and lower socio-economic groups tend to give a higher proportion of their income to good causes than those on 'middle' incomes.

■ *Race/ethnicity*   Race and ethnicity are used in demographic segmentation by some nonprofits. Different issues impact different racial and ethnic groups, and these groups differ in their media habits and organizational ties, with all the major minority groups having a plethora of specific newspapers, magazines, radio and television programming, which permit very precise targeting of messages. Creative images and messages can also be tailored to appeal to the various racial and ethnic groups and segments.

Table 4.3 Socio-economic groups

UK		USA	
Category	Description	Category	Description
A	Senior professional/ managerial	Upper-uppers	Social elite living on inherited income
B	Middle professional/ managerial	Lower-uppers	Individuals often from the middle class who have earned very high levels of income from success in business or the professions
C1	Junior management, clerical or supervisory	Upper-middles	Professionals or managers with unexceptional wealth
C2	Skilled manual labour (e.g. electrician)	Middle class	White and blue collar workers on 'average' levels of pay who live on the 'right' side of town
D	Unskilled manual labour (e.g. labourer)	Working class	Blue collar workers on 'average' income leading working class lifestyle
E	Unemployed, students, etc.	Upper-lowers	Employed in the workforce but earning income frequently just above poverty levels
		Lower-lowers	Living on welfare, public aid or charity

Note: US categories adapted from work of Richard P. Coleman (1983)

Geographic segmentation

In terms of historic development, segmentation on the grounds of where people live was the first system developed. Nonprofits would tend to look for support from individuals living close to the headquarters of the organization. However, segmentation and profiling on the basis of location alone is now very rare and it tends to be used in concert with one or more of the other bases for segmentation that are available. Geodemographics is an attempt to improve significantly on some of the limitations of the simple geographic model.

Geodemographics

In geodemographics information on geographical location is combined with lifestyle information to provide descriptions of neighbourhoods. In the USA this approach is typified by the PRIZM system, which is based on the core notion that people who live near each other are likely to have similar interests and behaviours. PRIZM was developed by the Claritas Corporation. Claritas collects a vast amount of information on the 42,000 zip code areas of the USA, including standard demographic data, product and service purchases and media use. Clustering procedures are used to group zip code areas into 62 categories and 15 social groups, which are given names such as 'Shotguns and Pickups', 'Money and Brains' and 'Second City Elite'. Fundraisers can use the PRIZM system to help define markets and target areas which appear to match those of existing donors. Other systems such as ACORN, ClusterPlus and MicroVision are also available to USA nonprofits.

UK geodemographic studies arose from work carried out by Webber in 1973. He was interested in studying urban deprivation and classified neighbourhoods using cluster analysis techniques to produce a system comprising 25 neighbourhood types, each of which exhibited different mixes of problems and required a different type of social policy. Using census data he was later able to extend this analysis to derive 38 neighbourhood types with which to classify the whole of the UK.

Webber's work was further developed by the British Market Research Bureau which overlaid purchasing patterns on to the neighbourhood types. There are now a number of commercially available geodemographic systems in the UK such as MOSAIC, ACORN and PINPOINT. All the systems use census data that is updated every ten years when every household in the country receives a questionnaire gathering data on some 300 variables. Census information is published only at the level of the 'enumeration district', which typically contains around ten postcodes. The geodemographic systems match the census data to the relevant postcodes and then reduce the high number of census variables down to a manageable number that are capable of explaining key differences in consumer behaviour. To develop market segments a technique such as cluster analysis is then used to group together postcodes with similar behaviours.

All the major suppliers of geodemographic data employ slightly different sets of census data and employ different statistical techniques to derive the final segments that will comprise their system. Typically, this includes information on: age, marital status, household composition, household size, employment type, travel to work, unemployment, car ownership, housing tenure, amenities, housing type, socio-economic group. Some of the suppliers conduct additional market research among representative samples of each of their segments to provide additional data on purchasing behaviour by group.

Systems such as ACORN and MOSAIC can be purchased as additions to nonprofit databases so that geodemographic data is appended automatically to every donor record, or data from the existing base can be exported and classified by the data providers as a 'one-off' or occasional profiling exercise to see which of the set categories predominate. This information can then be used in list selection or the purchase of other media. Geodemographic systems are sometimes criticized as being too homogeneous, and the groupings used critiqued as subjective and potentially misleading.

Behavioural segmentation

In the commercial arena individuals are segmented according to their 'knowledge of, attitude toward, use of, or response to a product' (Kotler and Keller 2006:254). This form of segmentation does not translate readily into nonprofit donor recruitment since by definition the organization has had no contact with these individuals before and as a consequence holds no data on their behaviour. It is widely used, however, in donor development communications where the organization looks to establish a relationship with the donor over time. The Royal Society for the Protection of Birds, for example, segments donors according to the level of interest and knowledge that they have in the subject. They send different forms of communication to committed birdwatchers than to individuals who merely like to attract birds to their garden and in reality understand very little about them. Organizations also target donors with specific campaigns based on their value (i.e. how much they have given in the past) and have a separate strategy for dealing with major givers.

Psychographic and lifestyle segmentation

There are also a number of bases for segmentation that can be considered as psychological or psychographic variables. Some researchers have argued that personality can be used as a suitable basis for segmentation and several studies have demonstrated links between personality variables and consumer buying behaviour.

In the nonprofit sector, segmentation by attitudes, values and value systems is more common, especially where organizations are actively attempting to change societal attitudes and behaviours. Data on the values and attitudes of existing donors can be gathered through survey instruments and used to add to the picture of the ideal prospect.

Lifestyle has been defined as 'a person's pattern of living in the world as expressed in the person's activities, interests and opinions. Lifestyle (as a consequence) portrays the whole individual interacting with his/her environment' (Kotler 1991:171). It can therefore be considered to be different to personality. Personality variables describe the pattern of psychological characteristics an individual might possess but say nothing of that individual's hobbies, interests or activities. Lifestyle data supply these missing variables. When the term lifestyle was first introduced into marketing research it was viewed as consisting of three basic components: activities (work, hobbies, social life, entertainment, shopping, sports), interests (family, home, job, community, recreation, media, achievements), and opinions (of oneself, social issues, politics, business, education, products and culture).

The basis of lifestyle profiling and segmentation is that very substantial numbers of people can be persuaded to provide comprehensive information about themselves, their households, their possessions, behaviour and interests. A huge amount of lifestyle information on millions of individuals is available commercially. Lifestyle data providers collect information at the level of the individual. Huge databanks are compiled from product registration cards and large consumer surveys that are often over 200 questions long (with some questions 'sponsored' by individual companies) and are incentivized to encourage completion.

Lifestyle data houses will take existing donor lists (or lists of 'best' donors) and match the names and addresses against their file. If a match rate of 10 per cent or more is attained a 'reliable' profile of the donors can be provided, illustrating characteristic lifestyle variables and indicating the extent to which the donors differ from the 'norm' in the display of these characteristics.

The key weakness of lifestyle data is that they contain a self-selected, and therefore unrepresentative, sample. It is therefore not possible to extrapolate from a lifestyle study to make a universal statement. Where nonprofits use direct mail in recruitment and development communication, lifestyle bases remain valuable as they are made up of mail-responsive people. Where different, non-direct mail responsive donors are recruited, lifestyle data may be inappropriate.

SEGMENTING BUSINESS MARKETS

In preparing a strategy for corporate fundraising, it is equally essential to decide exactly which segments of the market should be targeted. It is unlikely that the nonprofit will have global appeal, but it may have resonance with a number of very specific commercial organizations.

In the commercial context segmentation operates at two levels. The nonprofit has first to consider which organizations it will target and second who within these organizations should be contacted. This is not so straightforward as it may appear initially as the decision to support a nonprofit may be taken not by one individual, but by a number of people within the organization. Marketers refer to this group as the decision-making unit or DMU. It typically comprises:

- *Initiators* Those within the organization who raise awareness of the nature of the cause, or trigger the initial consideration of whether or not to offer a gift. They may have personal links to the cause, or have raised the issue with management in response to a communication from the charity. Either way they are important since they initiate the decision-making process.
- *Deciders* Those individuals who will effectively take the decision over whether support will be offered. They may be managers, or more senior staff such as a director or the chair if higher value forms of support are being suggested. They may have no direct contact with the nonprofit and simply take the decision on the basis of evidence presented to them by other members of their team.
- *Participants* Members of this group are nominated by the corporate to take responsibility for the decision. They may serve in a committee or meet on an ad hoc basis to consider the merits of a particular approach from a nonprofit. In some cases, where the decision is to be taken by a committee, their views will carry equal weight. In other cases, their views are sought to inform the decision that will be taken by the responsible manager.
- *Influencers* These may be influential people within the organization or they may be external contacts or consultants. These members of the DMU are important since their views are highly regarded by other members of the group. Again, they may have no direct contact with the nonprofit and may have no direct interest in the support that will be offered. They are merely opinion leaders.
- *Gatekeepers* These individuals 'guard' the senior staff in a corporate and thus make it difficult for the nonprofit to get its message across. Frequently, a secretary or personal assistant will filter calls to senior members of staff and will intercept mail, binning anything perceived as not being of relevance. They are thus an important category to consider since they control access to other members of the DMU.

Indeed, all these categories are important, since the nonprofit needs to ensure that it develops a separate strategy for getting its message across to as many of these groups as is practical. Each will likely have very different information needs and aspirations and this should be reflected in a segmented approach to fundraising practice.

Wind and Cordozo (1974) suggest that business segmentation should be undertaken in two stages. The first stage involves defining the segments in terms of size, profitability, industrial sector and Standard Industrial Classification (SIC) code (a two- to four-digit code which defines the company's industry and the nature of its work). The second stage they advocate is to define the segments in terms of the behavioural characteristics of their DMUs. The result is a hybrid segmentation system, which reflects not only the type of business, but also the manner in which it operates. To help illustrate the variety of criteria that are available it is worth briefly reviewing the work of Bonoma and Shapiro (1983) who developed one of the most comprehensive reviews of industrial segmentation currently available. The criteria the authors identify are given in Exhibit 4.1. The authors originally suggested that these criteria are arranged in descending

EXHIBIT 4.1 CRITERIA FOR SEGMENTING OF INDUSTRIAL MARKETS

Demographic

- Industry type – Which industries should be targeted?
- Company size – What size of company should be targeted?
- Location – In what geographical regions should firms be targeted?

Operating variables

- Technology – What kinds of technology do potential customers employ?
- User status – Would they be heavy, medium or light users of the service?
- Customer capabilities – Should customers having many or few needs be concentrated on?

Purchasing approaches

- Buying criteria – What would customers be looking for? Cost, convenience, service?
- Buying policies – Are decisions made locally or centrally, and what duration of relationship would be desirable?
- Current relationships – Should the organization focus on only those customers who have a track record of support?

Situational factors

- Urgency – Should customers with immediate needs be targeted?
- Size of order – Should customers requiring high- or low-value relationships be targeted?
- Applications – Should customers looking to use the association in different ways be targeted?

Personal characteristics

- Loyalty – Should only companies exhibiting high degrees of loyalty to their suppliers be targeted?
- Attitudes to risk – Should risk-taking or risk-avoiding customers be targeted?
- Buyer–seller familiarity – Should companies with similar characteristics to the seller be targeted?

Source: Adapted from Bonoma and Shapiro (1983).

levels of importance. In the context of fundraising, however, many of the criteria towards the bottom of the list can actually offer considerably more utility than those towards the top. As an example, companies whose customer profile would be likely to match the profile of a non-profit's typical donors, would clearly warrant consideration with an appropriately tailored approach.

Similarly the purchasing approaches adopted will have considerable relevance. Those organizations likely to make a genuinely philanthropic gift would require treating rather differently from those that would look to measure the 'success' of their donation by its impact on the bottom line.

Since criteria such as company size and location will clearly determine the likelihood and amounts of funding to be supplied it would seem that charities should give the greatest consideration to a mix of demographic, purchasing approach and personal characteristic variables when considering how best to segment the corporate donor market.

EVALUATING THE SUITABILITY OF SEGMENTS

The reader will by now appreciate the diversity of variables that could potentially be used as the basis for market segmentation. While there are many potential segments that an organization could look to pursue, it is almost certain that only a few of them will actually be worth exploiting. The difficulty facing fundraisers is exactly how to evaluate the possibilities.

In practice there are seven criteria that can be used to evaluate the potential offered by each segment proposed. Only if the analysis is favourable in each case should the segment be pursued. The segment must be:

1 *Measurable* The segment should be easily measurable and information about the segment and its characteristics should therefore exist or be obtainable cost-effectively.
2 *Accessible* It should be possible to design a fundraising approach to target the segment cost-effectively. One would therefore need to look, for example, at appropriate media opportunities that could be used with the minimum of wastage.
3 *Substantial* It should be cost-effective to fundraise from the segment. Clearly the segment should be large enough in terms of volume of donations (or small with high profit margins) to warrant exploitation.
4 *Stable* The segment's behaviour should be relatively stable over time to ensure that its future development may be predicted with a degree of accuracy for planning purposes.
5 *Appropriate* It should be appropriate to approach a certain segment given the organization's mission, resources, objectives and so on. A children's charity, for example, may wish to avoid seeking donations from corporations that have links to companies in the Third World which exploit child labour.
6 *Unique* The segment should be unique in terms of its response (to fundraising activity) so that it can be distinguished from other segments.
7 *Sustainable* Sustainability is an issue that is rapidly growing in importance. It refers to the extent to which particular categories of donor can be sustained by the organization. The National Trust, for example, would only hope to attract members/donors who will treat their properties with appropriate respect, stick to signposted paths, take home their litter and so on. Not every segment of society will thus be sustainable and fundraising activity, particularly where membership is offered as a product, will need to take this into account.

Criterion 6 warrants elaboration. A segment may meet all of the other criteria but may behave identically to other segments in terms of its response to different types and timing of strategy. If this is the case, Kotler and Andreasen (1991:170) identify that 'although it may be conceptually useful to develop separate segments in this way, it is not managerially useful'. As an example, many charities now have two distinctive demographic groups in their direct marketing database. Older individuals (i.e. 60+) and younger donors (age 25–40) recruited through one or more of the new media channels (see Chapter 6). The fundraiser responsible for donor development could look at the demographic differences, decide that he/she is looking at two distinct segments and develop a separate communications programme for each. However, this only makes sense if these individuals differ in their response to different forms of communication. If they react in an identical way to receiving direct mail, find the same topics/issues of relevance and are stimulated to give by the same motives, it does not make sense to treat these two groups differently. Segmentation is not necessary.

As a further example Figure 4.3 shows the allocation of a fundraising budget between two geographically separate markets, North and South. It can be seen from the slope of the two graphs that the North is more fundraising elastic (i.e. more sensitive to fundraising expenditure) than the South. The points FS1 and FN1 represent equal fundraising expenditures in the two markets. This allocation strategy yields total response results of RS1 and RN1. However, if the expenditure is shifted around between the two regions and $2,000 is moved from the South to the North, then the total amount raised will rise (RS2 + RN2) even though total expenditures remain unchanged. Clearly fundraisers should continue shifting their fundraising budget to the North until such time as the incremental gain in one market just equals the incremental loss in the other. One would normally take advantage of any differential responsiveness until there is no variation in total responsiveness given any small changes that might be instigated. It should be remembered that in this simple example the only variable under consideration was fundraising expenditure. In reality segments may exhibit differential responsiveness to a wide range of differing criteria and these data can be utilized to great effect in fundraising planning. Clearly if no differential responsiveness is exhibited one might question the value of segmenting the market on that basis since no managerial advantages accrue.

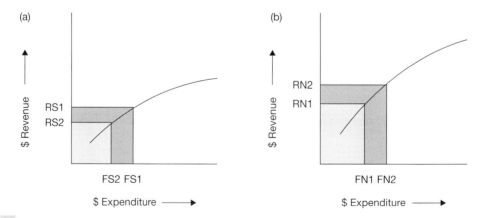

Figure 4.3 *Hypothetical responses of two markets to fundraising activities*

Source: Kotler and Andreasen (1991). © 2003 adapted by permission of Prentice Hall Inc, Upper Saddle River, NJ.

POSITIONING STRATEGY

Once the organization has decided on appropriate segments for the fundraising plan to address, it will be necessary to develop a strategy that will shape the message that the nonprofit wishes to project in the minds of these targets. This is in essence what marketers refer to as 'positioning' and it may be defined as:

> The act of defining in the minds of the target audience what a particular organization stands for and can offer in relation to other nonprofits.

In simple terms positioning defines what is unique about an organization and thus what distinguishes it from other nonprofits seeking to raise funds from similar sources. Positioning is key since it indicates to donors the distinctive nature of the work that is being undertaken and/or the distinctive nature of the benefits that might accrue as a result of being a member or donor. It is important that donors are clear from the outset about the nature of the work the organization undertakes and why this is different from that undertaken by other nonprofits they could look to support. Positioning is thus a general statement about perceptions of the organization as a whole and will later drive the specific 'case for support' that is created for each segment of donors, or in the case of major donors, each individual donor. It should be reflected in all the communications the organization sends out and be tightly linked to the issue of branding (see Chapter 13).

As an example, the UK has a number of large national children's charities. Figure 4.4 gives an example of how these different organizations might be positioned in terms of key organizational facets.

CASE FOR SUPPORT

The case for support is a critical concept in fundraising. It provides a rationale to donors for their support of the organization and should engender a sense of immediacy, excitement and importance. It should also draw on the positioning strategy and make it clear why the particular organization is distinctive. It must be well articulated and be capable of being thoroughly understood by all the charity's donors. Exhibits 4.2 and 4.3 provide examples for two very different categories of nonprofit.

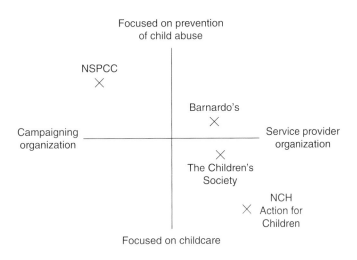

Figure 4.4 *Positioning of children's charities*

EXHIBIT 4.2 CASE FOR SUPPORT: AUTISM SPEAKS

Autism Speaks, the only UK charity raising funds for biomedical autism research, exists because it believes that autism is the most serious challenge facing medical science today. That claim is based on two simple realities; first, the huge financial burden which autism imposes on society as well as the individual and, second, the yawning gap in our knowledge about the causes of autism.

A third important factor for Autism Speaks is that autism benefits from far less research funding than any other comparable medical condition. It attracts less than 0.5 per cent of state medical research funds even in developed countries such as the UK and USA and to date attracts little private or charitable support.

Autism research struggles to attract the sympathy and the money of the wider world because autism does not kill; it merely disables. That disability can be extreme and it is life-long. It is this which has led health economists to conclude that the true annual cost of autism in the UK is £28 billion a year, a much larger figure than for any other costed medical condition.

It is now estimated that around one in every one hundred people is on the autistic spectrum. The impact of autism, emotionally, physically and financially, is huge and will continue to be so while there remains little knowledge about what causes the condition. Autism Speaks believes that no truly effective remedies or interventions for autism can be developed without this understanding, but the hopeful news is that recent scientific research is now bringing us little by little towards this goal.

Autism Speaks exists therefore to remove the biggest obstacle to significant and rapid progress along the road to full understanding by ensuring that the funds available to autism research match the scale of the challenge.

The key to Autism Speaks' approach is funding only high-quality research subject to rigorous peer review. Another important objective is to increase the number of people engaged in autism research, ensuring the field attracts the brightest and the best. Long term, the aim is to move funding for research towards the same level as that in such areas as cancer or cystic fibrosis. To achieve parity with spending on cystic fibrosis, the budget for autism research would need to be increased by a factor of a hundred.

The Autism Speaks research programme focuses on four main areas: the causes, biology, diagnosis and treatment of autism. It has a range of funding mechanisms to stimulate interest and support across the medical and research communities.

Above all Autism Speaks seeks to give hope to the whole autism community and intends firmly to see that hope fulfilled. The target of Autism Speaks is to achieve major progress in its key objective of determining and understanding the causes of autism within ten years.

Source: Museum of Life and Science, Durham, North Carolina. Reproduced with kind permission.

EXHIBIT 4.3 CASE FOR SUPPORT: NORTH CAROLINA MUSEUM OF LIFE AND SCIENCE

Our case for support

Building on a 60-year record of success, the Museum is growing indoors and outdoors to provide engaging experiences with science and the natural world. The Museum's fundraising priorities for this year are annual fund support to fuel our mission and the Dinosaur Trail Campaign.

History and mission

The Museum began in 1946 as a small trailside nature center. Generations of families have participated in joyful, enlightening experiences that spark wonder, touch the heart and expand the mind. Today, the Museum is an 80-acre site with 90,000 square feet of indoor space.

To meet a growing demand for learning and quality family experiences, the Museum is expanding with a larger campus and more learning experiences. Under the leadership of Barry Van Deman, President and CEO, the Museum is focused on a new mission: to create a place of lifelong learning where people, from young child to senior citizen, embrace science as a way of knowing about themselves, their community and their world. The Museum's Board of Directors is committed to a new strategic plan that will secure the resources to deliver this vision.

Improved service as a community resource

With our unique indoor/outdoor environment, the Museum serves over 300,000 annual visitors and helps define us as a community committed to learning and innovation. We are expanding our traditional educational role with children and families to a platform for *lifelong learning* serving visitors of all ages. To help our community learn about contemporary science, the Museum has recently won a major grant to educate the public on nanotechnology.

In May 2006, we opened Explore the Wild, a six-acre woodland and wetland site with habitats for black bears, red wolves and lemurs, featuring interactive exhibits and multi-media kiosks. Visitor response to our new Explore the Wild outdoor experience has been particularly positive.

The Museum consistently improves or re-invents the experiences that we offer to our visitors and members. Perennial favorites like Carolina Wildlife or Magic Wings Butterfly House gain new appreciation when visitors interact with our staff and volunteer docents or sign up for a behind-the-scenes tour. The Museum offers fresh features including forums for adult learners, visiting exhibits and special events. We also launched a partnership with a local restaurateur for a significantly upgraded café and on-site catering service to support increased Museum visitation and rental activity. Thanks to a planned gift from the Teer family, the Museum has purchased a new train locomotive to replace our 30-year-old model. The new locomotive was officially christened and began operation is January 2007.

How does the Museum make a difference to our children's education? Our hands-on, enquiry-based learning opportunities reinforce and supplement classroom experience. With over 50,000 students visiting on field trips annually, we provide environment-based learning with all-new focused field trips that provide engaging outdoor experiences. Leading corporations, including GlaxoSmith-Kline and Bayer CropScience, have made significant investments in the Museum to fund these important new educational programmes. The Museum also provides direct support to Durham Public Schools (DPS) through educational programming and kit programmes. In the last year, nearly 25,000 DPS students (75 per cent of total enrolment) visited the Museum or participated in Museum educational programming. Nearly 800 DPS classrooms used *Science in a Suitcase* kits maintained by the Museum on over 50 topics to strengthen hands-on science learning.

According to researcher Jon Miller, students participating in hands-on science programmes show 'increases in creativity, positive attitudes toward science, perception, logic development, communication skills, and reading readiness.' In an age when most children have uninterrupted access to sedentary, indoor activities, such as television, video games and computers, the Museum offers them an enhanced outdoor experience, filled with exploration possibilities and opportunities to appreciate our natural world and science in a safe and innovative environment.

For lifelong learners of all ages, the Museum's brand of experiential and social learning is a key building block of scientific literacy. As an environment where we can grow, play, and appreciate natural beauty, the Museum enhances our quality of life and helps to attract highly skilled workers and investment to our community.

Master plan growth

We are at an important point in the Museum's history with the phased opening of 12 acres of outdoor exhibits. This BioQuest project is large and rich enough to be considered a new museum in itself. This expansion offers both incredible new opportunities and challenges requiring continued and enhanced support.

In 2007, the Museum opened Catch the Wind, a new four-acre outdoor experience with a 5,000-square-foot radio-controlled sailboat pond, a flight experience and wind-related interactive exhibits. We will soon debut Investigate Health!, an indoor exhibit that will improve our understanding of the science behind health and wellness. The Museum's strategic plan calls for additional focus on building the experience for members, our loyal repeat visitor base; forging new partnerships and grant opportunities to enhance science access and understanding in our community; and launching a campaign to complete the funding package for a new Dinosaur Trail.

From FY2005 to FY2008, our annual operating budget is growing by $1.5 million to meet needs that include additional staff, animal care, and maintenance of a larger campus with more interactive exhibits. Durham County and the State provide just under one-third of our operating budget; therefore, the Museum must earn over 70 per cent of our funding through admissions, memberships, fees, contributions and other revenue.

Current investment priorities

This year, our priorities for investment are annual support of $450,000 to fuel our mission and raising the remaining $695,000 in needed capital funding to build the Dinosaur Trail.

The Museum's Annual Fund is critical to create memorable educational experiences, including:

- Magic Wings Butterfly House provides a source of wonder and an engaging educational experience for our visitors. Annual operating costs include about $60,000 in power and utilities, and about $80,000 in butterfly chrysalises and supplies. The chrysalises come from Central and South America, Asia and Africa and are a means of sustainable agriculture in the developing world whereby farmers can make a living from the forest's natural resources.
- Our annual educational supplies budget is about $70,000 annually for materials from paper and glue to Petri dishes and microscopes. These materials provide hands-on learning excitement in the nearly 100,000 children who are served in our programmes.
- The Museum's 130 species of live animals connect people with the natural world, and encourage us to consider better stewardship of our shared environment. It takes nearly $85,000 a year to feed and care for our animals – bears, the donkey, muskrats and tarantulas – just to name a few. Our grocery list includes 40,000 crickets, 3,000 apples, 2,500 pounds of bear chow and 365 bunches of kale.

■ Special exhibits help keep the Museum fresh and provide unique family experiences. Bringing a visiting exhibit to the Museum costs from $30,000 to $75,000 per exhibit.

The Dinosaur Trail Campaign is a $1.49 million public–private partnership to create a state-of-the-art Cretaceous experience. The Dinosaur Trail is supported by a Durham County bond investment of $675,000, and the Museum is raising the remaining $815,000 needed.

In addition to being a fun and healthy outdoor activity, the new Dinosaur Trail is an excellent way to learn. While some children may be intimidated by science and math, they amaze us with their accomplishment in learning how to pronounce dinosaur names, research the latest findings, or understand complex biological relationships. Students will tackle chemistry, physics, or math in order to understand what made dinosaurs tick, rumble or roar. Visitors will learn basic science concepts and are more likely to make connections with other knowledge, building science literacy skills. Many parents find themselves learning from their children about dinosaurs, and this inter-generational conversation will make the Dinosaur Trail a popular family activity.

Leveraged by Durham County's investment, donors to Dinosaur Trail will enjoy a long-lasting legacy of recognition in association with the dinosaur models that will populate the trail.

Summary

We envision a one-of-a-kind place, a science park, offering extraordinary experiences indoors, outdoors, and through virtual media where children and adults learn through the pursuit of their own interests and curiosity. Realizing the full potential of the Museum will require enthusiastic users, committed partners and engaged stakeholders.

As the Museum moves forward, investment to support our key annual priorities as well as exhibit fabrication and maintenance, educational programs and ongoing refurbishment will be critical to our success as an important community resource. We invite you to visit us, experience what the Museum is all about and learn more about what an investment in the Museum of Life and Science can do for our region.

Source: Museum of Life and Science, Durham, North Carolina. Reproduced with kind permission.

In designing a case for support, the Association of Fundraising Professionals (2008) propose that the document should be able to address each of the following questions:

■ Who is the organization and what does it do?
■ Why does it exist?
■ What is distinctive about the organization?
■ What must be accomplished?
■ How will this campaign enable it to be accomplished?
■ How can the donor become involved?
■ What's in it for the donor? Why should they give to this effort?

To answer these questions case writers will need to assemble a wide range of resources. The Fund Raising School at Indiana University (1999) suggest that this portfolio should include:

■ The mission statement and ultimate goals of the organization.
■ The specific objectives that the organization is now seeking to achieve.

- An outline of the programmes and services that the nonprofit provides. Here the organization should clearly express how it implements its objectives and the impact it has on the cause or the people it aims to assist. This must be much more than a bland statement of operational strategy; it should stress the real impact the nonprofit is having on people's lives.
- A description of the governance structure; the composition of the board, how it is elected or appointed and its relevance to the beneficiary group. This is particularly important for social welfare organizations since potential funders will often look to ensure that the board is representative of those it exists to serve.
- *Staffing plans*   The nonprofit should express how both paid staff and volunteers will be used in the appropriate and effective delivery of programmes.
- *Statement of non-financial resources*   This consists of a description of the facilities the nonprofit can offer and a list of the resources that can be brought to bear on service or programme provision.
- *Financial statements*   A detailed set of the organization's accounts should be included in the pack of case resources, including both the published accounts and the more detailed management accounts. Fundraisers may also solicit the help of the finance or programmes departments to secure any meaningful graphics, which help illustrate how resources are expended, or current levels of financial need.
- *Planning documents*   It would be helpful to include both a statement of the nature of the planning process itself and copies of any organizational or strategic plans the nonprofit may have produced.
- *History*   A brief summary of when and why the organization was created and a list of its past achievements.

To this list we might reasonably add the requirement to assemble any documentation the organization might have on the needs and preferences of its donors. While much of giving remains genuinely philanthropic, it is important to recognize that some segments of donors may have very specific needs or expectations of the organization. Such needs must be genuinely understood if the case for support, however worthy it might be, is to be made relevant and attractive to donors.

Fundraisers can employ this organizational case for support to assist them in designing the content of specific campaigns and appeals. All fundraising should reflect the agreed case for support so that a consistent message is delivered to donors over time. That said, the case conveyed in each campaign will obviously be tailored, to focus on one need or group of needs and to match these to the likely interests of donor(s). It will typically be helpful to write a case expression for each segment and, in the case of significant funders such as corporates and/or major donors, to develop one for each individual/organization. The same process will also be necessary in the case of trusts/foundations, but the form that the case expression must take will often be defined by the grant-maker in its application literature.

STRATEGIC WEAR-OUT

Thus far in our discussion of strategy we have been considering the overall direction an organization will take towards the fulfilment of its fundraising objectives, the segments of donors that will form the basis of the target audience for each form of fundraising undertaken and how the organization wishes to be perceived by the individuals or organizations that comprise this audience. These dimensions comprise the overall fundraising strategy of the organization.

It is important to recognize that this organizational strategy can easily become obsolete and inappropriate, particularly if the organization fails to undertake a regular fundraising planning exercise. This is known as strategic 'wear-out'. Its causes include:

■ *Changes in the macro-environment* For example, changes in legislation can limit the range of fundraising techniques available or make them uneconomic.
■ *Competitor activity* The strategy adopted by other nonprofits could impact negatively on an organization's ability to raise funds if it does not take account of their activities.
■ *Lack of investment* Some nonprofits fail to achieve targets, or set over-ambitious targets that cannot realistically be met given the level of investment. A direct mail strategy, for example, can easily become stale and inappropriate if the organization does not keep up adequate investment in database technology.
■ *Management complacency* The single biggest cause of strategic wear-out is management complacency where fundraisers believe that they have adopted the optimum strategy and there is no reason to consider change, or even to monitor it. Such individuals and/or fundraising departments are frequently overtaken by changes in the environment and recognize this only when it is too late to respond.

In seeking to prevent strategic wear-out fundraisers need to conduct regular and systematic planning exercises where all pertinent factors and changes are considered. The process of debating audit data and competitor activity should be open and constructive and all members of the fundraising team should be permitted and encouraged to challenge current ways of thinking and operating. The internal culture of the nonprofit should be stimulated to regard change as positive and an essential part of being responsive to donor needs and expectations. Finally, regular and ongoing communication within the fundraising team and with other departments or functions within the organization is essential. Often other teams working in service provision, IT or other areas may be aware of changes that could impact on the organization's future fundraising practice. Clearly the earlier this is shared and discussed with the fundraising team the stronger the likelihood that the organization can develop a cogent response.

TACTICAL PLANS

Having defined the strategy or overall approach that will be adopted, the next section of the plan contains the fine detail of the fundraising that will be undertaken. Thus separate plans will be provided here for direct marketing, major gift fundraising/planned giving, corporate fundraising, trust/foundation fundraising and community/local group fundraising. In smaller nonprofits, or those conducting only a limited range of fundraising activities, this may consist only of a list of actions to be taken (i.e. an action plan). In larger organizations, or those involved in a range of fundraising techniques, a separate sub-plan will be created for each form of fundraising and only the key points will be reported in the aggregate fundraising plan. If 'sub-plans' are used they will typically be structured in a very similar way to the aggregate plan and will have their own objectives, action plans, budget, schedule and series of controls.

Rather than elaborate further here, later chapters will consider each form of fundraising in detail.

BUDGET

Having detailed the steps that it will be necessary to take to achieve the fundraising objectives the writer of the plan should then be in a position to cost the various proposals and to derive

89

an overall fundraising budget for the planning period. Past experience or reference to bench-marking data (see Chapter 15) will provide guidance on what returns should be expected from each form of fundraising undertaken. These 'rules of thumb' can then be used to put together an Excel (or other) spreadsheet and the investment needed to raise the funds required from each medium calculated. This is known as the 'task' method of setting the fundraising budget and is the optimal approach.

Of course, in reality life is often not that neat. Rules of thumb are rarely 100 per cent accurate because the fundraising environment will be subject to change and fundraisers will inevitably have to argue a case for the investment they believe they need rather than just be awarded the necessary sum. Budgets are typically put together in an iterative way with proposals being evalu-ated and re-evaluated by senior management in the light of the nonprofit's budgetary constraints and other investment priorities. Perhaps inevitably, the total budget will be arrived at after a (sometimes lengthy) process of negotiation.

The task method is not the only way a fundraising budget can be determined. Other potential methods include:

- *Percentage of last year's donations*   Perhaps 10 to 20 per cent of income may be set aside to fund the following year's fundraising activity. While easy to calculate, this approach suffers from two key drawbacks. First, the budget may bear no resemblance to the cost of raising the requisite funding for the coming year's operations and, second, setting the budget in this way can have the effect of lowering the fundraising spend when income levels fall. It could be argued that this is the exact opposite of what should happen in these circumstances where many organizations must ideally look to invest in new forms of income generation to secure the nonprofit's long-term future.
- *Percentage of budgeted donations*   This approach eliminates the weaknesses alluded to above, but requires great care in the calculation of an appropriate percentage. Different fundraising techniques vary widely in the returns they are capable of generating and an aggregate percentage allocation can therefore be very simplistic.
- *Competitor matching*   Some nonprofits choose to monitor the expenditure undertaken by those they regard as their key competitors. While a careful choice of competitor against which to benchmark can often be insightful in suggesting the ballpark figures an organization might look to invest, this approach again fails to take account of the nonprofit's own objectives and need for funds, which could be quite different from that of a competitor.
- *What can be afforded*   This is perhaps the least rational of all the methods of budget calculation and involves the senior management of the organization deciding what they believe they can afford to allocate to the fundraising function in a particular year. Once again, little or no reference is made to the fundraising objectives.

Irrespective of the method actually employed, in practice it would be usual to specify how the eventual budget has been allocated and to include such a specification in the fundraising plan itself. It would also be normal for an allowance to be made for contingencies in the event that monitoring by the organization suggests that the objectives will not be met. Sufficient resources should then exist for some form of corrective action to be taken.

SCHEDULING

The reader will appreciate that a large number of tactics will have been specified in the main body of the plan. To ensure that these tactics are executed in a coordinated fashion over the

	Jan	Feb	Mar	Apr	May	June	July	Aug	Sept	Oct	Nov	Dec
Direct mail	X			X				X				X
Press ads	X										X	X
Display ads	X					X						
Telemarketing		X			X				X			X

Figure 4.5 *Gantt chart*

duration of the plan it is usual to present a schedule that clearly specifies when each activity will take place. This would often take the form of a Gantt chart (an example is provided in Figure 4.5). If the responsibilities for various fundraising activities are split between different groups of staff the schedule will act as an important coordination mechanism. Indeed if responsibilities are split in this way it would be usual to include an additional section to the plan specifying the individual postholder who will have responsibility for the implementation of each component of the plan.

MONITORING AND CONTROL

As soon as the plan has been implemented, fundraising management will then take responsibility for monitoring the progress of the organization towards the goals specified. Managers will also need to concern themselves with the costs that have been incurred at each stage of implementation and monitor these against the budget. Thus control mechanisms need to be put in place to monitor:

1   the actual donations achieved against the budget
2   the actual costs incurred against those budgeted
3   the performance of specific forms of fundraising
4   the appropriateness of the strategy/tactics adopted.

In the case of financial objectives, such as (1) and (2) above, it would be usual to break down the aggregate target for a given year into monthly targets, perhaps for each form of fundraising undertaken, each donor segment and so on. It should also stipulate how much variation it is prepared to tolerate from these monthly 'sub-targets' before the alarm is raised. The organization can then monitor actual performance against its targets each month, and where performance falls outside the band of permissible performance, bring the matter to the attention of fundraising managers who then have the opportunity to instigate some form of corrective action.

SELECTION OF AN APPROPRIATE PLANNING FRAMEWORK

Before closing this chapter it is important to say a word or two about the formats that might be used for writing up a fundraising plan. We introduced one such format in Figure 4.1 which consisted of an audit followed by objectives, strategies and tactics. There are other variants that might be more appropriate. In some cases it might make more sense to map out the audit, objectives, strategy and then to specify the tactics for each segment of donors.

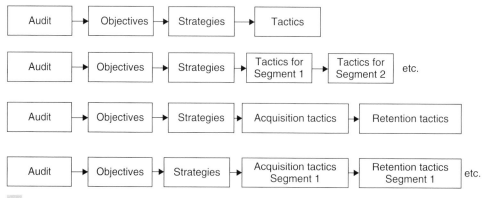

Figure 4.6 *Fundraising plan structures*

For organizations that do a lot of work with direct marketing, it can be more helpful to structure the plan by presenting the audit, objectives, strategy and then the tactics for recruiting donors to the organization and (separately) the tactics for developing the value of existing donors over time. It may even be helpful to develop a hybrid of these latter approaches by considering how the first segment of donors will be recruited and retained, how the second segment of donors will be recruited and retained and so on. These approaches are illustrated in Figure 4.6.

SUMMARY

In this chapter we have reviewed the final components of an aggregate fundraising plan. We have stressed the need for SMART objectives to guide the direction of the plan and to act as an effective form of control to ensure that scarce resources are applied appropriately across the range of fundraising techniques adopted. We have also examined the key elements of fundraising strategy, namely determining the overall direction that will be adopted, the donor groups that will be addressed with the plan and in general terms how the organization is distinctive in relation to its competitors (i.e. positioning). We have also explored the critical issue of the case for support and how tactical plans for each category of fundraising undertaken can be integrated in an aggregate fundraising plan. In subsequent chapters we will explain how each form of fundraising can be planned, implemented and controlled. Finally, we outlined the need to consider the fundraising budget, schedule and controls.

DISCUSSION QUESTIONS

1   What role do objectives play in the fundraising plan? What factors should be born in mind when setting fundraising objectives?
2   Distinguish between positioning strategy and the fundraising 'case for support'.
3   What is meant by the term 'segmentation'? How might a large national charity concerned with child welfare segment the market for corporate donations?

4 You are the fundraising director of a medium-sized nonprofit concerned with wildlife conservation. Your organization presently serves four counties and is considering using direct mail to solicit donations for the first time. Prepare a report for your Board indicating how the individual donor market might be segmented and highlighting the research you would propose to implement to explore this potential.

REFERENCES

Ansoff, I. (1968) *Corporate Strategy*, Penguin Books, London.

Association of Fundraising Professionals (2008) Case for Support and Case Statements, http://www.afpnet.org/ka/ka-3.cfm?content_item_id=8386&folder_id=907 (accessed 13 September 2008).

Banks, J. and Tanner, S. (1997) *The State of Donation* IFS, London.

Bonoma, T.V. and Shapiro, B.P. (1983) *Segmenting the Industrial Market*, Lexington Books, Lexington, MA.

Coleman, R.P. (1983) 'The Continuing Significance of Social Class to Marketing', *Journal of Consumer Research*, December, 265–280.

Drucker, P.F. (1990) *Managing the Non-Profit Organization*, Butterworth-Heinemann, Oxford.

Kotler, P. (1991) *Marketing Management*: *Analysis, Planning, Implementation and Control*, 8th edn, Prentice Hall, Englewood Cliffs, NJ.

Kotler, P. and Andreasen, A. (1991), *Strategic Marketing for Nonprofit Organisations*, 5th edn, Prentice Hall, Englewood Cliffs, NJ.

Kotler, P. and Keller, K.L. (2006) *Marketing Management*, 12th edn, Pearson Prentice Hall, Upper Saddle River, NJ.

MacDonald, M.H.B. (1984) *Marketing Plans*: *How To Prepare Them, How To use Them*, Heinemann, London.

Mullin, R. (1997) *Fundraising Strategy*, ICSA Publishing, London.

Philips, L.W. and Sternthal, B. (1977) 'Age Differences in Information Processing: A Perspective on the Aged consumer', *Journal of Marketing Research*, 14(4): 444–457.

Sargeant, A. (2004) *Marketing Management for Nonprofit Organizations*, 2nd edn, Oxford University Press, London.

The Fund Raising School (1999) *Principles and Techniques of Fund Raising*, Indiana University Center on Philanthropy.

Wells, W.D. and Gubar, G. (1966) 'Lifecycle Concept in Marketing Research', *Journal of Marketing Research*, 12(2): 301–335.

Wilson, R.M.S., Gilligan, C. and Pearson, D.J. (1992) *Strategic Marketing Management*, Butterworth-Heinemann, Oxford.

Wind, Y. and Cordozo, R. (1974) 'Industrial Market Segmentation', *Industrial Marketing Management*, 3(1): 153–165.

Part II

Fundraising from individuals

Chapter 5

Understanding giving

OBJECTIVES

By the end of this chapter you should be able to:
- Describe the profile of a typical charity donor.
- Describe a range of different motives for giving.
- Understand the criteria that donors use to select between charities.
- Understand why donors stop giving to specific organizations.
- Compare and contrast different models of donor behaviour.

INTRODUCTION

In the UK total individual giving to general charities stood at £11.5 billion in 2005/6 up 7 per cent on the previous year (NCVO 2008). In a recent Cabinet Office survey 81 per cent of adults claimed to have given to charity in the past four weeks, with women moderately more likely to have given than men (84 per cent versus 78 per cent) (Cabinet Office 2007). As impressive as this might be, charitable giving still represents less than 1 per cent of UK Gross Domestic Product and accounts for only around 1.3 per cent of weekly household expenditure compared with 2 per cent spent on tobacco and 4 per cent on alcohol. There is also considerable inequality in the pattern of giving. The richest 20 per cent of our society devote a mere 0.7 per cent of their household expenditure to charities while the poorest 20 per cent devote 3 per cent (Home Office 2005). Thus while the aggregate level of giving is impressive, there remains considerable scope for improvement.

In this chapter we look at how an understanding of giving behaviour might assist fundraisers in achieving this goal. We focus exclusively on the behaviour of individual donors as corporate and trust/foundation giving will be explored in later chapters. We examine who gives, why they give and, ultimately, why they stop.

WHO GIVES?

In the UK the Family Expenditure Survey regularly gathers data on the charitable giving of a representative sample of UK households. As the survey is wide-ranging and captures a lot of

Table 5.1 *Key characteristics of donor households*

Key characteristic	Probability of giving	Effect on levels of giving
Income	For each 10 per cent increase in household income, there is a 1.2 per cent increase in participation in giving	For every 1 per cent increase in expenditure, there is a 1.1 per cent increase in size of donations
Age	For every increase of 10 years in the age of the head of the household, there is an increased likelihood of giving of 3 per cent	For every increase of 10 years in the age of the head of the household, there is a 30 per cent increase in the value of donations
Children	Households with children are 3 per cent more likely to give than those without	(no information)
Wealth	Home owners are 6 per cent more likely to give than non-home owners and the effect of each additional room is to raise the likelihood of giving by 1 per cent	Home ownership increases size of donations by 14 per cent
Education	Households where the head has A levels are 5 per cent more likely to give and, where college-educated, 11 per cent more likely to give	The effect of having A levels is to increase the size of donations by 38 per cent and the effect of college education is an 80 per cent raise
Employment status	Households where the head is self-employed are 11 per cent less likely to give; where unemployed they are 7 per cent less likely to give	Those not in work are likely to give 20 per cent less than where the head is selfemployed, or employed

Source: Walker and Pharoah (2002), adapted from Banks and Tanner (1997). Reproduced by kind permission of Hodder Arnold.

demographic data, we now understand a great deal about how these variables impact on giving. A summary of their findings is provided in Table 5.1. Of course fundraisers are not so much interested in the general picture of who gives as they are in who gives to specific categories of cause/organization. The Cabinet Office survey (2007) referred to earlier provides some of this additional detail and the differences they identify by age and gender are reported in Table 5.2. As the table shows the proportion donating to medical causes increases markedly with age, with those aged 16–34 the least likely to have donated to medical research, hospitals and causes relating to physical and mental health. Those aged 35–44 were the age group most likely to have donated to schools, colleges and other educational causes.

Table 5.2 also indicates that women were more likely to have donated to most causes than men, a fact consistent with the higher prevalence of female giving we noted earlier. Women were found to be significantly more likely than men to have donated to animal welfare charities, causes related to social welfare and schools. They were also found to be significantly more likely to have donated to various medical causes including medical research, hospitals and disabled people.

Other studies have examined the role of additional demographic variables. Notable here is the role of religion or religiosity (the strength of an individual's faith). It is impossible in this brief

Table 5.2 *Causes donated to, by age and gender*

	Age						Gender		
	16–24%	25–34%	35–44%	45–54%	55–64%	65+%	M%	F%	All %
Medical research	41	49	57	54	57	48	47	55	52
Overseas aid – disaster relief	35	42	41	48	46	39	40	44	42
Hospitals and hospices	13	26	33	35	46	45	30	38	34
Animal welfare	22	30	38	28	33	34	25	38	32
Social welfare	26	33	34	37	31	25	26	36	31
Disabled people	25	24	31	37	36	33	28	34	31
Schools/colleges	23	35	45	35	24	20	27	35	31
Religion	27	28	29	32	30	36	30	32	31
Children and young people	19	27	32	29	25	21	24	27	26
Elderly people	15	22	24	28	34	28	23	28	26
Physical and mental health	12	16	22	28	38	27	21	25	23
Conservation, environment, heritage	7	15	20	24	24	19	21	17	19
Arts and museums	9	17	21	23	18	13	17	18	17
Sports/exercise	12	13	17	16	13	5	14	11	13
Hobbies/recreation	3	7	9	12	10	8	10	7	9

Source: Cabinet Office (2007: 83). Reproduced with kind permission.

chapter to fully address the impact of the world's great faiths and their traditions of giving, but it is probably fair to say that all have promoted voluntarism and the need to support the welfare of others. As Pharoah (2002:38–39) notes:

> In Islam the concepts of zakat and sadaqa enshrine the giving of money or gifts in kind. In Hinduism the central concept of daanam (the act of giving) takes many forms. Sikhism has the concept of kar seva (service to each other). Confucian teachings highlight 'humaneness,' and there is a long history of private benevolence for public good in China. Jewish concepts of charity have both long religious and secular traditions.

It is therefore not surprising that an individual professing a religious faith has been found to be more likely to engage in giving. People of faith tend to be more likely to give and to give at higher levels. However, the results of a recent study conducted by the Commonwealth of Australia (2005) suggest that the picture is actually more complex than these headlines suggest. Their results reinforce the findings of earlier work in that those having a religion and attending religious services were found to be significantly more likely to give and to give higher amounts (those with a religion gave at a rate of 88.9 per cent at an average value of $460AU per annum compared with 83.5 per cent of those who did not have a religion, at an average value of $223AU per annum). However, when giving by those with a religion *to* that religion is taken out of the equation the overall rate of giving and the amounts given are about the same as for those who do not have a religion. In addition, for those who have a religion, the less often they attend a religious service, the more likely they are to give to non-religious nonprofits. We can therefore conclude that secular organizations will find it of little value to focus on individuals of faith.

Until recently comparatively little research had been conducted into the impact of ethnicity on giving. This was due in part to the complexity surrounding the difference between race and ethnicity (hampering categorization) and also to the sensitivity surrounding the issue, making it difficult for researchers to handle the matter in an appropriate way. Nevertheless there is now a body of evidence to suggest that individuals from particular ethnic backgrounds do tend to support causes that benefit others matching that profile. In many communities of colour, for example, there is a strong sense of tradition and desire to express a unique identity. Such philanthropy has played an important role historically and continues to play a vital role in supporting individuals who might otherwise not reach their full potential.

In the UK, the Cabinet Office survey (2007) indicates that the majority of causes are significantly more likely to be supported by white people, but Asian and to a lesser extent black people are significantly more likely to support religious causes. This difference also appears to be reflected in the motives that individuals ascribe to their giving. The details of this analysis are reported in Table 5.3. Asian respondents were most likely to say that they donated because of their religion, while black respondents were most likely to say that they gave because it made them feel good.

WHY DO PEOPLE GIVE?

The issue of why individuals elect to offer their support has received considerable attention, with researchers from many different fields studying the topic. A variety of potential motives for giving have been identified including self-interest, altruism, empathy, sympathy, fear, guilt, pity, social justice and the existence of social norms. In this section we address the most widely cited of these variables.

Table 5.3 *Reasons for donating in the last four weeks, by ethnic group*

	White %	Asian %	Black %	Mixed/Other %	All %
Work of charity important	53	32	37	53	52
Right thing to do	40	49	46	59	41
Results of something that happened to me/friend/ relative	27	13	11	15	25
May benefit in future	23	6	22	22	22
Makes me feel good	16	26	31	28	17
Because of my religion	10	37	23	18	12

Source: Cabinet Office (2007: 97). Reproduced with kind permission.

Self-interest versus altruism

Self-interest can manifest itself in a variety of different ways including:

- *Self-esteem* Donors can be motivated to give because it offers them the opportunity to feel better about themselves for having made the gift (Piliavin et al. 1975).
- *Atonement for sins* Some donations may be motivated by the desire to atone for past sins – again with the ultimate goal of allowing the donor to feel better as a consequence of having made the gift (Schwartz 1967).
- *Recognition* Donors may also be motivated by the recognition they will receive from the organization, their family, peers or the local society in which they live (Dowd 1975).
- *Access to services* Donors may give to a nonprofit because they believe that they may benefit from the work it undertakes at some point in the future. Donations to cancer research, for example, may be driven by a donor's fear of developing the disease themselves.
- *Reciprocation* Equally donors may give in reciprocation for assistance or services that have been provided in the past. Donors whose lives have already been touched in some way may feel obligated to give to 'reciprocate' for the services offered. It is interesting to note that the notion of reciprocation also has a wider application, since we know from the psychology literature that sending tangible 'gifts' to donors can also generate the need for reciprocation. Many direct mail packs include pens, free address labels and other small items designed to stimulate a response. Plate 5.1 depicts a direct mail solicitation based on this principle, where the donor is sent 2p by the Children's Food Fund, in the hope that it will be returned with a donation.
- *In memoriam* Donors frequently give in memory of a friend or a loved one. In such cases the gift acts as a celebration of the individual's life and/or allows the donor to express their feelings of loss and perhaps solidarity with those left behind. Such gifts are often intensely personal and may offer the donor considerable utility in bringing meaning to the loss of a loved one.
- *Tax* There is considerable empirical evidence that the smaller the cost to a donor of making a gift, the more likely they are to contribute. A number of studies have examined the relationship between income tax rates and charitable support and although there has been variation in their findings the responsiveness of individual giving to changes in taxation appears relatively great. A change in the price of donating of a given percentage results in a 24 per cent greater percentage change in donations. Thus a shift in the marginal

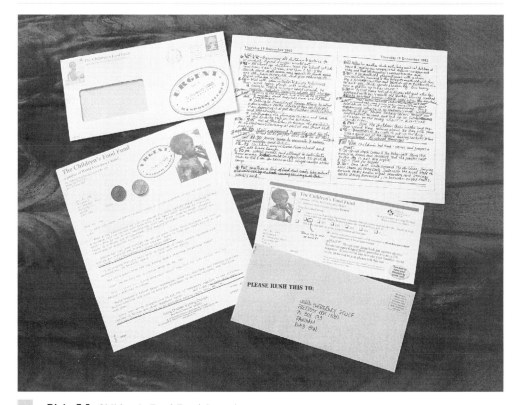

Plate 5.1 *Children's Food Fund Appeal*

Source: © Children's Food Fund Appeal. Reproduced with kind permission.

tax rate from say 40 per cent to 30 per cent results in a roughly 15 per cent increase in the cost of giving and would therefore reduce giving by some 18.6 per cent (i.e. 15 per cent × 1.24) (Weisbrod 1988).

The notion of tax relief on giving is thus considered an important motivator of charitable giving and as Odendahl (1987:21) notes:

the saving of taxes is not ever far from a person's motivation … it is in mine, and it is in almost everybody's I know. I think if it were not for the savings in taxes – the notion that the government really is participating in a gift – I think there would be an awful lot less giving.

Nevertheless it is important not to overstate the influence of taxation. Whatever way one looks at giving and whatever the marginal rate of taxation, the donor will always be better off not making a donation and keeping their money to themselves. Indeed, this is reflected in studies that have sought to rank motives for giving, where the impact of favourable tax breaks is typically a long way down the list.

The leading economist Andreoni (2001) offers a more succinct way of looking at the utility that derives from giving. He argues that so-called 'selfless' giving may be explained by:

■ *Public Good Theory* which postulates that people will support nonprofits because they recognize that society as a whole will benefit from the donation. They are thus rational since as a member of that society they too will derive benefit from the donation.

- *Exchange Theory* which posits that donors will give because of the tangible rewards they receive for their donation. This may take the form of membership benefits that may accrue as part of their subscription, or it may take the form of acknowledgement devices such as plaques or citations on a Roll of Honour.
- *Warm Glow Effect* some economists believe that the utility offered by a gift can be psychological in nature and thus completely intangible. People give because they feel better about themselves for having made the donation.

By contrast there have been arguments raised in favour of genuinely altruistic giving, whereby the donor recognizes a need and decides to offer a gift even in circumstances where they themselves will derive none of the benefits alluded to above. The sending of an anonymous donation or the leaving of a unsolicited bequest are two commonly cited scenarios where self-benefit would be hard to quantify. Becker (1976) however still argues that even these seemingly selfless acts can ultimately be traced back to self-interest. These might include:

> the desire for one's life to matter, to improve one's self picture, to feel happier about life and self, to relieve the distress of empathy with the victim, or to obey religious or societal norms.
>
> (Simmons 1991:16)

Perhaps as Simmons goes on to say, the underlying motive should not really be of interest to us at all. Helping should remain admirable even where at root the action may have been inspired by these subtle self-rewards.

Empathy

The arousal of empathy in a donor has consistently been shown to precipitate donations. Empathy may be defined as an individual's emotional arousal elicited by the expression of emotion in another (cf. Shelton and Rogers 1981). Thus donors are motivated to give because they are themselves distressed by the suffering endured by another. Numerous studies have found that the higher the level of empathy the greater the likelihood of a donation being made. To maximize this effect Davis et al. (1987) established that nonprofits should ask prospective donors to imagine how the beneficiary must feel, rather than asking the donor to imagine how they would feel in their place. The distinction is subtle but important. In one case the donor is compelled to look at a problem from the beneficiary's perspective, in the other they are not. Equally, to be effective the arousal of empathy must be powerful enough to overcome indifference but not so powerful that it becomes personally distressing to the donor. In such circumstances the message will be ignored (Fultz et al. 1986). Images in fundraising communications thus have to strike an appropriate balance.

Sympathy

The motive 'sympathy' has also received attention from fundraisers. Sympathy is a *value expressive function* that allows the donor to conform to personally held norms (Clary and Snyder 1991; Schwartz 1977). In other words, when confronted with a request to give donors will feel sympathetic if they believe it is inappropriate for the beneficiaries to be suffering in the manner depicted in the fundraising communication. Again, there would appear to be a relationship between the degree of sympathy engendered and both the propensity to donate and the chosen level of support (Batson 1990; Fultz et al. 1986). Greater sympathy leads to a higher level of gift.

Fear/guilt/pity

A variety of other potential motives for giving have been identified including fear, guilt and pity. These have been found to impact positively both on giving and the amount of that giving (Krebs and Whitten 1972; Pieper 1975). In general, the findings are similar to those reported above in the sense that the development of each motive in fundraising communications should be strong enough to demand action, but not so strong that it becomes personally distressing to the donor.

Social justice

Miller (1977) argued from social justice motivation theory that if people witness undue suffering their belief in a just world will be threatened – consequently they will be motivated to respond to restore their faith in that just world. Donors with this motivation have a strong sense of equity and believe that people 'get what they deserve'. They will thus be more motivated to respond to a campaign raising funds for breast cancer victims than for lung cancer victims whom, rightly or wrongly, they may regard as partially responsible for their own condition.

Miller also identified that helping behaviour would be increased when the need is not widespread and the duration of the need (persistence) is short. It is interesting to note that most charity communications appear based on the exact opposite of this position. Appeals tend to stress the ongoing nature of the need for support and make much of the number of individuals currently being impacted by the issue. Large numbers such as thousands or even millions are difficult for a donor to relate to and can lead to the conclusion that a donation from them would have little impact on the problem and would therefore not be worthwhile. A much better approach would be to explain what tangible difference a donation would make of the likely size the target individual could offer.

Norms

Giving may be motivated by a desire on the part of the donor to conform to social norms. Donors will give if they believe that other similar individuals have also given to support the nonprofit. Reingen (1978), for example, illustrated that showing prospective donors a fictitious list of others who had contributed to the cause tended to generate higher numbers of gifts and higher levels of gift. He identified that the length of the list was also an issue, with longer lists outperforming shorter ones. Judgements in respect of giving are therefore made in terms of beliefs about what is normative for the group (Clark and Word 1972).

More recent work by Shang et al. (2008) has reinforced the significance of norms. The authors found that social information about the amount of another donor's contribution influenced the level of the target donor's giving. In one series of experiments, the researchers amended the script that telemarketers used when listeners called in to a public radio station (in the United States) to make their donation. After being greeted by the operator, callers were told 'we had another donor who gave $X dollars. How much would you like to give today?' The amounts that callers were told another donor had given were varied so that the optimal amount to use as a specimen could be calculated. The researchers found that providing social information generally increased the amounts that people would donate, but that there was an optimal 'specimen' amount that would increase giving by an average (for new donors) of 29 per cent. This is illustrated in Figure 5.1 where the average gift in the control condition (i.e. where donors are given no social information) is shown alongside the cases where the caller is told about another donor having made a gift of $75, $180 or $300. In this case citing a prior donation of $300 was optimal.

Average amount contributed by social information condition

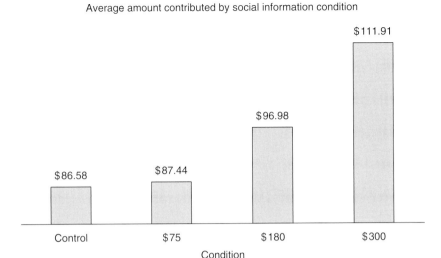

Figure 5.1 *Social information increases the contribution levels of new members*

Average amount increased from previous contributions by
social information condition

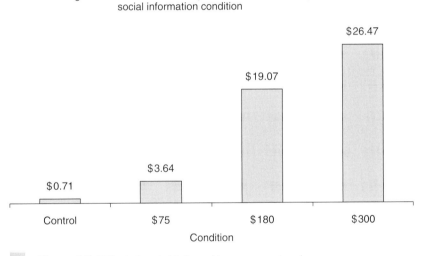

Figure 5.2 *Effect of social information on renewing donors*

A similar picture was obtained with donors who were calling in to renew (i.e. make a second or subsequent gift). Figure 5.2 shows that donors not exposed to the social information gave pretty much the same amount as last year (up only 71 cents). Those donors exposed to social information, however, gave markedly more and in the $300 condition, $26.47 more.

It turns out that the ideal amount to choose as a comparator is between the 90th and 95th percentile of the value of previous gifts to the organization. In plain English, if you line up all the gifts to a previous campaign in order of value, the best approach is to take a value somewhere between the 90th and 95th per cent highest gift. For example, if your average giving last year was

105

$120, the median was $75, the 90th percentile was $240, the 95th percentile was $360 and the 99th percentile was $600, then any amount between $240 and $360 would be the right amount to suggest as another person's contribution. Move any higher than this and giving is actually decreased as a consequence. Of course, in all of this, it is also important to be honest. Amounts can only be selected that an individual has actually given.

Now at this point, direct marketers might be developing some scepticism. Perhaps what we are seeing here isn't the impact of social information at all? Perhaps these uplifts are achieved simply because we are prompting people to think about gifts at particular levels? Shang and her team addressed this issue by changing the wording of the telephone script from 'we had another who gave …' to 'we had another donor he/she gave …'. In cases where the gender of the caller was matched with the gender of the example, the value of the giving was increased by an average of 34 per cent. If the comparator were only a prompt this uplift would not be achieved, so what this result tells us is that individuals *do* pay attention to social information and in particular social information that links in some way to their own identity. It also tells us that this information has the capacity to increase giving dramatically.

What is particularly exciting about this early work is that gender is of course only one identity that we possess and quite possibly one of the least relevant to the context of donations. Intuitively we might expect that other identities might be more powerful. In the context of environmental groups, for example, individuals might see themselves as a supporter, conservationist, environmental advocate, campaigner or perhaps as someone who behaves responsibly when it comes to their own impact on the environment. Each of these identities could be primed in the same way as gender in communications and we would expect to see an uplift in response as a consequence. Nonprofits need to think through all the possible identities that might be important to their donors and prime the most critical.

THE IMPACT OF CHARITY APPEALS

Thus far in our discussion we have concentrated specifically on the characteristics and motives of donors. At this point it is our intention to move on to consider the 'inputs' to the donor's decision-making process and to consider the impact that factors such as branding, the mode of ask and the content of fundraising communications might have in stimulating giving.

Branding

Nonprofits currently engage in a variety of different fundraising techniques employing media such as direct mail, telemarketing, face-to-face canvassing, door-to-door distribution, press advertising and, increasingly, radio advertising and DRTV (Direct Response Television). The use of each of these media is potentially capable of generating a response from the prospects targeted. In the case of a number of the larger charities it has been argued that this process has been greatly facilitated by the presence of a well-known and 'trusted' brand.

Roberts Wray (1994) was one of the first to explicitly debate the relevance of branding to the charity sector, with subsequent work by Saxton (1995) suggesting that in the voluntary sector context a strong brand should both draw on, and project the beliefs and values of, its various stakeholders. While these are perhaps rather less tangible than the facts about why an organization exists and the nature of the beneficiary group, this latter class of variables can greatly aid a donor's understanding of the charity concerned and suggest very potent reasons why it might be worthy of support (Dixon 1997). It is only comparatively recently, however, that there has been much formal interest in branding within the sector, but while as Tapp (1996:335) notes, some 'charities do not describe much of what they do as "branding", organizations have long been concerned with maintaining a consistent style and tone of voice and conducting periodic reviews of both policies and actions to ensure that a consistent personality is projected'. The clarity with which this 'personality' is projected will have a direct impact on an organization's ability to fund-raise. More recent work by Sargeant et al. (2008) has identified why this might be. The research shows that a large part of a charity brand is actually shared with other nonprofits. The idea is illustrated in Figure 5.3. The shared traits are illustrated in the outer ring of the diagram. There are many *benevolent* traits such as being 'fair', 'honest', 'ethical' and 'trustworthy' that the public attributes to organizations simply because they are charitable. Nonprofits do not need to earn these traits. Instead people start with the assumption that these traits apply until evidence appears to the contrary. Similarly, individuals see nonprofits as agents of change and imbue organizations with traits that reflect the nature of this *progressive* engagement with society. They viewed personality traits such as 'transforming', 'responsive' and 'engaging' as being common charitable traits.

Organizations that share a common cause, be it the environment, arts or a religious faith, will also share common personality traits. The Mission Aviation Fellowship, for example, strives to provide aid to Third World communities investing in projects such as sanitation and the provision of fresh water, while simultaneously raising awareness of the Gospel in the communities in which it works. Its donors are therefore supporting both practical and spiritual aid when they offer a donation. The Christian values that the organization embodies can therefore differentiate it from many secular international relief agencies, such as Oxfam, but not from other faith-based organizations.

Sargeant et al. (2008) also found evidence that some causes were perceived as being 'upper class', 'intellectual' or 'sophisticated'. Education and arts nonprofits were frequently referred to

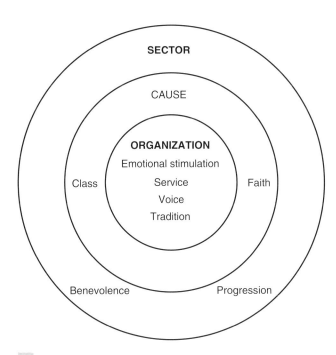

Figure 5.3 *Shared nonprofit traits*

in these terms and regarded as 'elite'. This again will be a characteristic shared with other non-profits in the same category.

Identifying which aspects of brand personality are shared within the sector and/or cause is important because the shared and unique aspects of personality affect giving in different ways. A belief that nonprofits are progressive and benevolent is a necessary prerequisite to becoming a donor in the first place. Similarly, an understanding that an organization is faith-based may be a necessary prerequisite for a follower of that faith to consider including it in what marketers refer to as their 'consideration set' (i.e. the range of nonprofits they will consider supporting). But none of these dimensions will have any impact at all on the amounts that people will give or on the level of loyalty a charity might engender.

What does affect both these aspects of a donor–nonprofit relationship are the facets of brand personality that are genuinely distinctive, the ones grouped in the inner circle of Figure 5.3. Projecting a unique or differentiated brand personality makes it more likely that an individual will give at a higher level and for extended periods of time.

Sargeant et al. (2008) show that there are currently four sources of brand differentiation. There may of course be others not exploited by the charities in their sample, but at a minimum charities can look to each of the following four areas in their bid to be distinctive.

1   *Traits connected with emotional stimulation*   Traits such as exciting, heroic, innovative and inspiring all have the ability to evoke an emotional response in donors and since there are many different categories of emotion that may be evoked (or combinations of categories), there are many potential avenues for differentiation here.
2   *Traits connected with voice*   Brands can also be differentiated on the basis of the tone of voice they project in the media. The NSPCC, for example, regards itself as challenging, courageous and protecting and its media voice reflects those traits. It also takes a strong but unpatronizing stance on social issues such as smacking. What a nonprofit says and critically *how* it says it can make it distinctive in the minds of the public.
3   *Traits connected with the service*   The style or philosophy behind how an organization delivers its services can also be an effective route to differentiation. Human service charities in particular might carve out a unique personality on the basis of characteristics such as inclusive, approachable and dedicated in the way that they deal with their service users.
4   *Tradition*   Donors view some nonprofits as traditional and regard giving as a duty, particularly during different events and seasons. In the UK the Royal British Legion sells poppies in advance of Remembrance Sunday to recognize those that have lost their lives in the service of their country. These symbols of remembrance have become such a powerful component of national life that no politician, newscaster or person of influence in the media will be seen without a poppy in the run-up to that event.

To maximize the performance of their fundraising, nonprofits need to be clear about how their brand is distinctive from others and ensure that these characteristics are consistently communicated over time to donors and other stakeholder groups.

Media

Nonprofits currently engage in a variety of different fundraising techniques employing media such as direct mail, telemarketing, face to face (on the street), door to door, press advertising, radio advertising and DRTV (Direct Response Television). An emergent body of literature on benchmarking the performance of specific media suggests that both initial returns and the lifetime value of supporters recruited will vary by the media employed (Sargeant and McKenzie 1998;

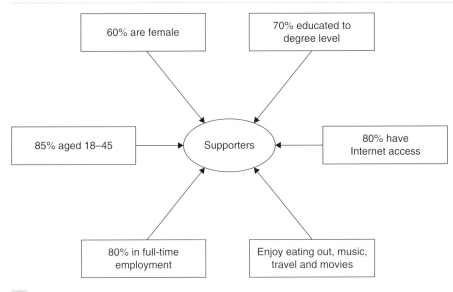

Figure 5.4 *Profile of face-to-face supporters*

Sargeant et al. 2006). We also know that the profile of the donors recruited by each media will vary in terms of their demographic, lifestyle and behavioural characteristics (e.g. Jay 2001; Aldrich 2004). An example of face-to-face donors (i.e. individuals who are recruited to make a regular gift by agency fundraisers approaching them on the street) is provided in Figure 5.4.

Role models

In soliciting funds a number of nonprofits make use of celebrities or community leaders who demonstrate their support for an organization and act as a 'role model' for others. The provision of role models can influence giving behaviour by leading to the creation of social norms thereby legitimizing and encouraging the giving behaviour (Krebs 1970). Role models can be through the presence of well-known high-profile donors at events and also in less personal forms of communication such as direct mail. Role models work particularly well in encouraging behaviours that are relatively rare. In the fundraising context this may be when an organization is looking to raise funds from a new audience, or when they are making a request for donors to give in a way that may previously have not been considered. In such examples donors exhibit a degree of 'social ambiguity' (Festinger 1954) and are not sure how to behave. A role model can be used to demonstrate the appropriate behaviour. Figure 5.5 contains an example of a communication designed to solicit a legacy/bequest. Visitors to the Remember a Charity website can download a copy of a video hosted by the newscaster Michael Buerk. The ad is fronted by the strapline 'I Will. Will You?'

Communities of participation

Communities of participation are networks of formal and informal relationships entered into either by choice or by circumstance (e.g. schools, soup kitchens, soccer groups) that bring an individual into contact with need. Authors such as Paul Schervish (1993, 1997) argue that a basic connection to a cause (e.g. being a graduate of a school) is not enough in itself to prompt

Figure 5.5 *Remember a charity*

Source: Remember A Charity. Reproduced with kind permission.

subsequent donations to that school and that some degree of socialization is required. This, the author argues, is experienced through communities of participation and thus donors will be predisposed to give to causes connected in some way with these communities.

More recently, Conley (1999) in a study of the predictors of alumni giving found that involvement in school activities and involvement in alumni activities were both primary indicators of whether an individual would give. Lohmann (1992) also found that giving frequently related to personal membership of networks, societies, political groups, social movements or religious, artistic or scientific communities. People can give to reinforce aspects of their social identity.

A further dimension of social identity lies in the realm of social networks. We typically have many of these. As individuals we may have a network of work colleagues, a network of people who attend the same church, a network of people we know who support the same football team and so on. As we get to meet more people who enjoy the same activity and/or embrace the same identity, the more likely it is that we see membership of this group as an important part of our lives and that the norms of behaviour for that group become an important set of influences on our own behaviour. Shang et al. 2008 investigated the role that social networks might play in the context of giving. Figure 5.6 shows the results of a further study of donors calling in to make a donation to a public radio station. In this case donors were asked by the fundraiser how many people they knew in the station catchment area or how many people they knew who also listened to the station. These questions were posed before the individual was asked how much they would like to give. In a control group donors were asked neither of these questions. As the graph clearly illustrates, donors who knew greater numbers of listeners gave greater amounts than those who lacked these acquaintances. Interestingly, having a large social network is not in itself enough. The key to enhanced giving lies in knowing greater numbers of people who share the common interest, in this case listening to the station. Further experiments showed that this effect is most pronounced when the fellow listeners are family and friends rather than just co-workers and that

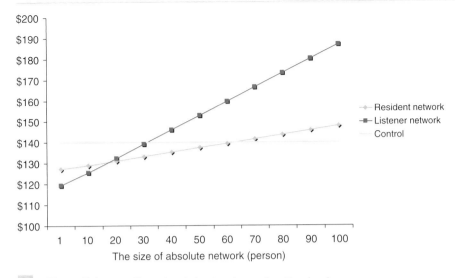

Figure 5.6 *The effect of social networks on donation level*

donors who believed their listener networks were bigger than those of other people tended to give more than those who believed they were smaller ($265 versus $139).

These results are easily applied to many other fundraising contexts. In telephone solicitations individuals can be asked how many other family and friends share their interest in the organization, cause or behaviour. Individuals whose social networks are larger than the average can be prompted to reflect on that during the course of the conversation. Their giving will be enhanced as a result. Equally, individuals can be encouraged to increase the size of this related social network. Online fundraising offers many opportunities to 'tell a friend' about the work of the organization and some automated donation-processing systems now offer this as a standard feature. Equally, many nonprofits offer supporters the opportunity to become part of a wider community. This is easy to accomplish online, but nonprofits may also achieve success through special interest groups and events. As the social network of donors begins to grow, so too will their support of the organization.

Portrayal of beneficiaries

The manner in which recipients of the charitable 'product' are portrayed can have a considerable impact on attitudes towards support and actual giving behaviour. Donors will tend to support those charities that represent the needy in an acceptable way (Eayrs and Ellis 1990). Pictures (for example, of an overtly handicapped child) have been shown to actually decrease the response to fundraising solicitations. Donors can find such images distressing and ignore the communication concerned. Reactance theory (Brehm 1966) also suggests that individuals have what they like to regard as a number of behavioural and attitudinal freedoms. A hard-hitting campaign can thus fail because it may threaten a donor's ability to choose to spend their monies elsewhere. It is thus somewhat ironic that a picture of an aided beneficiary can be much more effective, because donors then feel they have the freedom not to give and are statistically much more likely to give as a consequence (Bendapudi and Singh 1996).

Similarly appeals for charities concerned with disability often emphasize how dependent on the organization's work individuals with the disability are. There is now considerable evidence that such appeals are very successful in engendering feelings of sympathy (Brolley and Anderson 1986; Feldman and Feldman 1985) and feelings of guilt and pity (Feldman and Feldman 1985; Krebs and Whitten 1972; Pieper 1975). A key issue for fundraisers, however, is the extent to which dependency should be exhibited. While one might assume that depicting a greater degree of dependency is desirable and that it would be best to maximize this, this need not necessarily be the case. It depends on whether the dependency on the organization is perceived as temporary or permanent. Wagner and Wheeler (1969) identified that when the need is perceived as permanent, the level of dependency has no effect on the amount likely to be given. However, if the need is only temporary, increasing the level of dependency depicted in fundraising communications will increase the number of donors who both give and give at higher levels.

Interestingly Adler et al. (1991) identified that portraying recipients as succumbing to their condition (by contrast to coping) has no impact on the pattern of donations. They do however identify a strong impact on the subsequent attitudes of the donor towards the recipient group. This latter point is of particular interest since many authors argue that portraying people with disabilities as dependent may well harm the long-term interests of the beneficiary group by reinforcing negative stereotypes and attitudes (Elliot and Byrd 1982; Harris and Harris 1977). Positive portrayals on the other hand seem to engender positive attitudes (Harris 1975; Shurka et al. 1982) and fundraisers thus need to ensure that they take adequate steps to preserve the best interests of the community they serve, consulting as widely as possible before running a potentially contentious campaign. Those messages likely to raise the most funds can on occasion be entirely inappropriate given the nature of the cause and the wider needs of the beneficiary group.

Finally, other work on the portrayal of beneficiaries has suggested that attractive people are perceived as more worthy of support than unattractive people (Latane and Nida 1981) and that female subjects are considered more worthy of support than male subjects (Feinman 1978; Gruder and Cook 1971). The portrayal of the responsibility of recipients for their own condition can also impact on a willingness to support. Piliavin et al. (1975) identified that the extent to which an individual could be blamed for his/her needy condition would directly impact on both the number of donations and the levels of support proffered.

Fit with self-image

Coliazzi et al. (1984) noted that individuals are more likely to help those that are perceived as being similar to themselves. They will thus tend to filter those messages from charities existing to support disparate segments of society. Of course, charities exist to support work, not only with other members of human society but also wider environmental or ecological concerns from which every segment of society can ultimately stand to benefit. Dichter (1972) offers some explanation for support of this category of cause, suggesting that giving can greatly aid one's self-image or self-worth. Indeed generous giving to all manner of different causes has long been a source of prestige for individuals in the USA. Donors may thus prefer to concentrate on those categories of cause which are either perceived as most relevant to their segment of society, or which are perceived more widely as supporting how they wish to see themselves, or have others see them. As Schwartz (1967) notes, donating can confer an identity on both the recipient and the donor. Work by Yavas et al. (1980) suggests that possessing a generous, loving self-image is more important for donors than non-donors. Donors should therefore be portrayed in communications as generous and loving to help them project the self-image that they would wish others to accept (Douglas et al. 1967).

Strength of the stimulus

A variety of authors have chosen to focus on the strength of the stimulus generated by a particular nonprofit. Clearly the stronger the stimulus, the easier it will be for nonprofits to cut through the 'clutter' of other charitable appeals. There is evidence that the strength of the stimulus is related to a number of variables. The first is the perceived urgency of the recipient situation. In general, high degrees of urgency would appear to engender high degrees of support (see for example Chierco et al. 1982; Farrington and Kidd 1977). It would also appear that approaches which build up the degree of personal responsibility on the part of the donor will be more effective at engendering a response (see e.g. Geer and Jermecky 1973). Other key variables warranting consideration under this general heading include the degree of personalization attained (Weldon 1984) and the clarity of the request. Personalized, clear and unambiguous requests for support are more likely to engender giving than those that are vague or general in nature.

SELECTION CRITERIA

In the modern era most individuals have the opportunity to support a wide variety of causes. In this section we consider how individuals decide between competing solicitations and select the specific organizations they will give to. Notable here is the perceived performance of the nonprofit organization. Donors will generally prefer to give to organizations that are both effective (in the sense that they do what they say they will do) and efficient (in the sense that they make the best possible use of the monies available to them).

A number of well-publicized abuses of donated monies have served to sensitize donors to these issues. In the USA, for example, the National Kids Day Foundation raised $4 million between 1948 and 1963 and spent the entire amount on fundraising and administrative costs (Cutlip 1980). When challenged, charity administrators said the foundation's purpose was to promote the idea of needy children rather than actually providing aid. Similarly, the United Way suffered a dramatic fall in support following the Aramony scandal when its CEO was accused of having misused the funds of the organization to pay for (among other things) business flights on Concorde.

Glaser (1994:178) found that the variable 'an adequate amount spent per program' was the most important factor in the decision to contribute to specific charitable organizations. Donors appear to have a clear idea of what represents an acceptable percentage of income that may be applied to the cause as opposed to being 'squandered' on both administration and fundraising costs. Warwick (1994) identified that donors expect that the ratio between administration/fundraising costs and so-called charitable expenditure would be 20:80. It is interesting to note that despite this expectation most donors believe that the actual ratio is closer to 50:50. Harvey and McCrohan (1988) found that 60 per cent was a significant threshold, with charities spending at least 60 per cent of their donations on charitable programmes achieving significantly higher levels of donation. Steinberg (1986) suggests that this is something of an anomaly since fundraising costs are sunk (i.e. have already been incurred by the time the donor receives the solicitation), and should therefore not enter into a donor's decision of whether or not to support a given charity.

On a related theme, perceived mismanagement by charity administrators and trustees can impact negatively on donations (Baily and Bruce 1992) with donors reportedly seeking a degree of professionalism from the organizations they support. There is also an interesting anomaly here, however, since while donors seem to want to see high-quality professional management, they appear to favour organizations that do not resemble business organizations and are actually 'amateurish but effective' (Nightingale 1973). Work by Sargeant et al. (2001) concludes that while donors may purport to demand professionalism they are in reality drawn to organizations that retain the ethos of voluntarism.

Donors can also and very obviously be drawn to organizations that have a good match with their own particular motivation. We dealt with these at length earlier, but to summarize donors may prefer to give to organizations that offer them the highest level of:

- *Emotional utility*   In the sense of the 'warm glow' considered by the economist Andreoni and others. Donors will be more likely to give to organizations where the sense of having done the right thing, accomplishment or self-worth will be highest.
- *Familial utility*   Donors may also prioritize organizations that they or their family and friends might benefit from (or might in the future). They may also elect to give in memory of a loved one.
- *Demonstrable utility*   In the sense of where they can 'see' the biggest impact for their donation. Donors can rationally decide between competing organizations to see where they believe their donation would make the greatest difference to the cause.
- *Practical utility*   Where donors may give simply because they want the practical benefits that accrue from giving. They might thus join the National Trust to gain access to the properties they wish to visit, or to enjoy a variety of the other membership benefits the nonprofit is able to offer. As we discussed earlier, giving can be motivated by a plethora of extrinsic rewards particularly in the context of membership.
- *Spiritual utility*   Where donors select a nonprofit because it has the strongest fit with their spiritual identity and needs.

Donors who have given previously may also be motivated, at least in part, by the quality of the previous giving experience. If the gift was banked within a reasonable time, the donor was thanked appropriately and their preferences for further communication were solicited and actioned, they will be more likely to give again than where the process was flawed. Donor satisfaction with the quality of service provided will therefore be a highly significant factor.

FEEDBACK

Having decided to offer a donation to a nonprofit, donors will typically be thanked by the respective organization in the hope that this will be the first stage in building an ongoing relationship. There are two broad concepts from fundraising research that fundraisers can employ in designing these communications.

Labelling

In thanking donors for their gift organizations often append labels to the donor such as kind, generous and/or helpful. Work by authors such as Swinyard and Ray (1977) has identified that this elicits a greater motivation to help and fosters favourable attitudes on the part of the donor. The impact of labels will be particularly potent when there are concrete prior behaviours to be labelled and when the label stresses the uniqueness of the donor's behaviour (McGuire and Padawer-Singer 1976). To be effective the labels should be used consistently over time. They should also be credible and supplied by a credible source (Allen 1982). Thinking back to our earlier discussion of identities, these too could be introduced in labels and reinforced over time.

Recognition/rewards

The fundraising literature is replete with references to the need for adequate donor recognition (e.g. Warwick and Hitchcock 2001; Irwin-Wells 2002). Failure to provide adequate and

Table 5.4 *Reasons for non-support*

Reason	% of sample
I cannot afford to offer my support to charity	23.3
Charities ask for inappropriate sums	22.5
The government should fund the work undertaken by charities	19.3
I find charity communications inappropriate	12.0
The quality of service provided by charities to their donors is poor	6.8
In the past charities have not acknowledged my support	4.0
I feel that charities are not deserving	2.8
Other	9.3

Source: Sargeant et al. (2000). Reproduced with kind permission.

appropriate recognition, it has been argued, will lead either to a lowering of future support or its withdrawal. Sargeant et al. (2001) provide the first empirical support for this proposition, indicating a link between the perception of adequate recognition and the level of subsequent loyalty. Recognition may be as simple as a thank-you from the fundraiser, or it may be more complex, particularly where higher value gifts are concerned. In such circumstances the recognition should be carefully tailored to the needs of the donor.

INHIBITORS

Sargeant et al. (2000) identify a number of inhibitors or barriers to giving. These are presented in Table 5.4. In a large-scale survey of non-donors they determined that a lack of money was the primary issue, although this was only marginally more significant than being asked for inappropriate sums, or believing that the government should be funding the work undertaken by charities. It is interesting to note that communications and service quality issues are also significant factors in non-giving.

MODELLING GIVING BEHAVIOUR

Aside from the plethora of studies addressing specific aspects of charity giving, a few studies have also made attempts to synthesize the available literature and to develop a rather broader perspective on how and why individuals elect to give. Notable amongst these is the work by Sargeant and Woodliffe (2007) and Burnett and Wood (1988). The respective models are depicted in Figures 5.7 and 5.8.

The Sargeant and Woodliffe (2007) model is the basis for how we have chosen to structure this chapter. Their model is an attempt to group together the numerous studies of giving behaviour in a meaningful way. Although it is presented sequentially it makes no attempt to map the complex processes that individuals go through in deciding whether or not to offer a donation. Instead it focuses on broad categories of research. It is therefore an example of a *content* model of giving behaviour. The Burnett and Wood (1988) model by contrast is an example of a *process* model where often complex interrelationships between the variables are all highlighted. The reader is left with a clear idea of how a giving decision may be formulated.

There are other differences between the two models. Sargeant and Woodliffe highlight 'processing determinants' or the criteria that may be used to identify which specific organizations will be supported, such as efficiency, effectiveness and the quality of service provided. There are

115

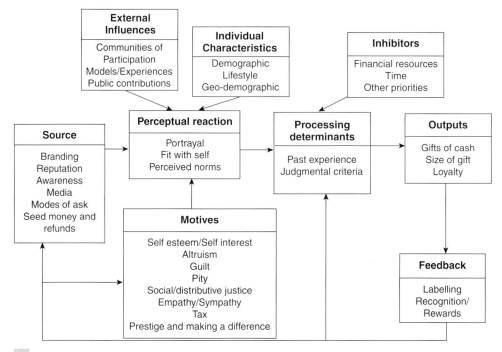

Figure 5.7 *Sargeant and Woodliffe's model of donor behaviour*

also differences surrounding the handling of what Sargeant refers to as the intrinsic determinants of giving. While Burnett and Wood include the category 'personal traits' in their model this does not address the full range of intrinsic motives an individual might have for responding to a particular appeal (e.g. sympathy, empathy, belief in social justice, etc.).

Sargeant and Woodliffe also consider the contribution of a wide range of charity 'inputs' to the donor's decision-making process including brands, a variety of facts/images about the organization that may be attained from various media and the specific charitable appeal in question. Whether that appeal will be recognized as relevant to the donor will be a function of their perceptual reaction to the message. This in turn will depend on the manner in which recipients are portrayed, the perceived fit with the donor's self image, the strength of the stimulus engendered and the extent to which other 'perceptual noise' might be present (e.g. other charity appeals, or other commercial marketing communications of various types). Those messages that are perceived as potentially relevant to the donor will be evaluated to determine whether support will be offered. Donors may look at the efficiency/effectiveness of the organization asking for support and, if they have past experience of dealing with the organization, the quality of service provided. Where a favourable view is formed a gift of cash, time or goods will be made. The more favourable the view the more likely a higher value gift will be made and the more likely it will be that the donor will remain loyal over time.

According to Sargeant and Woodliffe (2007), there are other categories of variable that will shape giving. First, some categories of individual will be more likely to offer support to nonprofits than others. Variables such as age, gender, social class and so on will influence whether an individual will elect to respond to a particular appeal. The authors also acknowledge that the extent to which a particular appeal is successful at arousing emotion will impact on the response. Those appeals that successfully engender sympathy, empathy, guilt, pity and so on will therefore tend both to stimulate giving and at higher levels.

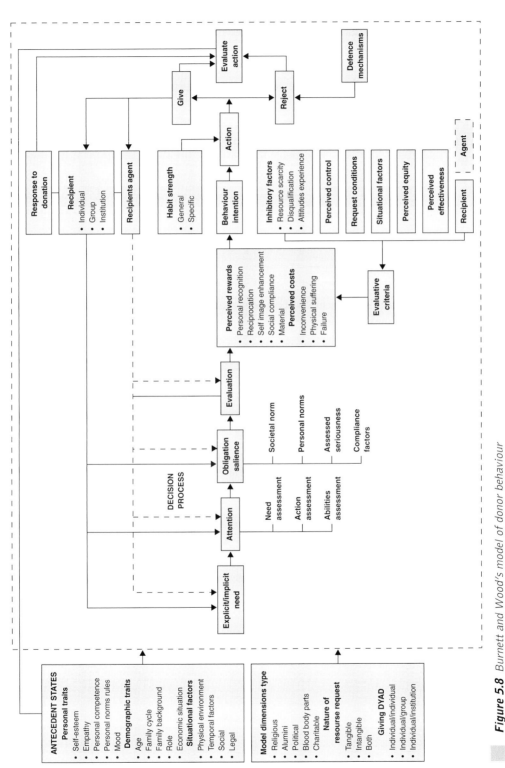

Figure 5.8 Burnett and Wood's model of donor behaviour

Source: Burnett and Wood (1988). Reproduced by kind permission of the authors.

Burnett and Wood (1988) acknowledge the impact of personality traits, demographic and situational factors on the donation-making process. They postulate a complex process of decision-making beginning with the identification of need on the part of the nonprofit. Donors will then evaluate the level of the need, whether action is required and their ability to make a difference. It is then necessary to determine whether the obligation to support the organization applies to them. They will decide whether this is the case by reference to pertinent norms and the extent to which they believe the level of the need is urgent. The authors argue that where need is perceived as salient, they will then decide whether a gift should be offered by evaluating the costs and benefits of taking action. At this stage the donor will thus examine the rewards, either economic or psycho-social, that will accrue as a consequence of giving, and compare these with the economic costs of giving, the inconvenience of making a donation and the risk that their gift will not make the difference they believe it will. On the basis of this complex process donors will decide whether to offer their support or not. The authors argue that where the decision is taken to reject the appeal a number of defence mechanisms will be employed such as 'they don't really need the money', 'what possible difference could my money make?' or 'it's just not my responsibility'.

The final stage of the model is to evaluate the outcome, examining whether the rewards were as expected, whether the impact of the gift was as expected, whether the quality of service provided was as expected, and so on. This final stage typically involves the assessment of intangibles and is thus highly subjective. Nonprofits are advised to be aware of this process of evaluation and attempt to influence it by providing donors with explicit information to input to this evaluation process, perhaps through the nature of the thank-you or data in respect of how the gift has been used.

WHY DO INDIVIDUALS STOP GIVING?

Having now considered why individuals give to nonprofits we will move on to consider why they stop. Sargeant (2001) conducted the first comprehensive study of why donors in both the UK and the USA stop giving to specific nonprofits. In a large-scale survey of lapsed donors the author identified a remarkable degree of similarity between the feelings of donors in both countries. The results are depicted in Table 5.5. In interpreting the table it is important to recognize that donors could select as many reasons as they wished for the termination of their support. Thus the columns do not sum to 100 per cent.

It seems clear that many donors lapse because of a change in their financial circumstances or because of a desire to allocate their resources elsewhere. It is important to note, however, that a good many donors appear to be simply switching their support to other organizations that they perceive as equally or more deserving. This is clearly good news for the nonprofit sector, but bad news for the particular organization. Rather less encouragingly it seems that a number of donors quit because of poor quality service from the organization. Many nonprofits appear not to thank the donor adequately, inform them how their monies were spent or offer them sufficient choice in communications.

The study also examined the underlying reasons why donors quit, looking at the impact of a range of other determinants of giving. The following factors were identified as impacting on retention:

- *Recognition*   Donors were significantly more likely to quit if the recognition offered to them was seen as being inappropriate or insufficient given the size and nature of the gift.
- *Personal benefit versus altruism*   Interestingly donors motivated by a desire to attain some personal benefit in return for the gift were significantly more likely to lapse than those motivated by more altruistic concerns.

Table 5.5 *Reasons why donors terminate their support in the USA and UK*

Reason	UK (%)	USA (%)
I can no longer afford to offer my support	22.3	54.0
I feel that other causes are more deserving	26.5	36.2
Death/relocation	23.1	16.0
No memory of ever supporting	11.4	18.4
X did not acknowledge my support	0.9	13.2
X did not inform me how my money had been used	1.7	8.1
X no longer needs my support	1.2	5.6
The quality of support provided by X was poor	0.9	5.1
X asked for inappropriate sums	3.1	4.3
I found X's communications inappropriate	3.6	3.8
X did not take account of my wishes	0.7	2.6
Staff at X were unhelpful	0.5	2.1

- *Pressure* Those donors who felt under significant peer pressure to make a gift were more likely to lapse.
- *Impact* Those donors who were reassured that previous donations had had the impact the nonprofit had suggested were significantly less likely to lapse. This stresses the need for nonprofits to provide adequate feedback when thanking donors and asking them for further resources.
- *Relationship* The perceived strength of the relationship was also an issue, with donors who felt that they had genuinely been able to interact with the organization significantly more likely to remain loyal. Donors who felt that they had been able to shape the relationship, perhaps by exercising choice over the number and nature of communications received, or who felt that they had received a personalized service, tended to remain loyal.
- *Service quality* The perception of the quality of service provided by the fundraising department to its donors impacted on retention. Donors with more favourable perceptions in respect of the communications they received were significantly more likely to remain loyal. Indeed donors who described themselves as 'very satisfied' with the quality of service were twice as likely to remain loyal as those who indicated that they were merely 'satisfied'. This highlights the need for nonprofits to measure and reflect on the quality of service provided and is an issue that will be returned to in Chapter 7.

More recent work by Sargeant and Woodliffe (2007) has looked at the role of donor commitment in driving loyalty. Defining commitment as an enduring passion for the cause, the researchers identified a strong and positive impact on loyalty. The greater the degree of commitment, the greater the level of loyalty a given donor will exhibit. Importantly the researchers were also able to identify a number of the drivers of this commitment:

1 *Service quality* Although satisfaction with the quality of service provided has a direct impact on loyalty, it also has an indirect effect with favourable perceptions also driving the sense of commitment.

119

2   *Risk*   Donors who believe that if they cancel their donation no one will suffer harm as a consequence were found to be significantly more likely to lapse. By contrast, when donors believed that by cancelling their donation the beneficiary group would be impacted, they were significantly more likely to remain loyal.

3   *Shared beliefs*   As donors begin to buy-in to or share the beliefs of the organization their sense of commitment begins to grow. This is more than sharing a sense of the work that needs to be accomplished; it also includes sharing beliefs about *how* it should be accomplished.

4   *Learning*   Donors who feel that they are deepening their understanding of the work the organization is conducting and why this is important are significantly more loyal than those who do not. The researchers therefore recommend that organizations plan the supporter journey that they will take each category of donor on, as the relationship with the charity develops.

5   *Trust*   Donors who trust that the organization will have the impacts it says it will have on the beneficiary group will be significantly more loyal than those who lack this trust. The provision of regular feedback is therefore important in driving loyalty, as is being able to justify the pattern of performance achieved.

6   *Personal link*   For some causes, it is possible that supporters will have a personal link to the organization. Many medical research charities, for example, gain the support of those whose life has been touched by the disease or disability. It is no surprise that the existence of strong personal links is a determinant of loyalty.

7   *Multiple engagements*   This was found to operate at two levels. In the first, donors who were also campaigners and service users and volunteers were significantly more loyal than individuals who had only one such linkage. In the second, the researchers found that each time a nonprofit had a two-way interaction with a donor their level of loyalty would increase. Activities such as conducting research, offering choice in communication, inviting participation in a community, attendance at an event and so on all have the capacity to build commitment and subsequent loyalty.

SUMMARY

In this chapter we have provided a summary of the extant research on giving behaviour. We have reviewed a large number of studies examining specific aspects of giving and ended with a discussion of the merits of two composite models of giving behaviour. We also briefly examined the factors that drive donor loyalty. From all the studies cited it is clear that a variety of factors can shape giving and nonprofits would be well advised to review the fundraising activities they presently undertake in the light of these findings. Donor behaviour remains one of the most researched issues in the social sciences, drawing on work conducted in the disciplines of marketing, economics, clinical psychology, social psychology, anthropology and sociology. All have much to contribute to our knowledge of the topic and all have much to contribute to professional practice.

A greater degree of reflection on the needs of the donor and a greater degree of understanding of why donors behave as they do is long overdue in fundraising. Lee (1998) warns fundraisers that they risk becoming the 'used car salesmen' of the sector, if they increasingly embrace 'techniques' and lose sight of the real reason for their existence. Future marketing activity must be based on a sound understanding of how and why donors elect to give and the practice of fundraising must reflect this. Ongoing research would greatly assist fundraisers in enhancing the quality, precision and performance of their communications with donors and thereby ensure the future health and stability of the voluntary sector.

DISCUSSION QUESTIONS

1   In the light of your reading, critically appraise the fundraising practice of your own organization, or one with which you are familiar. Can you identify ways in which the fundraising practice could be improved taking account of the findings of the donor behaviour literature?

2   In your role as the head of fundraising of a large national charity, prepare a report to your CEO explaining how the organization might reduce its attrition rate (i.e. the percentage of donors it loses each year).

3   'There is no such thing as altruism. At its root all giving can ultimately be explained by reference to enlightened self interest.' Using your knowledge of giving behaviour, critically evaluate this statement.

4   You are the head of fundraising for a small nonprofit working to educate children with special needs. What are the issues you will have to deal with in developing a direct mail campaign to cover the running costs of the organization?

5   Compare and contrast the two composite models of giving behaviour. What do you see as the strengths and weaknesses of each? How could they be improved?

REFERENCES

Adler, A.B., Wright, B.A. and Ulicny, G.R. (1991) 'Fundraising Portrayals of People with Disabilities: Donations and Attitudes', *Rehabilitation Psychology*, 36(4): 231–240.

Aldrich, T. (2004) 'Do-it-yourself DRTV: A Practical Guide to Making Direct Response Television Advertising Work for Charities,' *International Journal of Nonprofit and Voluntary Sector Marketing,* 9(2): 135–144.

Allen, C.T. (1982) 'Self Perception Based Strategies for Stimulating Energy Conservation', *Journal of Consumer Research*, 8 (March): 381–390.

Andreoni, J. (2001) 'The Economics of Philanthropy', in N.J. Smelser and P.B. Baltes (eds) *International Encyclopedia of the Social and Behavioural Sciences,* Elsevier, London.

Baily, A. and Bruce, M. (1992) 'United Way: The Fallout after the fall', *Chronicle of Philanthropy*, March: 2–6.

Banks, J. and Tanner, S. (1997) *The State of Donation,* IFS, London.

Batson, C.D. (1990), 'How Social an Animal? The Human Capacity for Caring', *American Psychologist*, 45: 336–346.

Becker, G.S. (1976) *The Economic Approach to Human Behavior*, University of Chicago Press, Chicago, IL.

Bendapudi, N. and Singh, S.N. (1996) 'Enhancing Helping Behavior: An Integrative Framework for Promotion Planning', *Journal of Marketing*, 60(3): 33–54.

Brehm, J.W. (1966) *A Theory of Psychological Reactance*, Academic Press, New York.

Brolley, D.Y. and Anderson, S.C. (1986) 'Advertising and Attitudes', *Rehabilitation Digest*, 17: 15–17.

Burnett, J.J. and Wood, V.R. (1988) 'A Proposed Model of the Donation Process', *Research in Consumer Behaviour*, 3: 1–47.

Cabinet Office (2007) *Helping Out: A National Survey of Volunteering and Charitable Giving*, Cabinet Office, London.

Chierco, S., Rosa, C. and Kayson, W.A. (1982) 'Effects of Location Appearance and Monetary Value on Altruistic Behaviour', *Psychological Reports*, 51: 199–202.

Clark, R.D. and Word, L.E. (1972) 'Why Don't Bystanders Help? Because of Ambiguity?', *Journal of Personality and Social Psychology*, 24: 392–400.

Clary, E.G. and Snyder, M. (1991) 'A Functional Analysis of Altruism and Prosocial Behaviour: The Case of Volunteerism', *Review of Personality and Social Psychology*, 12, London, Sage, pp. 119–148.

Coliazzi, A., Williams, K.J. and Kayson, W.A. (1984). 'When Will People Help? The Effects of Gender, Urgency and Location on Altruism', *Psychological Reports*, 55: 139–142.

Commonwealth of Australia (2005) *Giving Australia: Research on Philanthropy in Australia*, Commonwealth of Australia, Canberra.

Conley, A. (1999) '*Student Organization Membership and Alumni Giving at a Public Research University*', unpublished doctoral dissertation, Indiana University.

Cutlip, S.M. (1980) *Fundraising in the United States: Its Role in America's Philanthropy*, Transaction Publishers, New Brunswick, NJ.

Davis, M.H., Hull, J.G. Young, R.D. and Warren, G.G. (1987) 'Emotional Reactions to Dramatic Film Stimuli: The Influence of Cognitive and Emotional Empathy', *Journal of Personality and Social Psychology*, 52(1): 126–133.

Dichter, E. (1972) 'Giving Blood or Lending Blood', presented before the Deutsche Gesellschaft fur Bluttransfusion, Giesen, Germany.

Dixon, M. (1997) 'Small and Medium Sized Charities Need a Strong Brand Too: Crisis' Experience', *Journal of Nonprofit and Voluntary Sector Marketing*, 2(1): 52–57.

Douglas, J., Field, G.A. and Tarpey, L.X. (1967) *Human Behaviour in Marketing*, Charles E. Merrill Books, Columbus, OH.

Dowd, J.J. (1975) *Stratification of The Aged*, Brooks Cole, Monterey, CA.

Eayrs, C.B. and Ellis, N. (1990) 'Charity Advertising. For or Against People with a Mental Handicap?', *British Journal of Social Psychology*, 29(4): 349–360.

Elliot, T.R. and Byrd, E.K. (1982) 'Media and Disability', *Rehabilitation Literature*, 43(11–12): 348–355.

Farrington, O.P. and Kidd, R.P. (1977) 'Is Financial Dishonesty a Rational Decision', *British Journal of School and Clinical Psychology*, 16: 139–148.

Feinman, S. (1978) 'When Does Sex Affect Altruistic Behaviour?', *Psychological Reports*, 43: 12–18.

Feldman, D. and Feldman, B. (1985), 'The Effect of a Telethon on Attitudes Toward Disabled People and Financial Contributions', *Journal of Rehabilitation*, 51: 42–45.

Festinger, L. (1954) 'A Theory of Social Comparison Processes', *Human Relations*, 7(2): 117–140.

Fultz, J.C., Batson, D., Fortenbach, V.A., McCarthy, P. and Varney, L.L. (1986) 'Social Evaluation and the Empathy Altruism Hypothesis', *Journal of Personality and Social Psychology*, 50: 761–769.

Geer, J.H. and Jermecky, L. (1973) 'The Effect of Being Responsible for Reducing Others' Pain on Subjects' Response and Arousal', *Journal of Personality and Social Psychology*, 27: 100–108.

Glaser, J.S. (1994) *The United Way Scandal – An Insiders Account of What Went Wrong and Why*, John Wiley, New York.

Gruder, C.L. and Cook, T.D. (1971) 'Sex Dependency and Helping', *Journal of Personality and Social Psychology*, 19: 290–294.

Harris, R.M. (1975) '*The Effect of Perspective Taking, Similarity and Dependency on Raising Funds for Persons With Disabilities*', unpublished Master's Thesis, University of Kansas, Lawrence.

Harris, R.M. and Harris, A.C. (1977) 'Devaluation of the Disabled in Fund Raising', *Rehabilitation Psychology*, 24: 69–78.

Harvey, J.W. and McCrohan, K.F. (1988) ' Fundraising Costs: Societal Implications for Philanthropies and Their Supporters', *Business and Society*, 27(1): 15–22.

Home Office (2005) *A Generous Society: Next Steps on Charitable Giving in England*, Home Office, London.

Irwin-Wells, S. (2002) *Planning and Implementing Your Major Gifts Campaign*, Jossey Bass, San Francisco, CA.

Jay, E. (2001) 'The Rise and Fall? – of Face to Face Fundraising in the United Kingdom', *New Directions for Philanthropic Fundraising*, 33 (Fall): 83–95.

Krebs, D. (1970) 'Altruism – A Rational Approach', in *The Development of Prosocial Behaviour*, ed. N. Eisenberg, Academic Press, New York (1982), pp. 53–77.

Krebs, D. and Whitten, P. (1972) 'Guilt Edged Giving – The Same of It All', *Psychology Today*, January: 42.

Latane, B. and Nida, S. (1981) 'Ten Years of Research on Group Size and Helping', *Psychological Bulletin*, 89(2): 308–324.

Lee, S. (1998) 'What Goes In Must', *Third Sector*, 25 June: 14–15.

Lohmann, R. (1992) 'The Commons: A Multidisciplinary Approach to Nonprofit Organization, Voluntary Action and Philanthropy', *Nonprofit and Voluntary Sector Quarterly*, 21(3): 309–324.

McGuire, W.J. and Padawer-Singer, A. (1976) 'Trust Salience in the Spontaneous Self Concept', *Journal of Personality and Social Psychology*, 33: 743–754.

Miller, D.T. (1977) 'Altruism and Threat to a Belief in a Just World', *Journal of Experimental Psychology*, 13: 113–124.

National Council for Voluntary Organizations (NCVO) (2008) *Civil Society Alamanac*, NCVO, London.

Nightingale, B. (1973) *Charities*, Allen Lane, London.

Odendahl T. (1987) *America's Wealthy and the Future of Foundations*, The Foundation Center.

Pharoah, C. (2002) 'How Much Do People Give To Charity?', in C. Walker and C. Pharoah (eds) *A Lot of Give*, Hodder and Stoughton, London.

Pieper, E. (1975), 'What Price Charity?' *Exceptional Parent*, 5(1): 35–40.

Piliavin, I.M., Piliavin, J.A. and Rodin, J. (1975) 'Costs of Diffusion and the Stigmatised Victim', *Journal of Personality and Social Psychology*, 32: 429–438.

Reingen, P.H. (1978) 'On Inducing Compliance with Requests', *Journal of Consumer Research*, 5: 96–102.

Roberts Wray, B. (1994) 'Branding, Product Development and Positioning the Charity', *Journal of Brand Management*, 1(6): 26–42.

Sargeant, A. (2001) 'Relationship Fundraising: How to Keep Donors Loyal', *Nonprofit Management and Leadership*, 12(2): 177–192.

Sargeant, A. and McKenzie, J. (1998) *A Lifetime of Giving: An Analysis of Donor Lifetime Value*, Charities Aid Foundation, West Malling.

Sargeant, A. and Woodliffe, L. (2007) 'Gift Giving: An Interdisciplinary Review', *International Journal of Nonprofit and Voluntary Sector Marketing*, 12(4): 275–307.

Sargeant, A. Ford, J. and West, D.C. (2000) 'Widening the Appeal of Charity', *International Journal of Nonprofit and Voluntary Sector Marketing*, 5(4): 318–332.

Sargeant, A., West, D.C. and Ford, J.B. (2001) 'The Role of Perceptions in Predicting Donor Value', *Journal of Marketing Management*, 17: 407–428.

Sargeant, A. Jay, E. and Lee, S. (2006) 'Benchmarking Charity Performance: Returns From Direct Marketing in Fundraising', *Journal of Nonprofit and Public Sector Marketing*, 16 (1/2):77–94.

Sargeant, A. Ford, J.B. and Hudson, J. (2008) 'Charity Brand Personality: The Relationship with Giving Behavior', *Nonprofit and Voluntary Sector Quarterly*, 37(3): 468–491.

Saxton, J. (1995) 'A Strong Charity Brand Comes From Strong Beliefs and Values', *Journal of Brand Management*, 2(4): 211–220.

Schervish, P.G. (1993) 'Philosophy as Moral Identity of Caritas', in P.G. Schervish, O. Benz, P. Dulaney, T.B. Murphy and S. Salett (eds) *Taking Giving Seriously*, Center on Philanthropy, Indiana University, Indianapolis.

Schervish, P.G. (1997) 'Inclination, Obligation and Association: What We Know Now and What We Need to Learn About Donor Motivation', in D. Burlingame, (ed.) *Critical Issues in Fund Raising*, Wiley, Hoboken, NJ.

Schwartz, B. (1967) 'The Social Psychology of the Gift', *American Journal of Sociology*, 73(1): 1–11.

Schwartz, S. (1977) 'Normative Influences on Altruism', in L. Berkowitz, (ed.) *Advances in Experimental Social Psychology*, 10, New York, Academic Press, pp. 221–279.

Shang, J., Reed, A. and Croson, R. (2008) 'Identity-based Gender Congruency Effect on Donations', *Journal of Marketing Research*, 45: 1–10.

Shelton, M.L. and Rogers, R.W. (1981) 'Fear Arousing and Empathy Arousing Appeals to Help: The Pathos of Persuasion', *Journal of Applied Psychology*, 11(4): 366–378.

Shurka, E., Siller, J. and Dvonch, P. (1982) 'Coping Behaviour and Personal Responsibility as Factors in the Perception of Disabled Persons by the Non Disabled', *Rehabilitation Psychology*, 27: 225–233.

Simmons, R.G. (1991) Presidential Address on Altruism and Sociology, *Sociological Quarterly*, 32: 1–22.

Steinberg, R. (1986) 'Should Donors Care About Fundraising?', in S. Rose-Ackerman (ed.) *The Economics of Nonprofit Institutions: Studies in Structure and Policy*, Oxford University Press, New York, pp. 347–364.

Swinyard, W.K. and Ray, M.L. (1977) 'Advertising–Selling Interactions: An Attribution Theory Experiment', *Journal of Marketing Research*, 14: 509–516.

Tapp, A. (1996) 'Charity Brands: A Qualitative Study of Current Practice', *Journal of Nonprofit and Voluntary Sector Marketing,* 1(4): 327–336.

Wagner, C. and Wheeler, L. (1969) 'Model Need and Cost Effects in Helping Behaviour', *Journal of Personality and Social Psychology*, 12: 111–116.

Walker, C. and Pharoah, C. (eds) (2002) *A Lot of Give*, Hodder and Stoughton, London.

Warwick, M. (1994) *Raising Money By Mail: Strategies for Growth and Financial Stability*, Strathmoor Press, Berkeley, CA.

Warwick, M. and Hitchcock, S. (2001) *Ten Steps to Fundraising Success: Choosing the Right Strategy for your Organization,* Jossey Bass, San Francisco, CA.

Weisbrod, B.A. (1988) *The Nonprofit Economy*, Harvard University Press, Boston, MA.

Weldon, E. (1984) 'De-Individualisation Interpersonal Affect and Productivity in Laboratory Task Groups', *Journal of Applied Social Psychology*, 14: 469–485.

Yavas, U., Riecken, G. and Parameswaran, R. (1980) 'Using Psychographics to Profile Potential Donors', *Business Atlanta,* 30(5): 41–45.

Chapter 6

Donor recruitment

OBJECTIVES

By the end of this chapter you should be able to:

- Outline the key stages in donor recruitment planning.
- Develop supporter acquisition objectives.
- Segment donor markets.
- Profile and target appropriate prospects.
- Implement a supporter acquisition campaign.
- Analyse and interpret the results.

INTRODUCTION

The recruitment of new individual donors at an acceptable cost is a challenging and complex activity.

In fundraising, as in commercial marketing activity, it costs roughly five times as much to engage with a new customer than an existing one. While fundraisers can expect to generate a return on investment (ROI) of about 4:1 from a campaign targeting existing (warm) donors, acquisition campaigns are more likely to require an investment, or at the very best achieve break-even, than to generate a positive return. More enlightened and informed nonprofits are content with this scenario in the confidence that they will be able to cultivate profitable relationships with the donors they recruit over the full duration of their relationship with them. Less well-informed and experienced organizations frequently find it hard to justify and explain high recruitment costs to board members.

> New donor acquisition efforts usually cost 75 to 150 percent of what they raise. The reality is that this has been the practice for decades. Many of the most prestigious and successful charities have developed very efficient multimillion-dollar appeals and major donor programs with donors originally acquired at 100 percent fund-raising costs.
> (Center on Philanthropy 1999:16)

In terms of the balance of fundraising resource, it makes sense to target the majority of the resources available at those donors who will generate the highest levels of profitability.

125

Typically, therefore, donor retention and development activity should account for 70 to 80 per cent of a fundraising budget. However, there will always be a need to recruit new donors to every organization. Even if relationships are excellent and levels of satisfaction high some donors will terminate their relationship as interests and financial circumstances change or they die or move away. Donor recruitment also provides an opportunity to refresh a database, as individuals often give most generously and demonstrate most enthusiasm for a cause during the 'honeymoon' period of the first few months of their relationship with a nonprofit. The addition of new donors also allows an organization to grow and broaden its support base, test new fundraising offers and to attract new audiences and constituencies to the cause.

In recent years acquisition activity has been complicated by the introduction of new communication channels, new methods of giving and increasing demands in terms of transparency and privacy protection. Data profiling and research among givers and non-givers have indicated that nonprofits are often competing to recruit from an identical and diminishing pool of potential donors.

Against this background, careful acquisition planning is more essential than ever if donors are to be recruited successfully both in terms of the quantity of those recruited and of their quality and likely long-term value. This chapter will focus on 'mass' individual donor recruitment via direct marketing techniques. The recruitment of wealthy individuals through Major Gift and Events is covered in Chapter 8.

RECRUITMENT PLANNING

In planning for donor recruitment, the initial 'macro' stages of the plan such as the audit and the development of overall fundraising objectives and strategies will be common to both acquisition and donor development activity (see Figure 6.1).

In implementing donor recruitment plans, however, we are focusing on the attraction of new supporters to an organization. Seven stages can be followed as a framework:

1   *Objectives*   Identifying the objectives to be achieved.
2   *Segmentation and profiling*   Research and analysis of the existing donor base to develop a broad profile to be used as a starting point in targeting recruitment efforts.
3   *Targeting*   Having developed a detailed donor profile, the information can then be used to tailor the nature of the communication to be received and the channel through which it will be communicated.
4   *Media selection and planning*   Allied to the above, media can be selected to reach the intended audience cost-effectively. Integration of the various media to be employed should also be considered at this stage.
5   *The nature of the fundraising message*   How best to communicate the fundraising 'ask' in line with the brand and mission of the organization. At this stage the parameters for the creative work and messages will be defined.
6   *Fulfilment*   How response to the campaign will be handled, followed up and the information stored on the fundraising database.
7   *Budgeting, control and evaluation*   Testing, response analysis and tracking.

SETTING RECRUITMENT OBJECTIVES

The first step in developing a donor acquisition programme or campaign is to decide on the objectives by which the success of the activity will be measured. As with all fundraising activity, the objectives need to be SMART (see Chapter 4).

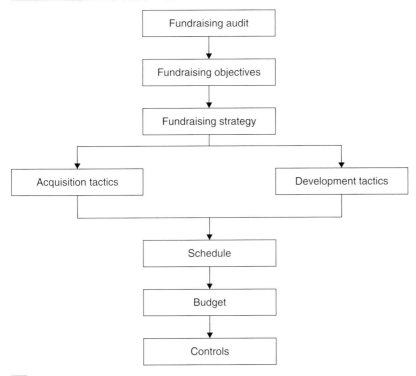

Figure 6.1 *Recruitment and development planning*

In donor recruitment the most common simple target set by fundraising managers is the recruitment of X new donors for Y cost, with overall levels of expenditure and investment set in accordance with a requirement to grow or maintain the total size of the organization's individual donor database.

More valuable and thoughtful objectives and targets involve the consideration of the quality as well as the quantity of the donors, and are further broken down by segment and activity. Most organizations now recognize the long-term value of recruitment directly on to a regular gift, so additional objectives may involve the percentage of regular versus one-off givers to be acquired. The recruitment of 'fresh' audiences may be set as an objective, for example an organization with an 'ageing' database may wish to recruit new donors from younger age groups. In more sophisticated fundraising organizations where lifetime value is calculated acquisition objectives will be set with the input of lifetime-value data. This may mean that certain media routes are favoured as tending to produce more valuable donors over time.

The distinction between regular and cash givers is important, particularly in the UK where each group may be defined as follows:

1   *One-off or cash givers*   Individuals who do not commit to a regular gift, but who will typically respond to one or more direct mail asks in a given year, by sending a cheque.
2   *Committed givers*   Sign up from the outset to give a regular monthly (or yearly) donation, direct from their bank account or credit card.

The economics of dealing with each group are quite different and separate objectives would therefore be derived. In the USA the need for the distinction may be less clear since relatively few organizations recruit directly in to regular or committed giving.

It is also essential that the objectives set for donor recruitment are tied in to those set for the subsequent development of the donors. Many organizations make the mistake of viewing acquisition and development as separate entities, working to separate unrelated and sometimes opposing targets. Over time this can cause problems if the donors recruited are found subsequently to be unprofitable or problematic: they may be unresponsive, exhibit high attrition rates or require a different programme of communication from the rest of the database. For example, many UK nonprofits have had great success in recent years in recruiting new donors with requests for a small regular monthly gift. These recruits tend to be much younger than the 'traditional' donor and to have very different lifestyles. While this can be seen as a success for the recruitment manager, these donors often prove difficult to retain and develop subsequently as they do not respond to direct mail, and prefer communication through alternative routes such as e-mail and text messaging – media which many nonprofits have not yet developed fully. The recruitment of younger donors is also likely in the longer term to work against the efforts of fundraisers promoting planned giving and bequest (legacy) fundraising. It is thus essential that recruitment and development targets are complementary and that planning for both is undertaken as a joint exercise.

Finally, it is worth noting that many organizations develop objectives for both 'cold' donor recruitment and for the recruitment of those individuals who are 'warmer' to the organization. This category might include previously lapsed supporters whose giving the organization is looking to reactivate, previous enquirers who have not made a donation and other stakeholder groups who are linked to the cause in some way, such as service users or campaigners.

SEGMENTATION

Having set recruitment objectives, the next stage is to determine which potential donors (or prospects) will be targeted. In essence there are two approaches, the appropriateness of which will be determined by the extent to which an organization has prior knowledge of its markets. These approaches can be categorized as being either a priori or *post hoc* (Green 1977). An a priori approach is based on the notion that fundraisers decide in advance of any research which categories of individual (perhaps by demographics or lifestyle) they intend to target. The fundraiser would then carry out market research to determine the attractiveness of each segment and make a decision on the basis of the results as to which target audience to pursue. *Post hoc* segmentation by contrast involves the fundraiser in carrying out research into their existing donor audience. The research might highlight attributes, attitudes or benefits that relate to particular groups of donors. This information can often be obtained by profiling discrete groups of donors on the database (e.g. cash givers or committed givers). If a certain type of individual emerges as 'typical' this information can be used to refine the criteria for list selection and other similar individuals can be targeted. Nonprofits commonly use geodemographic and/or lifestyle data for this purpose.

PROFILING

To inform the choice of segments to be targeted, those organizations that already hold a database of donors have a distinct advantage. Such organizations can profile their existing database to identify whether specific types of people seem to be:

- giving higher sums
- giving in certain ways

- responding to different media
- responding to certain types of message.

This profile can then be used in the selection of prospects – in other words, list and media selection can be undertaken to ensure that individuals who match the profile of the required category of givers are targeted with appropriate recruitment messages. At best, profiling can serve to bring audiences to life by painting pictures of their main differentiating characteristics and suggesting fundraising messages they are likely to find appealing.

In some instances this simple replication of the current donor profile may not be desirable, in which case the same techniques can be used instead to define a picture of alternative target audiences. If one of the objectives of a recruitment campaign is, for example, to recruit younger regular givers to supplement a database comprised of older cash donors, a supplemental profile of the new target audience will have to be generated. Equally, higher value donors or those who have pledged a legacy may be profiled as a separate group if it is feasible to conduct a recruitment campaign to enlist high-value givers, perhaps through the promotion of a high-value or committed product such as a child sponsorship package.

To work most effectively, the segments generated have to be:

- *Accessible* It should be possible to access the segment cost-effectively. If communication media do not exist to reach the market without a high degree of wastage attempts could be costly and potentially unprofitable.
- *Substantial* It should be cost-effective to market to the segment. Clearly the segment should be large enough in terms of the absolute number of donors to make it worthwhile targeting. It could also be small, but with the prospect of higher than normal gifts, again making it worthwhile to address.
- *Stable* The segment's behaviour should be relatively stable over time to ensure that its future development may be predicted with a high degree of accuracy for planning purposes.
- *Appropriate* It should be appropriate to target a particular segment given the organization's mission, resources, objectives, etc. While on the face of it, for example, it might seem appropriate to target sufferers of a particular condition to support a medical charity, the Board may well feel that this is inappropriate and that funding should be sought elsewhere.

TARGETING

Having developed a detailed prospect profile, the information can be used to tailor the nature of the communication to be received and to make decisions on the channel or channels through which it will most effectively be communicated. A 'picture' of the individuals a nonprofit is attempting to reach, even in outline or aggregate form, is an enormous advantage in designing recruitment materials, in deciding where such individuals are most likely to be reached, and what media and approach they are most likely to respond to. Targeting is the single most important consideration in cold recruitment campaigns. No matter how strong the creative treatment, if it does not reach the right people the campaign will fail. It is generally accepted in nonprofit as in commercial direct marketing that the prospect list is six times more important than the creative in the success of any campaign.

In seeking to reach prospect audiences to recruit new donors as cost-effectively as possible it makes sense to start by gathering prospect data from within the organization rather than embarking on the purchase of cold lists or using other broadscale media immediately. While it may prove difficult to obtain the names of service users, enquirers, campaigners and so on from within an organization, these are almost always the most worthwhile source of new donors. Lapsed donors, volunteers and traders (catalogue buyers) should likewise be tested. These lists will be free (or low cost if the data needs to be captured) and the individuals appearing on them will almost certainly be more sympathetic to the needs of the organization, and therefore more responsive to a recruitment message, than individuals who may not have had any prior contact with or knowledge of the nonprofit and its work. In planning a recruitment campaign, those prospects likely to be recruited at the lowest cost should be targeted first. Once the 'warmest' prospects have been identified the remainder of the budget can be allocated to 'colder' media.

An outline picture of the prospects being targeted will be of huge interest and utility to those designing recruitment materials. Information on the demographics and lifestyle of target audiences can be used to guide creative outputs generally (What sort of message is the audience most likely to respond to? What 'triggers' and cultural references are appropriate to the age/social group?) and practically – if an older audience is to be reached the typeface should be larger, for example, and copy may be written for male or female readers.

MEDIA SELECTION AND PLANNING

Once 'internal' warm lists of prospective donors have been assembled, the selection of external 'cold' media can begin. Media selection and planning is potentially one of the most complex areas of any recruitment plan.

Even if the profiling process has been undertaken for the first time, or profiles have been revized or refreshed, part of this process will involve the review of past experience and results. Nonprofits that are undertaking recruitment campaigns over time amass volumes of data on the response rates and profitability of certain recruitment routes, on response to a range of creative approaches and messages, and on the subsequent behaviour and lifetime value of the donors recruited. All this past history should be part of the planning process, though it is also important to rethink and review recruitment approaches regularly and to remain aware of new opportunities. In the nonprofit sector peer networks can also be used to gather generic information on the likely performance of new routes and media and compare notes on the pitfalls associated with new recruitment ventures. In the commercial world such information sharing would be impossible under commercial confidentiality. Specialist agencies and consultants can also provide valuable insights and experience on the likely performance of certain media and creative routes.

Some of the most commonly used recruitment media are discussed briefly here.

Direct mail

Cold mail remains the most common means of donor recruitment on both sides of the Atlantic, even though it has become far less cost-effective in recent years. Those charities using cold lists to recruit new donors would typically only generate 50 pence back for every pound of investment. The organizations concerned would only make money on the second and subsequent gifts. Achieving break-even in donor recruitment activity would thus represent very high-quality performance indeed.

Thousands of mailing lists can be provided to facilitate donor recruitment, so navigating the range of alternatives can be problematic if an organization has no past experience on which to draw. List buying is an area where the services of a specialist adviser (list broker) are therefore essential. If you provide a list broker with the profile of the prospect audience, he/she will provide recommendations and advice on the lists which best meet those requirements. Lists can be rented for once-only use, for repeat use, or can be purchased outright (a much more expensive option).

Lists fall broadly into the categories of geodemographic and lifestyle and an amount of profiling will usually be required to refine the criteria that are eventually used in list selection. Lifestyle list providers will run a profile against their own base to find those names on their file that most closely resemble the target group. Other lists, typically generated through mail order product sales, will have less information available against which to select. Lists vary considerably in terms of the level of sophistication that can be offered. Some key checks to make when purchasing lists are:

- *What criteria can be used in selection and what are the cost and timing implications of selecting by multiple criteria?*
  Many list owners will, for example, offer the opportunity to select males only, or males who bought a product within the last six months, have bought previously, and where the last product purchased cost at least £50. Typically each overlay will incur an extra charge per thousand names selected. More complex selections will also take longer to process and output. Before running selections based on multiple criteria one needs to be confident that the uplift in response rates or donation levels is likely to justify the extra cost.

- *What is the roll-out potential of each list, or of each selection, and when and how is the list refreshed?*
  Any list should be tested initially. If the list performance is acceptable, the list can then be rolled out in a subsequent campaign. Those lists that can deliver large quantities of names are preferable to those that will be quickly exhausted as a source of new recruits. The tendency is to target with great care in the selection of the test quantity – if this selection is successful it is essential that the same selection can be used in pulling out a higher quantity of names for the roll-out. Recency is often key to list performance, so it is also important to be aware of when and how lists are refreshed and added to.

- *What is the history of nonprofit usage?*
  List suppliers can give an idea of the response rates experienced by previous nonprofit clients, and can provide data on how heavily the list has been employed by nonprofits. This is key as lists become 'tired' very quickly and assessing whether competitors have already used the list can be very significant.

Before purchasing a commercially available list it is also imperative to check the 'cleanliness' of that list and to ensure that the relevant data protection or privacy legislation has been fully complied with.

A variety of opinions exist with regard to how intensively a cold mail programme should be run. At base, there is agreement that lists should only be mailed while doing so is profitable, and that every element of the list and the creative should be tested before it is rolled out or reused. Many organizations rent lists for once-only use, renting larger quantities later if the test meets the required standards. Some follow the advice of other experts such as James Greenfield and use lists far more intensively:

> A successful mail acquisition plan … should project a three-year, multimailing programme, a minimum of five to six mailings each year, and a total of between five and eighteen letter packages to be sent to substantially the same people.
>
> (Greenfield 1994:85)

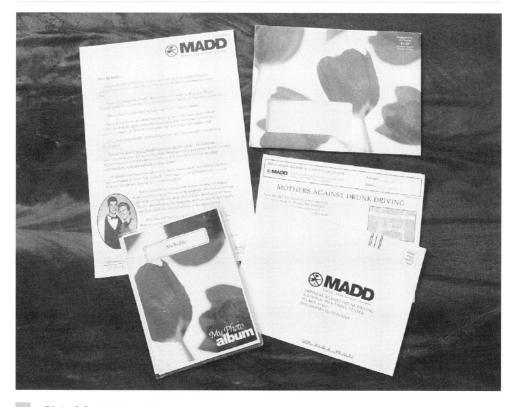

Plate 6.1 *MADD mailing*
Source: © MADD. Reproduced with kind permission.

Cold direct mail has been used very creatively and to great effect by many thousands of non-profits worldwide. Examples of successful recruitment mailings are provided in Plates 6.1 and 6.2. When using direct mail for recruitment, nonprofits over time identify mail packs that are particularly effective at recruiting donors and tend to stick with these until they are beaten in performance by other materials the nonprofit is testing. This was the case with the Mothers Against Drunk Driving (MADD) mailing in Plate 6.1. The inclusion of the photo album, although adding to cost, proved worthwhile because of the heightened response rate and value of gifts.

The campaign pack illustrated plate 6.2 was developed by the Denver Rescue Mission. It was sent to prospective donors over a holiday period and comprised a brown paper lunch bag indicating that $1.79 would provide a full Thanksgiving meal or a night's shelter to a homeless person. The appeal generated $25,651 from 1,248 people.

List swaps (reciprocals)

The nonprofit sector is unusual in that organizations often exchange the names of supporters for use in recruitment campaigns (again, exchanging customer names with competitors would be unheard of in the commercial world). These lists of known current givers are much more responsive than 'cold' lists, and are supplied free of charge by nonprofits or at a nominal cost by agency intermediaries. They thus recruit new donors very cost-efficiently.

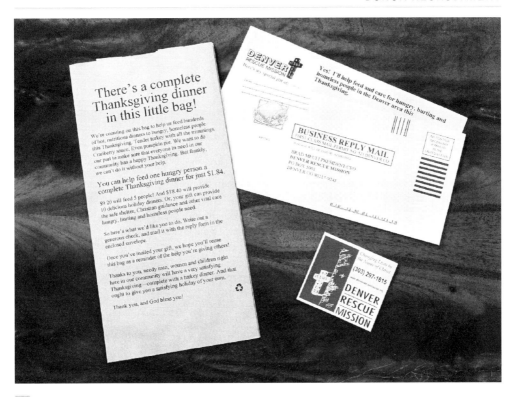

Plate 6.2 *Denver Rescue Mission mailing*
Source: © Denver Rescue Mission. Reproduced with kind permission.

However, there are a number of negative points associated with this practice. Few nonprofits monitor the subsequent giving patterns of donors whose details are supplied to competitor nonprofits through list swaps. Research has shown that the response rate to development mailings can drop by 10 to 20 per cent among donors whose names have been included in reciprocal deals. (Sargeant 1999). List swaps, though ostensibly an effective tool for recruitment managers, can in the longer term prove to be damaging. One of the most common complaints among donors is that they are 'deluged' with nonprofit direct mail appeals once they have given to one nonprofit. In countries such as the UK with strict data protection legislation in place names can only be exchanged if donors have previously had the opportunity to opt out of name exchanges.

Data processing and de-duplication

Every cold mail campaign will involve data processing as the externally supplied lists will need to be run against the existing donor file to ensure that current givers are not mailed. This de-duplication (merge purge) process will also involve the running of the external lists against each other so that no individual (whose name may appear on several different lists) will receive more than one copy of the mailing. At this point any 'stop' list of people who have made it known that they do not wish to hear from the nonprofit can also be excluded. On large campaigns this can become a complex, time-consuming and expensive exercise.

Valuable data can be gained from de-duplication reports. The degree of overlap between the 'house' file and externally supplied lists can be ascertained and used as a useful pointer, and 'multibuyers' (individuals appearing on a high number of lists) can be separated out and possibly treated differently (by remailing) as they should be the best prospects if the targeting has been effective.

Unaddressed mail

Mail can also be delivered unaddressed. These mailings are targeted by postcode/zipcode, and are distributed through a number of suppliers, either through the mainstream postal service so that the packs arrive with the normal mail, or through specialist delivery companies. The response rates to unaddressed mail are considerably lower than those generated through personalized direct mail as the targeting is less sophisticated and the mailings less personal. However, the costs of distribution are also much lower as there is no list cost and there is no de-duplication, data processing or personalization involved. Unaddressed mail can reach individuals whose names do not appear on mailing lists and therefore may comprise a fresher audience.

Successful unaddressed mailings tend to be amended versions of a successful cold direct mail pack. Some restrictions apply in terms of the delivery of bulky items or unusual sizes, so the creative options for this media tend to be restricted in comparison with cold mail. Delivery can be arranged as either 'solus' or as a 'shared' delivery.

As the mailing piece does not carry personal details in this case, many nonprofits find that up to 20 per cent of responses to unaddressed recruitment mailings are anonymous.

Telephone

In the USA outbound telephone calls are used in donor recruitment in conjunction with cold mailings. It is less common in the UK, where a national Telephone Preference Service (Do Not Call) is in operation. UK charities tend to work with list providers to call individuals who have indicated an interest in a cause or a nonprofit in consumer research surveys.

Telephone solicitation in enlisting new donors is used by American nonprofits in a variety of ways. 'Phonathons' are primarily used by educational institutions and conducted by volunteers who contact researched lists of prospects; 'Telefund' uses paid callers through an agency, again using researched lists provided to the agency by the nonprofit organization; and 'Telemarketing' sales or cold calls are made by an agency through random calling from unresearched lists. Tele-marketing is fast becoming unprofitable as response rates are low and a national 'Do Not Call' register begins to bite.

While the telephone can be used effectively in recruitment, especially where prospect lists are built of individuals known to be phone-responsive and/or where the use of the telephone is integrated with direct mail or other media, it is relatively expensive and often does not meet the minimum levels of cost-effectiveness required.

When integrated with other components of the campaign and particularly when offered as an inbound response mechanism (i.e. where the donor calls the organization) the use of the tele-phone can be highly profitable and creative. Donors, for example, wishing to donate money to the restoration fund for the Statue of Liberty in the early 1980s were invited to dial 1-800 THE LADY.

Press and magazine advertising

Press and magazine advertising is an expensive recruitment route, and press adverts tend only to be cost-effective if the nonprofit is recruiting donors on to a high-value or regular gift, if the advert is soliciting funds against a high-profile emergency event, or if the newspaper or magazine is carrying a great deal of supporting editorial coverage of the event or cause.

Nonprofit recruitment adverts tend to look very formulaic. This is partly because the cost of advertising space is prohibitive and nonprofits therefore buy the cheapest standard ad sizes, and to buy at the last minute to keep the costs down. Years of experience of press advertising have taught practitioners how best to use design and copy to maximize response. Headlines, coupons and response telephone numbers tend therefore to be of a certain size and prominence, with copy and images arranged in a certain way to ensure readability and impact within a small space and where the production values tend to be low. Best practice suggests that nonprofits should provide the donor with both the problem and the solution within the copy of the ad. A recruitment ad from the World Society for the Protection of Animals is included in Plate 6.3. The figure contains three versions of an ad that were piloted by the charity. The first advert outperformed the others undoubtedly because it provides the donor with a problem and an easy way in which they can resolve that problem: £10 buys a chaincutter!

As with all direct response recruitment, off-the-page advertising should be run over time as a series of tests; of copy and creative, of ad size, of media title, of placement of the ad within the publication, day of the week and so on.

Inserts

Some organizations use inserts into press and magazine titles in the recruitment of new donors. Like press advertising, there are a number of standard design and copy guidelines that should be followed in the preparation of the inserts themselves. Again, the key point is to attract the eye and, as inserts can fall out of the publication, both sides of the insert should be arresting and attractive. Inserts can be successful, especially in specialist publications where the reader profile

Plate 6.3 *WSPA press advertisements*
Source: © WSPA. Reproduced with kind permission.

is a suitable match against the prospect profile. They typically achieve a response rate of six times that which would be generated by off-the-page advertising, but are substantially more costly. As with all direct marketing media they should thus be tested to ascertain the return on investment that will ultimately accrue.

When arranging inserts it is important to ensure that no nonprofit competitors are placing inserts in the same publication on the same day, and to check the number of inserts that will be carried at any one time. As with cold lists, publications get 'tired' quickly, and may need to be 'rested' before another insertion is placed. It is possible to test a small number of inserts on a random basis initially before rolling out to the full run of any publication. Some publications can also offer segmentation by geographical area, or by subscribers versus newsstand copies.

Plate 6.4 contains an illustration of an insert developed by the charity Sightsavers. The pack which has an involving message and illustration on both sides, pictures an individual's eyelids rimmed by barbed wire. This powerful image is still one of the best performing the charity has ever developed. When opened up, the pack explains how a small donation can restore someone's sight.

Direct dialogue and door to door

In Europe a large proportion of donors are now recruited via direct dialogue or face-to-face fundraising (see Plate 6.5). The initial impetus for this new development was the imposition of

Plate 6.4 *Sightsavers insert*

Source: © Sightsavers. Reproduced with kind permission.

Plate 6.5
Face-to-face
fundraising

strict data protection legislation that made cold mail recruitment difficult. In this form of recruitment trained recruiters stand in the street or in private sites such as shopping malls. Recruiters are clearly identified as representing a nonprofit as they wear a brightly coloured tabard featuring the nonprofit logo. They approach passers-by and encourage them to sign up to support the nonprofit through regular giving. While this approach has proved unpopular with some sections of the media in the UK, where it is now an important source of new donors, it remains an attractive recruitment route for UK fundraisers. Face-to-face recruits tend not to have given to any nonprofit before, and to be much younger (80 per cent being under 40 years of age) than the 'typical' UK charity donor. It is impossible to undertake a great deal of targeting by this method as sites only work effectively if a high 'foot traffic' of passers-by is evident.

Face-to-face fundraising transformed the finances of Action for Blind People boosting its annual income from £2 million to £10 million in just over three years. The nonprofit originally decided to test the new media when its fundraising department was restructured. Since its inception this new media has generated £6 million and recruited 60,000 new supporters.

New donors are also solicited by trained recruiters going door to door in selected neighbourhoods, asking householders to consider signing up to support a nonprofit with a regular gift. This activity is targeted by zipcode/postcode. In door-to-door fundraising (which again is used mainly in the UK and Europe, but is also now working successfully in Canada) several nonprofits may be represented in a 'basket' approach. Prospective donors are offered the opportunity to give to one of a selection of nonprofits.

Direct response television

Direct response television (DRTV) advertising is an expensive media to enter, but can prove an effective means of donor recruitment. The cost of airtime has reduced considerably in recent years, whilst the number of channels available, and the number of niche specialist channels, have increased enormously, allowing nonprofits to begin to target specific audiences through television.

However, production costs and the costs of telephone fulfilment still mean that DRTV is complex to manage, and tends to be used most successfully only by high-profile nonprofits with a 'mass' appeal message. The most successful uses of DRTV have tended to be organizations asking for a low-value committed (regular) gift where the gift can be fulfilled over the telephone through a 'paperless' direct debit transaction. If the number of stages that are required to complete the transaction can be limited to one, the return on investment is substantially higher.

137

In the US, some charities are able to take advantage of public service broadcasting slots and may thus acquire free airtime from the media owner. This can have a dramatic effect on the economics of DRTV and make it cost-effective for even smaller local nonprofits to utilize the medium. In the USA a number of nonprofits also host their own television programmes on specialist channels. Life Outreach International is one of the most well known, offering *Life Today*. The programme has featured such celebrities as George W. Bush and Robert Duvall and is broadcast five times a week on cable stations including Pax TV and Fox Family. It features topics such as health, grief and relationships and also opportunities to buy products such as books and CDs alongside traditional fundraising appeals. Viewers of the show contributed $12 million dollars in response to appeals aired on the programme.

The Internet

The used of the Internet and e-mail in recruiting new donors is covered in Chapter 14.

INTEGRATED CAMPAIGNS

Acquisition campaigns that use several media within the same time period, carrying a common message, and which combine awareness development with fundraising objectives, are more successful than single media campaigns. By integrating a message across different media streams a nonprofit can build the momentum of a campaign. The promotion of the appeal or programme through public relations and communications work will likewise raise the profile of the campaign in the eyes of the public. Individuals who come across multiple messages are more likely to respond positively when given an opportunity to donate.

Some media routes tend not to be successful when used alone, but can provide uplift when used in conjunction with other routes. The most effective integration employs each route or discipline to carry out the functions it does best, while pursuing a common communications objective – ensuring that each element reinforces the others without compromising its own effectiveness. Direct response radio advertising, for example, rarely delivers new donors profitably despite the relatively low costs of production and airtime. However, if radio ads run at the same time as door drops or direct mail the response rates to the mailpacks will increase.

Integrated multimedia campaigns, where the aim is to coordinate different channels in a cohesive and seamless way can be extremely complex to schedule, manage and track, especially as awareness and direct response targets differ fundamentally and have to be measured very differently.

THE NATURE OF THE FUNDRAISING MESSAGE

In designing a case for support and producing the materials required for recruitment, both the target audiences and the position and brand of the nonprofit organization have to be considered. There can be a tendency in recruitment creative to 'oversell' in order to recruit support. In the longer term this can lead to high rates of donor attrition and to donor dissatisfaction.

Recruitment creative needs to be powerful in order to be seen and heard by the target audience – the strongest and most engaging message the organization has. Recruitment communications have by necessity to focus on and illustrate a limited part of the work of the organization, but that aspect should be representative, sustainable and should fit absolutely with the image and mission the organization wishes to project. For instance, it may be tempting for an art gallery or museum to tempt potential donors with a forthcoming blockbuster exhibition or exhibit and the benefits they receive should they become a donor rather than focusing their recruitment message on the depth and strength of the permanent collection, and Third World development organizations find that they will attract a different (and often less committed) donor if they emphasize short-term emergency disaster relief efforts as opposed to longer term sustainable development projects.

Premiums, benefits and fundraising products

Many nonprofits, especially in the US, use premium offers in recruitment campaigns. These may be 'front end' such as name stickers, stamps and notecards or 'back end' offers which can range from coffee mugs and certificates to plaques. Many UK and USA fundraisers likewise use 'involvement devices' (such as pens or photographs) to increase response rates to cold mail. Plates 6.6 and 6.7 illustrate the use of involvement devices. The first example (Plate 6.6) illustrates the use of a 'survey pack' where prospective donors are asked to complete a survey and to return this with a donation. Charities that employ this device often find that the inclusion of a pen enhances the response rate and that surveys are more effective than other categories of pack. On the down side donors who respond to these packs tend to offer lower value gifts and tend not to remain loyal for extended periods of time. They should hence be used with care. Plate 6.7 depicts a pack employed by Marie Curie Cancer Care in which the charity sends prospective donors a single daffodil bulb to stimulate a response. The key with such involvement devices is relevance to the cause, in this case the fact that the recipient can grow the organization's emblem. It is absolutely critical that charities stimulate involvement with the cause in this way rather than with the selected device per se. Only the former strategy will result in an enhanced response rate.

While in many cases such devices guarantee an uplift in recruitment response rates, the longer term impact of their use should be considered carefully. In many cases, as with survey packs, the donors recruited through these routes are not of the highest quality, and may prove expensive to retain if they require the provision of premiums as a constant feature of the relationship.

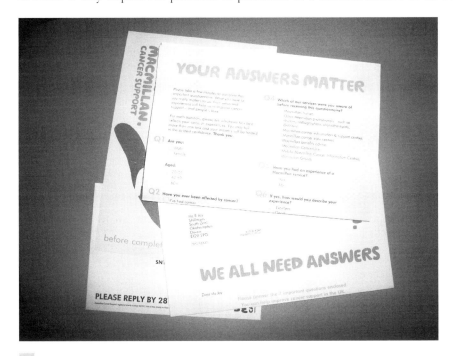

Plate 6.6 *Survey pack*

Source: Macmillan Cancer Support. Reproduced with kind permission.

Plate 6.7 *Marie Curie Cancer Care recruitment pack*
Source: © Marie Curie Cancer Care. Reproduced with kind permission.

Any involvement device or premium gift must also fit with the image, mission and message of the organization, or damage will be done to the brand over time.

Some nonprofits utilize benefit-led packages or donor products in the search for new fundraising supporters, such as membership schemes or sponsorship offers. Again, the costs of the maintenance of such schemes have to be monitored with great care, with thought given to how such relationships are to be maintained and grown over time.

Methods of giving

In the UK the economics of donor recruitment and development have changed dramatically in recent years with the growth of regular giving vehicles. Banks have promoted the use of single-step electronic and automated banking and paperless payment schemes, which are now widely accepted and used throughout the population. Automated banking puts the control of the payments in the hands of the initiating organization rather than the bank, and does not attract high bank administration costs.

This has paved the way for nonprofits to operate low-value monthly giving schemes, and to set up these regular giving arrangements electronically, without requiring the donor to sign any paperwork. New regular gifts can therefore be arranged over the phone in a single transaction rather than the previous two-stage arrangement whereby a new donor would have to phone in, pledge a regular gift, and then wait to receive the forms through the mail which would have to be completed and returned before the gift could be set up. These regular or monthly giving programmes are now also being used in the US, where regular gifts can be set up through banks or credit cards.

Besides improving the profitability of media such as DRTV and the telephone, which previously entailed 'multi-step' arrangements, UK fundraisers have found that regular giving schemes also broaden the 'traditional' prospect audience as younger sections of the population like to give in this way. The introduction of low-value monthly giving programmes has changed the nature of the supporter base for many UK nonprofits, and are rapidly becoming more important in the American fundraising sector.

FULFILMENT

The 'back end' fulfilment of a recruitment campaign is a further key feature of donor acquisition work. The way that response to the campaign will be handled and followed up is often treated as something of an afterthought, but the treatment of new donors is hugely important in terms of building the image of the organization and beginning the relationship with the new recruit.

At base, fulfilment planning should ensure that systems and materials are in place to thank all new donors quickly, to deal with complaints and enquiries arising from the campaign, and to bank the cash donations and set up regular giving arrangements quickly and accurately. In many instances a great deal of time and thought is put into profiling, media selection, targeting and creative work on a campaign that then fails because the thought process was not carried through to the next stage. There are many case studies of DRTV campaigns where the TV ad is hugely successful and generates a huge volume of calls, which cannot be handled by the telephone agency. Donors receiving an engaged tone or a holding message do not hold on or call back and the new recruits are lost.

Relationships can be made or broken with new donors during the initial or 'honeymoon' stage of the relationship with a nonprofit, so the timing, accuracy and tone of the first 'thankyou' or 'welcome' communication is extremely important. Fulfilment is a highly specialized operation and in many cases it is most cost-effective to outsource fulfilment to an external supplier rather than to attempt to handle responses in-house. Where fulfilment is outsourced, careful and detailed briefing is essential, alongside the testing of systems and communications between the chosen supplier and the nonprofit.

BUDGETING CONTROL AND EVALUATION

Testing

The control of donor acquisition campaigns initially involves the tracking and testing of pilots. The beauty of direct marketing techniques is that opportunities for testing abound, and therefore the risk of mistakes is lessened. Testing against controls is a way of life for direct marketing fundraisers, conducted on a cyclical basis as a source of continuous improvement. Creative, media, timing and response mechanism variants can be tracked and tested before any roll-out is arranged. The control of tests can become very complex and processes must be in place to ensure that only one variant is being tested at any time and that only significant variables are tested. Testing represents a sizeable investment of budget and always carries a risk of poor return on investment. For this reason test budgets are usually set as no more than 10 per cent of the total media budget. Sample sizes should likewise be limited to sufficient minimum quantities, so that the majority of the prospect base can be contacted with the most proven and cost-effective control communication.

Some direct marketing costs increase with quantity, while others, most notably the cost of printing, can be dramatically reduced at a unit level with increases in quantity. Straight-line extrapolation from test results can therefore distort the financial implications of a roll-out. Understanding the effects of quantity in each media stream is critical if the correct inferences are to be drawn from a test campaign.

Control

Direct marketing works entirely through measurement, both during a campaign to monitor the success of the tactics selected and after a campaign to decide what succeeded and what failed. The information needed in monitoring tends to be fairly straightforward and to derive from the logical flow of a campaign. Information on, for example, the volumes actually despatched and the date of despatch, whether advertisements or inserts appeared according to schedule, and the availability of response packs will be needed on a regular basis. Any suppliers should be briefed in detail on these requirements before a campaign is launched to ensure that the requisite statistics are always accurate and available.

Reporting and evaluation

In documenting and reporting on recruitment campaigns each media necessitates slightly different controls and requirements. Each media route should be evaluated against as well as in conjunction with the other media employed. Some key performance measures used across a range of media are given below. These calculations should be performed across the campaign as a whole, and by each segment, media and creative treatment.

- *Percentage response* The response rate received to the original communication.
- *Cost per response* The total cost of the campaign divided by the number of respondents.
- *Percentage conversion* If the purpose of the original communication was merely to solicit enquiries it will also be necessary to examine the percentage of enquiries that ultimately offered a donation.
- *Cost per donor* Total cost of the campaign divided by the number of donors attracted.
- *Revenue per customer* Total value of donations divided by the number of donors attracted.
- *Profit per customer* Total profit from a campaign (if any) divided by the number of donors attracted.
- *Lifetime value per customer* Mean projected lifetime value for each donor recruited by a particular campaign.
- *Return on investment* Either calculated as an immediate return (i.e. an ROI for the recruitment campaign itself) or a projected return given the forecast lifetime value of the donors recruited.

Lifetime value is a topic to which we will return in detail in Chapter 7.

In reporting the success of any given segment or media route there are some standard pitfalls to avoid. One is the effect of extreme data or outliers – i.e. an exceptional result that can radically distort the true picture and lead to a false interpretation of the results. Outliers can occur by chance because of the extreme behaviour of one or two recruits, especially those giving very high-value initial gifts. Likewise, there is a danger in relying on average measurements – often the measurement of the median (or middle) value is more reliable, though more complex to calculate.

The costs of fulfilment should also be included and set against the income generated. It may not be possible to allocate such costs in detail to specific media or segments, but it is essential that they are allocated at least at the top level of the campaign.

Table 6.1 *Donor recruitment suppliers*

Supplier	Function
List broker	Recommendation and purchase of mailing lists
Creative agency	Concepts, design and copy for packs, ads, scripts
Media buyers	Purchase of advertising space or airtime. Specialist media buyers may be used for DRTV and radio
Data-processing house	De-duplication and cleaning of mailing list data
Mailing house	Personalization of packs, insertion of involvement devices, collation and mailing of packs
Fulfilment house	Processing of response 'banking and thanking'
Telephone agency	Outbound calling or inbound call response
Product supply	Supply of premium gifts or involvement devices (e.g. pens)
Production studio	For TV ad production

A detailed assessment of the performance of any campaign is essential in building data over time and guiding future recruitment strategy and tactics. At this stage the results should be shared with those responsible for donor development to ensure that the whole process is managed holistically and that donor development and upgrade communications are appropriate for the newly recruited donors and likely to maintain and maximize their support over the full duration of their relationship with the nonprofit organization.

SUPPLIER RELATIONSHIPS

Donor recruitment campaigns can involve a bewildering array of suppliers (an illustration of the potential range of suppliers is illustrated in Table 6.1). Coordinating and briefing suppliers is a key skill in the management of recruitment campaigns, and harmonious relationships with suppliers are hugely important in avoiding problems and ensuring that things run as smoothly as possible. Suppliers should be respected, and should be involved as early as possible. They will be specialists and will be experienced in (often the least glamorous, but essential) aspects of the work. Communication channels should be kept open throughout the process with results and successes being shared. At some point there will be a need to 'lean' on a supplier for extra fast turnaround or to 'go the extra mile' in delivering a service – if the fundraiser has made an effort to understand the business of the supplier and to treat them as key and equal team members they are more likely to respond to calls for help with alacrity. A motivated supplier team is more likely to produce the extra effort required to solve your problems and prioritize your work.

SUMMARY

In this chapter we have drawn a critical distinction between acquisition and development activities. In respect of the former a planning process was delineated, including the derivation of objectives, segmentation and profiling, targeting, media planning, communication of the offer, fulfilment and response analysis. It is important to realize that this process does not occur in isolation and that in many ways it would be better regarded as a loop. Information about the performance of one recruitment campaign can be used to inform the development of those run subsequently and modifications to strategy can often result.

DISCUSSION QUESTIONS

1   List and describe the main steps involved in planning a donor acquisition campaign.
2   How can you use profiling information about existing donors to inform a cold list mailing recruitment campaign? Is there any information that it would be inappropriate to utilize in this way?
3   As the fundraising manager of a small charity, prepare a presentation of the arguments for and against undertaking an extensive programme of list swops/reciprocals.
4   In your role as the director of fundraising you have recently appointed three new staff who will undertake donor recruitment duties. Prepare a brief presentation to them explaining how the process works and the key points that should be borne in mind at each stage.

REFERENCES

Banks, J. and Tanner, S. (1997) *The State of Donation,* IFS, London.

Center on Philanthropy (1999) *Principles and Techniques of Fund-Raising,* Indiana University, IN.

Green, P.E. (1977) 'A New Approach to Market Segmentation' *Business Horizons,* 20(1): 61–73.

Greenfield, J.M. (1994) *Fund-raising Fundamentals: A Guide to Annual Giving for Fundraisers and Volunteers,* John Wiley, New York.

Kotler, P. (1991) *Marketing Management,* Prentice-Hall, Englewood Cliffs, NJ.

MacDonald, M.H.B. (1984) *Marketing Plans: How to Prepare Them, How to Use Them,* Heinemann, London.

Philips, L.W. and Sternthal, B. (1977) 'Age Differences in Information Processing: A Perspective on the Aged Consumer', *Journal of Marketing Research,* 14(4): 444–457.

Sargeant, A. (1999) 'Charity Giving: Towards a Model of Donor Behaviour', *Journal of Marketing Management,* 15: 215–238.

Chapter 7

Donor development

OBJECTIVES

By the end of this chapter you should be able to:

■ Outline the latest research on donor development and retention.

■ Discuss the theory, practice and advantages of relationship fundraising.

■ Understand how lifetime value, recency/frequency/value models and approaches such as the donor pyramid are used in donor development strategies.

■ Discuss the optimum use of segmentation in donor development communication programmes.

■ Isolate those issues that are critical to donor retention such as service quality, feedback and recognition.

INTRODUCTION

As we discussed in the previous chapter, the bulk of the income generated from donors comes through retention and development activity rather than at the point of recruitment. Nonprofits tend to have to invest in the acquisition of new supporters. That initial investment is repaid and additional income is generated over time if the donor continues to give. Few would question that existing donors will always be the most cost-effective source of additional donations (Lindahl and Winship 1992). Donor development is thus the main income stream for nonprofits, and as such should be the area in which the highest levels of investment are made.

Donor development techniques are used to maximize the profitability of every donor relationship. In practice this involves activity designed to retain donors over time and to develop and grow their giving to increased levels through the implementation of tailored fundraising communication and stewardship programmes. It should be recognized at the outset that not all donors are of the same worth to a fundraising organization. While the targeting and profiling work undertaken in the acquisition process should go some way to ensuring that newly recruited donors are all valuable additions to the supporter database, the identification of different types of donor, of their actual and potential value to the nonprofit, and of the optimum levels of investment that should therefore be made in them, is vital to successful donor development.

145

The database, and the effective and efficient use of the information that the database can provide, is the key to this process. As with donor recruitment, a plethora of routes, options and models are available to fundraisers in devising development plans for existing donors. In this chapter we will look in detail at some of the most effective tools currently used in donor development segmentation and measurement, such as lifetime value, recency/frequency/value analyses, and relationship fundraising techniques. These should form the basis of donor development planning and strategy. We will also look at the available research on what drives donor loyalty and what nonprofits can do to encourage retention.

DONOR DEVELOPMENT PLANNING

Development objectives

Donor development objectives typically focus both on general measurements of retention and campaign-by-campaign evaluations. Many of the measures we described in the previous chapter, such as revenue, profit, campaign ROI and so on would hence form the basis for donor development objectives. We may, however, add to this measurements such as:

- *Retention rate*   The percentage of current donors who will still be considered active donors at the end of the year (or planning cycle).
- *Attrition rate*   This is simply the converse of the retention rate and expresses the percentage of current donors who will lapse their support of the organization over the course of the year (or planning cycle).
- *Aggregate return on investment*   A global measure of ROI for development activities. Nonprofits need to set targets for the return on investment they achieve for donor development activities as a whole. This frequently sits alongside ROI objectives for specific donor development campaigns, but is an essential and more global measure of performance. This is simply because not all the communications donors receive are designed to raise funds. Some may merely be imparting news and information about the work the organization undertakes. Since these are not 'campaigns' they would not be measured in the same way as other fundraising communications and are simply a facet of good donor stewardship.

Development strategy

Development planning usually involves the testing and adoption of a broad programme or annual plan of regular donor communications, which is then broken down by segment. Within this overall picture individual campaigns will be planned and targeted to achieve maximum effect. Some campaigns will be driven by clear income targets, while others will be designed as retention vehicles, and thus are not likely to be judged solely in terms of campaign profitability.

Discussions of donor development tend to be based on the belief that once supporters have been recruited, they can be cultivated over time and their contribution to the organization can be grown. Thus a new recruit who gives a small cash gift to an emergency appeal can be 'moved up' the scale of support to ultimately become a major giver or a legator. The development process also involves the 'cross selling' of other philanthropic 'products', so the one-off cash donor might also be introduced to retail trading goods, prize draws, membership or adoption schemes, or to volunteering or advocacy roles within the organization as a means of increasing the depth and profitability of the donor/nonprofit relationship.

This process is often referred to visually as a 'Ladder' or 'Pyramid', as depicted in Figures 7.1 and 7.2. The 'Loyalty Ladder' was originated in principle by Raphel and Considine (1981).

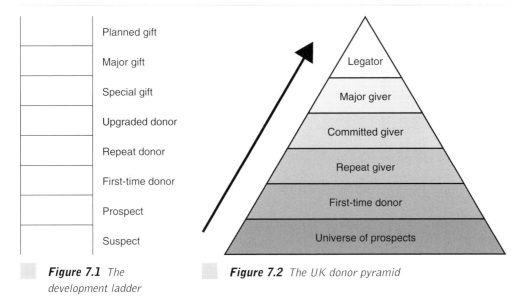

Figure 7.1 The development ladder

Figure 7.2 The UK donor pyramid

The 'Pyramid' model for donor development processes is intuitively attractive as it corresponds to the 'pyramid of giving', i.e. the observation that many small gifts are made, and few large gifts – so 80–90 per cent of the value of donations tends to come from just 10 to 20 per cent of the supporter base.

These models have been criticized in recent years as over-simplistic and static. Both assume a single route into a charity via a response to a first appeal at the base of the ladder or pyramid. In reality first donations can be a major or even planned gift, and major givers can 'descend' over time (if the relationship with them is not managed well) to lower value levels of support. Large legacy gifts are often received by UK charities from individuals who have never appeared on the charity's supporter database. Donor development planners must bear in mind that models are merely general guidelines, and that the reality is often more dynamic and less predictable than the theory would suggest.

Nonprofits commonly refer to their core donor development 'programme' or 'cycle'. This is the regular pattern of communications and events for donors that form the central development process for that organization. The cycle may be very simple, based around a single annual fund drive or a membership renewal system, or it can be a complex system of timed communications. An example of a more complex cycle is provided in Figure 7.3.

Many organizations treat a newly acquired donor differently during the first period of their support. It can be very difficult to persuade cash donors to give for a second time. It is therefore essential that the first stages of acknowledgement, welcome and re-solicitation are handled well, and that the first communications a new supporter receives are a logical development of the recruitment communication (in terms of both content and tone) that elicited their first gift. Special 'welcome' packages are often used, designed to thank the new donor, to introduce them to the organization and to renew or deepen their interest. Some organizations then continue to treat new donors as a separate segment for a certain time period, targeting them with a special series of communications (by mail, e-mail or phone) designed to foster interest and loyalty and to educate the donor about the organization and the ways in which they can become involved. After this set period the donor will be integrated into the main supporter base.

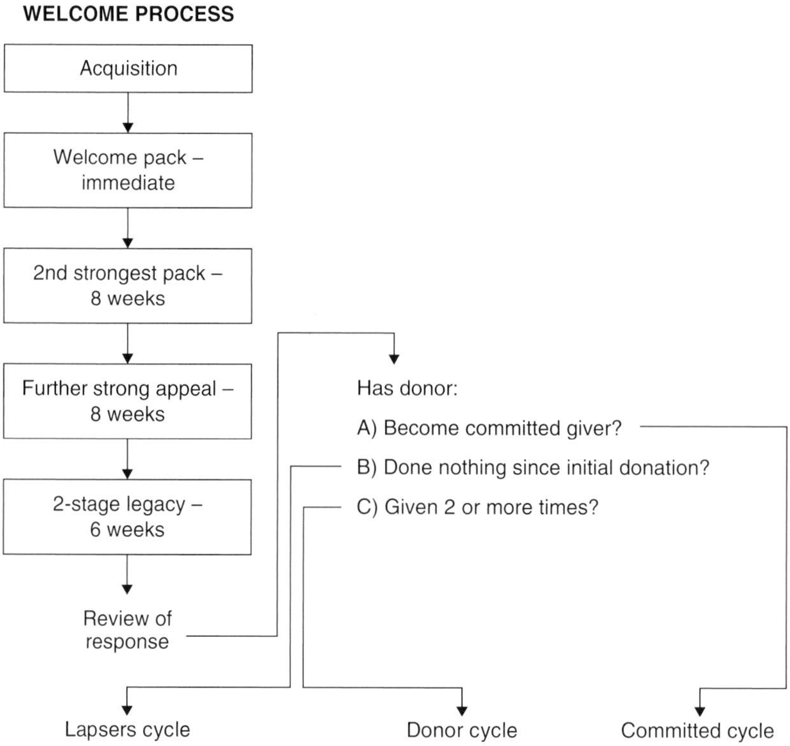

WELCOME PROCESS

```
┌─────────────────────────┐
│      Acquisition        │
└─────────────────────────┘
            │
            ▼
┌─────────────────────────┐
│   Welcome pack –        │
│   immediate             │
└─────────────────────────┘
            │
            ▼
┌─────────────────────────┐
│  2nd strongest pack –   │
│  8 weeks                │
└─────────────────────────┘
            │
            ▼
┌─────────────────────────┐        Has donor:
│  Further strong appeal –│
│  8 weeks                │        A) Become committed giver?
└─────────────────────────┘
            │                      B) Done nothing since initial donation?
            ▼
┌─────────────────────────┐        C) Given 2 or more times?
│  2-stage legacy –       │
│  6 weeks                │
└─────────────────────────┘
            │
            ▼
      Review of
      response

  Lapsers cycle          Donor cycle          Committed cycle
```

Figure 7.3 *RSPCA donor mailing cycle*

Source: © RSPCA. Reproduced with kind permission.

Donor development communications range from appeals for repeat support (by mail, phone or e-mail), updates and newsletter communications providing feedback and background information, to events invitations and higher value appeal approaches which might involve CD/DVD mailings and face-to-face visits. Donors may be invited to become members of clubs or schemes, to give regular gifts to the general fund or to sponsor an area of work or a beneficiary. Campaigning organizations might ask donors to take personal action through lobbying or protest activity. With such a plethora of options available, it is essential that fundraisers are equipped with information on the current and likely future value of individual donors, and with guidance on their likely future responses and behaviour. In the absence of this knowledge all donors will be treated the same, so some will not reach their full potential profitability while others will receive inappropriate levels of care and investment.

MEASURING DONOR VALUE

Relationship fundraising

Fundraising practice has undergone rapid change since the early 1980s and the dominant paradigm has shifted away from transactions to relationships. At the core of relationship fundraising is the development and maintenance of long-term relationships with donors, rather than simply a series of discrete transactions. Such a change in emphasis more accurately reflects real market behaviour, where few donation decisions are taken on a 'once-only' basis. Real market behaviour consists of a series of exchanges rather than purely one-off transactions.

While the move from a transaction to a relationship approach to donor development fundraising may seem little more than a play on words, the differences in terms of the impact on strategy and performance are profound. In a transaction-based approach, development activity is driven by the need to maximize the returns generated by each individual campaign (except perhaps where a campaign has been jointly designed to achieve other goals such as awareness, participation or education). Strategy is based on achieving the highest possible return on investment (ROI) when the costs and revenues of a campaign are calculated.

Fundraisers following such a strategy tend to offer donors little choice. They cannot afford to – to do so would merely add to the cost. Little segmentation takes place and donors typically receive a standard pack. The emphasis of the content is usually on the immediacy of each appeal and donors are exalted to give 'now' because of the urgency of a given situation. They may then be approached in a few weeks' or months' time with a further seemingly urgent issue the charity feels they should support. The donor thus receives a series of very similar communications each designed with an eye to achieving the maximum possible ROI.

A relationship approach by contrast recognizes that it is not essential to break even on every communication with a donor. The relationship approach recognizes that if treated with respect donors will want to give again, and fundraisers are therefore content to live with somewhat lower rates of return in the early stages. They recognize that they will achieve a respectable ROI over the full duration of the relationship. At the heart of this approach is the concept of 'lifetime value' (LTV). Once fundraisers understand how much a given donor might be worth to the organization over time, they can tailor the offering to that donor according to the individual's needs/requirements, and yet still ensure an adequate lifetime ROI. These differences between the transaction and relational approaches to fundraising are summarized in Table 7.1.

Relationship fundraising may therefore be defined as: 'An approach to the management of the process of donor exchange based on the long-term value that can accrue to both parties.' From a donor's perspective, this style of approach addresses how an organization

- finds you
- gets to know you
- keeps in touch with you
- tries to ensure that you get what you want from them in every aspect of their dealings with you
- checks that you are getting what they promised you.

Naturally, as Stone et al. (1996:676) point out, this depends on the effort being worthwhile to the organization concerned. This is clearly of paramount importance as donors themselves expect that the maximum possible percentage of their donation will be applied directly to the cause (Harvey and McCrohan 1988).

Table 7.1 *Comparison of transaction and relational approaches*

Differences	Transaction-based fundraising	Relationship fundraising
Focuss	Soliciting single donations	Donor retention
Key measures	Immediate ROI, amount of donation, response rate	Lifetime value
Orientation	Urgency of cause	Donor relationship
Time scale	Short	Long
Customer service	Little emphasis	Major emphasis

Burnett (1992:48) was the first to recognize the need for what he termed 'relationship fund-raising' which he defined as:

> an approach to the marketing of a cause which centres not around raising money but on developing to its full potential the unique and special relationship that exists between a charity and its supporter.

Burnett championed a move towards dealing with donors individually, recognizing each donor as unique in terms of their giving history, their motivation for giving and the overall standard of care that they expect to receive from the charities they support. The entire relationship with a donor, he argued, should be viewed holistically and fundraising decisions taken in the light of the perceived value of the overall relationship.

Relationship fundraising is characterized by donor choice. Recognizing the benefit of future income streams, fundraisers are not afraid to invest in their donors and to allow them greater flexibility over the content, nature and frequency of the communications they receive. As Jackson (1992) notes, this makes people feel important and thereby fulfils a basic human need. While the initial costs of implementing such a strategy are undoubtedly higher, the benefits in terms of enhanced patterns of donor loyalty – and therefore future revenue streams far outweigh this investment.

BOTTON VILLAGE – DONOR CHOICE AND SEGMENTATION

One of the most successful fundraising charities in the UK – Botton Village - had to write to its donors asking them not to send any further monies. They had literally received all the funds they needed to sustain the Village into the medium term. Key to the charity's success was the concept of donor choice and allowing donors to specify exactly what they wanted to receive from the charity and when. On the back of every communication donors received from the organization was a form inviting them to specify their individual choices. Donors could elect to receive only one mailing a year, to receive mailings, but not to be asked for money, to receive back editions of the newsletter, to receive information on how to make a legacy and, even, never to hear from the organization again. So successful was their fundraising that an Xmas mailing achieved a response rate of over 50 per cent - quite phenomenal in direct marketing terms and a testament to the move away from 'intrusion' in development activity to 'invitation'.

Fundraising departments operating relationship fundraising therefore make every effort to segment their donor base and to develop a uniquely tailored service and importantly 'quality of service' for each of the segments they identify. At the core of this approach is the concept of lifetime value. It is this that drives the nature of the contact strategy and the dimensions of the relationship.

Lifetime value

Bitran and Mondschein (1997:109) define lifetime value (LTV) as 'the total net contribution that a customer generates during his/her lifetime on a house-list'. It is therefore a measure of the total net worth to a fundraising organization of its relationship with a particular donor. To calculate it one has to estimate the costs and revenues that will be associated with managing

Let The Camphill Family help you

**Your support means a great deal to us and we want to help you in return.
Please let us know your preferences by ticking the relevant boxes below.**

Choose when you want to hear from us

1. **If you receive four issues of our newsletter each year:**
   ☐ *I would prefer to hear from you just once a year, at Christmas.*

2. **If you only receive a newsletter once a year,
   you may like us to contact you more often:**
   ☐ *I would like to receive Camphill Family Life four times a year.*

3. **If you would rather not receive appeals:**
   ☐ *I would like you to keep me up to date with news through
   Camphill Family Life, but I do not wish to receive appeals.*

4. **If you would rather not receive any further
   information from The Camphill Family:**
   ☐ *I would prefer you <u>not</u> to write to me again.*

To set up or change a regular gift

Giving The Camphill Family your regular financial support helps
us to plan for the future. By setting up or amending a Banker's
Order you'll continue giving our communities regular help, but
your bank will be doing all the paperwork.

5. **If you would like to set up a regular gift:**
   ☐ *I would like to give to The Camphill Family on a regular basis –
   please send me a Banker's Order form.*

6. **If you would like to amend your existing
   regular gift:**
   ☐ *I already give regularly by Banker's Order and would like to
   amend it – please send me a form.*

Thank you.

Your guide to
The Camphill Family

You can be sure of a warm
welcome at any of the eleven
communities supported by
The Camphill Family. This
guide gives you all the
information you need to
plan a visit, including our
opening times.

☐ *Please send me a free
copy of the guide.*

Do you want a word with someone?

Our office team of
Kelly, Fran, Sue, Jackie
and Joanne is here to
help you. **Just ring our
helpline 01287 661294
or our switchboard
01287 660871, 9am
to 4pm weekdays,**
and one of us will be

pleased to talk to you. Do let us know if you have moved
to a new address, if we are sending you more than one
copy of our newsletter by mistake, or if there is anything
else you would like to tell us.

Find out more about what life is like in
The Camphill Family at Botton Village

7. **Our video of life in Botton**
   Botton Village: This is our home is set against the changing
   seasons in the rural beauty of Danby Dale and will help you
   to get to know us better. It tells the story of our community
   through the lives of our villagers and is a charming portrait
   of special people and the challenges they meet in sharing
   life together.
   ☐ *Please send me a complimentary copy of the video,
   Botton Village: This is our home.*

8. **The *Botton Village* photo book**
   Featuring wonderful images of the people and places that
   make Botton special. Photographer Keith Allardyce used
   to live in the village and his close relationship with our
   community shines through.
   ☐ *Please send me a free copy of the* Botton Village *photo book.*

9. **Our *Sounds of Botton* audio tape**
   Our tape follows villager Jane Hill as she tours the village
   and meets her friends. It gives you a unique insight into
   life at Botton.
   ☐ *Please send me a free copy of the* Sounds of Botton *tape.*

10. **Visiting Botton Village**
    Visitors are always welcome at Botton. If you can, please ring
    us in advance on 01287 660871 and we can give you details
    of workshop opening times as well as directions.

11. **Sending you past issues of our newsletter**
    Interesting stories from the village's history feature in past
    issues of our newsletter, *Botton Village Life*. You may ask
    for any of the past issues you would like, or another copy
    of ones you may have mislaid.
    ☐ *Please send me issue no._____ (most issues are available).*

The Camphill Family supports eleven communities which help adults in need of special care and understanding, and which are registered
as the Camphill Village Trust Limited, a non-profit-making company limited by guarantee 539694 England and registered as a Charity 232402.

Plate 7.1 *Botton Village donor response form*
Sorce: © Camphill Village Trust Ltd. Reproduced with kind permission.

the communication with that donor, during each year of his/her relationship. If, for example, the relationship extends over a period of four years, one can subtract the costs of servicing the relationship with that donor from the revenue so generated. In essence the contribution each year to the organization's overheads and charitable appeals can be calculated. Of course there is a certain amount of crystal ball gazing involved since it becomes increasingly difficult to predict costs and revenues the further one looks into the future. To take account of this uncertainty and to reflect the fact that a £20 donation in four years' time will be worth much less than it would today in real terms, it is also important to discount the value of the future revenue streams that will be generated. After all, instead of investing the money in donor acquisition activity the charity could simply place the money concerned in an interest-bearing account. Unless the return from the fundraising activity can be expected to match, or hopefully exceed, what could be generated by an interest-bearing account, it will clearly not be worthwhile. If this analysis is conducted right across the database a key advantage accrues. Charities can employ an LTV analysis to increase their overall profitability by abandoning donors who will never be profitable and concentrating resources on recruiting and retaining those who will (see also Lindahl and Winship 1992).

There are two key decisions to be taken in this examination of donor value. First, nonprofits must choose between the uses of historic or projected future value. Second, they must choose to calculate value on either an individual basis or, more usually, on a segment-by-segment basis, examining specific groups of donors on the database.

The majority of voluntary organizations continue to equate lifetime value with 'total historic value' and thus to calculate lifetime value by conducting a simple historic analysis of their database. The question fundraisers are asking, by conducting their analysis in this way, is simply 'How much has this particular individual, or segment, been worth to my organization in the past?' However, lifetime value can and should be used as a projective measure, offering information in respect of how much a given donor or segment will likely be worth in the future.

Calculating the LTV of individual donors

The formula for calculating LTV in the case of an individual donor is as follows:

$$\text{LTV} = \sum_{i=1}^{n} C_i(1+d)^{-i}$$

Where:

C = net contribution (i.e. revenue minus cost) from each year's fundraising activities
d = discount rate
n = the expected duration of the relationship (in years).

This somewhat complex-looking equation merely indicates that it is necessary to calculate the likely future contribution by a donor to each year's fundraising activities, discount these future contributions and then add them all together. The grand total is the LTV of a given donor.

In examining the contribution each year, an organization should subtract all the relevant costs of servicing the relationship with a given donor from the revenues so generated. The issue of what constitutes a relevant cost is driven by the purposes for which the analysis is being conducted. Thus it may be appropriate to include the costs of recruitment where the aim is to compare the performance of various recruitment media. If the aim is simply to apportion a donor to a given standard of care, these costs are sunk and therefore of no relevance. Similarly a major issue for many organizations is the appropriate assignment of joint/overhead costs. There are many applications of lifetime value analysis where such costs are not of relevance (see e.g. Sargeant and MacKenzie 1999).

Of course the lifetime value of a donor should take into consideration much more than just the revenue from their direct donations and the costs of the communications they receive. Donors are worth much more than this to an organization, because, for example, they often purchase goods from trading catalogues, sell raffle tickets, donate their time to fundraising events and so on. Each of these contributions needs to be accounted for in the equation. As an example, the net contribution figure for each year could, therefore, take account of the following costs and revenues:

Costs

- newsletters
- appeal communications
- acknowledgement/thank you communications
- cost of promotional merchandise/donor gifts
- cost of telemarketing activity, if any.

Revenues

- cash donations
- tax reclaimed (in the case of tax-effective giving)
- cash value of donations in kind
- cash value of any volunteering undertaken
- cash value of referrals (i.e. introductions of other donors)
- revenue from sale of promotional merchandise.

Table 7.2 shows a worked example. In this very simple example a donor has started their relationship with the charity as an uncommitted giver. Suppose for the sake of argument that this person is female, aged 45, lives in a certain type of accommodation (identifiable from her postcode information) and responded to a very specific type of appeal (e.g. famine relief) conveyed through an equally specific recruitment media - perhaps a list swop mailing. On the basis of a historical analysis of the database, the fundraiser understands that donors matching this profile would typically upgrade to committed giving in the third year of their relationship with the charity and would tend to be regular purchasers of raffle tickets. Indeed it is not unusual for this type of person to persuade friends or relatives also to sell raffle tickets on the charity's behalf. On the basis of this information, coupled with forecast donation levels and projected costs, it is possible to produce the forecast given in Table 7.2 of the contributions that this donor will make to the organization over the duration of their predicted five-year relationship. As previously indicated, the value of the future contributions must be discounted and on this basis the predicted lifetime value of the donor is calculated as £387. This information can then be used to assign the donor to an appropriate pattern of contact and quality of care.

Major gifts

No mention has yet been made of major/estate gifts, or, in the case of the UK fundraising arena, legacies, which remain a major source of income for many voluntary organizations. The issue of whether or not to include an estimate of likely major gifts is one of predictability. In the UK it remains extremely difficult to predict legacy income and organizations thus tend to exclude it from models used to shape day-to-day fundraising activity. In the USA where planned giving is a

Table 7.2 *Example LTV analysis for an individual donor (£)*

	Year 1	Year 2	Year 3	Year 4	Year 5	Total
Revenue						
Cash	50	50				100
Raffles	10	20	30	30	40	130
Covenants + tax						
refunded			100	100	100	90
Referrals				10	10	20
Total income	60	70	130	140	150	550
Costs						
Newsletters	2	2	2	2	3	11
Appeals	4	4	5	5	5	23
Thank yous	1	1	1	2	2	7
Raffles	2	2	2	3	3	12
Incentives				5	5	10
Total costs	9	9	10	17	18	63
Contribution	51	61	120	123	132	487
Discounted value	51	55	99	92	90	387

Discount rate of 10 per cent per annum

key facet of fundraising and where fundraisers have a much more detailed understanding of the incidence of this category of gift, it may well be appropriate to include variables pertaining to the costs and revenues associated with this form of giving.

Calculating the LTV of discrete donor segments

In the example quoted above we were concerned with how lifetime value might be calculated in the case of an individual donor. More usually, charities want to understand whether specific segments of their database exhibit higher lifetime values than others. This calls for a more sophisticated degree of analysis. In attempting to measure lifetime value the following process is recommended.

1   The first stage is to decide what the purpose of the analysis will be. Although this sounds rather obvious, many organizations are not clear from the outset exactly what they are hoping to gain from it. The technique typically employed is to determine whether specific segments of the database have a higher or lower value than others. Thus if female donors appear to be worth more than male donors, or donors recruited by direct mail have a higher lifetime value than those recruited by press advertising, fundraising resources can be allocated accordingly. Not only can recruitment resources be more appropriately targeted, but contact strategies employing appropriate degrees of care can be developed to ensure the highest possible degrees of loyalty amongst those segments with the strongest lifetime values. Lifetime value analysis is therefore commonly employed to determine the LTV of donors who have specific characteristics. The nature of these characteristics needs to be determined from the outset. Clarity in respect

of the purpose of the analysis can also guide the organization in assigning appropriate categories of cost for inclusion in the calculations.

2   The next stage is to decide the period of analysis to use. It is not essential here that the chosen time period selected is based on the longest standing donors (Carpenter 1995). Since predicting behaviour becomes progressively more difficult the further one looks into the future, and since contributions arising in the medium to long term will be heavily discounted, it is only important that the time period selected captures the majority of the contribution for a given segment of donors. Previous research in the commercial sector with similar value products suggests that a time frame of three to five years might be most appropriate for application in the fundraising context (see e.g. Jackson 1992). The value of future contributions that occur beyond this period will be increasingly difficult to predict, as will the rates of donor attrition. In a sense, therefore, the term 'lifetime' value is something of a misnomer. It is entirely up to the organization concerned to set a suitable time frame for the analysis and to look at the lifetime value of its donors over this very specific horizon.

3   The next step should be to segment the database into a manageable but distinct group of cells on the basis of the primary variable to be explored. Suppose one wished to explore the LTV of donors who give their first donation at differing monetary values. To investigate this issue the database should be divided into a number of cells based on the level of the initial donation. In theory, the greater the number of cells the more accurate the predictive capability of the eventual model. But, in practice, there is a trade-off between accuracy and simplicity; increasing the number of cells adds greatly to the complexity of the model. As a general rule, in the fundraising context, between 10 and 30 cells are recommended. One might therefore allocate donors to cells on the basis that their initial donation was between

- £1 and £10
- £11 and £20
- £21 and £30

and so on

4   It is then necessary to establish the giving behaviour of each of the cells identified at (3) above. A historical analysis of donor behaviour for each level of donation should yield valuable information in respect of

- *Attrition rate*. This will almost certainly vary from year to year. For example, comparatively few uncommitted givers will give a second donation. Those that do will probably exhibit a much reduced, but thereafter fairly even, pattern of attrition. This information can be used to calculate the percentage of donors within the cell likely to be active in year 2, year 3 and so on.
- *Giving history*. It should be possible to calculate typical response rates for members of each value cell according to the type of donor development activity employed. It should also be possible to track any trends in the actual amount donated in response to each campaign. Indeed a number of donors will typically migrate from one cell to another, as they decide to give more (or less), or upgrade, for example, to committed giving.

5   The final stage is to outline the intended development strategy, including, for example, the number of mailings and the projected costs thereof. This should include the costs of

maintenance and stewardship communications a donor would typically receive (e.g. newsletters), even though they are not specifically aimed at raising funds.

6   The preceding information can then be employed to predict future value. Armed with information about likely attrition rates, the future costs of servicing donors, the predicted revenue streams and an appropriate discount rate, one can then proceed to make predictions about the projected lifetime value of each cell, or category of giver.

AN LTV CASE

LTV analysis employing the methodology above was conducted on behalf of a large International Aid organization in the UK. The charity ranks among the Top 100 Fundraising Charities (as ranked by voluntary income) and is involved in a number of development projects worldwide. In the case of this analysis, the aim was to determine which recruitment media generated the highest donor lifetime values. Only uncommitted giving (i.e. gifts from donors who give only a series of 'one-off' donations and do not commit themselves to future gifts) was considered. A random sample was therefore taken of 1,000 individuals who had been recruited from each of five primary recruitment media. This allowed the researcher to explore the behaviour of all the variables alluded to above and to build a model capable of predicting the lifetime value of donors that would be recruited by each method over the forthcoming recruitment campaign. The results of the analysis were employed to inform the allocation of recruitment resources between the various media available and to forecast the likely (lifetime) ROI of the campaign. A 10 per cent discount rate was employed and the duration of a donor lifetime was taken as five years. As we are concerned here with the relative performance of each recruitment medium, the costs of recruitment have been included in the LTV calculation. The results obtained are presented in Table 7.3.

Table 7.3 Forecast LTV by recruitment media

Medium	Mean LTV (£)
Direct mail (cold mailing)	121.73
Direct mail (reciprocal mailing)	110.54
Door-to-door distribution	102.89
Direct response press advertising	95.78
Direct response television	76.76

The benefits of LTV analysis

Lifetime value can be used to drive four management decisions:

1   assigning acquisition allowances
2   targeting donor acquisition campaigns
3   setting selection criteria for donor marketing
4   investing in the reactivation of lapsed donors.

1 Assigning acquisition allowances

An understanding of the lifetime value of a charity's donors can guide the determination of how much should be spent to recruit each new donor. Many charities conscientiously strive to achieve as closely as possible a break-even position at the end of each of their recruitment campaigns. While commendable this is not at all necessary, so long as the future income stream from the donors being recruited is a healthy one. Charities employing the lifetime value concept would therefore tend to assign somewhat higher acquisition allowances. In financial terms this is simply because a fundraiser employing a transaction-based approach will calculate campaign ROI thus:

$$\text{ROI} = \frac{\text{immediate revenue generated}}{\text{cost of acquisition campaign}}$$

A fund-raiser adopting a relational approach based on lifetime value (LTV) would by contrast calculate ROI as:

$$\text{ROI} = \frac{\text{initial revenue} + (\text{sum of all future contributions less discount})}{\text{cost of acquisition campaign}}$$

Where:

ROI = return on donor acquisition investment
Future contribution = estimated annual contribution to profit
Discount = reduction in value of future cash to today's rate (discounted cashflow).

2 Targeting donor acquisition campaigns

Fundraisers engaged in the perennial problem of donor recruitment are well versed in the necessity of asking questions such as

'Which media should I be using for my recruitment activity?'

'What balance should I adopt between the media options that are available?'

The traditional approach to answering these questions would have been to calculate the immediate ROI for each media and consider the response rates typically received from each media in the past. Such analyses suggest sub-optimal allocations of fundraising resource, because they ignore certain known donor behaviours. Donors recruited from one medium may never give again, while donors recruited by another medium exhibit much greater degrees of loyalty to the cause. The overall profitability from one relationship can therefore vary considerably from that of another. This is reflected in the results reported in Table 7.3.

LTV analysis can also be used to select appropriate prospects to contact. If an organization has a good database and accompanying geodemographic/lifestyle data it can generate a clear profile of its higher value and/or most loyal supporters. If this profile differs significantly from the balance of the database it will be possible to use the differences to drive how recruitment activity is conducted. If higher LTV donors are male, tend to enjoy hobbies such as gardening and are aged between 50 and 65, this knowledge can be used to guide the purchase of mailing/e-mail lists and/or guide the choice of media that will be employed for recruitment. In essence the fundraiser will look for media that can reach individuals matching this profile cost-effectively, minimising the wastage involved in recruiting other individuals who will never be loyal and offer only a low or even negative LTV.

3 Setting selection criteria for donor marketing

Lifetime value calculations can prove instructive for more than just recruitment planning. The information can be used to guide contact strategies for ongoing donor development. If a charity calculates a projected lifetime value for each donor on the database, donors can be assigned to specific segments, and contact strategies can be customized to build value. Initially, this may involve simply recognizing the difference in contribution, so as to offer particularly high-value donors a differentiated pattern of care that reflects their status. This might involve more detailed, higher quality mailings, invitations to events, personal thank you calls and so on. As charities become more experienced in the use of LTV analysis, it would also be possible to associate the impact of differentiated standards of care, or forms of contact, upon the LTV for a given donor. In a sense, one then begins to model the optimal lifetime value. An example will illustrate this point.

Suppose a Third World charity has conducted a LTV analysis. They have divided donors into segments on the basis of projected LTV and decide to mail the highest value segments with an expensive mailshot designed to solicit funds to support Third World families. On the basis of the projected LTV they have calculated that sufficient funds exist to include a detailed case history of one family that warrants support, photographs of each of the family members and a promotional DVD highlighting the work the organization could do with that family. While the LTV calculations suggest this is a very viable form of contact, which will generate an acceptable rate of return, the charity has no way of knowing whether this is optimal. Through experience a charity can monitor the impact of different contact strategies on lifetime value (e.g. a standard mailshot, including/not including the photographs, including/not including the DVD). Contact strategies can then be selected which maximize the overall lifetime value of a given segment of donors. In our example, it may be that the inclusion of a DVD is perceived as wasteful and therefore lowers the value of subsequent donations, or it could have such an emotive and tangible pull that donors feel a greater sense of commitment and the longevity of their relationship is extended. As Peppers and Rogers (1995:49) note:

> Instead of measuring the effectiveness of a marketing programme by how many sales transactions occur across an entire market during a particular period, the new marketer will gauge success by the projected increase or decrease in a customer's expected future value to the company.

4 Investing in the reactivation of lapsed donors

Few fundraisers would disagree with the notion that reactivating lapsed donors can be profitable. Having been sufficiently motivated to give at least once in the past, with the proper encouragement it is eminently possible that donors will do so again. The problem, however, for many organizations lies in deciding which lapsed donors should be selected for contact. While one could do this easily on the basis of the total amount donated, the level of the last gift, or the length of time since the last donation, it can be instructive to use projected lifetime value, to inform the decision. With the right persuasion to respond, targeting those with a higher forecast LTV is likely to prove a most efficient use of resources. A 'reactivation allowance' can be built into the budget. How much an organization is prepared to commit to reactivating one donor would inform the nature and quality of the contact strategy employed.

never advisable, as there is a great deal of anecdotal evidence to suggest that sizeable legacy bequests can come from donors who have given little during their lifetime.

Efforts should therefore be made to maintain a relationship and to retain low-value donors if this is possible, while also obtaining a positive ROI. Low-value donors might therefore receive a restricted number of appeal and update communications each year, and will also be approached to convert their giving to a regular commitment in order to reduce administration and retention costs. Some categories of charity may even find it a viable option to switch to electronic communications for members of this group.

Low-value donors can also be used in reciprocal mailings (list swops). As the least valuable donor segment, it may be considered worthwhile to use these donors (where data protection legislation permits) in exchanges with other nonprofits in order to minimize recruitment costs. However, as we discussed in Chapter 6, reciprocal mailings are inherently risky ventures and should be used with care.

Lapsed donors

We have discussed the worth of LTV analysis in assigning a potential value to lapsed donors and guiding levels of investment and communication. Investment in lapsed donor reactivation is undoubtedly worthwhile, especially when the levels of ROI are compared with the costs of recruiting a new donor from a commercial list. However, it is easy to invest too high an amount in this group. When a lapsed donor is reactivated their subsequent giving history should be tracked carefully. In many instances reactivated donors lapse again, and the investment of the nonprofit in keeping that donor on board is therefore not recouped.

KEEPING DONORS LOYAL

Why is loyalty important?

Loyal donors are those who give support time after time. While data analysis and segmentation exercises may indicate that certain types or groups of donors are not likely to be very profitable over time, and that little should therefore be invested in retaining and growing their support, there are very few instances where the loss of a supporter would be an optimum result. Major gifts, and especially legacy or bequest gifts, are highly unpredictable sources of charity income. There is much anecdotal evidence that even the lowest value giver in life can become a major benefactor after death. While segmentation based on profitability is essential, studies have shown that a small increase in customer retention can produce a significant impact on profitability (Reichheld and Sasser 1990).

As is the case in consumer marketing, it appears that there are several different levels of loyalty. Nonprofits in the field of disaster relief, for instance, commonly find it extremely difficult to elicit repeat gifts from donors who give for the first time in response to an emergency appeal. In this instance, the giving of the gift has been motivated by the urgency of the cause or event and the perceived needs of the beneficiaries, while the identity of the facilitating nonprofit agency has barely registered. The donor therefore feels no loyalty to the nonprofit and is unlikely to consider themselves to have any sort of relationship with them.

The giving of a second gift is always seen as a key point in the donor/nonprofit relationship. As we have seen, most nonprofits report that over half of new cash donors never give again. First gifts can be seen as a 'test', with the donor (consciously or unconsciously) waiting to see what feedback they receive before going further.

In the 'middle' levels of loyalty a donor may give repeat gifts, but may also support other similar causes and may not feel any great involvement with or preference for a particular organization.

At the 'top' level donors feel that they have a strong relationship with a particular nonprofit organization and will continue to support them even though competitors exist in the same field of work. At this level of loyalty the donor would be likely to be receptive to major gift or planned giving approaches, and would act as a strong advocate for the nonprofit.

How can loyalty be increased?

In Chapter 5 we examined the reasons why donors stop giving to nonprofits. The results of the research undertaken into reasons for quitting suggest a number of ways in which nonprofits may seek to retain their donors. While there may be little that can be done to facilitate the retention of those donors who experience a change in their financial circumstances, there is much that can be done to deal with many of the other common causes of lapse. Building on the learning from Chapter 5 we offer the following suggestions:

1   Nonprofits should begin by developing an understanding of the economics of loyalty and identify for themselves the difference in the LTV of the fundraising database that would be attained as a consequence of small improvements in the level of donor loyalty (e.g. 1 per cent, 2 per cent, 5 per cent, etc.). This is essential if staff and Board members are to understand the rationale for an enhanced focus on loyalty and therefore to 'buy-in' to the process necessary for this to become a reality. Knowledge of these figures can also assist in motivating donor-facing members of staff to provide a high quality of service because small increases in loyalty are very achievable. We know from research that as little as a 10 per cent improvement in the level of loyalty can increase the lifetime value of a fundraising database by over 200 per cent (Sargeant and Jay 2004), so even small changes matter.

2   Perceptions of the quality of service offered to donors are the single biggest driver of loyalty in the fundraising context. Donors who indicate they are very satisfied with the quality of service they receive are twice as likely to be supporting the organization in a year's time as those who say they are merely satisfied (Sargeant and Jay 2004). Organizations should therefore take steps to measure the quality of service provided by their organization and take steps to improve on those areas where weakness is detected. It should be remembered that in measuring the quality of service provided it is necessary to measure separately the importance that individuals place on each aspect of the service. As Figure 7.4 illustrates, effort may then be expended on those aspects of the service that are perceived to be important and yet currently underperforming.

Care should be taken to measure satisfaction on at least a five-point scale, thus:

1   Very dissatisfied
2   Dissatisfied
3   No opinion/neutral
4   Satisfied
5   Very satisfied.

As was noted earlier, individuals who claim to be very satisfied will exhibit much higher levels of loyalty than those who regard themselves as merely 'satisfied'. Any measurement system must therefore be sensitive enough to capture this distinction.

In seeking to develop a measure of service quality, organizations will want to develop a scale tailored to their specific context and needs. It will need to reflect their existing pattern of communication, the different ways in which donors can interact with the organization, the pattern of benefits offered (particularly in the membership context) and so on. The scale in Figure 7.5 is

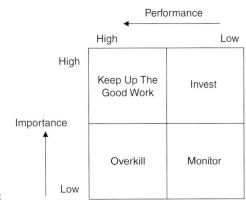

Figure 7.4 Importance/performance matrix

offered as a generic example. An aggregate satisfaction score can easily be created by calculating the average rating across all the various dimensions, or by simply calculating the total score. This might then form part of the appraisal of an organization's fundraising performance. An identical scale can be employed to measure importance, modifying the five-point scale to range from 'very unimportant' to 'very important'.

It may also be helpful to measure the quality of service provided by other organizations the donor supports so that a comparative strand to the analysis can be developed. Satisfaction with service quality is rarely an absolute. How donors feel will depend in no small measure on what they were expecting. Donors whose expectations were met or exceeded will be satisfied, while donors whose expectations fail to be met, will not. The difficulty lies in measuring this additional dimension as many donors will probably not have thought through their expectations of a fundraising team. In seeking to measure this it therefore makes more sense to ask them about the quality of service they receive from 'other' charities on the basis that whether they realize it or not this will certainly be driving their expectations of the focal organization.

3 Organizations should think through and ideally conduct their own primary research programme to understand why donors support their organization, or more specifically, from

Please rate your level of satisfaction with each of the following aspects of the service that XXX provides you with as a donor, where 1 = very dissatisfied and 5 = very satisfied

	Very Dissatisfied	2	3	4	Very Satisfied
Informing me how my money is spent.	❑	❑	❑	❑	❑
Not asking for support too often.	❑	❑	❑	❑	❑
Offering me some choice in the communications I receive.	❑	❑	❑	❑	❑
Thanking me appropriately.	❑	❑	❑	❑	❑
Recognizing the contribution I've made in the past.	❑	❑	❑	❑	❑
Demonstrating they care about my needs.	❑	❑	❑	❑	❑
Making it clear why my continued support is needed.	❑	❑	❑	❑	❑
Giving me opportunities to support XXX in other (non-financial) ways.	❑	❑	❑	❑	❑
Using an appropriate style/tone in their communications.	❑	❑	❑	❑	❑

Figure 7.5 Example of satisfaction questionnaire

which aspects of the organization's operations (or fundraising) individuals derive the most value. Value can then be engineered in fundraising communications that directly reflects and satisfies donor motives for supporting the organization. If donors are drawn to particular aspects of an organization's work, this can be developed in newsletters, e-mails and web content.

4   Allied to the above, nonprofits should consider how and under what circumstances they might contribute to a donor's sense of self-identity. Are there circumstances where a donor would be likely to start defining themselves, at least in part, through their support of the organization? Donors may, for example, derive value because they identify with aspects of an organization's brand or personality. They may also identify with an issue, an activity, with specific categories of beneficiary or indeed other stakeholder groups such as senior members of staff or celebrity endorsers. The psychological benefit that accrues from making the gift is enhanced because these positive associations reinforce the donor's own sense of self-worth or esteem. Looking for ways of strengthening the bond of identification is therefore a critical step in fostering loyalty.

5   Nonprofits can seek to build donor commitment to their cause, by considering each of the drivers we listed in Chapter 5. They can therefore:

- Clearly articulate their organization's values.
- Make it clear to the donor the difference that their support is or has been making and therefore the consequences to the beneficiary if they withdraw.
- Consider the 'journeys' that they will take supporters on through ongoing communications. This might be as simple as considering what 'a year in the life' of each category of supporter might look like, or it may be more sophisticated, looking at how each segment of donors will be educated about the cause (and brought closer to it), over time.
- Allied to the above, consider ways in which donors can be actively encouraged to interact with the organization. In the electronic environment, for example, this is relatively easy. Supporters can be asked to sign up for specific forms of communication, to offer recommendations or suggestions, to take part in research, to 'ask the expert', to campaign on behalf of the organization, to 'test' their knowledge in a quiz and so on. The more two-way interactions that are engendered, the higher will be the level of loyalty achieved.

6   Similarly, organizations can recognize that trust is a major driver of loyalty. They can look to foster this by:

- Demonstrating to the donor that they have exhibited good judgement in their dealings with beneficiaries, stewarding organizational resources and, where applicable, in respect of their approach to campaigning.
- Stressing that they adhere to appropriate standards of professional conduct (e.g. subscribe to codes such as the Fundraising Promise or the Donor Bill of Rights).
- Ensuring that all members of fundraising staff receive appropriate training in customer service.
- Designing and instigating a complaints procedure so that individuals who wish to can take issue with the quality of an organization's fundraising or approach.
- Communicating the achievements of the organization and where possible relating these to the separate contributions made by individuals or segments of supporters.
- Ensuring that all promises made to donors are adhered to and, critically, seen to be adhered to.

7   Nonprofits can provide donors with ongoing cues as to the quality of the organization's overall performance. Drip-feeding relevant data, rather than merely providing annual accounts, for example, will improve donor perceptions of the nonprofit and greatly facilitate loyalty.

8   Organizations should consider the development of regular or 'sustained' giving programmes. Levels of attrition are much lower than those achieved in traditional annual or cash giving. Younger donors are also significantly more comfortable with regular giving than their older counterparts, so offering regular giving, particularly as an online giving option, will greatly reduce the level of attrition experienced.

9   Nonprofits should evaluate the continuation of activities that lower loyalty, such as list swap programmes. Managers need to assess the impact on donor lifetime value, rather than looking at the short-term attractiveness (i.e. ROI) of such programmes.

10   Nonprofits should consider the creation of donor welcome cycles. E-mail and mail versions of these communications should be considered. Newly acquired donors should be exposed to a differentiated standard of care while their relationship with a nonprofit develops. The historically strongest recruitment messages would be likely to be the most effectual components of such cycles.

11   Where donors are offered gifts as recognition for contributions at specific levels, nonprofits should ensure that these gifts are linked in some way to the service they provide and thus tap in to 'intrinsic' rather than 'extrinsic' motives. Such gifts should be tied to the cause and thus not be capable of being supplied by any comparable organization. Thus, for example, in the case of the Royal Opera House, offering discounts at nearby restaurants or discounts at local traders in response to a gift will not be an effective way of engendering loyalty. Such schemes develop loyalty to the promotion, not loyalty to the organization. Providing CDs of music linked to the programmes and thus only obtainable from the charity, by contrast, would be likely to be highly effectual.

12   Finally, those organizations seeking to facilitate higher levels of loyalty would be advised to maintain regular contact with their donors, researching ongoing needs and preferences. As a consequence of this research database segmentation can then be regularly reviewed and updated. It would also be helpful to conduct regular exit polling of lapsed supporters to identify the most common reasons for this behaviour and thus facilitate corrective action.

SUMMARY

This chapter has introduced and explained some of the latest research undertaken on what can be done to retain the support of donors over time and to develop their giving. The concept of relationship fundraising and the differences between this approach and the more traditional transactional route is explained, and the core measurement of lifetime value was introduced and discussed in some detail.

Segmentation is key to the implementation of successful donor development strategies, and we also examined some of the main categories of donor and the sort of treatment each might receive in an optimal development plan. Finally, we have addressed the critical issue of loyalty and discussed how to address the big three drivers of retention, namely: satisfaction, commitment and trust. We concluded by offering a number of practical recommendations for how loyalty can be developed.

DISCUSSION QUESTIONS

1   List the reasons for donor lapse that can effectively be addressed by the fundraising function. How would you go about improving these areas in your own organization (or one that you know well)?

2   In your capacity as head of fundraising for an arts organization, make notes for a presentation to your CEO on the merits of undertaking a lifetime value analysis of your donor base.

3   Put yourself in the position of a donor who gives regularly to two nonprofit organizations working in a similar field. One of the organizations has adopted relationship fundraising techniques while the other uses a transactional approach. How would your perceptions of the two nonprofits differ?

4   What is meant by the term commitment? How might an understanding of this construct help an organization to achieve improvements in donor loyalty?

5   In what ways might a nonprofit seek to build up the levels of trust that donors have in the organisation?

REFERENCES

Bitran, G. and Mondschein, S. (1997) 'A Comparative Analysis of Decision Making Procedures in the Catalog Sales Industry', *European Management Journal*, 15(2): 105–116.

Burnett, K. (1992) *Relationship Fundraising*, White Lion Press, London.

Carpenter, P. (1995) 'Customer Lifetime Value: Do the Math', *Marketing Computers*, January: 18–19.

Harvey, J.W. and McCrohan, K.F. (1988) 'Fund-raising Costs - Societal Implications for Philanthropies and their Supporters', *Business and Society*, 27 (Spring): 15–22.

Jackson, D.R. (1992) 'In Quest of the Grail: Breaking the Barriers to Customer Valuation', *Direct Marketing*, March: 44–47.

Lindahl, W.E. and Winship, C. (1992) 'Predictive Models for Annual Fundraising and Major Gift Fundraising', *Nonprofit Management and Leadership*, 3(1): 43–64.

McKinnon, H. (1999) *Hidden Gold*, Bonus Books, Chicago, IL.

Magson, N. (2002) 'Database Fundraising', *Customer Relationship Management*, September/October: 111–117.

Peppers, D. and Rogers, M. (1995) 'A New Marketing Paradigm: Share of Customer Not Market Share', *Managing Service Quality*, 5(3): 48–51.

Raphel, M. and Considine, R. (1981) *The Great Brain Robbery*, Business Tips Publications, New York.

Reichheld, F.F. and Sasser, W.E. (1990) 'Zero Defections: Quality Comes to Services', *Harvard Business Review*, September/October: 105–111.

Sargeant, A. (1998) 'Donor Lifetime Value: An Empirical Analysis', *Journal of Nonprofit and Voluntary Sector Marketing*, 3(4): 283–297.

Sargeant, A. and MacKenzie, J. (1999) *A Lifetime of Giving*, Charities Aid Foundation, West Malling, Kent.

Sargeant, A. and Jay, E. (2004) *Building Donor Loyalty: A Fundraisers Guide to Increasing Lifetime Value*, Jossey Bass, San Francisco, CA.

Squires, C. (1994) 'Picking the Right Gift to Ask For: Donor Renewal and Upgrading', *Fund Raising Management*, 25(5): 37.

Stone, M., Woodcock, N. and Wilson, M. (1996) 'Managing the Change from Marketing Planning to Customer Relationship Management', *Long Range Planning*, 29(5): 675–683.

Chapter 8

Major gift fundraising

OBJECTIVES

By the end of this chapter you should be able to:

■ Describe the extant research into major giving and the motives of major givers.

■ Explain the process of major donor recruitment and development.

■ Understand the concept of stewardship.

■ Provide an overview of the key tools and techniques used in major gift fundraising.

■ Discuss donor recognition and events management as part of major gift fundraising.

INTRODUCTION

Major donors are individuals who make sizeable personal contributions. Major gifts are, broadly speaking, those that are large relative to the majority of the gifts the organisation receives. The definition of a major giver thus varies from one organisation to another, and the donor will also have their own perspective on what constitutes a significant gift for them personally at any time.

The Institute of Fundraising defines a major donor as one who has:

> The potential to make or procure a gift which would have a significant impact on the work being conducted, who is approached and/or cultivated using personal development fundraising techniques for the mutual benefit of the organisation and the donor. The gift may be of capital, revenue, time, or influence.
>
> (IOF Major Donor and Major Donor Fundraising Code of Practice)

In the USA it is now not unusual for 90 per cent or more of the money a nonprofit raises from individuals to come from just 10 per cent of their donors. In the UK, according to the Institute of Philanthropy, 6 per cent of the population contributes 60 per cent of all monies donated to charities.

Unlike companies and foundations, major donors are not regulated by time frames, restrictive giving policies or committee judgements. They can give as much as they wish, with few or no bureaucratic strings attached. As major donors are likely to have extensive contacts in business, political or social circles, they can themselves be vital sources of new prospects, and can be the most valuable of ambassadors. Major donor support can also have drawbacks – they may exert excessive influence if they are a major giver and are also a member of the board of directors, for example, and may wish to influence programming in a way that compromises the mission of the organisation.

The solicitation of major gifts is a very different process to that involved in the solicitation of small donations:

- it evolves over a lengthy period of time as the relationship with the prospect is cultivated;
- it involves face-to-face solicitation by peers who are often volunteers;
- throughout the process the donor is often encouraged to become involved personally in the work and running of the organisation;
- major givers often require some form of acknowledgement or reward for their gift;
- major gifts may be paid immediately or pledged over time.

Major gifts may also come in the form of deferred or planned gifts and legacy bequests. This form of major giving is dealt with in Chapter 9.

In this chapter we will summarize the research that has been undertaken on the motivations that drive major giving and on what major givers look like. We will explain how the process works and the main techniques that are used in major gift solicitation and will discuss some of the concepts and experiences that lie behind this area of fundraising.

CHARACTERISTICS OF MAJOR GIVERS

Major donors are likely to be people with a strong interest in and good knowledge of the charitable organisation, to have given in the past and to have a personal contact within the organisation at some level. 'They run the spectrum from a person who wants all the fame that money can buy to an anonymous donor' (Fredricks 2001).

Practitioner guides recommend that when identifying and rating major gift prospects the three main criteria should be:

1   they have the financial means to make a major gift
2   they have a high degree of attachment to your institution
3   they have a high degree of affinity with your institution (Wylie and Lawson 2006).

Major donors often have assets in mixed forms such as stocks and shares, property, retirement funds, insurance policies and savings. They are generally protective of these assets and cautious about giving them away. Some view the gift process as an investment and expect a return. They may involve solicitors and accountants in the process of giving, which can take years. Many support a range of nonprofits, and most will expect a significant level of communication and feedback from a chosen cause.

Individuals with major gift potential are likely to demonstrate some of the following factors: over 55 years of age, male, married, conservative, religious, approaching retirement, have a history of giving and involvement, hold mixed assets, a family foundation, a business and/or inherited wealth (Williams 1991).

Research studies conducted by the Boston College Social Welfare Institute (Schervish and Havens 1995) have examined the connections between giving and wealth in the USA. One important contribution of the analysis was to correct the popular misconception that lower income USA households were relatively more generous than upper income households. The research found that in fact lower and upper income households were equally generous, While very high income households were markedly more generous. Among the wealthy:

> virtually all the rich are contributors, they donate very large amounts to charity, and they give greater proportions of their income to charity than the poor or affluent. Fundraisers generally do not need to turn the rich into donors, usually that has already occurred.
>
> (Schervish 1993:87)

MOTIVES OF MAJOR GIVERS

It is generally accepted that the decision-making process associated with major gifts is far more complex than that entailed with the making of a small gift in response to a direct mail piece or telephone fundraising call. Major gifts are 'Stop and Think' gifts (Sturtevant 1996) and involve a complex and lengthy process. As the gift decision grows in magnitude the donor will require a stronger set of motives for giving. There are likely to be more influences and inputs into the gift decision, and while the decision is emotional the donor is more likely to express decision-making parameters in rational terms.

> A major gift is not something that donors do on a whim or a lark, or on the spur of the moment. ... They do not flow into an organisation at the rate of one a week, and in all likelihood they do not materialize without a great deal of time, talent or effort attached.
>
> (Fredricks 2001:23)

Until recently, large-scale research among major donors was limited, despite their relative importance. This area is now beginning to receive increased attention from nonprofit academics and researchers engaging in studies to establish the needs, motivations and strategies of major givers.

In a study of a sample of wealthy philanthropists, Teresa Odendahl (1990) used four broad philanthropic groupings in explaining key characteristics of major givers. The first of these, 'Dynasty and Philanthropy', concerns those families that maintain a prominent position in a community for a long period of time, with capital being accumulated, preserved and transmitted down several generations.

'Lady Bountiful' is used to describe wealthy female major givers. Odendahl (1990:100) explains that 'sexism is as prevalent among the rich as elsewhere in society' and that the wealthy women she interviewed tended to be active volunteers throughout life, having assumed the responsibility for the family's philanthropy alongside childrearing, household management and social and cultural activities. 'First Generation Man' is the term appended to elite givers who are self-made, the newly rich who have made money through the high-technology industries, manufacturing, property, oil or retail. These givers tend to take philanthropy seriously when their businesses are stable and mature and they feel less pressure to put profits back into the company, and therefore more comfortable about giving to charity. Odendahl's final category is 'Elite Jewish Givers'. While the history of Jewish charity in the USA parallels that of Protestant giving to a great extent, Jewish philanthropy is characterized particularly by the sympathy and kinship exhibited with Jews around the world, and the willingness to support them in times of hardship. The tradition of giving is an important aspect of the community life, ethnicity and religion for Jews of all classes, and hence wealthy Jewish people contribute to and lead nonprofit enterprises across the USA.

The motives that lie behind major giving by the wealthy have also been investigated at length by the Boston College Social Welfare Institute:

> What motivates the wealthy is very much what motivates someone at any point along the economic spectrum. Identify any motive that might inspire concern – from heartfelt empathy to self-promotion, from religious obligation to business networking, from passion to prestige, from political philosophy to tax incentives – and some millionaires will make it the cornerstone of their giving.
>
> (Schervish 1997:70)

Those who hold great wealth and direct it to social purposes also invariably want to shape rather than just support a charitable cause. This tendency is summarized by labelling wealthy big givers 'hyperagents' – people capable of establishing the institutional framework in which they and others live. This research has also looked at the spiritual foundations of giving by the wealthy, and at the associations and identifications which motivate giving by this group. It was found that the level of contribution depends on the frequency and intensity of participation, volunteering and being asked to contribute, that larger gifts are generated from those already making substantial gifts, and that, generally, charitable giving among the wealthy derives from the forging of associational and psychological connections between donors and recipients (Ostrander and Schervish 1990).

> Donors contribute the bulk of their charitable dollars to causes from whose services the donors directly benefit. It is not by coincidence that schools, health organisations and (especially) churches attract so much giving. It is here that donors, because they are also recipients, most identify with the individuals whose needs are being met by the contributions.
>
> (Schervish 1993:87)

Hyperagency does not mean that all wealthy major givers achieve major innovative philanthropic interventions, but they are more likely to than givers in general. Some become proactive producers of philanthropy rather than passive supporters of existing projects or causes – when a wealthy contributor provides a sizeable enough gift the whole agenda of a nonprofit may be changed and the giver can become the director or architect of the work.

As well as the inclination to make a difference in a significant way, the top wealth holders also have the material wherewithal and the tax incentives to do so. In recent years larger and larger numbers of households have achieved the resources for modest to substantial philanthropic giving:

> It is the first time in history that large proportions of a population can materially afford to consider charitable giving as a principal component of their financial strategy and moral agency.
>
> (Schervish 1997:67)

Schervish and Havens (2001/2) and Shervish (2005) put forward a number of what they refer to as 'supply-side vectors' in motivating major giving:

■ *Happiness* As more individuals come to recognize at an earlier stage in their life cycle that their financial resources now exceed their material needs and those of their families, they begin to focus more 'on how to allocate their excess wealth for the care of others in a way that brings deep satisfaction' (Schervish 2005:17–18). In essence, individuals give because it makes them feel good to do so.

- *Financial security* Not surprisingly, perceptions of financial security were also found to influence giving, but interestingly it appears that both objective and subjective wealth drive behaviour.
- *Identification* The authors define this as a wish to help others like themselves, their spouse, their parents, their siblings or their children.

> The disposition of identification contrasts sharply with that of altruism to the extent the latter term connotes the prominence of selflessness. Our research has consistently revealed that wealth holders like all others who make charitable gifts, regard their philanthropy as an engagement rather than an absence of self.
>
> (Schervish 2005:18)

- *Gratitude for blessing* Some donors desire to give back and share their good fortune with others:

> Just as my fortune is not due entirely to my own merit, others' misfortune may not be entirely attributable to their own failure. This realization, it turns out, is a generative one. It forges identification between donor and recipient as the offspring of a common destiny. As such, those who recognize that they have been blessed with good fortune become more inclined to care for those who have been less blessed.
>
> (Schervish 2005:18)

- *Entrepreneurial disposition* Philanthropy can be an attractive outlet because it offers individuals a welcoming place in which to be creative, purposeful and effective producers of the world around them. Many donors are attracted to be a supporter because they perceive that an action has a higher probability of being undertaken because of them.
- *Philanthropy as financial morality for self and family* Donors can use philanthropy to eschew a more positive and productive financial morality. Through their giving they seek to explore the more profound aspects of financial care and frequently aim to teach these issues to their children.
- *Self-reflective discernment* Finally, Schervish (2005:35) argues that approaches based on guilt or dictated expectations are doomed to failure. Instead, he believes that significant gifts accrue where donors explore for themselves to seek 'the point of convergence where what needs to be done coincides with what they *want* to do'. The notion of self-reflective discernment does not neglect a sense of 'duty', it merely makes it self-discovered.

Other literature on the reasons for giving major gifts applies classic theories of motivation to fundraising (Williams 1991) and maps out motivations as: religious belief, guilt, recognition, self-preservation and fear, tax benefits, obligation and pressure, with other factors listed as: acceptance, altruism, appreciation, enlightened self-interest, approval, being asked, belief in the cause, community interest, competition, gratitude, immortality and sympathy. The practitioner literature also promotes involvement as a primary motivator for major giving.

There is a debate around the importance of tax incentives in the giving of major gifts. It is agreed that tax is important, especially with regard to the timing and the size of any gift. Practitioners appear to conclude that tax incentives are unlikely to 'spark' the giving of a gift, although they are important in enabling the donor to retain control of their money. As such, legal and financial advisers are seen as important players in the major gift scenario. Affluent people are accustomed to making financial decisions based on reason, so although the initial prompt to give

173

may be emotional, a nonprofit has to be prepared to provide a valid and fact-based rationale to affirm the initial emotional response (Goettler 1996).

> Major donors give because they are asked, they give to people, and they give to meet opportunities not to meet needs. They want to make an impact; they want to change the world.
>
> (Lawson 1998:18)

Prince and File have undertaken a long programme of research to establish a donor-centred framework that can be used in 'understanding the concerns, needs, interests and motivations of individual affluent donors' (Prince and File 1994). Their work on the 'seven faces framework' categorizes and segments wealthy donors into seven motivational philanthropic types:

1   *The communitarians*   This is the largest segment (26 per cent). Communitarians give because 'it makes sense to do so ... they believe in active philanthropy as they help their own communities prosper by supporting local charities'.
2   *The devout*   (21 per cent) This group is motivated to give for religious reasons, and channel almost all of their giving to religious organisations.
3   *The investor*   (15 per cent) Investors organize their giving to take advantage of tax and estate benefits. They are most likely to support 'umbrella' nonprofits and donate to a wide range of causes.
4   *The socialite*   (11 per cent) Members of local social networks who 'find social functions benefiting nonprofits an especially appealing way to help make a better world and have a good time doing it' (Prince and File 1994). They tend to support the arts, education and religious groups.
5   *The altruist*   (9 per cent) 'Altruists embody the perception of the selfless donor – the donor who gives out of generosity and empathy to urgent causes and often modestly wishes to remain anonymous' (Prince and File 1994). Altruists tend to give to social causes and tend not to want active roles in the groups they support.
6   *The repayer*   (10.2 per cent) 'A typical Repayer has personally benefited from some institution ... and now supports that institution from a feeling of loyalty or obligation' (Prince and File 1994).
7   *The dynast*   (8 per cent) Dynasts do good because it is a family tradition. Giving is something their family always stood for, and they believe it is expected of them to support nonprofits. Dynasts support a wide range of nonprofits, often selecting those that are not 'mainstream'.

These groupings can be used by practitioners in categorising donors and prospects, in preparing solicitation presentations, preparing responses to objections and questions that donors might have, and in planning recognition vehicles.

MAJOR DONOR RECRUITMENT

Major donor fundraisers use three key routes to the research, sourcing and development of prospects. The first is to draw prospects from among a nonprofit's existing supporter base, the argument being that many major donors will begin their association with the cause through lower value giving. The second approach (often used simultaneously) also identifies 'colder' prospects using a variety of research sources including prospecting agencies and online data research tools. Peer networks, including the address book of board members remains the third key source of potential contacts.

Major giver prospecting from the existing donor base

The theory behind this approach is that individual donors can be brought up through the ranks:

> The donor first gives through a small annual gift. Over time and based on capability, the donor is moved upward in gift size and type. Using this model, the development officer begins with the annual gift programme and later introduces major and planned gift opportunities. It is assumed that major and planned gift prospects will thus emerge from the annual fund.
>
> (Dean 1996:26)

This is often illustrated as a donor pyramid or ladder as shown in Figure 8.1.

Major gifts can appear at any stage, but are most likely to be generated once the donor is cultivated and approached through face-to-face personal methods rather than through direct mail or the telephone. In this system potential major givers are 'prospected' from the main donor file. Individuals who have made larger than average gifts or where a high degree of affluence is suspected will be drawn from the database to be researched, the theory being that some of these donors may have the financial capacity to make substantial gifts after appropriate involvement and cultivation:

> A person may give ten times the amount they give through the mail if they're asked face to face. Gifts through the mail are impulse gifts – when asked in person the donor must give a major gift more serious consideration. You have potential major donors hiding on your donor base.
>
> (Reuther 1998:46)

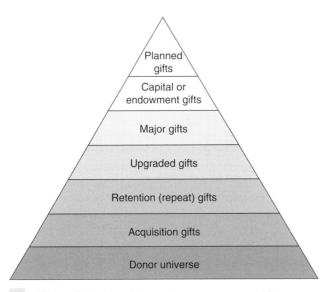

Figure 8.1 *The US donor development pyramid*

Prospect research

Prospect research began as a profession in the 1980s. It is widely understood that prospect research plays a critical part (which can be up to 80 per cent) in the work involved in securing a major gift. Many charities now employ specialists to carry out this work either as staff members or consultants.

Prospect research is often aided by the use of research agencies and specialist software providers that hold data on wealth, assets, family, business and community connections and on previous giving. Researchers must be expert in information management as well as information sourcing and especially aware of the obligations and restrictions data protection legislation places on fundraisers.

Major giver prospecting through peer contacts

This method of 'discovering' prospects starts from the premise that personal and peer contact with the prospect is all-important. Fundraisers will therefore require board members to provide details of qualified individual contacts through their own business and social networks, and will ask them to volunteer to make initial approaches to these contacts to introduce the cause and the appeal.

Major gift fundraising is unique in the degree to which the involvement of senior staff, trustees and high-level volunteers is required at every stage of the process. The trustees and the CEO are key in researching and providing links to high-level prospects, and in the solicitation and cultivation of their peers as both donors and volunteers. The creation of a major gift committee is widely recommended where committee members agree to represent the charity to the community, contribute a personal leadership gift and work to provide and cultivate potential major donor contacts. Such a committee may also be responsible for identifying and researching projects for big gift funding:

> Studies show that strong, committed, informed boards that are involved in resource building make for financially healthy and respected organisations. Weak, inactive boards make for financially troubled and short-lived organisations.
>
> (Maude 1997:24)

Likewise, existing donors are used as advocates in major giving campaigns in recommending and introducing potentially wealthy friends and colleagues.

The recruitment process

The successful recruitment of major donors through any of the above routes requires access (you must know them personally or at least know someone who can make the introduction), belief (the prospect must believe in the organisation's work) and ability (the financial ability to make the gift) (Reuther 1998).

The many practitioner texts available emphasize the need for a long period of research and cultivation prior to the 'ask' being made. Kotler and Scheff (1997) recommend a six-point plan for successful solicitation of major gifts: *Discover and qualify, Plan, Involve, Ask, Negotiate and close and Thank and plan.* Fundraisers, through desk research, initially identify a sufficiently wealthy individual who could conceivably have a strong interest in the organisation.

They identify others who could supply information and arrange an introduction. They cultivate the person's interest in the organisation without requesting a gift and evaluate his or her capacity for making a large gift. Eventually they make the 'ask'. Upon receiving a gift they

> ### PETERBOROUGH CATHEDRAL
>
> In the mid-1990s the cathedral administration recognized the need for major renovation work that would cost the organisation £7.3 million to accomplish. To bring in the funds, teams of volunteer fundraisers were established, each with their own speciality, ranging from business, music and local authorities to farming, parishes and major gifts/grants. The appeal treasurer recognized the need to bring in several large donations of over £100,000 if the target was ultimately to be met and sought to leverage the contacts of the volunteers and other friends of the cathedral to identify individuals with the ability and interest to make contributions at this level. Wherever possible the fundraising 'ask' was made by individuals who had themselves contributed to the restoration work so that they could have the highest possible credibility when approaching others. Ultimately £1.3 million was raised from private benefactors with a further £100,000 pledged in legacy gifts. The balance was funded by grants from government, business and grant-making trusts.

express appreciation and lay the groundwork for establishing further involvement. Throughout the process approaches are made on a personal level through face-to-face contact.

In the early 1960s, G.T. 'Buck' Smith developed a five-step process that has been described as the 'secret to securing major gifts': *Identification, Information, Interest, Involvement* and *Investment*. These steps should comprise a continuing cycle seeking to nurture and develop those people who are committed to the nonprofit's mission. This has become known as the 'cultivation cycle' or 'moves management theory', and is still taught today as the route through which an individual can be 'moved' through a cycle until the relationship is developed to the point of investment (Smith 1997). The five 'I's are actually the four 'R's – *Research, Romance, Request and Recognition* – according to Ernest Wood (1997) and the process parallels courtship and marriage.

MAJOR DONOR RETENTION AND DEVELOPMENT

While there is a vast array of practical 'how-to' guidance available on locating major donor prospects and on soliciting the first major gift, there is relatively little detailed information available on how to renew and develop major donors over time. Once a significant gift has been made it is recommended that an intensive and lengthy programme of thanking and recognition (if required by the donor) is undertaken. The donor then becomes part of the organisation's stewardship programme.

Stewardship is a key concept – the idea that, as best practice, fundraisers should become responsible guardians of donor assets that are held on trust for the public good. Stewardship is considered a guiding principle of philanthropic fundraising:

> The means by which an institution exercises ethical accountability in the use of contributed resources and the philosophy and means by which a donor exercises responsibility in the voluntary use of resources.
>
> (Tempel 2001:34)

As such stewardship focuses primarily on concern and respect for the needs and rights of those who give and of those who receive – the beneficiaries of the charity organisation. The ultimate extension of stewardship would be a scenario whereby a fundraiser would be employed by donors rather than by nonprofits.

Stemming from Judeo-Christian tradition (Jeavons 1997), stewardship now implies a deep burden of trust, responsibility and accountability for the proper management and administration of the resources under the steward's care. Within the context of contemporary nonprofit governance and management, the role of steward and its corresponding obligation of stewardship are used to apply to any person in a position to manage or account for financial resources: trustees, the CEO, the finance director and fundraising staff.

Fundraising stewardship incorporates acknowledgement, recognition and gift management and is closely bound with ethical philanthropy practices: 'Stewardship is trust, responsibility, liability, accountability, integrity, faith and guardianship' (Conway 1997: 12). Planned and major giving sits particularly within this construct of stewardship, with estate and financial planning seen as an opportunity to service the needs of the donor and facilitate their philanthropy, requiring the nonprofit to look towards the longer term and take an active role in the stewardship of the assets entrusted to them. Reports on asset management and investment performance are fed back to the donor as stewardship reports, increasing the confidence of the donor in the investment advice of the nonprofit/the nonprofit's financial representatives.

> Major gift stewardship is the continuous personal interaction and information exchange that you and others from your organisation have with your donors. It paves the way for your donors to make repeat larger gifts. It is a form of cultivation.
>
> (Fredricks 2001:23)

In practical terms, stewardship of major givers could include the provision of regular feedback on how the gift has been used and on the effect it has had, a regular programme of communications such as annual reports and newsletters, plus invitations to participate in a range of events both large scale and private. The solicitation, cultivation, development and stewardship of major donors works as a cycle, as shown in Figure 8.2.

TOOLS AND TECHNIQUES

Capital campaigns

Capital campaigns can be considered a subset of major gift fundraising. While it is not necessary to conduct a capital campaign to solicit major gifts the process of making the case for major giving tends to reveal special requirements and discrete needs that can be used to focus the fundraising effort and to provide indications of tangible outcomes for prospective donors. Institutions embark on a capital or endowment effort when they have a significant one-time need. These campaigns are intense, carefully organized and highly structured efforts to raise a large and specific amount of money over a finite period of time (typically three or five years). External consultants are often used to provide advice, and extra staff are often drafted in at every level. Various types of capital appeal are mounted:

- The '*Bricks and mortar*' campaign – for new construction (or major renovation) of buildings or major new equipment purchases.
- The '*Endowment*' campaign – where funds are raised to add to the organisation's capital investment fund from which income is earned to support programmes.
- The '*Combined*' campaign – where the campaign is targeted to raise funds for a mixture of capital and endowment needs. Current running costs may also be part of this sort of campaign.

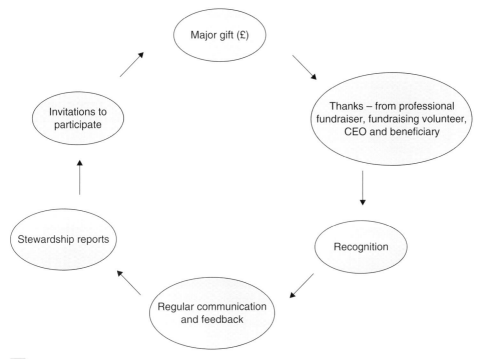

Figure 8.2 *Stewardship and major donor development cycle*

■ The '*Project*' or '*Programme*' campaign – where funds are to be raised to fund a specific project or area of programme activity that is packaged using a capital campaign model and where a tangible and specific outcome can be cited.

Capital campaigns typically involve a volunteer campaign chair and committee, who work through the operational side of the campaign and develop recognition and naming opportunities. Essentially the solicitation process is identical to that employed in all major gift work, with the difference being that in a capital campaign a specific 'product' can be offered to the potential donor. The specific, often visually demonstrable nature of the need and the time-limited nature of the campaign lend themselves to PR and events work.

Campaign structure and the use of volunteers

Major gift campaigns usually involve the setting up of a formal structure of campaign committees and subcommittees. These voluntary bodies serve to direct and steer the campaign, and, importantly, also undertake the bulk of the actual fundraising effort. Fundraising staff primarily service these committees, train and equip the volunteers and facilitate the running, coordination and monitoring of the campaign. Committee members are also expected to be 'lead givers' themselves. Exhibit 8.1 details the role and responsibilities of major gift campaign chairs, honorary chairs and committee members.

Volunteers are thus used extensively in major gift fundraising, forming the main fundraising 'workforce', and delivering a high proportion of the income goal personally. There has been some debate in the USA about the role of volunteers in major gift fundraising and the degree to

EXHIBIT 8.1 KEY ROLES AND RESPONSIBILITIES OF COMMITTEE MEMBERS

Campaign chair

Primary role
To lead the fundraising effort

Responsibilities

- Identify and recruit volunteers.
- Hold regular committee meetings to steer and review the campaign as it progresses.
- Maintain contact with committee members and provide them with help and encouragement.
- Assist in identifying potential donors.
- Speak on behalf of the campaign.
- Host campaign events.
- Solicit key lead gifts.
- Make a generous personal gift

Honorary co-chair

Primary role
To raise the public profile of the campaign

Responsibilities

- Facilitate the use of your name and photo in campaign promotional materials.
- Attend events.
- Assist in identifying volunteers and prospects.
- Make a generous personal gift.

Committee member

Primary role
To implement the campaign plan

Responsibilities

- Personally solicit gifts as per the campaign plan.
- Help plan solicitation strategies.
- Attend events.
- Make a generous personal gift.

which campaigns can succeed without them. Some of the largest educational institutions in the USA are now extending their staff rather than relying on volunteers. However, volunteers are still widely thought to be essential to a successful campaign because:

- Organisations usually do not have sufficient staff to undertake face-to-face solicitation with a long list of prospects.
- The enthusiasm and motivation of a dedicated 'volunteer salesforce' is supremely effective.
- Fundraising staff do not usually have the right sort of contacts or background to solicit gifts from prospective major donors.
- When staff solicit gifts the prospect may feel that they are merely raising income to cover their own salaries rather than being able to inspire the giving of a gift to forward the mission of the organisation.

Volunteers suitable for major gift campaign work are generally found amongst the 'inner circle' of an organisation and are already committed to the work the organisation undertakes. As such volunteers may be found from amongst current trustees and board members, former trustees and board members, programme volunteers, donors and service users. Volunteers are recruited best by their peers and, as with gift solicitation, they need to be motivated by the campaign vision and by the personal benefit that will accrue to them if they agree to help.

Once a volunteer has agreed to join the campaign committee he or she must receive training to increase their levels of knowledge about the campaign and the work of the organisation. Training should be prolonged, both formal and informal, with the aim of enabling the volunteer to speak confidently and accurately about the campaign. In many cases professional training agencies are employed at this stage to complement staff efforts, and a full 'tool kit' of information, solicitation and briefing materials are provided.

The case for support

The case for support document is a fundamental tool in major gift solicitation. At base, the case for support for major gift fundraising will rest on the mission statement formulated for the

CHILDREN'S HOSPITAL BOSTON

In 2000 the Children's Hospital saw big increases in its large donations, increasing the number of donors who gave between $100,000 and $500,000 from 31 to 46. In the $10,000 to $20,000 range numbers jumped from 95 to 157. The organisation attributes its success to specialization, and trains nine senior major gift officers to become experts on two to five departments by shadowing nurses, doctors and researchers on the job. One major gift officer, for example, covers genetics, neurology and orthopaedics.

The hospital has also established Philanthropic Leadership Councils, which bring together donors to raise funds for specific medical divisions of the hospital. By 2001 the hospital had established three such councils, comprising 10–25 members, each of whom has provided the hospital with $25,000 or more. Council members are able to bring in friends for tours and events or presentations by senior medical staff. The oldest of the three councils mails a biannual newsletter to 20,000 current and prospective donors and holds an annual Valentine's Day Dinner to recruit new donors.

organisation in the early stages of the fundraising planning process. However, the justification of why an organisation is deserving of major gift support requires a special treatment, especially in terms of an articulation of the benefits accruing to the donor, and of the impact a big gift might have on the community. A clear vision of the future is essential in major gift fundraising as donors are asked to consider the 'big picture' and will need to be inspired to invest significantly in the cause. 'People give to a vision rather than a need' (Matheny1994:12).

A draft case for support should be tested among a sample of potential major givers (this process in itself can be a useful donor cultivation tool). It should also be fully endorsed by senior staff, trustees, and all those staff and volunteers who will take part in solicitation and cultivation. Asking for input at this stage can increase the sense of ownership in a campaign and make these individuals more effective as representatives. Typically the document would cover:

- For what purpose will funds raised from major gifts be used?
- What need does this meet?
- What happens if this need is not met?
- What benefits result from meeting this need?
- Why is this organisation the best one to do this?
- Why should the prospective donor care?
- How does the donor benefit?

The case should be expressed throughout from the perspective of the donor rather than the organisation:

> The solicitor should not say 'If you give us this money for a minority scholarship, we can attract more high-quality African-American and Hispanic applicants'. Rather the benefit should be stated in the donor's terms saying: 'If you give us money for a minority scholarship, you can feel that you are helping your alma mater increase the richness of the educational experience it can give future students like you.'
>
> (Kotler and Andreasen 1996:260)

The gift range chart

Major gift campaign fundraisers use gift range charts and tables of gift levels extensively in campaign planning and monitoring. These are statistical representations of patterns of giving generated through past experience of major giving campaigns and guide the fundraiser in terms of the numbers of gifts required of particular £/$ levels if the campaign target is to be reached. An example is provided in Table 8.1. In this case the campaign target has been set at $100,000.

To prepare a gift range chart the following rules are applied:

1 the first two gifts of the campaign are set to equal 10 per cent of the goal (i.e. 5 per cent each);
2 the next four gifts are set to provide a further 10 per cent of the goal.

The remainder of the chart will be developed flexibly taking account of the past experience of the nonprofit in running such campaigns. The figures given in the example are not untypical and serve to illustrate that it would generally be expected that 60 per cent of the total would be provided by 10 per cent of the donors and that 80 per cent of the goal would be provided by 20 per cent of the donors. This pattern of performance is very common.

Table 8.1 *Gift range chart*

Gift Number ($)	Number of gifts	Cumulative number of gifts	Prospects required	Cumulative number of prospects	Per range ($)	Cumulative ($)
5,000	2	2	10 (5:1)	10	10,000	10,000
2,500	4	6	20 (5:1)	30	10,000	20,000
1,000	10	16	40 (4:1)	70	10,000	30,000
750	20	36	80 (4:1)	150	15,000	45,000
500	30	66	120 (4:1)	270	15,000	60,000
		10 per cent of donors			60 per cent of goal	
300	67	133	201 (3:1)	471	20,100	80,100
		20 per cent of donors			80 per cent of goal	
Under $300 average gift ($60)	333	466	666 (2:1)	1,137	19,900	100,000
		100 per cent of donors			100 per cent of goal	

When developing the gift range chart it should be noted that the ratio of prospects to gifts tends to fall as one moves down the pyramid. It is typically necessary to identify five prospects to give at the highest level, to ultimately acquire one donor. At lower ends of the pyramid it will typically be necessary to name only two prospects to provide a gift of $60 for each eventual donation.

Of course this example is only fictional and in reality the sums involved when addressing major donors will be substantially higher, but it serves to illustrate how the tool is utilized in practice.

The construction of a gift range chart should allow the fundraiser to ensure that an adequate number of qualified prospects are available to meet the goal and that the overall financial goal is realistic. One of the most common causes of failure in major gift fundraising is the lack of adequate prospects.

The gift range chart is used throughout a campaign in monitoring and reporting progress and problems, and should be formally revized at intervals as prospects are solicited and actual results obtained.

Solicitation techniques

Practitioner texts offer a huge amount of practical advice on how to handle the solicitation (the 'ask') itself at a face-to-face meeting. This includes tips on listening and questioning skills, sample solicitation scenarios and scripts, advice on body language and on how to handle objections (Irwin-Wells 2002; Williams 1991). Fundraisers are encouraged to think of every solicitation as a separate campaign, with a distinct financial goal, set of strategies and timeline.

The case for support is used as the basis for the 'ask'. The Fund Raising School at the Indiana Center on Philanthropy (Seiler 2000) recommends that the case is made in a solicitation by:

- stating the need
- documenting the need you are meeting
- proposing strategies and tasks
- identifying who will benefit
- demonstrating organisational competency
- specifying the resources required
- stating how gifts can be made
- communicating the benefits of making a gift.

The most effective 'askers' or advocates are volunteers who have a peer relationship with the prospect (i.e. they are of a similar economic status and move in the same social circles) as this tends to guarantee that the meeting takes place against a background of mutual respect. Ideally both parties should have similar levels of interest in and engagement with the fundraising organisation, and the volunteer will himself or herself have made a significant contribution in support of the campaign. 'They should not be put in the position of asking someone to do something they have not already done' (Irwin-Wells 2002).

If a high-level volunteer is not available a 'proportional giver/volunteer' can be employed, i.e. someone who would still engender mutual respect in the prospect but who may not be as closely matched in terms of economic or social status. In this case the solicitor will have himself or herself given a gift which is significant to them personally, but which may be much lower than that which is being asked of the prospect. The 'worst case' option is that a staff member is employed to make the ask. In this case the likelihood of success, and any amount donated, is likely to be much lower.

In every case the solicitation is unlikely to succeed if the person charged with making the ask is unknown to the prospect. Ideally they should be familiar with each other as friends or colleagues, but at the very least the 'asker' should have been introduced by someone known to the prospect, and to have been involved in cultivating a relationship with the prospect beforehand. Where the solicitor does not have a peer relationship with the prospect a team of two people should be involved in the solicitation process, such as a committee member and the development director, or the campaign chair and a committee member. 'Comfort, capacity and connections to the prospect are more important than job titles' (Irwin-Wells 2002).

DONOR RECOGNITION

While individuals offering small gifts in response to direct mail or telephone approaches are unlikely to expect a high level of recognition for their support, and often insist that the whole of their gift should go direct to the programmes they are supporting, people giving significant gifts are more likely to expect that this will be marked, and that they will receive something in return for their gift.

In theory the potential recognition need of a donor should be discussed as part of the donor cultivation process. By the time a gift is pledged the solicitor should have a good idea of what level and type of recognition might be appropriate. Recognition of the biggest gifts can involve the naming of buildings or projects, While devices such as framed certificates, citations in publications and reports, and publicity through press announcements are also used. Special events may be appropriate either in recognition of a particularly significant contribution or of a group of contributors. Donor recognition events, societies and activities tend to focus on exclusivity and privileged access, whether to an event, to information and feedback or to senior staff. Table 8.2 provides some examples of four donor recognition clubs.

Table 8.2 Donor recognition clubs

Environmental Health Foundation of Canada	New York General Hospital Foundation	Shriners Hospitals For Children	Luther College
Patron – Gift of $5,000 or more	*Cornerstone Society*: Friends who have donated a total of $250–$9,999 to the Foundation – receive a certificate recognizing their support, together with hospital publications	*The Gold Book Society* recognizes seven levels of giving from $2,000 to $25,000 and represents these in the form of one to seven stars. Each donor may progress through all the awards, each of which attract distinctive statues made from materials such as brass, lucite and walnut	*The President's Council* honours donors giving personal gifts of $1,000 or more annually
Benefactor – Gift of $2,500 to $4,999			*President's Executive Cabinet*: Gifts of $50,000 or more
Advocate – Gift of $1,000 to $2,499	*Chairman's Circle*: Membership offered to those making a gift of $10,000 or more. Members' names are listed in the entry area and are honoured guests at the Chair's annual luncheon		**President's Associates: $25,000 to $49,999**
Supporter – Gift of $100 to $999		*Five-star, six-star and seven-star* donors are further honoured in their local Schriners Hospital on a 'Because We Care Givers' panel (and also at the Shriner Headquarters In Tampa)	*President's Academy: $10,000 to $24,999*
Donor – Gift of $25 to $99	*Heritage Circle*: Individuals committed to a future gift are invited to an annual luncheon to hear presentations from senior staff. They may also have their names placed in the main lobby and receive a regular newsletter	*Philanthropic Society* – honours contributions in excess of $250,000 and provides additional recognition in a further four levels, culminating in the Spectrum Gold Philanthropic Society award for gifts exceeding $2 million	*President's Society: $1,000 to $9,999*
			The President's Circle honours gifts at higher levels offering four different levels of status for gifts of over $100,000

You can call them something traditional, like The Founders Society, or a bit more unusual, like the Mount Everest Club. You can commemorate them with a token as simple as a bookmark or a tribute as elaborate as a black-tie dinner. However you operate them, donor recognition societies are a time-honored technique for thanking good friends and encouraging them to give even more generously.

(Ruda 1998:34)

EVENTS

Special events such as galas and benefits have been a popular fundraising aid for many years and are part of every major donor programme as means of recognition and cultivation.

Special events are notoriously labour-intensive and can lose money because of the high costs involved. The most effective events employ volunteers at every level of operation, and involve a group of 'leaders' in special event committees – prominent individuals with wide influence who will help generate funds through their prestige and encouragement of friends and colleagues to attend. Events are not commonly used as occasions to solicit funds directly, though they may well be the point at which agreement is reached that a further meeting can take place, and they are enormously valuable as networking opportunities when a prospective donor can be introduced to nonprofit programme and fundraising staff.

UK EXPERIENCE

The biggest gifts from wealthy people in the UK over the past fifty years have gone to universities, and to museums, galleries and cultural organisations such as the Royal Opera House. The NSPCC Full Stop campaign, launched in 2000, was the first time a welfare charity in the UK had attempted to secure the very major sums previously only attracted for higher education and the arts.

Big gifts have been sought in the UK so far mainly through capital campaigns, using the USA model. The Tate Gallery of Modern Art worked through a USA-style fundraising development committee structure using high-level volunteers to introduce and cultivate prospects.

The fundraising campaign was planned to follow the strategic model established by major fundraising campaigns in the USA, the big gift pyramid. The focus was to begin with the biggest gifts and the supporters closest to the gallery, moving through to smaller gifts and donors who are not quite so warm and culminating with appeals to the Tate membership and general visitors.

(Ballard 1999)

The main effort was expended in obtaining leadership gifts of £1 million and more. Gifts were solicited against named spaces in the gallery – many of the TGMA's individual galleries, education facilities and public spaces have been named after donors.

A case study from the British Museum Development Trust evidences the same influences and techniques (Marland 1999): 'Look to the USA as a model and use periodic big pushes with capital campaigns' and warns that most UK organisations need to undergo a change of culture before they are ready to fundraise successfully in this way.

In recent years many more 'major gift' staff and departments have been set up within UK fundraising organisations. While in many cases capital campaigns have been used, increasing numbers of UK charities are now introducing the technique as a permanent part of their fundraising effort.

In introducing major gift fundraising UK fundraisers have typically found certain areas particularly challenging:

Senior staff and trustee attitude

It is essential that trustees and senior staff 'buy in' to the concept of major giving, and that they take part in recommending contacts, making leadership contributions and actively 'making the ask' on occasion. Many UK trustees are extremely reluctant to make personal gifts, to surrender their address books and to ask directly for funding. In some cases this problem has been overcome by means of the creation of a separate high-level major gift committee, or a group of major gift advocates or representatives who are willing to take leadership roles in major gift fundraising initiatives.

Cultural and fiscal barriers

Differences between the USA and the UK in terms of tax incentives for individual giving and cultural behaviours are often cited as the main reason why major giving 'will not work' in the UK. The tax changes introduced by the UK government in 2000 went a long way towards invalidating the 'tax barrier' argument, as individuals can now give very tax-effectively both in terms of cash giving and especially in the donation of stocks and shares, effectively lowering the cost of donating. Higher rate tax givers can also now benefit as they can claim back some of the tax they have paid on donations.

There is no doubt that cultural differences are still a factor in the translation of USA practice into UK fundraising. However, those UK fundraising nonprofits implementing major gift fundraising are finding that the similarities far outweigh the differences and that the USA model can be used as an effective template in developing major giving in the UK individual donor marketplace.

The wealth profile of Britain has changed over the past twenty years, and there are now many more people who have attained great wealth. These newly rich individuals are making gifts, sometimes in millions or tens of millions. A new intermediate group of prospects who are not 'rich' but have significantly greater means than the majority is also evident. Like the rich, this new affluent group can be targeted to give large sums if they are sufficiently motivated, which is most likely to be through major giving or planned giving approaches.

SUMMARY

In this chapter we have summarized the research that is currently available on how and why individuals make major gifts to charity, and what is known about the key motives behind the giving of large gifts.

We have also worked through the major gift fundraising process to see how donors are recruited and developed, and to look at some of the main tools and techniques that have been developed to help in this form of fundraising. It is clear that major gift fundraising requires a very different approach and that fundraisers engaging in this process are required to think and work in a way that contrasts dramatically with the practices and techniques used, for example, in direct mail fundraising.

Major donor fundraising is a key route in the USA and is growing rapidly in the UK. As we have seen, the concept of stewardship is all-important as a theory and ethical underpinning in major gift fundraising.

DISCUSSION QUESTIONS

1   In your role as head of fundraising at a medium-sized UK charity, prepare a report for your CEO arguing the case for the introduction of major giving techniques to run alongside existing direct mail fundraising.
2   Draft a template to be used in the gathering of information about major giving prospects. What information would be most important?
3   Draft a gift range chart for a capital campaign where the target is £500,000 over three years.
4   Using your own organisation as an example (or one that you know well), outline the concept of stewardship and how it fits with your current practice.

REFERENCES

Ballard, F. (1999), 'The Balance of and Difference between Revenue and Capital Campaigns', Presentation at Fundraising for Museums, the Arts and Heritage, Henry Stewart Conferences, June.

Conway, D. (1997) 'Interview with Henry Rosso on Stewardship and Fundraising', *New Directions for Philanthropic Fundraising*, Fall: 11–22.

Dean, J. (1996) 'The Key to Major Gifts: Cooperative Relationships', *Fund Raising Management*, April: 26.

Fredricks, L. (2001) *Developing Major Gifts*, Aspen Publications, New York.

Goettler, R.H. (1996) 'Announcing the "Four Ws" of Major Gift Solicitation', *Fund Raising Management*, April: 40.

Institute of Fundraising (IOF), Major Donor and Major Donor Fundraising Code of Practice, http://www.institute-of-fundraising.org.uk/

Irwin-Wells, S. (2002) *Planning and Implementing Your Major Gifts Campaign*, Jossey-Bass, New York.

Jeavons, T.H. (1997) 'Stewards for Whom? Problems with Stewardship as a Model for Fundraising', *New Directions for Philanthropic Fundraising*, 17 (Fall): 35–42.

Kotler, P. and Andreasen, A. (1996) *Strategic Marketing for Nonprofit Organisations*, 5th edn, Prentice Hall, Upper Saddle River, NJ.

Kotler, P. and Scheff, J. (1997) 'Standing Room Only: Strategies for Marketing the Performing Arts', Harvard Business School Press, Boston, MA.

Lawson, R. (1998) 'Involving the Board in Major Giving' *Fund Raising Management*, July: 18.

Marland, J. (1999) 'Developing Major Gift and Membership Programmemes for the British Museum', presentation at Fundraising for Museums, the Arts and Heritage, Henry Stewart Conferences, June.

Matheny, R.E. (1994) 'Major Gifts Solicitation Strategies', Council for the Advance and Support of Education, Washington DC.

Maude, M. (1997) 'Catapult Your Development Efforts with an Advisory Council', *Fund Raising Management*, May, 24.

Odendahl, T. (1990) 'Charity Begins at Home: Generosity and Self-Interest Among the Philanthropic Elite', Basic Books, New York.

Ostrander, S.A. and Schervish, P.G. (1990) 'Giving and Getting: Philanthropy as a Social Relation', in J. Van Til (ed.) *Critical Issues in American Philanthropy: Strengthening Theory and Practice*, Jossey Bass, San Francisco, CA.

Prince, R.A and File, K.M (1994) *The Seven Faces of Philanthropy: A New Approach to Cultivating Major Donors*, Jossey Bass, San Francisco, CA.

Reuther, V. (1998) 'Debunking the Myth of Bill Gates; Finding Major Donors', *Nonprofit World*, March/April: 46.

Ruda, T.L. (1998) 'Principles of Stewardship', in I. Bunin, J. McKown and S. Noden (eds) *Donor Relations: The Essential Guide to Stewardship Policies, Procedures and Protocol*, Jossey Bass, San Francisco, CA, pp. 27–35.

Schervish, P.G. (1993) 'Philanthropy as a Moral Identity of Caritas', in P.G. Schervish et al. *Taking Giving Seriously*, Indiana University Center on Philanthropy.

Schervish, P.G. (1997) 'Inclination, Obligation and Association: What We Know and What We Need to Learn about Donor Motivation', in D.F. Burlingame (ed.) *Critical Issues in Fund Raising*, Wiley, New York.

Schervish, P.G. (2005) 'Today's Wealth Holder and Tomorrow's Giving: The New Dynamics of Wealth and Philanthropy', *Journal of Gift Planning*, 9(3): 15–37.

Schervish, P.G. and Havens, J.J. (1995) 'Wherewithal and Beneficence: Charitable Giving by Income and Wealth', *New Directions for Philanthropic Fundraising*, 8 (Summer): 67–82.

Schervish, P.G. and Havens, J.J. (2001) 'The New Physics of Philanthropy: The Supply Side Vectors of Charitable Giving – Part 1: The Material Side of the Supply Side', *CASE International Journal of Educational Advancement*, 2(2): 95–113.

Schervish, P.G. and Havens, J.J. (2002) 'The New Physics of Philanthropy: The Supply Side Vectors of Charitable Giving – Part 2: The Spiritual Side of the Supply Side', *CASE International Journal of Educational Advancement*, 2(3): 221–241.

Seiler, T. (2000) *Developing Leadership for Major Gifts*, Fund Raising School, Indiana University Center on Philanthropy, IN.

Smith, G.T. (1997) 'CEOs and Trustees. The Key Forces in Securing Major Gifts', in *Developing Major Gifts, New Directions for Philanthropic Fundraising*, Indiana University Center on Philanthropy, IN/Jassey-Bass, New York, pp. 123–128.

Sturtevant, W.T. (1996) 'The Artful Journey: Seeking the Major Gift', *Fund Raising Management*, April: 32.

Tempel, E. (2001) 'The Ethics of Major Giving', in T. Seiler, *Developing Leadership for Major Gifts*, Fund Raising School, Indiana University Center on Philanthropy, IN.

Williams, M.J. (1991) *Big Gifts*, Fund Raising Institute, Taft Group.

Wood, E.W. (1997) 'The Four Rs of Major Gift Fundraising', in *Developing Major Gifts, New Directions for Philanthropic Fundraising*, Indiana University Center on Philanthropy, IN Jossey-Bass, New York.

Wylie, P. and Lawson, D. (2006) 'Why Bill Gates Might Not Be Your Best Prospect', in *Major Donors: Finding Big Gifts on Your Database and Online*, John Wiley, Hoboken, NJ.

Chapter 9

Legacies and in memoriam giving

With special thanks to Meg Abdy (Legacy Foresight), Emma Bockhop (Remember A Charity) and Kevin Kibble (Whitewater) for supplying text and other resources for this chapter.

OBJECTIVES

By the end of this chapter you should be able to:

■ Understand the significance of legacy income for nonprofits.
■ Describe trends in legacy giving.
■ Describe donor motivation for offering a legacy.
■ Understand the barriers to legacy giving.
■ Understand how legacy giving is currently promoted.
■ Develop a legacy promotion campaign.
■ Develop a strategy for In Mem and Tribute Fund giving.

INTRODUCTION

Legacy Foresight estimate that the UK legacy market is now worth £1.9 billion. Over the past 24 years, the market has grown eight-fold in 'money of the day' terms. Even after accounting for inflation, it has more than trebled. It currently provides around 13 per cent of overall voluntary income, although this is only an average figure and charities such as the RNLI and RSPCA regularly derive over two-thirds of their income from this source (Legacy Foresight 2008). A key characteristic of this income stream that makes it so critical for many organizations is the fact that legacies are usually 'unrestricted' so that they can use the money as they wish. Legacies also have the merit of being comparatively cheap to raise. The charities that comprise the legacy foresight consortium currently spend only around 2 per cent of their legacy income on this category of fundraising. The work of the consortium is described below:

LEGACY FORESIGHT

Legacy Foresight (www.legacyforesight.co.uk) is a research programme, funded by charity consortia. The programme aims to understand and predict the drivers of legacy income, both for individual charities and for the voluntary sector overall. They analyse the state of the legacies market, produce market forecasts, and research into legator motivations. Legacy Foresight was founded in 1994, when a consortium of 13 large legacy charities commissioned them to produce a 20-year outlook for the legacy market, taking into account a wide range of economic, social and structural trends. The research findings triggered considerable debate - both in the voluntary sector and beyond. The original consortium members went on to set up the Legacy Marketing Campaign, now called Remember A Charity. Today, Legacy Foresight works with some 50 clients, including 18 of the top 20 legacy charities. It also works closely with colleagues at Remember A Charity, the Institute of Legacy Management and Clearwater to promote the concept of legacy giving, and the principles of effective legacy management.

Use of logo by kind permission

Legacy gifts may be either pecuniary or residuary. Pecuniary gifts are gifts of specific sums, while residuary gifts are gifts of a percentage of the balance (or residue) of the estate after specific legacies (e.g. to family) and any debts have been paid. They are very different in terms of value to a nonprofit since pecuniary gifts, however generous they might be at the time a will is written, will inevitably decline in value over time. A £1,000 donation is worth a lot less today than it would have been 20 years ago! Individual estates are also typically worth a lot more when the assets are realized than the donor might have envisaged when the will was originally drafted. The value of the estate will have increased over time. For both these reasons the average value of a pecuniary donation is £3K, while the average value of a residuary gift is £50K.

The legacy market is dominated by major players, with the ten largest charities accounting for around one-third of the total (by value). The 20 largest account for almost half and the largest 500 fundraising charities account for 75 per cent (Legacy Foresight 2007). As Figure 9.1 illustrates,

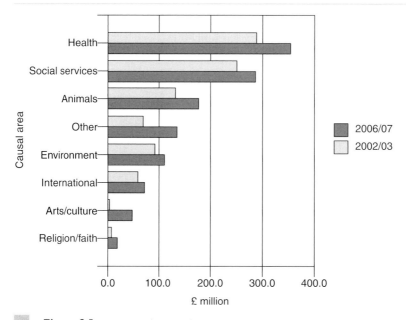

Figure 9.1 *Top 100 charities legacy income*
Source: Guidestar UK Data and Legacyforesight.co.uk
Reproduced with kind permission.

within the top 100 charities it is health, social services and animals that are the most favoured causes. It is interesting to note though that the most rapid growth in legacy income is taking place elsewhere in the sector. Legacyforesight research using data from Guidestar reveals that the greatest increase is taking place in small organizations with annual income of under £0.5 million, as Figure 9.2 illustrates. The causes experiencing the most rapid growth are depicted in Figure 9.3.

While the figures for legacy income are impressive they belie a significant opportunity for improvement, since comparatively few of us will remember a charity in our will. While over 80 per cent of individuals will give during their lifetime it is estimated that only around 5 per cent

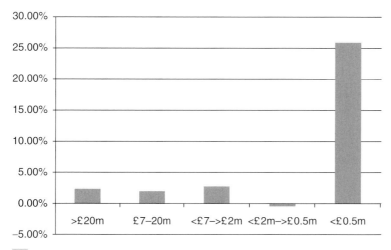

Figure 9.2 *Growth in legacy income, 2000/1–2004/5*
Source: Guidestar UK Data and Legacyforesight.co.uk
Reproduced with kind permission.

192

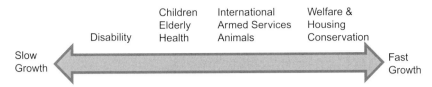

Figure 9.3 *Causes experiencing growth in legacy income*
Source: CAF/NCVO/Guidestar Databases – (2000–2004). Reproduced with kind permission.

of those who die leave a bequest to charity, a figure which has remained remarkably static for over a century. Females are slightly more likely to remember a charity than men with 6.4 per cent of female deaths resulting in a charitable legacy compared with 4.3 per cent of male deaths. Unsurprisingly, single people are the predominate source of legacies, supplying over half the number of legacies. This is highly significant since the number of single women in our society is continuing to decline.

Although the number of wills containing a charitable bequest has recently been growing at around 2 per cent per annum (thanks largely to a fall in intestacy) there remains a substantial opportunity to grow participation. Recent work by James (2008), for example, has established that even among donors, the individuals who care for us the most, only 10–12 per cent will die with any charitable estate provision. It is therefore not without cause that writers such as Smith (1996) regard the bequest as one of the last great fundraising opportunities. He derides the lack of creativity and energy in legacy fundraising thus:

> we plod around the opportunity as if we were undertakers ourselves, clad in black with crêpe bands hanging from tall hats. We need not to just admit the scale of the legacy opportunity but to admit its joy, its promise, its inherent customer satisfaction. For it is the only donation that never reflects in the donor's current account. It is the only donation that most of us will ever make in thousands, tens of thousands pounds, hundreds of thousands of pounds. It is the only donation that just about everyone *can* make.
>
> (Smith 1996:196)

In this chapter we begin by examining some of the latest research with the capacity to inform legacy fundraising practice. We will also examine how legacy fundraising is currently conducted, provide examples and offer a number of recommendations for change. The chapter will then conclude with a consideration of in memoriam giving, the tools and techniques that can aid a charity in developing this category of income and, again, illustrate this with examples of best practice.

WILL MAKING IN THE UK

Although levels of intestacy are falling, almost 20 per cent of us will die without making a will. Clearly if an individual is to offer a legacy to charity they must first make their wishes clear! For this reason the barriers to will making should be of interest to fundraisers.

Rowlingson (2004) identified a series of triggers for an individual making their first will. These were:

- illness of the individual him/herself or the illness of a relative or friend
- death of a relative or friend
- the difficulties associated with having to sort out the estate of a family member
- some form of family change, such as marriage, divorce, remarriage, etc.

193

- planning long distance travel
- the purchase of a house.

The learning here is that none of these variables will appear on a typical charity's database. There is therefore a need for legacy communications to consist of a constant 'drip feed' of awareness of how individuals could help in this way. Newsletters and other communications should carry legacy information as a matter of course, so that when an individual is in the position of making or remaking their will, they may be prompted to consider the inclusion of a legacy.

Rowlingson (2000) conducted a similar study of the key barriers individuals cited to making a will. These included:

- a belief there were, or would be, no assets to leave
- the absence of anyone obvious to leave anything to
- a feeling that it was morbid to think about death
- the individual had not yet 'got around to it'
- the individual did not expect to die for some time and would make a will before they did
- it was felt that there were too many things happening in life, so it would be best to wait until life had settled down before making a will
- it was perceived as too difficult to sort out their affairs.

Many of these barriers can be tackled by fundraisers, particularly the issue of complexity with 'Make A Will' guides and free will schemes, where a charity may arrange access to a lawyer free of charge, in the hope that the donor will reciprocate with a gift.

Rowlingson and McKay (2005) track the pattern of will-making by age. Their results are illustrated in Figure 9.4. Levels of testacy increase with age with last wills being made at age 69 for men and 73 for women. Other key findings from their study included:

- People with assets to leave are more likely to have made a will than others – nevertheless a substantial minority of owner-occupiers (25 per cent) had not made a will.
- Only 17 per cent of Asians and 12 per cent of black people had made a will compared with 47 per cent of white people.
- Knowledge of issues around inheritance and taxation was poor: 39 per cent of respondents believed, incorrectly, that a long-term cohabiting couple would receive equal treatment under inheritance law as a married couple. People who were themselves cohabiting were no more knowledgeable on this matter than others.
- When asked about inheritance tax, most people either had no idea how the system works, or believed that more people pay it and pay more than is actually the case. At the time of their study only around 6 per cent of estates were caught by this tax, whereas of those who gave an answer 25-49 per cent of estates were viewed as being caught. Only 6 per cent of respondents answered all questions correctly about the operation of the tax.

The study also explored the intention of all age groups to leave an inheritance (i.e. which includes a bequest to family, friends and potentially a charitable bequest). As the data in Figure 9.5 makes clear, there are a number of interesting differences by age. Younger people regard the leaving of an inheritance as fairly important, but as these individuals hit their fifties their enthusiasm wanes. It is possible that at this age children start to become independent and the minds of individuals turn to the issue of retirement. At this point, reality dawns and they become concerned about their standard of living in retirement, perhaps feeling that they will need the

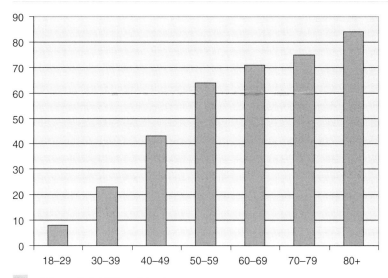

Figure 9.4 *Will-making by age*
Source: Rowlingson and McKay (2005). Reproduced with kind permission.

money themselves. Equally, they may just feel that the years are passing them by and want to enjoy life a little more than they had previously thought. As individuals age into their sixties and beyond the percentage viewing leaving an inheritance as 'very important' climbs steadily.

Of course, it is important to stress a major caveat at this point. The study in question was cross-sectional, so the researchers were not in a position to track how the views of an individual might change over time. One interpretation of these results, for example, may be that the generation now passing viewed the issue of an inheritance as important, but that the baby boomers that will follow may prefer to spend their resources themselves. As yet we have no way to know.

We elaborate on this idea in Table 9.1 where the life experiences of each generation are mapped. From 2008-2015 the core of people dying will have been born between 1915 and 1937. Their formative years were spent during times of austerity and while they experienced the growth of consumerism it will have been as a parent, rather than as a single adult. As a consequence of

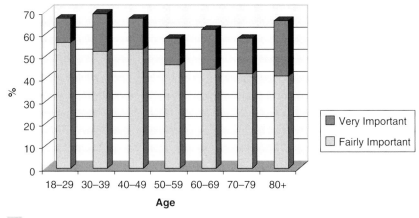

Figure 9.5 *Importance of leaving an inheritance*
Source: Rowlingson and McKay (2005). Reproduced with kind permission.

195

Table 9.1 *Life experiences of legacy cohorts*

Todays legacy cohort	Core boomers
Experienced one or both world wars	Grew up in austerity but came of age in prosperity
Grew up in era of austerity, without television, telephones, washing machines or cars	Product of universal secondary education, under the grammar school system
Largely too old for the swinging sixties	Dramatic increases in female participation in work and with it pension coverage
Experienced emerging consumerism as parents, not children	Benefitted from shift from manual to white collar jobs. Occupational mobility high
Original beneficiaries of the welfare society, with expectations of cradle to grave provision	Enjoyed increasing home ownership and the house price booms of the 1970s, 1980s and late 1990s
Benefitted from housing boom of the 1970s and 1980s, but also facing uncertainty over pensions and financing long-term care.	Supplemented their state pensions with occupational (and more recently) personal pensions

Source: Adapted from Legacy Foresight (2007). Reproduced with kind permission.

their background and upbringing they tend to have rather traditional views about duty and service and are relatively accepting of the notion of a genteel old age. Their parents and all previous generations (who lived long enough) would have experienced this. The life experiences of baby boomers who will begin to push up the death rate around the middle of the next decade, were very different. Boomers are confident consumers who demand choice and control. They are also more idealistic than the previous generation although given the breadth of the experience have developed a healthy cynicism too. Legacy fundraisers need to develop an understanding of how boomers think and develop and adapt their communications accordingly.

MOTIVES FOR LEGACY GIVING

While many of the motives for lifetime giving we discussed in Chapter 5 are of equal relevance to the realm of legacies, there are also a growing number of studies that have examined the specific issue of bequests. Research in the discipline of economics has revealed that the probability of an individual leaving a charitable legacy increases with wealth and age (Boskin 1976; Joulfaian 1991). Auten and Joulfaian (1996) have also shown that the income of children affects the amount that parents will contribute to charity. Their results indicate that where children are better off, parents are likely to increase charitable giving. We also know that the presence of a surviving spouse and children generally diminish the size of a charitable legacy. A strongly stated religious preference also has an impact (Chang et al. 1999; James 2008) with legacies to religious organizations being the least sensitive to wealth (Joulfaian 1991). Poor people are just as likely to support the church as wealthier people. Finally, legacies have been found to vary by the number of dependents and the inclusion of non-charitable legacies (people who leave gifts to friends are significantly more likely to remember a charity) (Clotfelter 1985).

Studies involving talking to donors about their motives for legacy giving are rarer and have tended to ask individuals very simplistically to indicate from a list the motives that apply. The largest study

Table 9.2 *Reasons donors make planned gifts*

Reason	%
Desire to support the charity	97
The ultimate use of the gift by the charity	82
Desire to reduce taxes	35
Long-range estate and financial planning issues	35
Create a lasting memorial for self or loved one	33
Relationship with a representative of a charity	21
Encouragement of family and friends	13
Encouragement of legal or financial advisers	12

Source: NCPG (2001). Reproduced with kind permission.

of its kind, the National Committee on Planned Giving (NCPG 2001) in the United States, determined that a genuine desire to support the charity and how the monies would eventually be used were the two primary motives for offering a planned or legacy gift. By comparison, tax is cited as a motive by a fraction of respondents. Their results are reported in Table 9.2

More recent work conducted by Sargeant and Hilton (2005) and Sargeant et al. (2007) in the UK is summarised in Figure 9.6. The authors found that a variety of 'generic' motives for giving to charity was of equal importance to individuals who had pledged to leave a charitable legacy. They also found that legacy pledgers were significantly more interested in data on the organisation's performance and had higher expectations of the quality of service that would be supplied to them as donors. As the authors note, given that a legacy will probably be the largest single gift they will ever make to a charity, it is not at all surprising that they will (a) seek reassurance that the money they donate will be used wisely and (b) expect to be well treated by the organization as a consequence. It is therefore sad to note that relatively few nonprofits treat their legacy pledgers with a differentiated standard of care. In the NCPG (2001) survey in the United States, for example, only 25 per cent of donors who had informed a charity of their legacy intentions experienced being treated any differently as a consequence.

Figure 9.6 also illustrates a number of motives for giving that are legacy specific. Legacies can be offered by individuals who believe their family have no need of their money or, in circumstances where family need might exist but where relationships have broken down, the legacy is a mechanism for ensuring that actively disliked relatives will not get their hands on the estate. Thankfully individuals will also give for more philanthropic reasons, including the desire to be remembered by continuing to support the work of the nonprofit after they have gone. It is interesting to note that this seems to occur in part because individuals perceive some similarity between their personal values and the enduring values of the organization. By playing a part in securing the organisation's future they can see a little part of themselves 'live on' (Sargeant and Shang 2008).

LEGACY FUNDRAISING

The gift of a legacy is generally seen as the peak of the giving pyramid in donor development, the theory being that a donor moves from initial low-value single gifts, through to repeat or regular gifts, on to gifts of an increased size and, once committed to the aims of the charity and happy

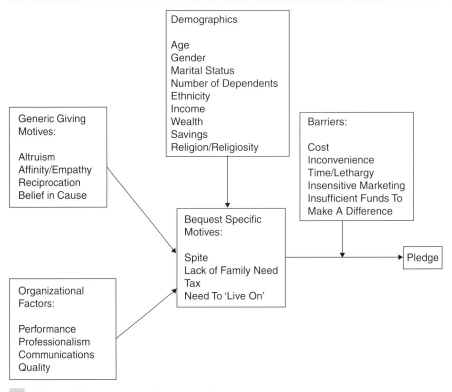

Figure 9.6 *Motives and barriers to legacy giving*

with the relationship, then may pledge to leave that charity a gift in their will. Legacy fundraisers therefore target committed donors from the base who have an established relationship with the charity. They may also target by age if the data are available.

Direct mail has frequently been employed for the purposes of legacy fundraising. Donors are sent a personally addressed mail package that introduces the idea of legacy giving, explains the importance of legacies to the organization, talks about the importance of will making for the donor and provides information on how to go about leaving a legacy to the charity. Sometimes the donor is asked to send a response card or form to the charity to provide feedback on whether they have already made a legacy provision in favour of the organization, or will now do so. Within this broad approach charities take many different creative approaches to asking for a legacy. An example is shown in Plate 9.1. The mailing tells the moving story of a volunteer who went out to clear mines in Afghanistan. Tim Goggs was in his mid-twenties and had served in the army. He was driving along with a colleague in a Jeep when they hit a mine. Tim was thrown clear but his Afghani colleague was trapped in the burning Jeep. Tim went back to get him out. … and they both died. Not only had this young man written a will before he died but he had left a legacy to Christian Aid in it. The mailing is a very emotion-laden letter from the boy's mother recounting the story, talking of her pride and loss and encouraging others to join her son in supporting the work of the organization.

Research on the efficacy of such mailings is scant, due in part to the complexity and sensitivity of the legacy gift. A large percentage of individuals moved by the communication will not notify the organization that they have included them in their will. Work by Sargeant et al. (2005)

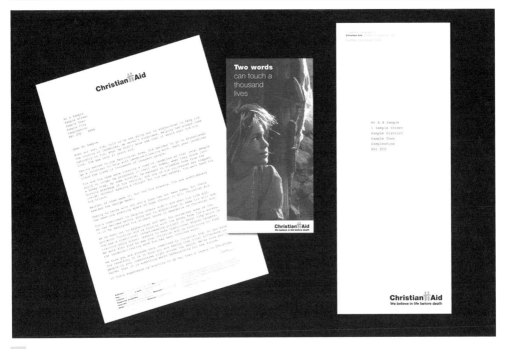

Plate 9.1 *Christian Aid legacy mailing*

Source: Christian Aid. Reproduced with kind permission.

indicates that only around 40 per cent of individuals who make a change to their will would notify the nonprofit concerned.

In the only study of its kind, DameGreene (2003), after a 15-year study of records at a large national nonprofit with a mailing programme of one million, concluded that:

- Donors who received a letter directly asking them for a legacy were 17 times more likely to give a legacy than donors who were not asked.
- Donors who were asked and thanked gave twice as much as those who were not thanked.
- Those who were cultivated (notes, letters, visits, etc.) after the thank you gave three to four times as much.
- Fewer than 1 donor in 14 had informed the charity that they had named them as a beneficiary in their will.

Donors electing to respond to mailings such as the example in Plate 9.1 should be flagged on the charity database as a legacy pledger and treated as a special group in terms of future communications. Crawford and Hartwick (2001) argue that these pledger programmes or bequest societies can provide four clear benefits:

1   They provide a forum for the charity to express appreciation to its members.
2   They serve as an incentive for non-members to make similar plans.
3   Since most estate plans can be changed at any time before the donor dies, a planned giving society can provide a regular reminder to donors of the importance of their future gifts.
4   They can bring members closer to the charity and may provide the opportunity to ask for current gifts.

In the view of the authors, club members should receive:

- A membership gift for all new members. Something not expensive but tied in some way to the charity's work. There is support for this in the wider literature and such gifts are genuinely effective at building commitment *if* they are linked to the nature of the cause.
- An annual event – perhaps a tour of a facility or a talk by researchers. In the view of the authors these must be exclusive so that only members are invited. They further advocate that after the event its success is advertised in the general newsletter to encourage others to do what is necessary to join next year.
- Special newsletters and communications can be used to make members feel like insiders. If there is a special piece of news or a news release, mail a copy to members as soon as possible.
- Birthday and holiday cards. The authors make the point that for a number of bequest pledgers this may be the only card they receive. They also argue that holiday cards may work better than Christmas cards as if they are sent in the New Year they have a greater likelihood of standing out.

Incentive gifts such as pens, pins or prints are often offered in recognition of a legacy pledge, and on receipt of a legacy gift many charities offer the opportunity for the donor to be recognised (ultimately) through an entry in a Book of Remembrance or, for larger gifts, a plaque, the planting of a tree or flower, or indeed the naming of a room or a building in the case of substantial legacies or 'in memoriam' gifts.

While direct mail is still the core of most legacy promotion strategies, an increasing number of UK charities are now also undertaking legacy fundraising through face-to-face solicitation. This is undertaken in much the same way as with major gifts with legacy fundraisers or fundraising volunteers approaching donors in their own homes. This approach, while costly in terms of staff/volunteer time, enables charities to engage donors on a very personal level and facilitates a dialogue during which many of the traditional barriers and concerns surrounding legacy giving can be addressed with sensitivity. Trained face-to-face legacy fundraisers also arrange group presentations to prospective legacy donors in local communities, perhaps at the invitation of groups such as the Women's Institute or Rotary Club.

While the existing donor base tends to be the starting point for legacy promotion strategies, legacy giving is also promoted to other audiences, and through intermediaries. In some instances service users are an important source of legacy gifts to charity, and so are included in legacy solicitation planning. Some promotion is also undertaken to 'cold' audiences, mainly through two-stage press adverts which typically state the importance of will making and invite the reader to send in a coupon or call a telephone number. An example is provided in Plate 9.2

Some charities also target solicitors who specialize in probate and estate planning through direct mail and through adverts in legal press titles. Solicitors are sent information on the charity and cause to encourage them to recommend the charity as deserving of support if clients ask for guidance, and to ensure that the correct charity registration details are at hand should the solicitor require these in the making up of a will. The efficacy of this approach has been called into question, however, as most solicitors are reluctant to offer advice on giving and prefer to serve merely the function of noting the gift and ensuring that the details of the recipient organization are properly recorded.

More creatively, some charities have sought to work with solicitors to tackle some of the barriers to will making, notably the cost and complexity. They offer a service to their donors where the individual can access a free or reduced-price will scheme in conjunction with local solicitors (see Plate 9.3)

...with a legacy to the Royal Academy

The RA receives no public funding, so the continuity and development of this exceptional institution is entirely in the hands of Friends like you who love the arts. A legacy will help us continue our unique contribution to cultural life which began over two hundred and thirty years ago. It will also help us maintain our high standards of creativity and excellence in all areas of our work, especially projects like these:

- Maintaining the quality and diversity of our exhibitions
- Supporting our education programme and students in the historic RA Schools
- Conserving and exhibiting the works in our Permanent Collections
- Preserving Burlington House and the Burlington Estate for the nation

Please contact us so that we may tell you more about how your legacy, large or small, can contribute to our plans for a creative future. We can offer advice on changing your will, inheritance tax and tell you how your gift will be remembered.

Please contact Sally Jones, Legacy Manager at the Royal Academy of Arts, FREEPOST 33 WD1057, Piccadilly, London W1E 6YZ or telephone her on 020 7300 5677 weekdays between 10am and 5pm.

Royal Academy Trust Charity number 1067270

Plate 9.2 *Legacy appeal*

Source: © Royal Academy of Arts. Reproduced with kind permission.

Plate 9.3 *Free will offer*

Source: © Tozers Solicitors. Reproduced with kind permission.

Sector schemes and products

There are also national schemes such as Free Wills Fortnight supported by a wide range of charities. Under this scheme members of the public aged 55 and over contact one of the firms of solicitors taking part in the campaign at some time during the fortnight to request an appointment. The solicitor will help draw up a will that accurately reflects the wishes of the individual or couple. Those taking up the offer are under no obligation to leave a gift to one of the Free Wills Fortnight charities. However, the charities hope that many will see this as a chance to help their favourite cause. The scheme will then pay the solicitor for their time. Free Wills Fortnight takes place in specific cities and towns within the UK each year. Notification of the areas covered by the scheme is provided through the organization's website two to three weeks prior to each campaign.

The Will Aid scheme (see Plate 9.4) is a similar idea. It offers individuals the opportunity to have a basic will professionally drawn up by a solicitor free of charge. Users of the website can search for a local solicitor who is a member of the scheme. In return for the service solicitors hope that the individual will choose to donate to the Will Aid charities the fee they would normally charge. Since the campaign started in 1988, almost £7 million has been raised in donations.

The Charities Aid Foundation have developed their own legacy 'product' that should be of interest to many charity fundraisers. It offers donors the benefit of additional flexibility and choice over the organizations they might choose to support. The scheme works as follows. The donor specifies a pecuniary or residuary gift in their will to the Charities Aid Foundation (CAF) and notifies them which nonprofits they would like to see benefit from this money. On the donor's death CAF collects the donation from the estate and distributes the money to recipient

Plate 9.4 *Will Aid website*

Source: Will Aid. Reproduced with kind permission.

REMEMBER A CHARITY

everyone can leave the world a better place

remember a charity in your will

Remember A Charity, hosted by the Institute of Fundraising, is a consortium of over 140 UK registered charities working to increase the value of legacy income to the voluntary sector by increasing the number of people who remember a charity in their wills.

Since its launch in 2002, Remember A Charity has targeted both the general public and will-writing professionals alike with a media and PR campaign including national press, radio and television advertising to significantly increase awareness of this method of support. Building on this success, in 2008 the campaign commissioned new research which forms the foundation of its new Social Marketing strategy for achieving the desired long-term behaviour change of making charitable wills a social norm.

Similar campaigns have subsequently been launched in the Netherlands in 2003 (www.nalaten.nl), Australia in 2006 (www.includeacharity.com.au) and Spain in 2007 (www.legadosolidario.org).

Currently the campaign is funded almost entirely by the fees of its member charities who pay according to a sliding fee scale. The size and diversity of membership has continued to grow and now includes the education and arts sector and NHS Hospital Trusts.

Remember A Charity logo used by kind permission © Remember A Charity 2008 charities in accordance with the donor's wishes. The benefit of this scheme is that, having promised a legacy to CAF, if a donor should change their minds about the ultimate recipients they need only notify CAF of this change. There is no need to engage a lawyer to write a codicil to the existing will, or redraft it to reflect the change. There are therefore no extra costs to the donor. They may change their minds as they wish. Gifts can be made to any recognised UK charity.

LEGACY DECISION-MAKING

Before leaving the topic of legacies, it is worth conducting a brief review of research conducted in the domain of temporal decision-making. It acknowledges that donors taking decisions about the future will take those decisions rather differently from donors deciding to give now to an annual campaign. People think differently about decisions that will be actioned in the future (Trope and Liberman 2003) and in essence there are five key differences.

Abstract versus concrete

When taking decisions about the present individuals prefer to think in terms of concrete information. Asking for a one-off donation by indicating what a donation at specific levels will buy is therefore a good strategy to adopt. Telling a donor that £10 would buy a tent or immunize two children would both be examples of a 'concrete' appeal. When taking decisions about the future individuals prefer to think in the abstract and would thus pay more attention to the general approach that would be taken to providing aid. This general approach should play to the abstract values of the organization, for example, compassion in international relief, human respect and dignity in health and welfare provision and so on. All these themes would work better in soliciting legacies than talking about specific and immediate needs.

Superordinate versus subordinate

This is a fancy way of saying that in the present, informing people about the mechanics of how an organization is achieving its goals would be the optimal strategy. For a hospice, talking to donors about the medications, the numbers of beds, the number of nurses and so on would all be appropriate. These are the nuts and bolts that allow a hospice to pursue its mission. In persuading individuals to leave a legacy, however, research suggests that stressing the superordinate, or what the successful achievement of the mission will deliver, would be a better approach. Promotional messages stressing the organization's ability to improve the quality of the end of life experience and the support provided for families would therefore be more appropriate. 'Why' is more important in the future than 'how'.

Decontextualized versus contextualized

Giving in the present can be bolstered by focusing on the organization and the help it is providing now to beneficiaries. The rationale offered for support is very much set within the context of the organization. We can help X number of beneficiaries, touching their lives in the following ways … For legacies the organization should give consideration to illustrating why the work of the organization is of broader social significance. For instance, sticking with the hospice example, 'society has a duty to provide the best terminal care that it can', '*our* loved ones might one day benefit from palliative care', 'no-one should be allowed to suffer unnecessarily' and so on. Rather than talk about the immediate benefits of patient care per se, the benefit to the local community and/or the wider society should be emphasized.

Promotion of primary values

Legacies can also be stimulated by appealing to a donor's sense of self and in particular their moral identity. As individuals we all have an 'ideal' moral identity, which is our desire to become a compassionate, caring, kind, friendly, honest, generous, fair and helpful person (Shang and Reed 2008). When thinking about the future, people focus more on what ideally they would like to become than who they think they are now. As a consequence, it is more important to appeal to people's ideal self-definitions than their actual selves (Kivetz and Tyler 2007).

Shang and Reed (2008) were able to measure an individual's actual and ideal moral identity using the scale shown here.

• Caring	Actual:	Not at all	1	2	3	4	5	6	7	8	9	Completely
	Ideal:	Not at all	1	2	3	4	5	6	7	8	9	Completely
• Compassionate	Actual:	Not at all	1	2	3	4	5	6	7	8	9	Completely
	Ideal:	Not at all	1	2	3	4	5	6	7	8	9	Completely
• Fair	Actual:	Not at all	1	2	3	4	5	6	7	8	9	Completely
	Ideal:	Not at all	1	2	3	4	5	6	7	8	9	Completely
• Friendly	Actual:	Not at all	1	2	3	4	5	6	7	8	9	Completely
	Ideal:	Not at all	1	2	3	4	5	6	7	8	9	Completely
• Generous	Actual:	Not at all	1	2	3	4	5	6	7	8	9	Completely
	Ideal:	Not at all	1	2	3	4	5	6	7	8	9	Completely
• Helpful	Actual:	Not at all	1	2	3	4	5	6	7	8	9	Completely
	Ideal:	Not at all	1	2	3	4	5	6	7	8	9	Completely
• Hardworking	Actual:	Not at all	1	2	3	4	5	6	7	8	9	Completely
	Ideal:	Not at all	1	2	3	4	5	6	7	8	9	Completely
• Honest	Actual:	Not at all	1	2	3	4	5	6	7	8	9	Completely
	Ideal:	Not at all	1	2	3	4	5	6	7	8	9	Completely
• Kind	Actual:	Not at all	1	2	3	4	5	6	7	8	9	Completely
	Ideal	Not at all	1	2	3	4	5	6	7	8	9	Completely

The researchers were then able to calculate average scores for individuals participating in their research. Their results are presented in Figure 9.7a and demonstrate the average scores attained for both male and female subjects. It is clear that there is a marked gap between the actual and ideal moral identity. Figure 9.7b focuses on this gap and presents the gaps for both genders. Females have a significantly larger gap between the actual and ideal moral identities than do males.

So how is this relevant to bequests? Well, we have already established that, when thinking about the future, individuals are more focused on who they would like to be. That being the case fundraisers can assist donors in achieving their ideal by suggesting that leaving a legacy will help them become more caring, compassionate and so on. They can do this by priming some of these words in the way they describe others who have already taken the decision to leave a gift. Many charities use case studies of existing legacy pledgers or celebrate individuals who have already left a legacy to the organization. Seeding these cases with the moral words listed above or seeding the solicitation with these words can greatly increase the efficacy of the communication. So phrases such as the following would be effective:

'Caring donors like you. ...'
'Elsie's generous gift has helped us to. ...'
'Through the kind support of donors like. ...'

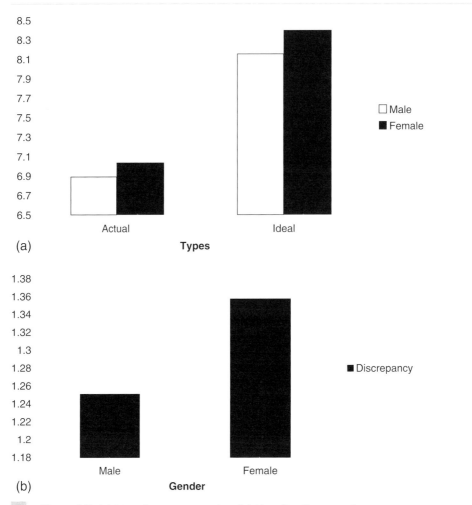

Figure 9.7 *(a) Morality: survey results; (b) Morality discrepancies*
Source: From Shang and Reed (2008, in preparation). Reproduced with kind permission.

Shang and Reed's (2008) work suggests that this approach would be particularly effective with female donors, which is good news for legacy fundraising since, as we already know, females live longer and will thus always be the critical legacy audience.

Structured versus unstructured

Finally, in seeking to promote take-up of legacies, nonprofits should think through their long-term mission for the organization. While annual appeals can be undertaken in a relatively unstructured way, focusing on the most immediate and pressing of needs, appeals for legacies need to articulate a longer term and coherent plan for what the organization is trying to achieve.

There are two further findings from the research on temporal decision-making that are of relevance to fundraisers. First, emotion discounts faster than logic. What this means is that when people make decisions about the future, they pay more attention to the logic underlying their decisions. As a consequence, while charities might use messages that evoke an emotion in their donors, for this emotion to offer utility in prompting a legacy donors need to be encouraged to think through why they experience that emotion. Thinking back to the Christian Aid example in Plate 9.1, some people may undoubtedly give because they experience sympathy with the mother, but this is an especially effective communication because the letter compels the reader to think through why sacrifice of the son was so significant and why what he was trying to achieve was so important.

Second, when thinking about the future, messages about well-being tend to work better than the prevention of suffering (Mogilner et al. 2008). Plate 9.5 provides an illustration. Here the National Trust discusses the 'Gift of a Lifetime' and focuses on how legacies will enrich the lives of generations to come. This message will be far more effective than an alternative focusing on the harm that would result to the nation's heritage if legacies were not forthcoming.

IN MEMORIAM AND TRIBUTE FUNDRAISING

People have given in memory or tribute following someone's death since time began. The urge to mark the passing of a life is a part of the natural grieving process, but in memoriam fundraising remains one of the most underdeveloped areas of charity fundraising. This valuable fundraising

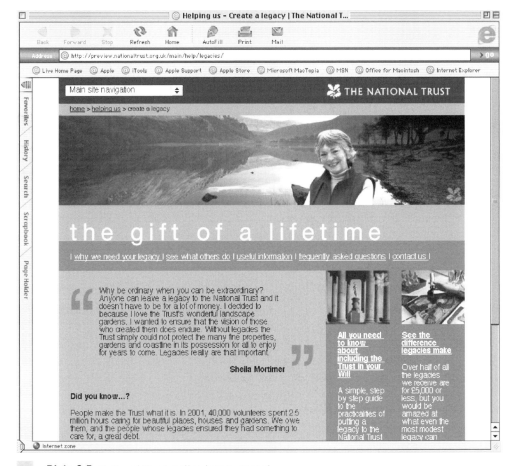

Plate 9.5 *National Trust online legacy appeal*

Source: The National Trust (c) 2008. Reproduced by kind permission.

tool is often mistakenly seen as being too intrusive – yet it can both deliver significant income and offer a valuable focus for grieving donors.

The value of in memoriam (In Mem) giving in the UK is huge; the charity that receives the second largest volume of In Mem donations by monetary value claims to have received £5.2 million in 2007–2008. Telephone research into funeral directors carried out by the communications agency Whitewater estimates this to be 9 per cent of the total.

In memoriam

In Mem gifts tend to come into charities via three routes: a direct donation sent from the donor, a collection sent in by the next of kin (or a close friend/relative), a collection undertaken on behalf of the family by the funeral director. The problem with collections is that the charity may have only one point of contact and therefore not know who each individual donor is. Is this an issue?

Charities like to thank all those who donate and to capture their details for further asks, but with In Mem donations this is entirely the wrong way to behave. Donors giving In Mem do not do so necessarily to support the cause, they give either as a way of dealing with their own grief/memories, or just because the family asks. It is therefore inappropriate to put In Mem donors in the warm donor file. In Mem giving is not about the charity, but about the donor and their memories.

There can often be a causal or life passion link to In Mem gifts but this is not, by any means, always the case. It is therefore necessary that the organisation develops a strategy to ensure that as many people as possible are aware that it can benefit and respond appropriately to In Mem gifts. By so doing it is possible to develop a robust and growing income stream that is, as near as is possible to get to, a recession-proof method of fundraising.

Secondary In Mem gifts

An In Mem strategy should include a programme of opportunities for donors to give secondary gifts. Greater frequency of contact allows donors to develop an emotional bond linking the memory of the person who died to the cause of the charity. These secondary donors can become good prospects for Tribute Funds (if you have them) or legacies, but the communication process to achieve this needs to be distinctive. The language used in the initial In Mem programme needs to continue to be reflected in the dialogue with secondary donors.

A strategy for encouraging secondary gifts might include visible signposts such as benches, plaques, trees and so on, but could just as easily be books of remembrance or special mailings around emotional trigger times such as Christmas or memorial services/events.

Tribute Funds

Tribute Funds offer the bereaved the opportunity to create a lasting memorial that they can manage at their own level. These funds are particularly effective where a life has been cut short. Modern Tribute Funds managed online offer the fundholders a range of options of engagement, from posting memories and pictures to effective support in fundraising on behalf of their chosen charity through sponsored events, special occasions and so on. The opportunity to see the fruits of their fundraising efforts embedded in the lasting memory they have created for the person who has died is very motivating to the bereaved and can help with the grieving process. An example is provided in Plate 9.6. In this case, once the tribute page is created on the charity's website, friends and relatives can be invited to give towards an appeal total decided on by

Plate 9.6 *Example Tribute Fund*

Source: Breakthrough Breast Cancer: Reproduced with kind permission.

the bereaved. In this example the appeal has been set at £300. Additional 'candles' can be purchased by visitors to the site to move the appeal towards its total. Progress here is recorded in a barometer, but other graphics may be selected or, indeed, none at all. Messages of love can also be posted on the site and a tribute to the life of the deceased be created in words and pictures.

From the charity's perspective, Tribute Funds offer a way of building lasting relationships with In Mem donors and not just with the fundholders, but also with those who support the funds through fundraising activities. A dedicated communication process maintains enthusiasm for the fund, ensuring longevity, and educating donors that legacies can be left to Tribute Funds opens a very powerful legacy proposition – it becomes personal – not just about the charity but about the family.

In Mem language

Undertaken effectively, In Mem and Tribute fundraising can be valuable income streams for charities, but there are some key issues to be addressed which should form the bedrock of any In Mem strategy or programme. The language used in communicating with bereaved people needs to be very carefully controlled, data need to be accurate, and the programme overall needs to be appropriate to the need of the donor and reflect the values of the charity. Some key words that would guide an In Mem strategy would include: Appropriate, Considerate, Consistent, Approachable, Personal and Caring.

The whole organisation needs to understand the ethos behind the In Mem strategy and programme to achieve effective 'buy in' from stakeholders, particularly in volunteer or community-led organisations.

SUMMARY

Gifts given through legacies and gifts given in memory of a loved one are important income streams for charities. Many charities do not commit much resource to the promotion of these forms of giving, and we have looked in this chapter at research which could help inform legacy promotion and marketing planning.

Predicting trends in legacy giving is difficult. In the medium term it would appear that the income stream faces a number of threats (from the slowing housing market, intense competition and fewer single women) but that opportunities also present themselves: more people are making charitable wills, younger charities are gaining ground in legacy giving and there are opportunities for charities to reach out to new legators including men, couples with children and baby boomers.

DISCUSSION QUESTIONS

1   What is the difference between a pecuniary and residuary legacy? Which is typically of most value to a charity? Why?
2   How do the motives for legacy giving differ from the motives for annual giving? How might these differences be reflected in fundraising communications?
3   Design a communication strategy for a group of donors who have recently pledged to leave a legacy gift to your organization. What sort of communications would you send them? How often would you contact them?
4   In your role as the head of fundraising at a regional hospice, prepare a presentation to the board making the case for the development of an In Mem and Tribute Fund giving.
5   How should the language employed in legacy solicitation differ from that employed for annual gifts? Using your knowledge of this, draft a legacy solicitation for your own nonprofit or one you are familiar with.
6   What is Remember A Charity? How is the work of this organisation relevant to fundraisers? What other sector initiatives exist to facilitate legacy giving?

REFERENCES

Auten, G. and Joulfaian, D. (1996) 'Charitable Contributions and Intergenerational Transfers', *Journal of Public Economics*, 59: 55–68.

Boskin, M.J. (1976) 'Estate Taxation and Charitable Bequests', *Journal of Public Economics*, 5: 27–56.

Chang, C.F., Okunade, A.A. and Kumar, N. (1999) 'Motives Behind Charitable Bequests', *Journal of Nonprofit and Public Sector Marketing*, 6(4): 69–83.

Clotfelter, C.T. (1985). *Federal Tax Policy and Charitable Giving,* University of Chicago Press, Chicago, IL.

Crawford, R.S. and Hartwick, F. (2001) 'Creating and Maintaining a Planned Giving Society', *Journal of Gift Planning*, 5(4): 19–52.

DameGreene, S. (2003) 'How to Develop a Successful Bequest Program: A Simple, Easy-to-Follow Plan for Starting, Increasing and Collecting Bequests at Your Nonprofit', *Journal of Gift Planning*, 7(2): 17–52.

James, R.N. (2008) *Causes and Correlates of Charitable Giving in Estate Planning: A Cross-Sectional and Longitudinal Examination of Older Adults,* report to the Association of Fundraising Professionals and Legacy Leaders, Washington DC.

Joulfaian, D. (1991) 'Charitable Bequests and Estate Taxes', *National Tax Journal,* 44: 169–180.

Kivetz, Y. and Tyler, T.R. (2007) 'Tomorrow I'll Be Me: The Effect of Time Perspective on the Activation of Idealistic Versus Pragmatic Selves', *Organizational Behavior and Human Decision Processes,* 102(2): 193–211.

Legacy Foresight (2007) *Ten Key Trends in the Legacy Market,* LegacyForesight, London.

Legacy Foresight (2008) *Legacy Monitor,* LegacyForesight, London.

Mogilner, C., Aaker, J.L. and Pennington, G. (2008) 'Time Will Tell: The Distant Appeal of Promotion and Imminent Appeal of Prevention', *Journal of Consumer Research,* 34(5): 670–681.

National Committee on Planned Giving (NCPG) (2001) *Planned Giving in the United States 2000: A Survey of Donors,* NCPG, Indianapolis, IN.

Rowlingson, K. (2000) *Fate, Hope and Insecurity: Future Expectations and Forward Planning,* Joseph Rowntree Foundation, York.

Rowlingson, K. (2004) *Attitudes to Inheritance: Focus Group Report,* University of Bath, Bath.

Rowlingson, K. and McKay, S. (2005) *Attitudes to Inheritance in Britain,* Joseph Rowntree Foundation, Policy Press, Bristol.

Sargeant, A. and Hilton, T. (2005) 'The Final Gift: Targeting the Potential Charity Legator', *International Journal of Nonprofit and Voluntary Sector Marketing,* 10(1): 3–16.

Sargeant, A. and Shang, J. (2008) *Identification, Death and Bequest Giving: A Report to AFP and Legacy Leaders,* Association of Fund Raising Professionals, Washington DC.

Sargeant, A., Hilton, T. and Wymer, W.W. (2005) 'Making the Bequest: An Empirical Study of the Attitudes of Pledgers and Supporters', *International Journal of Educational Advancement,* 5(3): 207–220.

Sargeant, A., Routley, C. and Scaife, W. (2007) 'Successful Bequest Fundraising: Lessons from Research', *Journal of Gift Planning,* 11(1): 11–39.

Shang, J. and Reed, A. (2008) 'The Effect of Moral Identity Discrepancy on Charitable Giving', *Journal of Personality and Social Psychology,* in preparation.

Smith, G. (1996) *Asking Properly,* White Lion Press, France.

Trope, Y. and Liberman, N. (2003) 'Temporal Construal', *Psychological Review,* 110: 403–421.

Chapter 10

Community fundraising

OBJECTIVES

By the end of this chapter you should be able to:

■ Discuss the range and types of activities commonly defined as community fundraising.
■ Understand how community fundraising has changed in recent years and what the major new developments have been.
■ Outline the levels of return on investment that can be expected from this form of activity.
■ Understand and manage the central role of the volunteer in community fundraising activity.

INTRODUCTION

Despite the increasingly professional stance of many nonprofit operations and the widespread use of TV, direct mail, the Internet and the telephone in fundraising solicitation, community fundraising activities are still what most members of the public call to mind if they are asked to describe the ways that fundraising happens.

Community fundraising comprises a wide range of participative events and activities, all of which are visible within the local community, raise funds from individuals within that community and usually involve a volunteer workforce. Initiatives that would fall under the umbrella term 'community fundraising' would include the distribution of collection boxes to stores and businesses, cash collections on the street, local flag days, fêtes, yard sales, sponsored events in local schools and workplaces, sponsored challenges like marathon running and mountain climbing and large-scale sponsored events such as fun-runs or danceathons.

Community fundraising can be as much (or more) about raising awareness of a cause within a given community as about raising funds. Although there are exceptions to the rule, in general community fundraising is one of the least profitable forms of income generation for nonprofits on both sides of the Atlantic. Given that it usually involves volunteers and apparently low-cost materials, this can be difficult to understand.

To an extent community fundraising is 'old-style' fundraising, and as such there are indications that it is becoming less effective and relevant as previous generations pass on and the demographics of giving and volunteering change. This is exacerbated by the fact that community fundraising is an area that is not easy to 'professionalize', in terms of centralizing, streamlining and controlling activities for maximum profitability.

In this chapter we will look at what community fundraising is, what rates of return can reasonably be generated by it and where it fits in the fundraising communications portfolio. We will also discuss the major trends affecting this area, including those impacting on volunteering and attitudes to volunteering.

COMMUNITY FUNDRAISING ACTIVITIES

Community fundraising works within the 'mass anonymous small gifts market' (Kotler and Andreasen 1991), generating a large number of small cash donations from individuals. This sort of fundraising is 'people intensive', involving the mobilization of large numbers of volunteers, often organized through committee structures.

The motives of donors in giving through community fundraising techniques are mixed. Some givers are no doubt motivated by 'pure' philanthropic motives, but community fundraising involves strong elements of exchange, whereby the donor derives a benefit from the giving of the gift too. Community events provide opportunities for socializing, entertainment, competition, recognition and networking, while raffles, auctions and sales provide opportunities to win prizes or to buy and sell goods. Giving in response to community fundraising initiatives is 'low-impact', involving no great depth of thought and requiring little by way of knowledge of the specific work of the nonprofit. The gifts are low value and impulsive, often triggered more by the person asking or by the event taking place than by the particular nature of the cause.

Participative community fundraising works by turning large numbers of people into agents on behalf of a nonprofit, getting other people to do the asking and thereby enabling fundraisers to broaden their audience. It turns social networks into chains of agents and supporters. When a fundraiser persuades a school to run a sponsored activity, effectively a personal 'ask' is being made for that charity by the teachers, and then by the children. If guilt-tripped parents then seek sponsorship for their child's activity from work colleagues the net is widened still further. The best community fundraising offers several ways for individuals to contribute, by volunteering time and skills to organize and run events, by taking part and seeking sponsors, by suggesting other individuals, or by giving directly. Plate 10.1 provides some examples of community fundraising ideas from a charity website.

Community fundraising thus depends on networks and concentrations of people. Fundraisers either go to where people are already and work through schools, workplaces, clubs and societies, or create events in order to draw people to them. The second option is often necessary for unpopular or controversial causes, where it may be difficult to gain entry to existing mainstream institutions.

The sections below briefly outline some of the most common community fundraising routes:

Schools fundraising

Many nonprofits seek to raise money through sponsored events in schools. In some cases the school allows children a 'non-uniform' day in return for a small donation to a cause, or distributes sponsorship forms to pupils. Children have been encouraged to seek sponsorship for a wide range of activities – from sports challenges through to sponsored silences, fasts, readathons and more. Most school fundraising has an educational aspect, whereby the children are provided information on the cause and on the beneficiaries and are encouraged to discuss the issues raised as a class exercise.

213

Plate 10.1 *Community fundraising ideas*

Source: Save the Children UK. Reproduced with kind permission.

As the number of nonprofits approaching schools has increased, schools have reacted by organizing their giving and fundraising activity more formally, often supporting the same cause through the same event each year, or rotating their support to different organizations on a regular basis.

School pupils will seek sponsorship from their families and from friends of the family, and thus raise awareness and donations from among their own circle. Nonprofits will also hope that support given by schoolchildren might be remembered fondly as the individuals grow to adulthood, providing a lasting sympathy and link to the work of the nonprofit.

Fundraising within local organizations

Other local organizations are likewise utilized by nonprofits for fundraising activity. Masonic guilds, recreational clubs, guilds, rotary clubs and workplaces all provide networks of people who can be motivated to raise funds, especially where the organization itself is generally charitably inclined and is designed in part to advance the social good. Workplace fundraising is usually categorized as corporate philanthropy, though it can involve many of the same events and tools as community fundraising and is often best delivered on a local basis.

Street and house-to-house collections

Most nonprofits have operated cash collections at some point, recruiting teams of volunteers prepared to collect with a bucket or collecting can in the street or in a shopping mall; or going door to door in their own neighbourhoods and asking for small donations.

While these activities can appear to be fairly spontaneous, all cash collections are in fact carefully orchestrated. Permission for cash collections in malls or on the street has to be given by the mall owners or the local authority, who often enforce rigid guidelines as to how long the collections can continue, and on the positioning and behaviour of the collectors. Door-to-door collections are generally not subject to this sort of permission, but areas have to be allocated without overlap, and good practice guidelines carefully adhered to with reference to the safety of the volunteer collectors and the good name of the nonprofit organization.

The recruitment, management and coordination of the large number of volunteers required for a large-scale collection campaign is also time-consuming and can be costly. The income generated has to be accounted for and banked. Volunteers will require recognition and thanks, and ideally will receive communications throughout the year in order to retain their good will and encourage them to repeat their involvement. Volunteers tend to be uncomfortable with making a direct ask for gifts, which is why many organizations prefer to use collection envelopes, which are put into mailboxes and collected some days later. Raffle/lottery tickets may also be sold door to door, giving volunteers the opportunity to offer prospective supporters the chance to win a prize.

House-to-house collections have been badly hit by the diminishing pool and increased age of fundraising volunteers, plus an increase in fears for personal safety. This has reached the point where the coordination of house-to-house collecting is no longer profitable for some charities even where a long history of the successful use of this method is in evidence.

Fundraising events

Fundraising events range widely from fêtes and local galas through to sponsored sports events, challenge events, entertainments, yard sales and fashion shows. Events can involve anywhere from a dozen people through to thousands, and can require weeks, months or years of planning and coordination according to scale and complexity. There is a portfolio of 'standard' fundraising events available, tested and experienced over years of charity fundraising across the sector. These proven formulas can be run using documents such as sponsorship forms, raffle tickets and entry forms, which are simple and require minimal amounts of staff time in explanation and advice to volunteers.

However, those events that work best are those where the core event has been creatively themed, where there is endorsement by a celebrity, or where the event is given a new twist that makes it relevant to the particular cause or community. The community fundraising market is crowded and competitive, and new initiatives have to stand out in order to succeed.

Fundraising events and initiatives tend to have a life cycle similar to that of a commercial product, whereby it takes time for the new product to become known and accepted, but once this happens sales rise rapidly and substantial profits can be made. In due course, however, the market becomes saturated, sales decline and, with many companies competing for business, profit margins fall sharply. This pattern can occur over a few years, or over decades as lifestyles and technology change. Many of the same factors such as novelty, costs and competition are at work in the charity events marketplace. Nonprofits respond to this either by shoring up the success of community fundraising products through ensuring they are not overused, and by introducing new novelty elements to keep them fresh, or by regularly developing and testing new community fundraising products. This latter option can be high risk, as many new ventures are likely to fail, and it tends to take a long time to disseminate successful practice to volunteer community fundraising groups, which by their nature tend to be conservative and slow to embrace innovation.

The possibilities for fundraising events are endless, and nonprofits are constantly devising new ideas. Some of the most well-tested sources of enjoyment and participation are listed below:

■ *'Fun-raising'* Events involving humour, jokes, dressing up and fooling around. Many 'good cause' events give an opportunity for people to play the fool, receive attention and make people laugh.

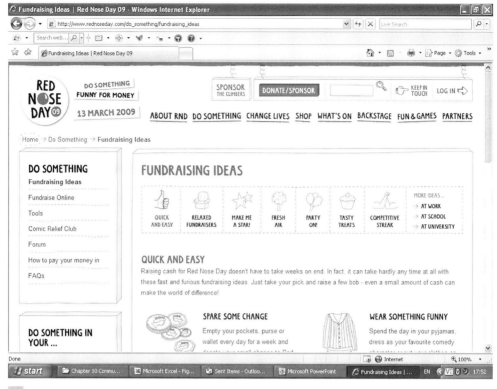

Plate 10.2 *Fundraising*

Source: Red Nose Day (c) 2009. Reproduced by kind permission.

- *Family events*   Events or activities that families can undertake or attend together.
- *Challenges*   Events involving teams such as tug-of-war and quizzes provide a spectacle for others to watch and stimulate competition. Individual challenges like bungee-jumping, parachuting and abseiling provide the chance to test yourself.
- *The chance to win a prize or secure a bargain*   Often the fact that the proceeds are going to a 'good cause' enable people to justify participation in raffles, prize draws and similar activities that they usually would not consider or would disapprove of.
- *Celebrities*   Local events often offer the chance to see or meet a celebrity, or to buy or win items donated by celebrities.
- *Fitness*   Sponsored walks, cycle rides, aerobathons, swimming galas and the like all enable people to enjoy physical activities and support a nonprofit at the same time.

Community fundraising events require a great deal of organization and are extremely labour-intensive. Small events will take months to organize properly, while larger sponsored events can take over a year. Sites and facilities have to be booked long in advance, as do celebrities, while police and local amenity authorities require applications to be processed with long lead times. The design and production of publicity materials is a lengthy process, especially if recognition and inclusion of sponsors and supporters is involved, and the support and coordination of a wide range of other bodies may be required to help with arrangements on the day. Advance warning and a gradual build-up of publicity over time is virtually essential to ensure good attendance figures.

Event organizers therefore have to be well organized, and to plan through the production of detailed schedules and checklists. Public events require the organizer to be well aware of public health and safety regulations, and to be able to carry out risk-assessment exercises as part of the event planning cycle. Planning a successful community event requires a blend of creativity and calculation, blending the enthusiasm that will motivate volunteers with the detachment and analysis required to make the event smooth-running and profitable. Exhibit 10.1 provides an example of a schedule for an annual sponsored bike ride.

Centrally coordinated and integrated campaigns

In recent years a trend has emerged of fundraising organizations using more centralized methods to coordinate and promote community activities, in order to take advantage of participative fundraising while reducing the overhead costs involved in setting up, controlling and servicing local fundraising bodies. This might mean that a new fundraising idea or theme is developed and tested centrally, with generic materials produced by a headquarters team that can be used locally. At the most extreme, fundraising 'packs' are generated containing a complete set of materials, instructions and support, and are distributed to local groups. While this makes good sense in terms of coordination, control and cost, many volunteer groups would argue that it stifles local ideas, energy and creativity, and that the strength of local activity lies in its local flavour and originality.

EXHIBIT 10.1 SCHEDULE FOR ANNUAL SPONSORED BIKE RIDE

Month 1   Agree dates for next year's event with Head Office and local volunteer group.

Month 2   First event committee to debrief on this year and begin to plan for next year.
Monthly meetings will be held from this point on.

Month 3   Identify top sponsorship fundraiser.

Month 4   Confirm sponsorship with local paper.
Send sponsorship proposals to drinks manufacturer, paper cup makers, clothing suppliers. Identify likely suppliers of prizes and approach.

Month 5   Agree route.
Prepare literature.

Month 6   Print literature.
Plan launch event.
Prepare administration systems and packs.
Book site facilities, PA system, transport.
Confirm booking of local celebrity.

Month 7   Hold publicity launch.
Contact suppliers of first aid, marshals and refreshments.

Month 8   Meetings to plan detailed arrangements on the day. Prepare route signs and direction materials.

Month 9   Draft scripts for speakers and commentators.
Draft press releases.
Final arrangements with sponsors and volunteers.

Month 10 Event takes place.

The centralising approach also helps to ensure that local fundraising activity is integrated with national campaigns, and that community fundraising can be coordinated with other fundraising activity to produce the maximum impact. A single campaign theme or message can be utilized across websites, fundraising mailings, telemarketing, advertising, radio and DRTV, while at the same time volunteers are active in their local communities running events, sponsorship events, cash collections and flag days promoting the same central message and call for funds. Examples of this are the Christmas campaign by the Salvation Army or, in the UK, Christian Aid Week.

Church fundraising

Fundraising within religious congregations is an important community fundraising exercise. This activity can range from the standard collection plate through to the organization of activities in which members of the congregation act as fundraising volunteers. Church fundraising may be undertaken by the church for the church, for related religious causes such as missionary activity, or for nonprofits unconnected with religious activity. Individual church leaders may integrate the nonprofit cause with education and information, providing displays or videos that present the background to the fundraising proposition, and featuring the appeal in church publications and communications. Individuals taking on sponsorship challenges in aid of good causes may also find potential sponsors from among members of their local religious community.

MANAGEMENT AND STRUCTURES

A community fundraiser primarily requires skills in organizing people and events. Success depends on the effective mobilization of supporters and resources. Many fundraising nonprofits create a range of volunteer committees to facilitate this, or encourage the formation of local branches and fundraising groups affiliated to the organization. In some cases these groups are a constitutionally important part of the organization, electing members of advisory or governing bodies. Other nonprofits opt for a less formal structure, working through other groups and organizations on a project or campaign basis rather than establishing permanent local committees.

Locally based committees or branches can be extremely effective, delivering funds, time and effort, and facilitating the organization of a demanding programme of fundraising events and activities. They can provide links into the social networks and institutions that make up the local community, and can add to the local credibility of a nonprofit, effectively making the cause relevant and popular on a local basis. Over time, volunteer committees or branches can become extremely knowledgeable and experienced local fundraisers and effective representatives and advocates for the nonprofit organization. That said, there are also significant costs and disadvantages associated with this sort of structure.

Groups and committees have to be serviced. The members will expect to be kept informed, and to be supported with information, training, materials and advice. They will require recognition for their efforts. If they form part of the governance structure of the organization their decision-making bodies will require administrative support. Groups and committees also have to be controlled. They may want to undertake activities that the main organization considers inappropriate, or even damaging. Their work has to be carefully monitored to avoid the situation where key donors or potential donors are approached with multiple requests from local and head office sources, and become irritated by the evident lack of professionalism and coordination.

The servicing, control and coordination of local fundraising groups thus carries a substantial cost. When this is coupled with the fact that the fundraising activities they undertake bring in relatively limited levels of income, it can be appreciated that the costs of supporting community fundraising can easily begin to outweigh the income generated. Nonprofits that make the decision to invest heavily in the creation of local fundraising offices and posts can therefore find that they fail to generate the requisite level of income to justify the infrastructure costs.

OUTCOMES AND PROFITABILITY

Despite the financial risks outlined above, many fundraising nonprofits continue to support extensive community fundraising work. These organizations may recognize that community fundraising is far less profitable than other forms of fundraising activity, but also contend that community activity generates additional and different benefits to the nonprofit, and hence that it should not be judged purely in terms of return on investment.

One of the main reasons for local fundraising is the publicity that can be generated for the organization, calling attention to the nonprofit, its work and its needs. Publicity may be generated through local media coverage, and directly among individuals through the visibility that accrues. Such publicity will help the organization to reach out to supporters and potential supporters, many of whom would be unlikely to be aware of the nonprofit otherwise.

Community fundraising events are also used to reward donors and to involve, thank and motivate volunteers, reinforcing their decision to support the organization and encouraging their renewed involvement and dedication. Many local initiatives also have an educational element, raising awareness of specific issues and providing information and advice. In making the organization visible at a local level, community fundraising activity can also have an impact on the levels of demand for the services that the nonprofit provides. Recognition of the value of one-to-one contact with many donor groups has made many organizations more aware of the value of a personal, local link to major donors, trusts and companies that may be located at a distance from the charity HQ.

Nonprofit organizations therefore have to consider carefully the balance of costs and benefits prior to making any investment in community fundraising. This balance will vary according to the nature of the cause and the structure and needs of the particular organization, and will be impacted upon by the requirements of the organization to raise its profile locally, to campaign or to educate.

In the UK, a third of the top 500 fundraising charities are estimated to engage in regional or 'local' fundraising activities. Recent research suggests that While a significant amount of income is typically generated, the returns from this form of activity are relatively poor. Across the top 500 the mean income generated per £1 of expenditure has been shown to be £2.14. It is interesting to note that no significant size or category effects could be discerned in these figures, suggesting that charities of a different size and nature of activity will tend to achieve the same level of performance. Returns on community fundraising activity in the USA are hard to tease out from the available figures, but are likely to be of the same sort of order.

THE ROLE OF THE VOLUNTEER

Community fundraising relies on volunteers, who participate in fundraising activities that promote or advance some aspect of the common good, without expectation of financial gain. According to the Corporation for National and Community Service (2007), over 26 per cent of adult Americans volunteered in some capacity in 2006. In the UK a Cabinet Office report of 2007 found 59 per cent of survey respondents had volunteered in the past year.

Trends in volunteering

It is difficult to draw general conclusions, but it is clear that changes in lifestyle, in the numbers of women entering the workforce and in working patterns have impacted on the nature of volunteer activity and on the demographic characteristics of the volunteer fundraising pool.

In the UK this volunteer pool appears to be shrinking. This is not the case in the USA, but the stated motives behind volunteering and the nature of volunteer involvement has altered.

Individuals take on volunteer work through:

- the desire to change society
- the desire to obtain experiences that can be useful in paid employment
- the desire to help a specific cause
- the desire to meet others
- the desire to prepare for a volunteer 'career' after retirement
- the desire to get inside institutions and organizations and ensure that they are doing what they profess to be doing.

Other trends:

- A wider spectrum of people is now volunteering. Rather than just the healthy middle classes, many elderly and handicapped people now offer their services, as do increasing numbers of professionals. Surveys consistently show a marked drop in volunteering among young people aged 18–24.
- Volunteers are becoming more demanding. They want more input into what they are doing.
- In the USA, increased numbers of African Americans and members of the Hispanic community are volunteering.
- The number of female volunteers aged 55 plus is dropping in both the USA and the UK. This group previously provided the main workforce for much local fundraising activity.

These trends are putting increasing pressure on nonprofits to improve their systems for volunteer recruitment and management, while the potentially contracting pool of volunteers (at least from some sections of the population) points up the importance to nonprofits of making every effort to retain volunteers for as long as possible once the investment has been made in recruiting and training them.

Recruiting fundraising volunteers

It tends to be more difficult to recruit volunteers prepared to undertake fundraising work than to attract voluntary help with programme work. For example, a group dealing with the welfare of domestic animals are likely to find it easier to recruit volunteers prepared to exercise dogs from the local animal refuge than to find volunteers to collect donations on the street. Fundraising ('asking for money') can be viewed as an unpleasant task, as well as being one step removed from the cause.

Generally, volunteers have to make a concrete connection with an organization before they will offer their time. This is often through being asked by a friend, through participation in the organization directly, or as a result of a friend or family member benefiting from the work of the organization. Volunteer recruitment thus operates primarily through 'word of mouth'.

As with donor recruitment, the profiles and sources of past volunteers will provide the best guidelines for locating and securing further recruits. The motivations of past and existing volunteer cohorts can be teased out and analysed to aid in presenting the offer that is made to volunteers.

For many, the only 'payback' required is the knowledge that society is gaining from their efforts, or that they will get the opportunity to meet new people and make new friends. An increasing number, however, will be looking for specific experience that they can use later in the workplace, or will be looking to use specific skills in their volunteer work.

Retaining and managing fundraising volunteers

Recruiting and training new volunteers is expensive, and efforts are better placed in retaining and developing those volunteers who have already signed up to help. Surveys of lapsed volunteers, and of satisfaction and dissatisfaction among current volunteers tends to yield the following issues:

- Unrealistic expectations when recruited. This can be the fault of the volunteer, who may have had an inaccurate picture of what volunteering would be like. It is often, however, the fault of the nonprofit, which may have 'oversold' the benefits of volunteering in its recruitment communications.
- Lack of appreciation from co-workers and beneficiaries.
- Lack of training and supervision.
- Feeling undervalued, especially by employed staff.
- Excessive demands on time.

Training is probably most commonly cited as a problem area, both in terms of a lack of training being offered and of the quality of training being perceived as poor and limited.

The use of volunteers can be problematic for a fundraising organization, and is certainly not an uncomplicated advantage for the nonprofit sector. Some volunteers prove difficult to manage because they are of the opinion that since they are donating their time free of charge they do not work (as such) for the organization and should therefore be requested rather than directed to undertake tasks. Some feel that they should have the right to exercise a great deal of control and independence in their work, and some require continual expressions of appreciation for their generosity.

Other problems come through in mixing professional paid staff with volunteers. Staff are often critical of the attitude of volunteers, who can appear to be:

- short-term members of the team and therefore not likely to assume responsibility for the long-term repercussions of their activity;
- insufficiently aware of the workings and ethics of the organization and thus likely to make mistakes when representing it;
- unwilling to take direction or guidance.

The attitude of management with regard to volunteers can thus be seen to be absolutely key to the maintenance of good relations between paid and unpaid staff. The optimum attitude is to treat volunteers entirely straightforwardly and as much as possible like paid professional staff. This should encompass full training, job descriptions and the setting and monitoring of targets, benchmarks and goals. This 'professionalization' of volunteering is challenging for nonprofits, and carries significant costs, but experienced organizations maintain that it brings results. 'The steady transformation of the volunteer from well-meaning amateur to trained, professional unpaid staff member is the most significant development in the nonprofit sector' (Drucker 1989:91).

NEW FORMS OF COMMUNITY GIVING

US nonprofit commentators (Bearman et al. 2005) have identified the rise of 'giving circles' as a 'new era in philanthropy'. This relatively new development in community giving is estimated to involve over 8,000 individuals in America and Canada. A giving circle has been described as a cross between a book club and an investment group. They entail individuals pooling their resources and then deciding together where these resources should be distributed.

Giving circles, to varying degrees, pool funds, give away resources, educate members about philanthropy and issues in the community, include a social dimension, engage members in volunteering and maintain independence by not affiliating with any one particular charity. The degree of each of these aspects varies depending on the type of giving circle – they may be loose networks, small groups or formal organizations.

Part of what makes giving circles special is their flexibility. They range from intimate 12-person groups that meet in a living room to 400-person organizations with their own nonprofit status. Although all circles require a financial contribution, the giving level also varies widely, from less than a dollar per day in some circles to up to twenty thousand dollars and more in others.

THE FUTURE FOR COMMUNITY FUNDRAISING

Community and local fundraising is an area in which there is currently little agreement across the sector as to the optimum structure and reasonable expectations and measurements. It is also an area of great turbulence, with many major nonprofits in both the UK and the USA reorganizing, restructuring and altering their local fundraising operations on a regular basis.

The key problems lie in the costs of maintaining an infrastructure to support community fundraising activity, and in making a local fundraising presence cost-effective in terms of a measurable ROI. Structurally the arrangements range from completely centralised nonprofits with no local presence at all, through to federated structures where the local groups are separately registered legal entities and work independently of the central organization.

This situation is complicated by the other advantages of a local presence such as publicity and credibility, which are not easy to measure in balance-sheet terms but which undoubtedly have a value to nonprofits in terms of both fundraising and service delivery.

Historically local and community fundraising has been heavily based on volunteer groups, and it is therefore an area in which changes in the demographics, motives and needs of volunteers impact heavily. Competition in local fundraising is also fierce as both national and local charities compete in the arena.

If community fundraising is to be maintained as a viable part of the nonprofit portfolio it would appear that its impact will have to be measured carefully, and not evaluated purely in terms of ROI. Those nonprofits likely to develop local fundraising activity most effectively in the years to come will be those that can maintain a sensible balance of overheads and infrastructure, likely to arise from increased levels of central control and increased integration of community fundraising activity with other fundraising routes.

SUMMARY

In this chapter we have discussed the wide-ranging fundraising activities that are undertaken within local communities. As we have seen, such activities generate relatively small gifts, and are labour- and people-intensive to organize and run. While reliant on volunteers to take on much of the workload, community fundraising carries substantial overhead costs and this, coupled with the relatively low income generated, means that the ROI across the activity is generally only of the order of $/£1: 2.1.

However, local fundraising activity is also of value because of the publicity it generates, the credibility it may add to the nonprofit and the increased accessibility it promotes in the local community. There is thus an argument for measuring its impact and value in terms beyond simple ROI.

Volunteers are key to local fundraising, and we have briefly discussed the levels of volunteering current in the USA and the UK, current trends in the volunteers market, and the likely impact of these trends on fundraising activity and profitability in the future.

DISCUSSION QUESTIONS

1   In your role as organizer of an annual sponsored walk, produce a timeline for the planning of the event. What documents and data would you look to gather from previous records?
2   Produce a job specification for a fundraising volunteer who will be expected to take part in a house-to-house raffle ticket sale.
3   Draft a projection of income and costs for a local fête event. What ROI would you expect from the event overall and how would you justify this to your fundraising director?

REFERENCES

Bearman, J., Beaudoin-Schwartz, B. and Rutnik, T. (2005) 'Giving Circles: A Powerful Vehicle for Women', *New Directions for Philanthropic Fundraising*, Winter: 109–123.

Cabinet Office (2007) *Helping Out: A National Survey of Volunteering and Charitable Giving*, Cabinet Office, London.

Corporation for National and Community Service (2007) 'Volunteering in America: 2007 State Trends and Rankings in Civic Life', Office of Research and Policy Development, Washington DC.

Drucker, P. (1989) 'What Business Can Learn From Nonprofits', *Harvard Business Review*, July August: 91.

Kotler, P. and Andreasen, A.R. (1991) *Strategic Marketing for Nonprofit Organizations,* 4th edn, Prentice-Hall, Englewood Cliffs, NJ.

Part III

Corporate/trust fundraising

Chapter 11

Corporate fundraising

OBJECTIVES

By the end of this chapter you should be able to:

- Describe trends in the corporate fundraising market.
- Assess the motives for corporate support of nonprofits.
- Develop a corporate fundraising plan.
- Develop an appropriate structure for corporate fundraising.
- Quantify the impact of the fundraising approach adopted.
- Develop plans for employee fundraising and payroll giving.

INTRODUCTION

In the UK there are few reliable figures on the value of support received from the business community. Pharoah (2008) estimates that cash support to our largest 300 charities is worth around £0.5 billion. This is a pathetically small percentage of the total fundraising income of these organizations, which stood at £14.4 billion in 2006/7. We estimate that the average percentage of pre-tax profit donated to good causes by businesses each year in the UK is correspondingly low and typically of the order of 0.2 per cent. In the United States the figure is much higher at 1.2 per cent. Although all these figures are small, it is important to note that there are a plethora of different ways in which companies can support nonprofits and many of these do not show up as cash in charity accounts. That said, even accounting for the value of donated goods and services, staff time, access to expertise and so on, the overall value of corporate support is much lower than many fundraisers and trustees believe.

Corporate fundraising should therefore not be regarded as a panacea for cash-starved nonprofits. It is a highly complex form of relationship fundraising that will not suit either the needs or capabilities of every organization. The potential to make money from this market must be carefully evaluated and a strategy for entry developed only where there is a clear rationale for doing so.

In this chapter we will review trends in corporate giving, explain why corporate support is offered, the forms that it might take and suggest a structured approach to corporate fundraising.

WHY DO COMPANIES GIVE?

At the beginning of the twentieth century corporate philanthropy was little more than an extension of individual philanthropy. High-profile individuals like Andrew Carnegie and John D. Rockerfeller endowed institutions in keeping with their own individual preferences and tastes. Until the early 1980s corporate giving still owed much to the interests and concerns of chief executives who usually made the final decision on the organizations they wished to support. Under this paradigm corporate giving could be viewed as a genuinely 'philanthropic' activity where the primary objective was for the business to give something back to the society in which it operated.

An alternative approach to corporate support first began to emerge in the late 1960s with a number of organizations beginning to expect benefits to accrue from their charitable giving. This 'opportunity'-based paradigm regarded a liaison with a nonprofit as a means of attaining key business objectives. Writers such as Mescon and Tilson (1987) or Wokutch and Spencer (1987) identified this as a shift towards what they call 'dual agenda' or 'strategic' giving whereby organizations will be predisposed to giving to charities that have a good fit with their own strategic objectives. As an example, the margarine brand Flora has been supporting the British Heart Foundation since 1996. The association raises money for the charity, but it also fits very well with the positioning of the brand and its role in relation to keeping fit. Similarly Chanel, when they wanted to launch an exclusive new fragrance to wealthy 'elite' consumers, sponsored an opening night dinner and fashion show connected with a performance at the Metropolitan Opera. The Met. received $1.2 million in donations and Chanel gained the exposure it required for its product.

The past 40 years has seen a gradual shift from philanthropy to strategic giving and in the United States there is evidence that the pace of this change has recently hastened. The Committee to Encourage Corporate Philanthropy (CECP), whose membership comprises companies that account for about 45 per cent of reported corporate giving, note a marked decline in 'philanthropic' giving. Between 2002 and 2003, for example, the incidence of this form of giving by CECP members declined from nearly 60 per cent to the low forties. 'Strategic' giving rose 15 per cent, and 'commercial sponsorship' doubled, from less than 10 per cent to nearly 20 per cent (Epstein 2005).

In strategic giving the benefits sought by a business from its relationship with a nonprofit might include increased sales; brand differentiation; enhanced brand image; improved employee recruitment, morale and retention; demonstration of shared values with the target market; enhanced government relations; a broadened customer base; and the ability to reach new customer segments (see e.g. Andreasen 1996; Sagawa 2001; Wymer and Samu 2003). Authors such as Shell (1989) have, in addition, emphasized the benefits of giving in strengthening ties to the local community and offering companies an opportunity to express corporate values in the public arena.

Putting aside the philanthropic and opportunity-based paradigms Himmelstein (1997) argues that in some communities where philanthropy thrives out of proportion to per capita income (e.g. Minneapolis/St Paul in the United States), there are further reasons why corporate philanthropy is stimulated. He argues that corporate leaders with strong links to the philanthropic community effectively set the agenda for their peers and encourage others to give by example. The more ties a given CEO has to these leaders the more their particular corporation will give away. It is interesting to note that so pervasive is the culture of giving in these communities that for a manager to succeed in business and become a powerful figure in the business life of that community s/he must publicly demonstrate their generosity and have a proven track record as a philanthropist.

Norms are enormously important. Where organizations collaborate on other business matters it would appear that they begin to develop very similar patterns of corporate giving. While it may not be possible for a business to share all the aspects of the corporate strategy it is adopting, those aspects that pertain to giving are not regarded as sensitive and are significantly more likely to be shared and perhaps copied by others. Extant research has identified that the more 'professional' an organization's approach to managing giving, the more likely its pattern of support is to resemble that of the corporate sector as a whole. Where managers have a strong tie to their professional community, they share their experiences of philanthropy through that community and thereby establish norms of support (Scanlan 1997).

FORMS OF BUSINESS SUPPORT

Overview

Whatever the initial motive for engaging with a nonprofit there are a variety of different forms of corporate support. A selection of the most common are listed here:

- *Cash donations*   This remains the most common form of corporate support of nonprofits and in many countries is popular partly because there are corporation tax benefits that can accrue as a consequence of the gift.
- *Donations of stocks/shares*   In some countries corporates can also give stocks and shares to a nonprofit of their choice. Again, this is typically tax efficient since the gift accrues a tax deduction equal to the value of the shares at the time of donation.
- *Publicity*   Nonprofits can gain from the association with a business since that business may promote its link to the cause and thereby heighten public awareness of the organization. The relationship in the early 1980s, for example between American Express and a little known charity 'Share Our Strength' served to greatly increase the standing of this organization (Himmelstein 1997). This enhanced awareness has been shown to lead to greater success in attracting public donations, members, volunteers, advocacy support and community understanding of the goals of the nonprofit (Wagner and Thompson 1994; Bragdon 1985). An example of a case where an organization was able to offer publicity to a nonprofit is provided in Exhibit 11.1. In this case the British Heart Foundation used their partner's network to spread their message.
- *Gifts of products/services (also known as gifts in kind)*   Often the goods or services produced by a company can be of value to the beneficiaries of a charity. The donation of food at or near its 'sell-by' or 'expiry date' to soup kitchens is one such example. The donation of computer equipment to schools and colleges is also common and gifts of office equipment, furniture, computer supplies or even photocopying facilities have been reported. There are now specialist charities that encourage corporates to provide gifts of this type and act as a clearing house for organizations that wish to find appropriate recipients. An example is depicted in Plate 11.1.

    In Kind Direct asks companies to donate surplus goods, mainly newly manufactured items. They might be ends of lines, seasonal items, samples, customer returns and things in damaged packaging or with slight defects. At the time of writing goods worth over £70 million have been donated by 750 companies, and thousands of charities have benefited. Gifts in kind can also be tax effective in some countries with the current value of the goods (i.e. not their full sale value) typically being tax deductible. Finally it is important to recognize the public relations value to some companies of this form of gift. If a clothing company disposes of 500 coats with slight imperfections at the local dump whilst inner-city children are freezing in the cold it could very well end up facing a major public relations challenge. Such gifts can therefore benefit both parties.

EXHIBIT 11.1 LLOYDS TSB AND THE BRITISH HEART FOUNDATION

Lloyds TSB reviewed the nature of its partnerships with charities. One major change made as a consequence of this review is that partnerships now last for two years, doubling their previous commitment. Lloyds TSB realized that by the time they had 'got to know' the partner and wound down from the relationship as the end of a year drew near, it had left them with a window of opportunity of only around four to five months to make a difference to the cause.

Their second innovation was to give their nonprofit partner a good lead time to prepare for the partnership. Lloyds TSB has 68,000 staff in 2,000 buildings spread across the UK. A charity can experience problems if a significant number of staff are interested in getting involved in the partnership; the charity needs time to put in place the resources to handle the demand.

The partnership between Lloyds TSB and the British Heart Foundation was built on these two principles. The partnership was designed to last for two years, and with a lead time of four months to prepare both organizations were ready to hit the ground running. The British Heart Foundation used the partnership to promote its healthy lifestyle messages through Lloyds TSB branches and in so doing reach communities right across the country. It has also had access to the bank's 16 million customers.

Lloyds also sees a benefit. Aside from the goodwill generated from staff involvement in fundraising, the organization hopes that the healthy living messages the charity communicates will ultimately benefit its insurance business Scottish Widows. Reducing the number of heart attack victims will reduce the number of claimants the organization has to deal with (Little 2008a).

Plate 11.1 *In Kind Direct*
Source: In Kind Direct. Reproduced with kind permission.

- *Staff time* Some corporates will agree to second staff to a nonprofit where specific expertise is being sought. This may be management expertise or perhaps technical skills where this would assist in improving the service provision to beneficiaries. Other corporates are willing to release staff who can act as volunteers to work with the nonprofit in whatever way desired (Sagawa and Segal 2000; Smith 1994.) Indeed some companies have even created their own volunteer departments, complete with their own budget and staff. The most successful employee volunteer programmes have several elements in common. First, employees drive the effort, and those doing the volunteering are allowed to select the causes they support. Also, successful programmes are vigorously supported by the company with volunteers being featured in the corporate newsletter and being recognized in other ways by management.
- *Sponsorship* Corporates are often willing to sponsor a particular aspect of a nonprofits service provision in return for an acknowledgement, or perhaps placement of the organization's name or logo. Organizations may also sponsor events or gala dinners that offer brand enhancement to the corporate whilst at the same time facilitating fundraising for the nonprofit from those present (Marconi 2002).
- *Fundraising from staff* A number of corporates are prepared to open up access to their workforce. Rather than give as an organization, such businesses will allow a fundraising team to solicit donations from their staff, perhaps through a simple monetary collection or by facilitating payroll giving. These are topics we will return to in detail later in this chapter.
- *Fundraising from customers* Finally, some corporates make it possible for nonprofits to fundraise from their customers. This may be either direct or indirect (Morton 2007). In the case of the former, nonprofits can solicit funds directly from customers – as in the Change For Good case cited here – perhaps collecting money on a business premises or placing a collection box in a retail outlet. In the case of the latter, the arrangement is more complex and would involve either collecting a donation from the customer when they pay their bill, or making a donation on the customer's behalf when a purchase of a product/service has been made. This final category of arrangement is known as cause-related marketing, which we will consider in further detail in the following section.

BRITISH TELECOM (BT) AND SCOPE

BT and the cerebral palsy charity Scope developed a more intimate partnership than most corporate collaborations. Their partnership emerged from work by BT's research laboratory with the charity to develop a device to help young disabled people with communication impairments. They developed the 'Wheeltop' which is a laptop attached to a wheelchair designed to allow users to speak, surf the net, text and download music. Scope was initially hoping that BT would provide the funding to build these devices but instead BT's charity team worked with Scope to put together a proposal to BT's corporate social responsibility board. The new proposal under the banner 'No Voice – No Choice' was centred on campaigning instead for the wheeltop technology to made available to as many people as possible as a statutory right. BT maintains an active role in guiding the project with senior executives sitting on the project's steering committee, as do two BT apprentices with cerebral palsy. Their collective role is to offer Scope advice and highlight opportunities the charity may not itself have been aware of.

Source: Little (2008b).

BRITISH AIRWAYS – CHANGE FOR GOOD

UNICEF and British Airways have been working in partnership since 1994, creating the ground-breaking Change For Good programme. Passengers on all British Airways flights are invited to donate any unwanted foreign currency to UNICEF using envelopes stowed in their seat pocket, or available from the flight crew. Change For Good has supported UNICEF's work in 50 countries.

Cause-related-marketing

McDonald's in the USA were the first organization to develop cause-related marketing, linking the purchase of their products to the Ronald McDonald House Charities. It was not until 1981 that the term was coined for first time by American Express who introduced the phrase 'Cause-related marketing' or CRM to define a new form of corporate 'giving'. Under CRM the link with

Plate 11.2 *Change for Good collecting envelope*

Source: © UNICEF (UK). Reproduced with kind permission.

a nonprofit is used to assist the business in increasing sales of its product. Its motivation is thus not philanthropic since such arrangements often make considerably more money for the corporate partner than they do for the nonprofit. As the senior vice-president of American Express noted in 1984: 'if your primary goal is to make money for a worthy cause, stay away from it. It's not meant to be philanthropy. Its objective is to make money for your business' (Josephson 1984:10).

Varadarajan and Menon (1988:60) define cause-related marketing as:

> A process of formulating and implementing marketing activities that are characterized by an offer from the firm to contribute a specified amount to a designated cause when customers engage in revenue providing exchanges that satisfy organizational and individual objectives.

The evidence from the United States is that CRM continues to grow in popularity with companies having spent $1.3 billion on CRM programmes in 2006, a 20 per cent increase over the previous year (Chiagouris and Ray 2007).

The exact form that the relationship takes varies considerably, but classically what this means in practice is that in return for using the nonprofit's brand name on a particular product (or service) the business will make a donation to the nonprofit every time a purchase is made. Mintel (2003) reports that the percentage of the public participating in CRM schemes has increased significantly over time from 56 per cent of adults in 2000 to 67 per cent in 2003. This undoubtedly reflects the growth in the number of such programmes over time, and it also suggests a growing consumer acceptance of such promotions as potentially serving a valuable purpose in raising money for charities (Farquarson 2000). Examples are illustrated in Plate 11.3

Large-scale surveys in both the UK and the USA have consistently shown that if key factors such as price and quality are equivalent, consumers are willing to break a previous tie with a product in favour of an alternative identified with supporting a particular cause (Cone Inc. 2002). In the UK Farquarson (2000) reports that consumers feel that companies supporting causes are more trustworthy and innovative than other companies. The study also reports that 77 per cent

Plate 11.3 *Cause-related marketing examples*

of consumers are positively influenced in their buying decisions by CRM programmes. It is interesting to note that this seems particularly true of female customers. Authors such as Ross et al. (1991) have consistently shown that females are more favourably disposed to pro-social appeals and hence more receptive to CRM appeals. Women also develop more favourable attitudes towards both the cause and the sponsoring company (see also Kropp et al. 1999). The evidence is therefore clear that there may be very real advantages for a business in developing a CRM scheme, particularly where a substantial proportion of their customer base is female.

Before leaving the topic of CRM it is important to note that such schemes are not without their critics. Work by Webb and Mohr (1998) has identified that some segments of consumers are highly sceptical of CRM activities and writers such as Corkery (1989) and Levine (1989) regard CRM as little more than a shallow sales ploy that will leave consumers largely unimpressed. More recent empirical work suggests that how consumers will feel about a particular scheme is likely to be a function of the degree of benefit that accrues to the nonprofit. Where only paltry sums are donated relative to the value of the product/service consumers are significantly more likely to react negatively to the scheme. There is thus a strong case for both partners to a CRM initiative to sit down together to work out a mutually beneficial arrangement. There is nothing to be gained on the part of the business by being seen to exploit the nonprofit partner (Daw 2006).

Where CRM schemes do work well they can raise significant sums. In 2006, for example, Pampers formed an association with UNICEF. For every pack of Pampers nappies (diapers) purchased in the two months before Christmas, the brand donated funding equivalent to one tetanus vaccination to UNICEF. By the end of 2006 Pampers had raised funding for 7.4 million vaccines and the campaign delivered record market share highs for the organization.

Finally, it should be noted that the sector's use of terminology is changing. While we continue to view CRM as a very specific form of corporate–nonprofit partnership, there are now many writers and practising fundraisers who use the term to refer to all categories of relationship a business might have with a nonprofit. Cause-related marketing is thus becoming a blanket expression referring to all forms of corporate engagement (Atkins 1999).

Payroll giving

In the UK it is possible to make a donation direct from an individual's payroll to a charity. To facilitate this form of giving it is normally necessary for the nonprofit to seek permission to address groups of employees at the place of business either directly themselves or through the use of a fundraising agent/intermediary.

In the UK payroll giving was first introduced in 1987 when Barnardo's pioneered work in this area. The present operation of the scheme in the UK is depicted in Figure 11.1. Employers willing to offer payroll giving as a service to their employees (there remains no statutory requirement for them to do so) must make their staff aware that the facility is available. Employees wishing to participate then authorize their employer to deduct a regular donation from their pay. This donation can be made to any registered charity currently in existence. There is no minimum or maximum limit for donations. Since the donations are deducted before PAYE (Pay As You Earn) tax, the employee gets tax relief for the donation at their top rate of tax. Some employers value the scheme as a means of fostering the retention of their staff and offer a system of matching, or part-matching, the donations made by their employees.

Once an employee has notified their employer of their intention to give through payroll giving, the employer makes the deduction and passes the donation to an 'agency charity' (which must be approved by the Inland Revenue). The agency charity claims the tax relief to which the recipient charity is entitled and then passes the donation to the organization concerned. In return for a small commission these agency charities typically assist an employer in creating a scheme, encourage

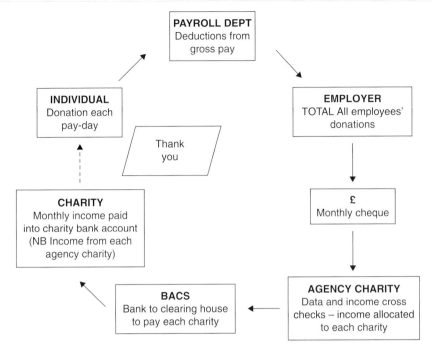

Figure 11.1 *Payroll giving scheme*

internal promotions of the scheme and provide information and statistics on how the scheme is progressing. The agency system also makes it possible for an employee to give, quite literally, to any charity of their choice. It was originally felt that the cost of dealing directly with all the charities their employees might choose to support could otherwise prove prohibitive for many employers.

For the year ending March 2007 payroll giving raised £89 million for charities. This figure was topped up with an additional £10 million from employers matching their employees' contributions. This figure of almost a £100 million represents a significant sum for the approximate 13,000 charities that are beneficiaries of payroll giving, but is small change in comparison with the balance of UK giving. It accounts for less than 1 per cent of all charitable donations and less than 3 per cent of all tax-efficient donations (Potter and Scales 2008).

During the year 2006–2007 there were around 644,000 payroll donors out of a total of 24 million employees paid through PAYE. Only 10.5 million (44 per cent) of these are employed by organizations with payroll giving schemes in place, so coverage is patchy despite the best efforts of the government to encourage participation. The average donation made through payroll giving is between £7 and £10 per month (Potter and Scales 2008).

The scheme has suffered from a number of problems, notably that the procedure for donor recruitment is quite bureaucratic and involves a number of different parties in establishing the relationship. It has also been quite difficult, historically, to retain and develop donors recruited in this way. As the scheme is linked to a particular employer, when individuals switch jobs their payroll giving relationship is terminated. The profile of a typical donor has also caused some problems because payroll givers are not typical charity donors. While one of the advantages of the scheme is that it is capable of reaching non-traditional audiences (a greater proportion of men, individuals aged 31–45 and those in blue collar occupations), charities have found developing the value of these individuals problematic.

Employee fundraising

As we have already noted, companies can sometimes open up access to their workforce for other forms of fundraising. In such cases there are a variety of activities that may be organized to solicit funds from members of the workforce. Each of these may be established either as a stand-alone programme or as part of an integrated pattern of corporate support where the organization too will participate in giving.

Employee fundraising can either be initiated by a corporate opening up access for a nonprofit to its workforce, or it may be initiated by individual members of the workforce who put pressure on the employer to support the philanthropic activity that they are already engaged in. Both forms are common and there are a variety of activities that come under this general heading.

- *Events*   The employer may donate time or space for the hosting of a charity event staff members may participate in. This may be a social gathering or dinner, but it may equally be a sponsored walk, golf, tennis, swimming or challenge event. While it is the employees themselves who fundraise, it is often the case that an employer will donate funds too, perhaps matching the funds generated by the employees.
- *Workplace collections*   Often where particular members of staff have a link or commitment to a particular cause they will raise funds simply by collecting cash donations from their peers. Typically, permission would be sought from the employer for this to happen on work premises and/or the employer's time.
- *Sales of merchandise and raffles*   Some corporates permit members of staff to distribute the trading catalogues of nonprofits they are involved with and for purchased goods to be held on the premises for collection by members of staff who have made a purchase, or to sell raffle tickets.
- *Group activities*   A further common form of employee fundraising involves the nonprofit in making a presentation to groups of staff who have expressed an interest in the cause. The goal here is to explain to members of staff how they can get involved with the work of the organization or in fundraising for it and to suggest activities that these groups of individuals may engage in. Such presentations are usually made on the company's premises and/or on company time.
- *Charity of the year/charity of choice*   The final category of activity is really only an amalgam of those noted above. Some businesses will focus attention in a given year on one specific cause or organization. Usually the corporate will offer a donation of cash, time or gifts in kind and take steps to encourage the employees to conduct additional fundraising of their own. The result is an overall commitment on the part of everyone within the organization to provide meaningful support to one particular nonprofit. Indeed, several large corporations now have 'Charity of the Year' schemes and since the value of support can in aggregate be very substantial, the competition among nonprofits to achieve this status is intense.

WHO TO ASK?

Selecting the right organization

Pick up any good practitioner 'how-to' guide on corporate fundraising and it will be guaranteed to exalt the need for a careful process of research to identify suitable corporate partners. Scrutiny of the local/national press, business directories and online data is suggested as a means of identifying the interests of particular organizations and the likelihood that they might be willing to support the fundraiser's nonprofit.

TRANSCO

Transco provides and maintains gas pipelines and has an ambitious commitment to an 'injury-free' working environment. In the mid-1990s despite increasingly high-profile campaigns within the organization the number of accidents taking place at work had not reduced according to the company's plan. In 1999 Transco took the radical step of creating a new initiative – the so-called Safety Charity Challenge.

The company challenged employees to identify and remove workplace hazards. For each hazard that was identified and removed Transco made a donation to disability charity MENCAP, or the Scottish equivalent ENABLE. The amount of the donation was half the amount of money the company expected to save from removing that hazard. The other half of the saving was retained in the business, making the scheme entirely self-financing.

Since the initiative began, there has been an 85 Per cent drop in the number of injuries that result in lost time. From the peak of 500 work-related injuries in 1998, in 2004 the company expected just 50. The company has donated over £3 million to charity so far.

While this process may well yield results, research into corporate fundraising has suggested a number of ways in which fundraisers can focus their prospecting efforts. These are summarized as follows:

- *Profitability*   Profitability is key to whether donations will be offered and the level of such donations. Less profitable organizations are less likely to engage in philanthropy (McGuire et al. 1988). The fundraiser may thus find it useful to look at the recent financial performance of potential supporters and to use this data to narrow the list of potential prospects.
- *Turnover*   Turnover is also key. Larger organizations are significantly more likely both to participate in giving and to offer higher value support (Adams and Hardwick 1998). Writers such as Watts and Zimmerman (1978) and Lenway and Rehbein (1991) have argued that this is because larger companies are likely to be more visible in their communities and also to government. Support of the nonprofit community may thus serve to enhance their reputation and mitigate any risk that the government might intervene in their sector with higher taxes or compliance costs. There are many advantages to being seen as a responsible corporate citizen.
- *Longevity*   The longevity of both the nonprofit and corporate partners is positively related to donations. In other words, firms that were created some decades ago are significantly more likely to offer support to nonprofits than firms created more recently. It also appears that nonprofits that have been around a while are more likely to attract support. While it would be wrong to speculate in the absence of research it does seem likely that these older nonprofits have had longer to establish a reputation/brand and may thus have more to offer any potential corporate partner.
- *Business sector/country of ownership*   Adams and Hardwick (1998) have identified that participation in giving and the level of giving varies considerably depending on the sector of business a particular firm might be operating in and the country of origin of its ownership. There are big differences in giving between the manufacturing and service sectors (the former are significantly more generous), but patterns of support also vary within these broad headings, reflecting the various needs of different sectors and

237

subsectors. Firms that are owned by others in countries with a strong tradition of corporate support also tend to be more generous than those without such links.

■ *Nature of the shareholding*   It is interesting to note that those firms with widely dispersed shareholdings are also felt to be more likely to donate money to nonprofits. The rationale here is that managers will often give, not for business reasons, but to enhance their own standing and influence in the community. A nonprofit association can enhance their reputation capital in both internal and external labour markets (Haley 1991). As Hart (1993:16) notes, 'it is not clear that (donations) … are made with the consent of the firm's owners or whether they are a form of self-aggrandizing, or self promoting behavior by management'. Companies with dispersed shareholdings present managers with more power in this regard than in circumstances of concentrated ownership (Grossman and Hart 1980). When stockholding is concentrated managers are unlikely to pursue strategies inconsistent with shareholder's direct interests (Hill and Snell 1989). Similarly, Ullman (1985) has argued that diverse ownership may act to increase the pressure for socially responsible behaviour since a breadth of shareholders increases the possibility that one or more of them will have a philanthropic motivation. It should be noted that whilst intuitive no empirical support has yet been provided in support of these assertions.

■ *Potential fit*   Nonprofits may well attempt, quite rationally, to identify potential partners based on simple accounting data as alluded to above. However, the concept of 'fit' is also relevant. The idea here is that an organization ought to look for certain characteristics in a potential partner, leading to a higher probability of successful outcomes. Samu and Wymer (2002) describe fit in terms of the degree of congruence between a cause and a business's product/service. For example, Gerber (baby food/products) would have a higher level of fit with the Great Ormond Street Children's Hospital than Exxon (petroleum products). We develop this theme in more detail in the next section.

The concept of fit

Drumwright (1996) views fit between a business and a cause as a type of affinity, in which supporters of a cause feel the business partner's core business has some relationship to that cause. More recent work by Drumwright et al. (2000) looked at seven distinctive dimensions of 'fit':

1 *Mission fit* The fit between a partner's mission and the purpose of the relationship formed.
2 *Management fit* The level of interpersonal compatibility between partner managers.
3 *Workforce fit* The fit between a company's workforce and the cause the company is supporting.
4 *Target market fit* The fit between the company's target market and the cause.
5 *Product/cause fit* The degree of congruence between the company's product and the cause.
6 *Cycle fit* The degree of synchronization between operational events in the collaborating organizations.
7 *Cultural fit* Similarities among partners regarding norms, behaviours and attitudes.

It is interesting to compare this list developed by an academic team with one developed by a nonprofit professional. Elischer (2001) suggests that fit should be evaluated by examining:

■ *Values*   Do the nonprofit and corporate partner share the same values base? Does the corporate respect the same issues as the nonprofit? Does the corporate take a strong (and compatible) stand in relation to business ethics?

- *Brand*   What will be the impact of a partnership on the brands of both organizations? How will this work, look and feel? How will stakeholders respond to this?
- *Objectives*   Is there a clear fit between the objectives of both parties? What do both organizations want to achieve? Can both sets of objectives be met?
- *Structure/geography*   Are they located in the same city? If they are both international, do they operate in the same countries? Most corporates will expect to engage with a nonprofit that can adequately match their needs and respond at an appropriately local level. In the UK, for example, UNICEF has a strong relationship with the soccer team Manchester United, even though the charity is based in London. The relationship works because the charity has been able to offer a dedicated (and local) member of their regional fundraising team to manage the relationship and to respond to the needs of the corporate partner (UNICEF 2002).

The central idea running throughout these two lists is that the greater the degree of fit between the nonprofit and corporate the stronger will be the resultant relationship and the more likely it will be to succeed. This presupposes, however, that both parties do want a 'relationship' and in fact many forms of corporate support, as we established earlier, do not require this level of engagement.

It is also important to note that although these lists have been offered as a means of appraising potential partnerships, many of the points made by both authors are difficult to appraise a priori. While they can certainly be appraised in the course of discussions it is doubtful whether they could genuinely be used to shortlist potential partners for support. Drawing from Drumwright et al. (2000), issues of management fit, cycle fit and cultural fit, for example, would be difficult to research in advance, as would Elischer's notion of 'values' fit. Thus whilst some of these criteria could be used in targeting potential new partners, the real utility of these lists probably lies in reflecting on the strengths and weaknesses of various relationships and fostering an understanding of when and why things may go wrong. They are thus most useful as a framework once discussions are under way and should be borne in mind as a checklist of points to consider before any form of contract is eventually signed.

Selecting the right level of contact

The starting point for many corporate fundraisers will be the Board. In essence the Board of a company exists to serve the shareholders interests and to monitor the way in which the organization is being managed. The composition of the Board is often quite diverse with individuals being drawn from many different walks of life. From a fundraising perspective it may well be the Board that drives the philanthropic involvement of an organization or sanctions the suggestions offered by management. It is possible to research board composition and nonprofits would typically look to identify whether anyone within their organization has a personal contact on the Board who could be approached to act as an advocate. The key here lies in building up the network of contacts and relationships a nonprofit has, particularly given that many board members are in fact members of more than one board.

Reporting to the Board is the executive management of the organization, most significantly the chairman, CEO or managing director. This individual would typically wield the most influence over the direction the organization might take and in some, particularly smaller, organizations any corporate philanthropy is likely to reflect their personal interests. Sadly, these individuals are easy for charities to target with solicitations and they are frequently bombarded with 'asks'. As Elischer (2002) has noted, many have thus developed sophisticated 'defence shields' to protect them from this blanket solicitation. It should also be noted that in medium and larger sized organizations, the decision over which nonprofit will be supported will frequently be taken lower down the organizational hierarchy, drawing on one of a number of departmental budgets. Contact with the CEO may therefore be neither desirable nor necessary.

The most notable of these budgets will be the marketing budget. Where a strong business case can be made to a director of marketing for increasing sales, it may well be most appropriate for a nonprofit to target this part of the organization first. Where the benefits are likely to accrue to the company as a whole, perhaps through building the overall brand image or reputation of the organization, it may be more appropriate to approach the public relations function, perhaps in tandem with an approach to the director of marketing.

If the nonprofit believes that the benefit to the corporate will lie primarily in the enhancing of its relationships with its workforce or local community it may be preferable to target the personnel or human relations (HR) department. Some organizations house their corporate giving budgets here, particularly after the introduction of payroll giving initiatives. It is also important to recognize that many forms of corporate support, such as staff secondments, volunteering, the provision of training and so on will all typically be controlled by the HR department.

Of course a typical business contains a number of other departments such as finance, corporate affairs, research and development and sales. It may be possible for a nonprofit to tap into one of these budgets with a particular approach, but whichever department is approached the rationale must be clear and the nonprofit should give adequate thought to the case for support, what this might be able to deliver in terms of benefits to the business and who within the business would be most affected. This should then suggest both the level at which contact should be initiated and, in the case of lower level contacts, the particular departments that might be most interested in the opportunity presented.

It is also worth noting that many, particularly larger corporations establish a charity committee, which typically comprises representatives from both management and the workforce and distribute the donation budget that many firms still have (Elischer 2002). The activities of these committees are generally well known in the nonprofit sector and the competition for their funds intense. Nonprofits seeking to raise funds from this source must have a strong case for support and accept that the ultimate decision may well be something of a lottery as the individual interests and biases of the members of the committee may be difficult to predict.

Finally, as Sargeant (1999) notes, too many nonprofits neglect the role that individuals can play in facilitating corporate fundraising. While a nonprofit might lack a network of contacts that extends to board members or even the individual managers of an organization, they may well find within their volunteer or donor base that there are individuals who work for the organization concerned. It may be appropriate to ask these individuals to take the lead in approaching the corporate since an approach from an employee can be an excellent way of cutting through the clutter of fundraising solicitations that businesses receive. Fundamentally, if the business believes its staff are interested in the cause they may well wish to demonstrate an interest too.

FOSTERING RELATIONSHIPS

Having selected and approached an appropriate corporate supporter, the nonprofit is then faced with the task of managing the relationship and where possible ensuring that the pattern of support becomes ongoing. Some nonprofits will find that the corporate dictates in fine detail the nature of the relationship the two organizations will have. Others, by contrast, may find that they can exert more influence and thus begin to 'tie-in' the corporate partner to the cause.

Academic writers such as Austin (2003, 2000) view nonprofit and business relationships as progressing through a series of three distinct stages, namely:

1   *Philanthropic stage*   In this stage the business is viewed by the nonprofit as a source of potential resources and primarily as a benefactor. The business views the nonprofit as a charity and

hence communication and interpersonal contact between the organizations is limited. There is no need for greater involvement.

2   *Transactional stage*   In this stage the business and nonprofit begin to look for benefits from the association. The relationship moves towards one based on exchange, where both parties recognize that they have something to offer the other and a dialogue opens accordingly.

3   *Integrative stage*   In the final stage, both partners seek to deepen their relationship. They find common values and overlapping missions, eventually blurring the identity boundaries of their own organizations as the two parties define themselves partially from their relationship with the other. The integrative stage approaches a merger between the organizations. Austin acknowledges that all nonprofit business associations do not evolve to the integrative stage, but he offers this stage as the ideal.

While clear benefits may result from this approach, some authors have expressed concern about the loss of a distinctive nonprofit identity that might result from an excess of corporate influence on an organization (Sargeant 1999; Bruce 2000). Such prescriptive approaches may also be criticized for failing to take account of the diverse and multiple relationships that often exist between a nonprofit and various ongoing supporters. While some might benefit from an integrative approach, this may clearly not be appropriate for all the organizations working with a given nonprofit.

Where closer relationships are sought however, there are a variety of issues that must be managed. Among these the issue of effective communication is paramount. Academic research into such relationships has consistently shown that open and regular communication among partners is highly important as it acts to build trust and can be an enabler for effective problem solving (Austin 2000; Berger et al. 1999). In building effective relationships partners need to develop multiple communication channels, both formal and informal, at different organizational levels (Austin 1999; Sagawa 2001).

Sagawa (2001) argues that the primary forms of communication in business nonprofit relationships are:

■   *Joint planning*   This form of communication involves various levels of the organizations in face-to-face interactions deciding jointly on the nature of the relationship and how it will develop. Joint plans are typically produced as a consequence and these may, or may not, form the basis of an agreed contract. Sagawa argues that joint planning with teams drawn from both organizations can facilitate problem solving and reduce conflict.

■   *Ongoing communication*   A variety of forms and channels of communication, both written and oral, will be initiated. To be effective these should be regular, candid and a balanced two-way flow of ideas and information.

■   *Internal communication*   While communications between the two organizations are important, it is also important to recognize the necessity of communicating with internal constituencies (e.g. employees, volunteers, board members, sponsors, and so on) about the relationship and its benefits.

■   *Intimacy*   Intimacy is perhaps the most difficult to define of these dimensions. Sagawa's view on intimacy is that it refers to the 'closeness' that develops between the two partners and thus the sense to which a strongly shared sense of vision and/or purpose emerges. The greater the extent to which this is present, the stronger and more enduring will be the relationship.

Other relationship variables are highlighted in the literature such as the need for a balance of power in the relationship and a sense of equality among the partners (Drumwright et al. 2000; Sagawa 2001). The notion of shared vision and goals (Austin 2000; Sagawa 2001) is also highlighted and, allied to this, Drumwright et al. (2000) add that relationships can fail because each category of organization can use different jargon to the other, fail to adequately understand the objectives of the other and, in the case of businesses, fail to understand the complicated politics typically operating within the nonprofit.

OUTCOMES

When a relationship is initiated it is important to determine from the outset how that relationship will be assessed and measured by both parties. This not only serves to reduce the capacity for conflict later, but it can actually serve as an aid to the retention of corporate support. A very high number of businesses do not assess the relationships they have with nonprofits even though these relationships may be entered into for clear business reasons. While this might be good for benefiting nonprofits in the short term, since they are freed from stringent evaluation, there is a danger that support will be abandoned in times of economic downturn, since no clear business case will ever have been established and any expenditure thus rendered impossible to justify. Steckel and Simmons (1992) suggest that businesses should use the following criteria to assess their relationships with nonprofits:

- impact on sales
- target market results
- retailer and distributor activity and response
- scope and timing of publicity
- employee involvement and attitudes
- managerial support and attitudes
- public reaction to partnership choice
- revenue and expense results
- the quality of the working relationships with partners.

Nonprofits should also assess the quality of any relationship from their perspective and consider factors such as the value of monetary and other support received, the exposure and media coverage generated, the public response to the partnership and the increased public awareness of the cause.

Data on the financial outcomes of business–nonprofit relationships are sparse. Work by Sargeant and Kaehler (1998) and the Centre for Interfirm Comparisons (2001) suggests that for the nonprofit an association with a corporate can be a highly lucrative venture. Sargeant and Kaehler (1998), for example, report that the mean revenue generated per £1 of fundraising expenditure in this area was found to be £6.62, noting a correlation between the size of a nonprofit and the rate of return it was able to generate. This was felt to reflect the fact that many large corporate donors wished to associate themselves with a top charity brand. The study by the Centre for Interfirm Comparison (2001), based on a much smaller sample, reported a somewhat lower rate of return from this activity at only £4.67 per £1 invested.

It is interesting to note that while data are available on the sums donated to good causes by business organizations, there has to date been no empirical study of the benefits that accrue to the business organization. This may be due in part to a reluctance on the part of business organizations to be seen to have exploited good causes, yet it remains a significant gap since better quality information may well serve to enhance corporate interest in this area.

THE PITFALLS

While we have painted a positive picture of corporate nonprofit relationships to date, it is important to note that from the business perspective these frequently fail as the result of unrealistic expectations, inappropriate implementation of marketing tactics, or a flawed partnership or programme (Barnes and Fitzgibbons 1992). Relationships can also fail because businesses can be perceived by the public to be exploitative. As we noted earlier, relationships that are perceived as being exploitative can actually have a harmful effect on a business's sales. There is also risk inherent in the planned longevity of a relationship. If a nonprofit decides to pull out early as a consequence of some unfavourable action on the part of the corporate partner, the resultant publicity could disproportionately damage the reputation of the organization.

Of course the risk accruing to a relationship can also affect the nonprofit partner. While the for-profit's brand may benefit from the values imbued, the nonprofit's brand may suffer disproportionately if negative publicity accrues to a partner (Andreasen 1996; Donlon 1998). A nonprofit can be viewed as being guilty by association and even accused by other nonprofits of 'selling out' (Charter 1994). This proved to be a particular issue for the British Red Cross, which was criticized for its relationship with Nestlé by Baby Milk Action and Save the Children. These charities felt that Nestlé was breaching World Health regulations in respect of its handling of the promotion of its baby milk formula in the developing world and that the Red Cross should not be accepting significant donations from an organization which, in their view, engaged in dubious and harmful business practices.

Nonprofits can also be accused of turning away from their core values, or somehow becoming more commercial in the minds of supporters (Caesar 1986). Indeed there can be a danger that traditional supporters may offer their support elsewhere when they learn of the corporate support. They may either not agree that monies from a particular corporate should have been accepted, or they could decide that their own support is no longer needed (Andreasen 1996; Caesar 1986). A further risk for the nonprofit is the potential for wasted resources. If the alliance does not work out, the nonprofit may have committed scarce resources and staff to the alliance that could have been used in other areas. Some corporate partners may seek to place restrictions on nonprofits which may limit their ability to criticize their partner should the need arise. This is of particular relevance in respect of alliances between environmental protection nonprofits and the corporate sector (Andreasen 1996).

FUNDRAISING PLANNING

So far in this chapter we have dealt with a range of corporate fundraising issues. In this section it is our intention to draw these various strands together and to posit a framework for corporate fundraising planning. The model is depicted in Figure 11.2.

Objectives

As with all other forms of fundraising the first stage in the process will be for the organization to set the objectives to be achieved by the corporate fundraiser or team. These objectives will undoubtedly emerge from the detailed fundraising audit we proposed in Chapter 2 and may be couched in terms of income targets, numbers of volunteers attracted, or volume in respect of various categories of goods in kind. Some organizations will just set overall targets whilst others will set targets for the development of both new and existing business.

Prospect research

If one of the objectives is to generate new corporate business the organization has then to decide which organizations it should target with the fundraising resources available to it. For larger

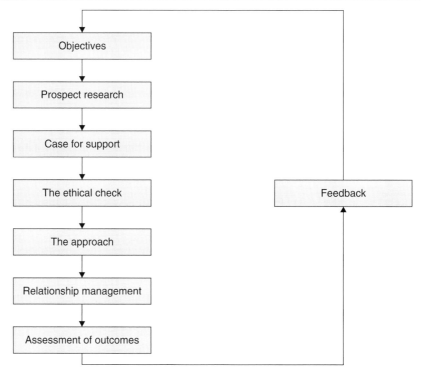

Figure 11.2 *Planning for corporate fundraising*

nonprofits this may involve profiling past corporate supporters to see whether certain categories of business have a propensity to support the cause. This information can then be used to identify other similar businesses that might have an interest.

Smaller organizations or those without a track record in this area will be forced to begin by examining trade and press reports of the corporate support that has been given to other similar nonprofit organizations. This might give them a sense of the kind of organization that might wish to support them too.

Similarly organizations of every size could begin by looking at what they have to offer a business and work up from this list of capabilities to those businesses that might have the required 'fit' with this profile. Again data can be gleaned from paper and online trade media, public media and business directories and journals.

In the UK the Directory of Social Change produces an online guide to corporate giving (www. companygiving.org.uk). Their database contains all the companies listed in their *Guide to UK Company Giving*, as well as newly discovered large givers. Over 500 companies are featured on this site, giving over £290 million in cash donations and more in other forms of community support. Entries contain full details on the various giving methods (cash donations, in-kind support, employee-led support, sponsorship and commercially led support), describing both what the company is prepared to fund and the organizations it has supported in the past. Contact details, exclusions and the application processes are listed alongside financial details of the company and its number of employees. Fundraisers may also find it helpful to consult the *International Directory of Corporate Philanthropy*, published by Europa publications in London. Data are provided on over 1,200 organizations, based in around 100 different countries.

We highlighted earlier that many good leads could also be generated from existing supporters, staff and/or volunteers. Many individuals connected with the nonprofit may already have strong links to a corporate, or even be working for a potential partner at present. These links need to be identified and examined to see whether potentially useful partnerships or other forms of support might result.

Case for support

Once a list of potential supporters has been assembled an appropriate case for support can be generated. This requires the nonprofit to consider carefully what it can offer a corporate, what the interests of the corporate are likely to be, the nature of the support the nonprofit will be looking for and the nature of the relationship, if any, it is looking to establish. It is the marriage of these factors that together combine to form the case for support. It should offer a business a strong, clear and highly attractive set of reasons for why corporate support should be offered.

The ethical check

Having delineated a list of prospects and specified appropriate cases for support many nonprofits then proceed to the solicitation stage. However nonprofits rushing into relationships with corporate partners have frequently had occasion to regret this decision as it can subsequently become clear that some relationships are wholly inappropriate. This is frequently because the organization is involved in activity directly or indirectly at odds with the nonprofit's cause. A children's charity, for example, can find that its corporate partner in the USA owns a toy manufacturer in Asia that employs large numbers of children in its workforce. Similarly an environmental charity in the UK might find that it is accepting donations from a company that is actually pumping lethal gases into the atmosphere in one of its chemical plants in Africa. In both cases, should these facts become public knowledge, significant and very damaging publicity could result for both the nonprofit and the corporate partners.

Many nonprofits have now generated ethical policies which map out the kind of organizations that the nonprofit will work with, the standards of behaviour that are expected and the consequences of any breach (e.g. immediate termination of the partnership). Such policies make it clear to fundraisers which organizations they can work with and in effect pre-empt problems by ensuring that the nonprofit only works with enterprises compatible with its own mission. An example of an ethical policy is provided in Exhibit 11.2.

Of course, life is rarely this neat and when one attempts to apply an ethical policy a number of issues commonly arise:

- *Chain of command* While it may be relatively easy to research the activities of a corporate partner directly, it is less easy to research the activities of the companies that might own this partner or be owned by it, particularly in Third World countries. Indeed, it is legitimate to ask at what point should this research cease? Is it only the partner organization, its parent company, its subsidiaries that should be addressed by the ethical policy, or literally every business that is owned or part-owned by the partner? The wider the scope of enquiry, the more difficult the task and thus the more time-consuming and expensive it will be.
- *Polluter pays?* It is no accident that many major oil companies are keen to invest in environmental charities. When a major oil spill occurs or a tanker sinks on the high seas, unimaginable damage can be done to wildlife and the environment. Some might therefore argue that it would be obscene to allow oil companies to fund the charities that may have to engage in the clean-up, or who exist to put pressure on companies to enhance their

EXHIBIT 11.2 CORPORATE CONTRIBUTIONS POLICY

Introduction

Under no circumstances will policy or programme decisions be affected by the companies that donate to support the work of Breast Cancer Action. BCA cannot be bought, influenced or discouraged from our mission to eradicate breast cancer. Throughout our history, Breast Cancer Action has relied primarily upon the financial support and generosity of our individual members. Nevertheless, financial realities dictate that Breast Cancer Action also seek funding from other sources such as foundations and corporations.

BCA recognizes, however, that the effectiveness of our work in public education, advocacy and coalition-building depends on the organization's credibility, particularly in the eyes of our members and the people we serve. The funding sources of any advocacy organization can appear to affect its political legitimacy, particularly in situations where corporate support raises the possibility of inference or perception of a conflict of interest.

BCA's corporate contributions policy aims to reconcile the need to ensure the long-term financial health and longevity of the organization with the desire to avoid potentially real or perceived conflicts of interest related to corporate giving.

Guiding principles

The following principles guide BCA's corporate fundraising strategy:

1   Providing unbiased information about breast cancer diagnosis and treatment necessitates that Breast Cancer Action be free of any appearance of conflict of interest. Accordingly, BCA will not accept financial support from corporate entities whose products or services BCA knows include cancer diagnosis or treatment.
2   BCA advocates the precautionary principle of public heath that calls for acting on the weight of the evidence that links environmental carcinogens to breast cancer and other cancers, rather than waiting for absolute proof of cause and effect. Consistent with this position, Breast Cancer Action will not knowingly accept funding from corporate entities whose products or manufacturing processes directly endanger environmental and/or occupational health or may possibly contribute to cancer incidence, nor will BCA knowingly accept donations from corporate entities that work to weaken or circumvent environmental and occupational regulations that would protect the public health and might decrease cancer incidence.

Unacceptable corporate contributions

Based on these guiding principles as well as BCA's mission and operating principles, BCA will not knowingly accept funding from the following categories of corporations (the following list is not necessarily exhaustive):

- Pharmaceutical companies
- Chemical manufacturers
- Oil companies

- Tobacco companies
- Health insurance organizations
- Cancer treatment facilities

This policy is intended to ensure that BCA is independent from outside influences in the pursuit of our mission and to avoid potential or perceived conflicts of interest. While we understand the impact of global capitalism and the structures of multinational corporations, this policy does not require BCA to engage in exhaustive review of every corporation to trace the sources of income. BCA does recognize that the activities of many corporations change rapidly, and that we will periodically need to evaluate new information about corporate donors and the implications of that information in light of this policy. We encourage our members and others to provide information about corporate activities that they believe has bearing on this policy.

Potential corporate contributions that may be problematic but are not adequately addressed by this policy will be evaluated by the Executive Director, and, if necessary, by the Board of Directors. In addition, as questions arise, an ad hoc committee comprised of staff, board and outside participants may be formed to recommend refinements of this policy. This corporate contributions policy will be used as a guide for BCA's Executive Director and Board of Directors to inform the organization's fundraising activities. BCA will continue to focus our fundraising efforts on individual giving, either through direct contributions or through workplace giving programs. This policy shall not be construed to prohibit BCA from accepting matching gifts from corporations that are initiated by donations from individual corporate employees.

Adopted August 1998

Source: © Breast Cancer Action. Reproduced with kind permission.

safety procedures. They argue that such nonprofits need their independence and must be free of 'tainted money' to have the maximum possible impact. There is also the opposite view, that this work would have to be undertaken anyway and thus why shouldn't the oil companies foot the bill? After all, they create the problem, so is it not right that they should also contribute to its resolution? There is no 'right' answer to questions of this type; it really depends on one's ethical perspective and a nonprofit needs to take a clear stance and to be ready to defend that stance when necessary.

- *History*   When does a tainted supplier become untainted? In other words when a corporate previously engaging in unacceptable behaviours ceases those behaviours, at what point may donations be accepted by the nonprofit? Does this happen immediately on cessation of these behaviours, or at some future date?

None of these issues are straightforward and a good ethical policy will help fundraisers to decide what is and what is not appropriate. Relationships should only be sought with corporates that meet the requirements of the ethical policy. Similarly unsolicited donations must only be accepted from those companies who meet the requirements of the ethical policy. Both dimensions are of equal importance.

The approach

The nonprofit must then decide how to approach potential corporate supporters. At its simplest level this will usually be a decision about whether to deal directly or indirectly with the organization. What we mean here is that if the nonprofit has only very limited resources and a large number of corporate prospects with only a weak case for support, it may be appropriate to simply initiate a mailing. Where a nonprofit has a corporate fundraising team, significant numbers of volunteers, a strong case for support and highly qualified prospects, it will be more appropriate to focus on a more personal approach.

Relationship management

Once a relationship is established the nonprofit needs to create a plan for administering and managing that relationship. This will have two key components. The first is the delivery of an appropriate quality of service to the corporate supporter. For some kinds of relationship this may be as simple as a timely and personalized acknowledgement of a gift. For other categories of relationship the nonprofit needs to ensure that it is honouring its obligations and that any objectives the corporate might have are likely to be met.

The second key component is a plan for developing and taking forward the relationship in the way that the nonprofit would prefer. This might include plans to deepen the relationship, cross-sell other fundraising products or increase the organization's share of the donation income available. In cases where the relationship is not working out as envisaged, this may also be a plan for withdrawal from, or the ultimate cessation of, the relationship.

Both components of a relationship management plan must be carefully integrated.

Assessment of outcomes

As we noted above, the nonprofit should seek to evaluate its relationships with corporate partners on an ongoing basis. This is essential to ensure that the quality of such relationships is developed and/or maintained. It is also essential to ensure that the relationship remains appropriate and that the costs/benefits of involvement are as envisaged.

It is also important that the corporate be invited (in all but the cases of philanthropic donations) to appraise the effectiveness of its nonprofit involvement. A clear rationale for support and demonstration of the achievement of corporate objectives will substantially increase the likelihood of future support.

Feedback

Finally, the nonprofit should reflect on the outcomes obtained and use this data to inform subsequent corporate fundraising planning. At the very least knowledge of the characteristics of successful relationships can greatly assist in the prioritizing of the recruitment resource available for subsequent year's activities. Fundamentally, however, all knowledge gained from the market will have value in informing subsequent planning.

STRUCTURES

So far in this chapter we have largely ignored the issue of organizational structure. While we noted that it may be appropriate to seek corporate partners who 'fit' with the nonprofits, existing structure, this matter was not elaborated on. In this section we return to this issue and explore how nonprofits typically structure their approach to corporate fundraising and the alternatives available.

Nonprofits serving a large geographic area such as a country or state have to decide whether to focus their corporate fundraising activity around their headquarters, or whether to attempt to fundraise across the whole of the geographic coverage of the organization. Where the nonprofit is based in a large city, there may well be a plethora of contacts that can be followed up locally that could result in corporate support. If it is based in a more rural location, this is likely to be more problematic and it may be better to focus attention on businesses operating near the programmes the organization is involved in running.

Focusing effort around the organization's base has the advantage that control can be retained centrally ensuring that only appropriate relationships are entered into and that the quality of these relationships is maintained. Proximity also makes it easier to package the kind of benefits a business may be seeking, such as access to celebrities, leveraging the brand and so on. Where appropriate, volunteers can also be easily recruited in centres of population and again trained by head office staff to ensure a consistent quality of skills.

The downside of this degree of centralization is that the organization may be missing out on significant opportunities in other parts of the country where businesses may very well wish to support the organization and often with large sums of money. The difficulty with fundraising in other regions is that it then becomes necessary to create regional teams of corporate fundraisers, either on a paid or volunteer basis. The distance can make it difficult to achieve appropriate recruitment, retention and supervision of the work undertaken. Unless these individuals work from home, overhead costs can also become an issue and the costs of corporate fundraising can spiral.

There is no one right approach. Many organizations struggle to find the optimal approach for them and there is frequently an element of 'trial and error' until the appropriate structure is identified. The best advice that may be offered is simply to:

- Appraise the scale of the opportunity for corporate fundraising in each of the regions in which the organization operates.
- These opportunities should then be banded indicating the likely financial worth of each region.
- In those regions with the greatest potential, a regional office may be created, including salaried corporate fundraisers and/or volunteers. If particularly large corporate accounts exist, one or more dedicated staff may be appointed to liaise with particular clients.
- In those regions with only minimal potential, the overheads associated with an office can be avoided by individual members of staff working from home in that region, possibly soliciting volunteer support and involvement to assist them in their task.
- Where the greatest potential is concentrated around the headquarters of the nonprofit, the temptation to expand wastefully into other regions should be avoided, unless it is possible to 'piggy-back' corporate fundraising on other forms of fundraising that are being undertaken in these areas. The temptation for too many organizations is simply to attempt to chase every corporate donation that might exist. This is not only an approach that is doomed to failure from the outset; it may very well achieve a highly negative return on investment and lose the nonprofit cash it has worked hard to earn from other sources.

SUMMARY

In this chapter we have provided a framework that may be used by nonprofits to consider the planning of their corporate fundraising activity. We have also conducted a review of the available research into this form of fundraising, explaining what is known about the kinds of businesses that support nonprofits, their motives for support, what they look for in a partner and how such relationships might be managed.

In reviewing this chapter, however, it is important to retain a sense of perspective. The significance of the corporate sector as a source of income should not be overstated. Businesses provide only a very small percentage (typically much less than 10 per cent) of the income generated by the nonprofit sector in most major Western countries. Businesses are notoriously ungenerous and offer only a small fraction of their pre-tax profits to good causes.

We have also noted how the trend in recent years has been away from philanthropy and towards dual agenda giving, where businesses expect to see very real returns for their investment. Perhaps inevitably it is not every nonprofit that is in a position to be able to deliver this return and as a consequence corporate giving tends to concentrate in the hands of a few large nonprofits with equally large and established brands.

Of course, there are exceptions to this – but in deciding whether to engage in corporate fundraising for the first time it is important to recognize that a large number of organizations either lose money on this activity or achieve returns that are little above break-even. When the opportunity costs of not being able to use fundraising resources elsewhere are taken into consideration, corporate fundraising can become a 'blind alley' that wastes significant time and monetary resource. It should thus not be entered into lightly.

DISCUSSION QUESTIONS

1 Explain the difference between 'strategic' and philanthropic company giving.
2 In your role as a fundraising consultant you have been invited to make a presentation to the Board of a nonprofit new to corporate fundraising. They have asked you to explain to them the process that they might establish to raise this category of funds.
3 What is CRM? What are the advantages and disadvantages of soliciting this form of funding?
4 Describe the approach to soliciting and managing payroll giving in the UK.
5 Why should a nonprofit engaging in corporate fundraising require an ethical policy?
6 Why may corporate fundraising not be appropriate for every nonprofit to engage in?

REFERENCES

Adams, M. and Hardwick, P. (1998) 'An Analysis of Corporate Donations: United Kingdom Evidence', *Journal of Management Studies*, 35(5): 641–654.

Andreasen, A.R. (1996) 'Profits for Nonprofits: Find a Corporate Partner', *Harvard Business Review*, 74 (November/December): 47–59.

Atkins, S. (1999) *Cause Related Marketing: Who Cares Wins*, Butterworth Heinemann, Oxford.

Austin, J.E. (1999) 'Strategic Collaboration between Nonprofits and Businesses', *Nonprofit and Voluntary Sector Quarterly*, 29 (supplemental): 69–97.

Austin, J.E. (2000) *The Collaborative Challenge: How Nonprofits and Businesses Succeed Through Strategic Alliances*, Jossey-Bass, San Francisco, CA.

Austin, J.E. (2003) 'Marketing's Role in Cross-Sector Collaboration', *Journal of Nonprofit and Public Sector Marketing*, 11(1): 23–40.

Barnes, N.G. and Fitzgibbons, D.A. (1992) 'Strategic Marketing for Charitable Organizations', *Health Marketing Quarterly*, 9(3/4): 103–114.

Berger, I.E., Cunningham, P.H. and Drumwright, M.E. (1999) 'Social Alliances: Company/Nonprofit Collaboration', *Social Marketing Quarterly*, 5(3): 49–53.

Bragdon, F.J. (1985) 'Cause Related Marketing: Cases to Not Leave Home Without', *Fund Raising Management*, 16(1): 42–47, 67.

Bruce, I. (2000) *Marketing Need*, ICSA Publishing, London.

Caesar, P. (1986) 'Cause-Related Marketing: The New Face of Corporate Philanthropy', *Business and Society Review*, 59 (Fall): 15–19.

Centre for Interfirm Comparisons (2001) *Fundratios 2000/2001*, Centre for Interfirm Comparisons, Winchester, Hants.

Charter, M. (1994) *Greener Marketing*, Greenleaf Publishing, Sheffield.

Chiagouris, L. and Ray, I. (2007) 'Saving the World with Cause Related Marketing', *Marketing Management*, (July/August): 48–51.

Cone Inc. (2002) Our Research. Cone Inc. Available online 11 March 2002 at: http://www.conenet. com/Pages/research.html

Corkery, P.J. (1989) 'What's In It For Me?' *Business Month*, 34 (November): 46–47.

Daw, J. (2006) *Cause Marketing for Nonprofits: Partner for Purpose, Passion and Profits*, John Wiley, San Francisco, CA.

Donlan, J.P. (1998) 'Zen and the Art of Cause-Related Marketing', *Chief Executive*, 138 (October): 51–57.

Drumwright, M.E. (1996) 'Company Advertising with a Social Dimension: The Role of Noneconomic Criteria', *Journal of Marketing*, 60 (October): 71–88.

Drumwright, M.E., Cunningham, P.H. and Berger, I.E. (2000) 'Social Alliances: Company/Nonprofit Collaboration', Marketing Science Institute Working Paper, Report No.100–101.

Elischer, T. (2001) 'Two's Company', *Professional Fundraising*, July:23.

Elischer, T. (2002) *Corporate Fundraising*, Directory of Social Change, London.

Epstein, K. (2005) 'How Today's Corporate Donors Want Their Gifts to Help the Bottom Line', *Stanford Social Innovation Review*, Summer: 21–26.

Farquarson, A. (2000), 'Marketing Campaigns Impact on Consumer Habits', *The Guardian*, 15 November, available online 25 February 2002 at: http://society.guardian.co.uk/voluntary/ story/0,7890,397881,00.html

Grossman, S. and Hart, O. (1980) 'Takeover Bids, The Free-rider Problem and the Theory of the Corporation', *Bell Journal of Economics*, 11(1): 42–64.

Haley, U.C. (1991) 'Corporate Contributions as Managerial Masques: Reframing Corporate Contributions as Strategies to Influence Society', *Journal of Management Studies*, 28(5): 485–509.

Hart, O. (1993) 'An Economist's View of Fiduciary Duty', LSE Financial Markets Group Discussion Paper No. 157, London School of Economics, London.

Hill, C.W.L. and Snell, S.A. (1989) 'Effects of Ownership Structure and Control on Corporate Productivity', *Academy of Management Review*, 32(1): 25–46.

Himmelstein, J. L. (1997) *Looking Good and Doing Good: Corporate Philanthropy and Corporate Power*, Indiana University Press, Indianapolis, IN.

Josephson, N. (1984) 'AmEx Raises Corporate Giving to Market Art', *Advertising Age*, 23 January: 10.

Kropp, F., Holden, S.J.S. and Lavack, A.M. (1999) 'Cause Related Marketing and Values in Australia', *Journal of Nonprofit and Voluntary Sector Marketing*, 4(1): 69–80.

Lenway, S.A. and Rehbein, K. (1991) 'Leaders, Followers and Free Riders: An Empirical Test of Variation in Corporate Political Involvement', *Academy of Management Review*, 34(4): 893–905.

Levine, J. (1989) 'I Gave at the Supermarket', *Forbes*, 144 (December): 138–140.

Little, M. (2008a) 'Lloyds TSB and the British Heart Foundation', *Third Sector*, 30 July: 20.

Little, M. (2008b) 'BT and Scope', *Third Sector*, 4 June: 20.

McGuire, J.B., Sundgren, A. and Schneeweis, T. (1988) 'Corporate Social Responsibility and Firm Financial Performance', *Academy of Management Journal*, 31(4): 854–872.

Marconi, J. (2002) *Cause Marketing: Build Your Image and Bottom Line through Socially Responsible Partnerships, Programmemes and Events*, Dearborn Trade Publishing, New York.

Mescon, T.S. and Tilson, D.J. (1987) 'Corporate Philanthropy: A Strategic Approach to the Bottom Line', *California Management Review*, 29 (Winter): 49–61.

Mintel (2003) *Cause Related Marketing*, Mintel, London.

Morton, V. (2007) *Corporate Fundraising*, Charities Aid Foundation, West Malling, Kent.

Pharoah, C. (2008) *Charity Market Monitor*, CaritasData, London.

Potter, V. and Scales, J. (2008) *Review of Payroll Giving*, Institute of Fundraising, London.

Pringle, H. and Thompson, M. (1999) *Brand Spirit: How Cause Related Marketing Builds Brands*, John Wiley, Chichester.

Ross, J.K., Stutts, M.A. and Patterson, L. (1991) 'Tactical Considerations for the Effective Use of Cause-Related Marketing', *Journal of Applied Business Research*, 7(2): 58–65.

Sagawa, S. (2001) 'New Value Partnerships: The Lessons of Denny's/Save the Children Partnership for Building High-Yielding Cross-Sector Alliances', *International Journal of Nonprofit and Voluntary Sector Marketing*, 6(3): 199–214.

Sagawa, S. and Segal, E. (2000) *Common Interest, Common Good: Creating Value through Business and Social Sector Partnerships*, Harvard Business School Press, Boston, MA.

Samu, S. and Wymer, W.W. (2002) 'Social Advertising: Effects of Dominance and Fit on Attitudes and Behavioral Intentions', *Academy of Marketing Science Conference*, 29 May/1 June, Sanibel Island, Florida.

Sargeant, A. (1999) *Marketing Management for Nonprofit Organizations*, Oxford University Press, Oxford.

Sargeant, A. and Kaehler, J. (1998) *Benchmarking Charity Costs*, Charities Aid Foundation, West Malling, Kent

Scanlan, E.A. (1997) *Corporate and Foundation Fund Raising: A Complete Guide from the Inside*, Aspen Publishers, Gaithersburg, MA.

Shell, A. (1989) 'Cause Related Marketing: Big Risks, Big Potential', *Public Relations Journal*, 45(7): 8, 13.

Smith, C. (1994) 'The New Corporate Philanthropy', *Harvard Business Review*, 72 (May/June): 105–116.

Steckel, R. and Simmons, R. (1992) *Doing Better By Doing Good*, Dutton, Boston, MA.

Ullman, A.A. (1985) 'Data in Search of a Theory: A Critical Examination of the Relationship among Social Performance, Social Disclosure and Economic Performance', *Academy of Management Review*, 10(1–2): 540–557.

UNICEF (2002) *Annual Report and Accounts 2000/01*.

Varadarajan, P.R. and Menon, A. (1988) 'Cause-Related Marketing: A Coalignment of Marketing Strategy and Corporate Philanthropy', *Journal of Marketing*, 52 (July): 58–74.

Wagner, L. and Thompson, R.L. (1994) 'Cause-Related Marketing', *Nonprofit World*, 12(6): 9–13.

Watts, R.L. and Zimmerman, J.L. (1978) 'Towards a Positive Theory of the Determination of Accounting Standards', *Accounting Review*, 53(1): 112–134.

Webb, D.J. and Mohr, L.A. (1998) 'A Typology of Consumer Responses to Cause-Related Marketing: From Skeptics to Socially Concerned', *Journal of Public Policy and Marketing*, 17(2): 226–238.

Wokutch, R.E. and Spencer, B.A. (1987) 'Corporate Saints and Sinners', *California Management Review*, 29 (Winter): 72.

Wymer, W.W. and Samu, S. (2003) 'Dimensions of Business and Nonprofit Collaborative Relationships', *Journal of Nonprofit and Public Sector Marketing*, 11(1): 3–22.

Chapter 12

Trust and foundation fundraising

OBJECTIVES

By the end of this chapter you should be able to:
- Describe the charitable trust and foundation marketplace.
- Conduct research and prioritize potential grant-makers.
- Write proposals or submit applications for appropriate grant funding.
- Describe the 'grant cycle' and the importance of feedback and reporting in this form of fundraising.
- Discuss the reasons applications to trusts and foundations might fail.

INTRODUCTION

A charitable trust or foundation is a body set up privately to make grants for charitable purposes. There are about 10,000 charitable trusts and foundations in the UK and they give in the region of £3 billion in grants each year, which makes them as important an income source as local authorities or central government departments. Data suggest that grant-making trusts are responsible for supplying roughly 10 per cent of an 'average' UK charity's income (Association of Charitable Foundations 2007). Grant-making trusts and foundations are regulated under the same laws as other charities, being required to register with the Charity Commission in England and Wales (the law is slightly different in Scotland and Northern Ireland) and to publish an annual report and accounts giving information about their grants. They are thus required to be transparent, though as independent bodies they are not publicly accountable. UK grant-making trusts have been classified (Clay 1999) into the following groups:

1. *Institutional*   Set up with a number of trustees. Institutional trusts tend to make grants according to detailed procedures, have established criteria and guidelines on which to base their decision-making, and employ professional staff.
2. *Private*   Set up by a single individual who takes most of the grant-making decisions alone or after discussion with a spouse.
3. *Family*   Often set up by one individual, often in memory of an earlier family member or as a result of a discretionary form of will, with trustees who are related or at least closely connected to each other. Decisions tend to be taken collectively but informally.

4   *Corporate*   These are trusts where the income of the trust is dependent upon the profits of a company or group of companies. Decisions tend to be made by committees and ratified by directors of the company. These trusts now increasingly take account of the views and interests of employees.

The Association of Charitable Foundations adds a fifth category reflecting the recent growth in such foundations. Community foundations are charitable trusts that support local community causes. Their role is to manage donor funds and build endowments as well as make grants to charities and community groups. They play an important role in linking local donors with local needs and their number has doubled since 2001 (Association of Charitable Foundations 2007).

Comparatively little is known about why people set up trusts or foundations (Lloyd 2004). Odendahl (1987) finds that motives such as seeking tax efficiency, leaving a living memorial to the founder (or others), paying back for good fortune in life, preventing heirs from inheriting wealth, spiritual and moral beliefs about the responsibilities of wealth, as well as wanting to improve society or help others, are common. Leat (2007: 115) observes that running through this list is the theme of control, controlling tax, controlling how you will be remembered, controlling children and so on.

> Even when the motivation is 'pure altruism', in many respects, the very act of creating a foundation, rather than giving directly to a charity/charities, may be seen as an exercise in control, even if, at the same time, the law somewhat constrains the power of the founder.

Given the importance of trusts and foundations as a funding source, comparatively little research has been undertaken in this domain, and as a consequence the decision-making process followed in awarding grants remains obscure in many cases. The basic tools and methods employed in raising funds from trusts and foundations have remained the same over many years, though technological developments have facilitated some advances (as well as an increase in competition for grant income). If it is managed well, trust and foundation fundraising can be creative, can deliver high returns and can produce lasting, profitable relationships with important funders.

GIVING PATTERNS AND PREFERENCES OF TRUSTS AND FOUNDATIONS

Most trusts and foundations derive their income from an endowment; a capital sum given by a wealthy individual, family or company. The endowment may take the form of cash, stocks, shares or land. It provides a tax-exempt income that funds grant giving. Some trusts derive income from other sources, such as gifts from a company's current profits, or from a regular public appeal (e.g. Comic Relief or Children in Need).

Overall, trust and foundation giving levels are closely tied to the performance of the stock-market, as most assets are held in the form of stocks and shares. In the late 1990s the market rose quickly and foundation giving rose alongside. With market drops in recent years, trust and foundation grant-making has been sustained by the formation of new trusts and foundations (both individual and corporate), by continued payments against multi-year commitments and by some large gifts of assets to existing foundations. In future years it is thought that the trust/foundation marketplace will continue to grow as an increasingly popular method of giving for individuals with significant personal wealth.

The giving decisions of trusts reflect individual and often idiosyncratic preferences and styles. These will depend on the history of the trust, on its stated policies and priorities, and also on the personalities and preferences of individual trustees at any given time. Many trusts are set up to give grants for 'general charitable purposes', While others have narrowly defined objects, and most fall somewhere in between. Trustees have to bear the origin and ethos of the trust in mind when allocating grants, but are also duty-bound not to ignore external changes in social, economic and political conditions. Where trusts date from previous centuries their objects sometimes have to be reinterpreted by trustees (with the agreement of the Charity Commission) to reflect present-day circumstances. All trusts and foundations are different, and they range from those where a single trustee makes giving decisions on an informal basis to those with a professional secretariat and formal application, selection and decision-making processes and materials in place. Within the terms of their trust, trustees can be creative, unorthodox and independent in the decisions they make on the awarding of grants.

Table 12.1 illustrates the current pattern of grant-making expenditure among the top 500 grantmakers in the UK. As the data clearly indicate, Social Care and Health are the primary recipients. The source of this funding is highly skewed towards a small number of very large players who provide the bulk of these resources. The top ten grant-makers account for over half of the top 500's grant-making expenditure. Table 12.2 lists these organizations, which represent a very diverse bundle of nonprofits; some are just grant-makers, while others, such as the British Heart Foundation, offer their own services too.

Generally, trusts and foundations like to fund areas that do not attract government funding or would not be easy to seek funds for from individuals or companies. According to the Association of Charitable Foundations (2008), key preferences include:

- new methods of tackling problems
- disadvantaged and minority groups which have inadequate access to services
- responses to new or recently discovered needs and problems
- work which is hard to finance through conventional fundraising
- one-off purchases or projects
- short- and medium-term work which is likely to bring a long-term benefit and/or to attract long-term funding from elsewhere.

In the USA and the UK the preference of trusts and foundations is usually for one-off or time-limited grants rather than for the provision of long-term funding. Leat (2007) also argues that the style of grant-making has changed significantly in the past 20 years. In the early 1990s British

Table 12.1 Distribution of grant-making by cause

Cause	Distribution of funding preferences %	Grants (estimated) £ million
Social care	18	489
Health	17	452
Education	10	273
Arts and culture	8	230
Environment	6	166
International	5	150
Faith Based	5	134
Other / general	31	836
TOTAL	100	2,728

Source: Charity Trends 2006. Reproduced with kind permission.

Table 12.2 *Top ten charitable grant-makers*

Charity name	Grant-making expenditure £million
Big Lottery Fund (New Opportunities Fund)	508
Wellcome Trust	344
Big Lottery Fund (Community Fund)	182
Cancer Research UK	96
British Heart Foundation	84
Comic Relief	54
Macmillan Cancer Relief	49
Football Foundation	45
Christian Aid	39
Gatsby Charitable Foundation	38
Top 10 total	1439
Top 500 total	2728

Source: Charity Trends 2006. Reproduced with kind permission.

foundations typically adopted the style of a gift giver, much more rarely adopting the stance of an investor or collaborative entrepreneur (Leat 1992). The largesse of these trusts was frequently offered with little attention given to the assessment of outcomes.

> There are (now) new demands for demonstrable 'impact' and 'effectiveness' as well as impending changes in charity law that will require a public benefit test as well as regular audits of effectiveness. 'Accountability', 'standards', and 'quality frameworks' are the orders of the day. Doing good is no longer good enough.
>
> (Leat 2007:117)

Fundraisers need to take account of this change and to have the systems and procedures set up in-house to ensure that data on these dimensions can be provided and tracked over time. There is likely to be a growing emphasis on funding to achieve specified, agreed outcomes and on post grant performance monitoring and measurement (Leat 2007).

RAISING FUNDS FROM TRUSTS AND FOUNDATIONS

As already discussed, trusts and foundations cover a huge range: from the small informal personal trust, operating on a voluntary basis from a home address, through to the large, professionally run concern. The first category of trust seldom has the capacity to communicate with applicants and is unlikely to acknowledge applications or reply to organizations that have been unsuccessful. In some cases the information available on the previous giving history and founding objects of such trusts is scant. Larger trusts and foundations by contrast are likely to have a professional staff, a range of printed information materials and a website (some organizations now encourage online applications) and will issue formal application forms or guidelines, deadline dates for submissions, requirements for supporting information and full details of previous grants given.

In seeking to raise funds, each trust should therefore be approached as a unique organization. As with the other forms of fundraising discussed in this book, there are essential stages that can be followed in the preparation and submission of any funding request to a grant-maker of whatever size and level of professionalism. Exhibit 12.1 outlines some of the strengths and weaknesses of trusts and foundations as a fundraising source.

TRUST/FOUNDATION RESEARCH

In seeking appropriate sources of funding, there are now a number of information sources open to fundraisers. Directories of grant-makers are plentiful and are regularly updated with information. Much of this material is now available online with the Directory of Social Change providing the core service in this area. Exhibit 12.2 provides an overview of the services available. A sample entry from the DSC/CAF online directory is provided in Figure 12.1.

While such entries provide the basic information required to make an application, more can often be gleaned from the Internet, or through enquiries to previous grant recipients. Trustees can also be researched as individuals (as in major gift prospecting) to ascertain whether any further information about the interests of individual trustees can be gathered.

Most trusts and foundations are hugely oversubscribed with applications. It is therefore essential that approaches are only directed at those grant-givers with a clear mandate to support the area of charitable activity the nonprofit organization is engaged in. Each trust will have stated *objects* and applications should only be made to those organizations whose objects appear to have a good match with the nonprofits' needs for funding.

Application guidelines should always be respected as grant-makers receive a high level of misdirected applications and will screen out any that are not presented in the required way,

EXHIBIT 12.1 STRENGTHS AND WEAKNESSES OF GRANT-MAKING TRUSTS AND FOUNDATIONS AS A FUNDRAISING SOURCE

Strengths

- availability of information. Online resources are multiplying and it is easy to obtain core information;
- many Trusts will fund over a three-year period, providing stability and the potential for planning;
- trusts exist to give money away;
- trusts will often fund projects or areas which are not attractive to other sorts of funders;
- applying to Trusts is relatively easy and inexpensive.

Weaknesses

- lack of in-depth information on giving patterns;
- lack of feedback, especially in the case of smaller Trusts;
- tend to fund only short-term projects, and not to fund overhead or staff costs;
- difficult to build relationships;
- high levels of competition for funding.

EXHIBIT 12.2: SOURCES OF INFORMATION ON GRANT-MAKING ORGANIZATIONS

A Guide to the Major Trusts – Vols. 1 and 2. Annual directories which include the largest 2000 grant-making trusts. Produced by the Directory of Social Change www.dsc.org.uk.

The Directory of Grant Making Trusts. Annual directory giving details of approximately 2500 grant-making trusts. Produced by the Directory of Social Change in hard copy and on CD.

Guides to regional and local trusts. The Directory of Social Change publishes a number of guides to local trusts across the UK. It also produces a range of sector specific guides such as the Arts Funding Guide, Sports Funding Guide, Environmental Funding Guide and others. Details are available at: www.dsc.org.uk.

Trustfunding.org is also a service provided by the Directory of Social Change. Subscribers can access information on any of the 4200 Grant Making Trusts featured in their range of publication. The web address is www.trustfunding.org.uk

FunderFinder.org.uk provides software that helps voluntary organizations and individuals seek funding from charitable trusts. www.funderfinder.org.uk.

Fundinginformation.org provides subscription-based information on sources of funding for the voluntary sector. www.fundinginformation.org.

Governmentfunding.org.uk is a free online directory of funding from five major government departments. It can be found at: www.governmentfunding.org.uk.

The Directory of European Union Grants contains details of grants available from the EC. It can be found at www.europeangrants.com.

The Association of Charitable Foundations provides a wealth of information and statistics on trust/foundation giving. It also provides a helpful guide for those looking to secure funding from this source. It can be found at: www.acf.org.uk

Caritasdata provides a facility to search for funders and research their policies online. It can be found at www.charityfunding-online.com

The Charity Commission may also offer value to charitable fundraisers. The register of charities may be viewed to identify sources of funding either in person at one of their offices (e.g London or Taunton) or online at www.charity-commission.gov.uk Some fundraisers use this source because new trusts and foundations can be listed on the register long before they appear in the sector's directories and are thus visible to everyone.

Guidestar UK is a further good source as their website contains an excellent search facility allowing fundraisers to look for potential grantmakers in the register by category of interest etc. It can be found at www.guidestar.org.uk

As one of the largest grantmakers the National Lottery Website will be of interest to many fundraisers. The site offers the ability to search for information on current funding programmes across the U.K. It can be found at www.lotteryfunding.org.uk

Finally, there are many good regional sources of information. The Northern Ireland Council for Voluntary Action for example offers the ability to search for grant makers in Northern Ireland. It can be found at www.grant-tracker.org/.

The Tilda Foundation

Grant total £25,000 (1998/99)
Beneficial area UK and Asia.

Health, education, Asian charities, general

The trust makes grants towards health, education, Asian charities and for other purposes.

In 1998/99 the Trust had assets of £112,000 and made 14 grants totalling £25,000.

Grants for the year included £15,700 to Sarvoday Yuvak Mandal, £5,000 to The Gujarat Hindu Society, £2,500 to Bharatiya Vidya Bhavan, £500 each to CYANA: Cancer – You Are Not Alone and Alzheimer's Disease Society, £200 each to Muscular Dystrophy Group and Age Concern, £100 each to Leukaemia Research Fund, Whizz–Kid, Saint Francis Hospice and The Children's Care Challenge and other smaller donations.

Applications In writing to the correspondent.

Contact details and other information

c/o Tilda Limited
Coldharbour Lane
Rainham
Essex
RM13 9YQ
Tel 01708 717777
Fax 01708 717700

Correspondent Shilen Thakrar, Trustee

Trustees S Thakrar; R Thakrar; V Thakrar; R Samani

Figure 12.1 *Sample entry for the DSC/CAF online directory*
Source: © Charities Aid Foundation and Directory of Social Change. Reproduced with kind permission.

clearly fall outside their area of interest or where deadlines have not been adhered to. Research is also essential on the level and type of grant that tends to be given to ensure that any application made is for a suitable gift amount. Many trusts stipulate that grants will not be given for certain types of cost such as staff or overheads and, again, given the level of competition for trust funding, there is little point in ignoring such guidance.

THE APPLICATION/PROPOSAL

Some trusts and foundations require an initial outline letter of enquiry to be sent for consideration prior to a full application. If this is the case, the letter should be very concise, providing initial information about the nonprofit, the project and the way a grant would be used. If this is seen to fall within their guidelines and current priorities, clearance will be given for a full application to be submitted.

Applications should be as concise as possible. Those organizations that issue application forms often severely restrict the word length as all trustees are required to read and consider a high number of applications (see Figure 12.2).

The application should include a short opening paragraph on the fundraising organization, its history, mission and objectives. This should be followed by more specific information relating to

APPLICATION FORM

Please complete this form in the spaces provided (please do not attach any supplemental pages). **Please ensure that you do not exceed the specified word limits, or we will be unable to process your application.**

Please send your completed application form, together with a copy of the **latest audited or independently examined accounts (as applicable) of your charity and a recent bank statement,** to:

Catherine Small
The Tubney Charitable Trust
c/o Nabarro Nathanson
The Anchorage
34 Bridge Street
Reading RG1 2LU

Telephone: 0118 925 4662
Fax: 0118 950 5640

Further copies of this application form can be downloaded from www.tubney.org.uk

CHARITY DETAILS

1. Name of charity

2. Charity address:

3. UK Registered charity number
    (if applicable)

4. Website address:

5. Contact's name:

6. Contact's position
    (e.g. Trustee, Senior Manager):

7. Telephone number:

8. Fax number:

9. E-mail address:

CHARITY BACKGROUND

10. Charity's objectives:

11. Activities: **in no more than 50 words** please provide a brief description of the activities carried out by your charity.

DETAILS OF APPLICATION

12. In no more than 50 words please describe the purpose for which funds are sought.

13. The Trustees as a matter of policy intend only to fund projects which provide a significant degree of outward provision and benefit to the community. Please therefore explain **in no more than 50 words** how you intend this to be achieved.

14. Amount requested:
    (please note the minimum grant level of £30,000 and the maximum grant level of £250,000 per annum)

Figure 12.2 Tubney Trust application form
Source: © The Tubney Trust. Reproduced with kind permission.

15. When would you like to receive the funds (indicate if in instalments):

16. (a) Indicate the overall total needed for the project;
    (b) Indicate how much money you have raised so far towards the project, and where this funding has come from;
    (c) Indicate how you are intending to raise the balance of funds and from what sources. If known, indicate when funding decisions will be made.

17. Have you applied to us before for funding, whether successfully or not?

    If yes, please give brief details including the date(s) of the application(s), the amount(s) applied for/awarded and what the funding was for.

18. Further Information:
    Please list any relevant additional documentation which is available. Any further information will be requested only if required.

19. How would you like to receive payment: tick as appropriate

    Cheque

    Made payable to:

    or

    Bank account:

If you would like funds paid directly into your charity's bank account, please provide details:

    Bank Name:

    Sort code:

    Bank address:

    Account name:

    Account No.

20. I enclose a copy of the charity's latest audited or independently examined accounts (as applicable). (Please note that we will not be able to process your application without this) ☐

21. I enclose a copy of the charity's entry from the Register of Charities or proof of the charity's exempt/excepted status. (Please note that we will not be able to process your application without this) ☐

22. I enclose a copy of a recent bank statement for the charity (Please note that we will not be able to process your application without this) ☐

I confirm that the details given above are correct and I acknowledge that these details may be provided to a third party individual or organization for the purpose of processing the application, including peer review of the application.

Signed: ....
                Trustee/Senior Manager

Name: ....

Position: ....

Date: ....

the nature and size of the need to be addressed, a more detailed description of the project or part of the organization for which funds are being sought and an indication of the impact a grant would have. Innovative or unique features of the proposal that may set it apart from others should be clearly featured.

The full cost of the project should be stated, and an itemized budget presented. A realistic timescale should be included, plus information on what other fundraising is being undertaken to resource the project, including the names of other grant-makers being approached, or from whom funding has already been secured. If the project is long term, information should be provided on how the work is likely to be sustained after the grant income is exhausted. Every application should include an outline of how the success of the work will be judged and monitored.

In terms of presentation, applications to trusts should be personalized and professional, attractively presented but not produced to such high standards that profligate spending on fundraising might be suggested. Where photographs are included they should be carefully chosen and limited in number. Clarity and simplicity is key.

If specific forms of supporting information are requested in trust application guidelines (such as supporting letters from beneficiary groups or letters of reference from partnership agencies) these, and nothing extra, should be submitted. Where no specific guidance is given, grant-makers should always be provided with evidence of the legal standing of the nonprofit, its governance structures, senior trustees and personnel, and of its current financial situation. The latest annual report and accounts of the nonprofit usually serve these purposes.

In some cases, often with larger grant-makers, a visit will be arranged by an assessor as part of the decision-making process. If this is the case, the trust representative is usually there to assess the need for the project and the extent to which the applicants have found a good and workable solution. They may also be looking for reassurance that the applicants are able to deliver what they promise. This is the chance for the nonprofit to bring the project to life, so the assessor should meet individuals who know about the project and are passionate about it. If the application is for a capital project it may be necessary for the potential funder to request technical plans, equipment specifications and specialist assessments to ensure that they understand what is intended and that the project is viable and well planned.

A recent survey asked UK trusts to rank the criteria they used to evaluate applications. The results are reproduced in Table 12.3 and serve to reinforce the notion that fundraisers must achieve a high degree of fit between the project and the objects of the trust/foundation.

Table 12.3 *Criteria used by trusts in evaluating applications*

Factor	Ranking
Strategic fit with Trust's mission	1
Figures requested realistic	3
Amount requested within acceptable parameters	4
Past experience of applicant	5
Amount of benefit to accrue to society	5
Evidence of support from other Trusts	6
Evidence of applicant's own efforts to raise funds	4

Source: © International Journal of Nonprofit and Voluntary Sector Marketing. Reproduced with kind permission.

INTERNAL PROCEDURES AND TOOLS

To fundraise successfully from grant-makers a nonprofit needs to have appropriate internal procedures in place. It is essential that programmes and support requirements can be costed and packaged into discrete units, and that budgetary procedures enable support services and overhead costs to be allocated to these units. Many trusts and foundations will only consider covering these essential costs if they are presented to them as part of a fundable unit or project.

Procedures must also be in place to facilitate financial management and accountability of grant funds received. Grant funders differ widely in the sort of feedback and reporting they require, but all nonprofits applying for such funding must be able to offer transparency in grant allocation and to ensure that where restrictions are imposed these are honoured (New and Quick 2003).

Tailored database applications relating to trust and foundation fundraising are available. These enable fundraisers to record details of trusts approached, their basic grant criteria, the size of grants given and application requirements and deadlines. All correspondence between the nonprofit and the grant-making trust can be recorded, alongside grants given and reporting required.

Whether a database or a less sophisticated system is in place for recording trust approaches and relationships, the marketplace should be segmented and targeted for best effect, with larger trusts prioritized over smaller ones, and those with remits closely matching the nonprofit organization prioritized over those with wider or less closely matching objects.

BUILDING RELATIONSHIPS WITH TRUSTS AND FOUNDATIONS

Once a grant has been obtained, a letter of thanks should be dispatched immediately, and any requirements for reporting, recognition, anonymity or feedback clarified. These should be recorded and adhered to strictly. Where no specific guidance is issued, reports on progress should be submitted every six months.

Designing a suitable 'stewardship' or relationship-building process for trust and foundation funders can be problematic, as they range widely in the way that they are structured, and in terms of what they deem suitable in terms of levels of communication from grant recipients. In most cases trustees and trust administrators will not wish to be added to general mailing lists or given subscriptions to magazines or newsletters, as this would add to the deluge of mail and information they receive. They may, however, respond positively to invitations to events, and often request that new annual reports and accounts should be sent to them (Dorner et al. 2004).

In each case the best rule for the fundraiser is to treat every instance as a separate and unique relationship. Table 12.4 reports on what feedback is preferred by UK trusts (Sargeant and Pole 1998). It is interesting to note that While 26.9 per cent of trusts welcomed invitations to visit the project, only 11.5 per cent of trusts when probed further said they would actually attend, with over 48 per cent saying that they would appreciate being asked but would be unlikely to attend!

Once a grant has been given a nonprofit can consider that a relationship of some sort exists and that prospects for further support are positive if the nonprofit proves responsible, communicative and respectful of the trust funder. Research should be a continuous process, and should build a comprehensive picture of the requirements and preferences of all the trusts and foundations that fund an organization. This ongoing research should include the tracing of any personal links between trustees of charitable trusts and individuals involved in the beneficiary charity, as any such personal links can be invaluable in fostering the relationship and enabling more direct and individual approaches to be made (Tovim 2004). However, it should also be noted that many

Table 12.4 *Additional feedback preferred by trusts*

Additional feedback welcomed	Percentage of respondents indicating
Financial information about how the grant was used	51.1
Invitations to visit the project	26.9
Requirements for likely future funding	26.7
Number of eventual beneficiaries	24.4
Nature/profile of eventual benefactors	22.2
Problems encountered with the project	20.0

Source: © International Journal of Nonprofit and Voluntary Sector Marketing. Reproduced with kind permission.

trusts and foundations deliberately maintain an impersonal and strictly businesslike approach and discourage unnecessary 'familiarity'.

THE GRANT CYCLE

Grant-making trusts and foundations differ greatly in relation to how often they will accept applications from an individual charity, and how long they will take to consider and make a decision on any application.

Figure 12.3 represents this as a cycle taking place over a one-year period. Many trusts will not consider submissions from a charity that has been given a grant more than once a year, though in

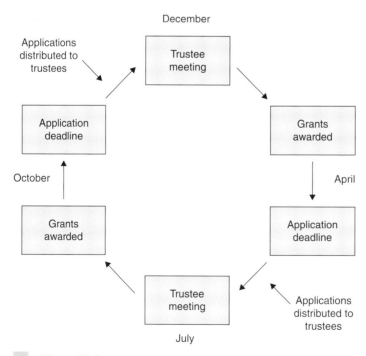

Figure 12.3 *The grant cycle*

special cases additional funding may be given before this date if a good relationship has been built and the charity can present a sufficiently urgent and impressive case for support. In the case of some larger trusts and foundations a three-year period is stipulated as a mandatory 'gap' between grants. Some trusts prefer to allocate the bulk of their funds each year to an established cohort of charities they have selected for ongoing support, While others will adhere to a policy that a proportion of all gifts given each year should go to new recipients. The fundraiser must be responsible for researching the grant cycle in the case of each trust or foundation to ensure that applications adhere to the correct timings.

Why applications fail

The first thing to realize is that even good applications will often be turned down. A trust may be swamped with applications in a given year, or have already committed funding to other organizations in the short to medium term. Data from the Association of Charitable Foundations indicate that the fundraising success rate varies a little depending on the size of the funder. Table 12.5 provides a summary of their findings, suggesting that around 40 per cent of received applications will be funded. A typical charity might therefore have to make three submissions to gain one grant.

Research undertaken among UK Trusts (Sargeant and Pole 1998) provides useful information on why applications for funding fail. Table 12.6 provides data on key mistakes made by applicants. Respondents in this research project were also asked what areas required most additional research by fundraisers. Table 12.7 records the findings.

In the US, similar findings are reported on why proposals are declined. The Fund Raising School at the Indiana University Center on Philanthropy provides the following list:

- Project hasn't been documented properly.
- Project does not strike reviewer as significant; statement of the project does not interest him/her.
- Prospective client groups appear not to have been involved in planning and determining project goals.
- Proposal is poorly written and hard to understand.
- Proposal objectives do not meet objectives of funding source.

Table 12.5 *Success rate of applications by grant-making expenditure*

Annual level of grant-making	Number of responses	Number of responses	Number of eligible applications	Eligible as a % of number received	Approved as a % of number eligible	Approved as a % of number received
Less than £500,000	82	19,709	11,121	56%	75%	42%
£500,000 to £1,999,999	31	27,273	12,023	44%	85%	37%
Over £2,000,000	25	55,894	35,847	64%	63%	40%
Total	138	102,876	58,991	57%	70%	40%

Source: Association of Charitable Foundations (2007, p8). Reproduced with kind permission.

Table 12.6 *Reasons for declining grant applications*

Category	Percentage of respondents identifying
Applicant did not read requirements	55.3
Applicant sent large amounts of unnecessary information	23.4
Application poorly presented	19.2
Applicant did not state how funds would be used	14.9
Applicant did not read the instructions for making an application	14.9
Applicant did not send a copy of accounts	14.9
Applicant did not make it clear that it was a charity	12.8
The application was impersonal and mass produced	12.8
No stamped addressed envelope was enclosed	10.6
Applicant was 'over-friendly' either in postal or telephone communications	8.5
Applicant sent insufficient information for a decision to be made	8.5
Applicant did not state the amount of funding that was sought	6.4
Application was too 'plush'	6.4
Other	8.6

Source: © *International Journal of Nonprofit and Voluntary Sector Marketing.* Reproduced with kind permission.

- Proposal budget is not within the range of funding available through the funding agency.
- Proposed project has not been coordinated with other individuals and organizations working in the same area.
- The funding source has not been made aware that those individuals submitting the proposal are able to carry out what is proposed. Not enough substantiating evidence is provided.
- Project objectives are too ambitious in scope.
- Proposal writer did not follow guidelines provided by funding agency.
- Insufficient evidence that the project can sustain itself beyond the life of the grant.
- Evaluation procedure is inadequate.

Table 12.7 *Additional research suggested by trusts*

Additional research	Percentage of respondents
Nature of causes supported	58.9
Past record of giving	30.6
Interests of Trustees	14.6
Submission dates	14.3

Source: © *International Journal of Nonprofit and Voluntary Sector Marketing.* Reproduced with kind permission.

It would seem that the availability of information on trusts and foundations and the increased ease with which nonprofits can produce application materials is leading to an increase in the numbers of applications and a decrease in their quality. While fundraising from grant-makers is always a 'hit-or-miss' activity at times, it remains profitable if fundraisers undertake research, tailor funding proposals with care and adhere to the guidelines and requests issued by trust funders. With levels of competition increasing there is little point in pursuing trust and foundation funding in any other way.

SUMMARY

Charitable trusts and foundations are an important source of funding for nonprofits across a range of subsectors. Grant-makers range from small private funds run on a very part-time and voluntary basis by one person who may be both chief administrator and sole decision-maker, to the huge foundations run by paid full-time staff and featuring formal application and decision-making procedures.

As such it is important that nonprofits research potential trust and foundation funders with great care, gathering all the available information before making any request for funding. Building relationships with trust and foundation funders is a mixture of the personal and the professional. Where personal links can be made or built the nonprofit will undoubtedly be at a great advantage, but many trusts operate on an impersonal, businesslike basis and state their preference for a formal and distanced relationship with the organizations they choose to fund. In both instances the trust and foundation fundraiser bears the responsibility of researching these communication preferences and reacting accordingly in order to build the most appropriate relationship.

While every trust requires individual attention, the core 'rules' of a good application can be laid out and followed. Nonprofits engaging in fundraising from grantmakers need to have systems in place to record and segment, and the financial controls in place to enable the packaging of requirements including staff and overhead costs into 'projects' that can be presented as fundable units. Trust and foundation fundraising can be one of the most profitable sources of income generation in terms of the return on investment produced, but fundraisers will be required to reach and maintain high standards to ensure continued success in an increasingly well-resourced and competitive fundraising marketplace.

DISCUSSION QUESTIONS

1   What are the primary sources of information for fundraisers seeking to research potential trust funders?
2   In your capacity as head of fundraising, draft the headings you would use to structure a grant application for a capital project to restore an Edwardian theatre in London.
3   Draft a question guide for use in telephoning charitable trust administrators to gather information from them prior to submitting an application. What key information would you wish to gather?
4   Why do trust applications fail? What actions can fundraisers take to improve their likely success rate?

REFERENCES

Association of Charitable Foundations (2007) *Grantmaking by UK Trusts and Charities*, Association of Charitable Foundations, London.

Association of Charitable Foundations (2008) *Applying to a Charitable Trust or Foundation*, Association of Charitable Foundations, London.

Clay, A. (ed.) (1999) *Trust Fundraising*, Charities Aid Foundation, West Malling, Kent.

Dorner, J., Seely, J. and Baumgartner-Cohen, J. (2004) *Writing Bids and Funding Applications*, Oxford University Press, Oxford.

Leat, D. (1992) *Trusts in Transition: The Policy and Practice of Grant-Giving Trusts*, Joseph Rowntree Foundation, York.

Leat, D. (2007) 'What Makes Foundations Tick?', in J. Mordaunt and R. Paton *Thoughtful Fundraising*, Routledge, London.

Lloyd, T. (2004) *Why Rich People Give*, Association of Charitable Foundations, London.

New, C.C. and Quick, J.A. (2003) *How to Write a Grant Proposal*, John Wiley, Oxford.

Odendahl, T. (1987) *America's Wealthy and the Future of Foundations*, The Foundation Center, New York.

Sargeant, A. and Pole, K. (1998) 'Trust Fundraising – Learning to Say Thank You', *Journal of Non-Profit and Voluntary Sector Marketing*, 3(2): 122–135.

Tovim, R. (2004) *Fundraising from Grant-makers, Trusts and Foundations*, Directory of Social Change, London.

Chapter 13

Branding and campaign integration

OBJECTIVES

By the end of this chapter you should be able to:

- Define branding and describe a number of models of 'brand'.
- Explain the various approaches to brand management an organization may adopt.
- Explain the role of branding in fundraising activity.
- Delineate brand values.
- Understand the importance of integrating fundraising campaigns with other nonprofit communications.

INTRODUCTION

The topic of branding is generating ever more interest in nonprofit circles and with good reason. A strong and effective brand offers a nonprofit a number of distinctive advantages that can greatly enhance the efficiency of both its fundraising operations and charitable service provision.

Roberts Wray (1994) was one of the first to explicitly debate the relevance of branding to the charity sector, arguing that one could brand charities in the same way as corporate organizations or their products. There is evidence that this may indeed be true – at least in part – and that although as Tapp (1996:335) notes, 'charities do not describe much of what they do as "branding"', they have nevertheless 'long been concerned with maintaining a consistent style and tone of voice and conducting periodic reviews of both policies and actions to ensure that a consistent personality is projected'. Such practices are the very essence of brand management, irrespective of whether the organization's management uses that term.

It is interesting to reflect on how times have changed. Branding was until recently regarded as something of a 'dirty' word by nonprofit managers afraid of being seen to grasp at some of the more 'disreputable' elements of for-profit marketing practice. There was a fear that in giving active consideration to branding, nonprofit organizations would somehow lose a sense of what made them distinctive (Ritchie and Swami 1999).

In reality nothing could be further from the truth; attempts to manage an organization's brand should actually enhance the character of the nonprofit, emphasizing its strengths and achievements alongside its modus operandi. Saxton (1995) suggests that the practice of branding in this context should differ from commercial practice in so far as it should both draw on and project the beliefs and values of its various stakeholders. This leads to what Hankinson (2000) regards as the greater complexity associated with managing charity brands. She argues that charity brands require a different approach that distinguishes between the 'functional attributes of the brands – their causes – and the symbolic values of the brand – their beliefs' (Hankinson 2001a:233). Hankinson (2001b) cites the example of the RSPCA whose cause is preventing cruelty to animals, While its values are 'caring', 'responsible', 'authoritative' and 'effective'. Both dimensions pervade its communications (see Plate 13.1).

In this chapter we examine the concept of 'brand' and explore what it can offer a nonprofit. We will also discuss a number of models of brand and discuss the implications for brand strategy and campaign integration.

WHAT IS A BRAND?

The American Marketing Association defines a brand as follows:

> A brand is a name, term, sign, symbol or design, or a combination of them, intended to identify the goods or services of one seller or group of sellers and to differentiate them from those of competitors.

In the nonprofit context a brand is thus a device to allow members of the public to recognize a particular nonprofit that may take the form of a name, trademark or logo. Legislation in Northern Europe and North America provides protection to the owners of these devices that

Plate 13.1 *RSPCA fundraising materials*
Source: © RSPCA. Reproduced with kind permission.

ensures that no other organization can impinge on their intellectual property. Brands may not be borrowed or copied without permission.

This degree of protection is important since brands are in essence a promise to the public that an organization possesses certain features, or will behave in certain ways. Aaker (1997) argues that in fact brands can convey up to six levels of meaning to a consumer:

1   *Attributes*   Brands can suggest certain attributes the organization might possess. These attributes may include the size of the nonprofit, the scope of its activities, the nature of the work undertaken and so on. In short the brand can act as a vehicle for summarizing what the organization does and how it does it.

2   *Benefits*   Brands also offer a series of functional and emotional benefits. From a donor's perspective, when they elect to associate themselves with a particular brand by offering their support they are buying a distinct set of functional benefits either for themselves, or more likely the beneficiary group. By giving to a branded organization that they are already aware of by virtue of the nonprofit's general communications, they will already be aware of the impact their gift could have long before a fundraising solicitation is actually made.

    Benefits can also accrue to the donor and these again could be functional in nature. As we discussed in Chapter 5, some donors may be motivated to give because of the status their association with the organization will confer. They may also wish to attract the awards on offer through a donor recognition programme. However, donors may also gain emotional benefits from their association with a brand. Wearing the logo or symbol of a nonprofit organization might confer an identity to the donor, just as in the commercial world wearing a brand like Nike conveys an identity to the young people who sport their shoes. Of course in the nonprofit context this process may be a little more thoughtful and can often involve a desire to express a sense of solidarity with the cause. A powerful UK example of this would be the Royal British Legion's Poppy Appeal, where many millions of small gifts are solicited in return for the token of a poppy that may then be worn in public from the time of purchase until Remembrance Sunday when the nation acknowledges the sacrifice of its armed forces (see Plate 13.2). It is interesting to note how many public figures elect to wear their poppy in the run-up to the commemoration and that over 33 million poppies are produced in total.

3   *Values*   The brand can also convey something of the organization's values, not only what it stands for, but also the way in which it will approach key issues related to the cause. A non-profit for example may have the values bold, authoritative and challenging, While another might be helpful, sympathetic and caring. The values of an organization will often be derived from the passion of the founders of the organization, from religious associations or from the nature of the work undertaken. What is actually happening here is that the values of the various stakeholders to the organization are being projected into how the organization communicates with the outside world. When the charity Botton Village, for example, began fundraising for the first time, it was keen to imbue its communications with the ethos of the Steiner philosophy that drives the organization forward. Fundraisers were thus keen to bring donors inside the organization and to make them feel a genuine and valued part of their community.

    Using brands to convey the values and beliefs of stakeholders can greatly aid a donor's understanding of the charity concerned and suggest very potent reasons why it might be worthy of support (Dixon 1996). This latter point is of particular significance since authors such as Dixon (1996), Kennedy (1998) and Denney (1998) have noted that an increased focus on branding, or indeed a complete rebranding exercise, can often be precipitated by a crisis in income generation.

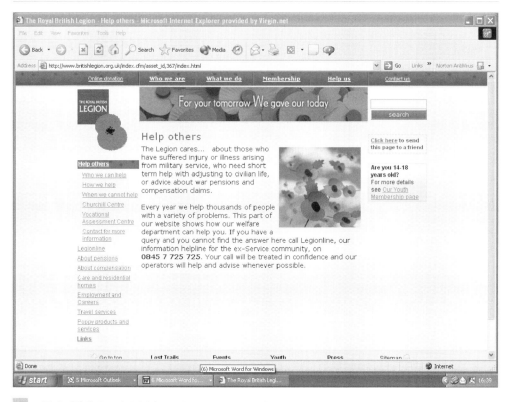

Plate 13.2 *Royal British Legion Poppy Appeal*

Source: © Royal British Legion. Reproduced with kind permission.

4   *Culture*   In the nonprofit context this element is hard to differentiate from values. In the commercial sector an individual brand may have distinctive values, but it will also communicate something of the corporate culture of the parent organization (i.e. the way it does business). For nonprofits, the culture of the organization will be driven in large measure by the values of the various stakeholder groups. Indeed a nonprofit organization is often a melting pot of such values, which in turn drive how the organization will behave. Greenpeace's culture, for example, has historically been very confrontational as the nonprofit seeks to put pressure on commercial organizations it sees as damaging the environment. On 14 June 2003, for example, Greenpeace volunteers from the 'Forest Crime Unit' visited 24 Travis Perkins stores across the UK. At the Dalston store in East London, a crew of eight people from the unit cordoned off what they claimed to be illegally logged Indonesian timber. They found 19 crates of Barito Pacific ply in one section and branded it a 'forest crime scene'. The volunteers then hung a banner which read 'Stop Rainforest Destruction'.

5   *Personality*   Aaker argues that some brands can convey a distinctive personality. In the case of commercial sector marketing, the Fosters lager brand drew heavily on the character of the Australian comic Paul Hogan in the late 1980s. Nonprofit brands can also convey a distinctive personality and there are often personal characteristics that can accrue to the image of an organization. This may occur because of the activities of a particularly flamboyant founder whose own personality becomes indelibly stamped on the organization's brand, but equally it can simply develop over time as the public come to view the nonprofit more as a

personality than organization per se. The charity Comic Relief is an excellent example of this. Grounds and Harkness (1998) have argued that the clarity with which this personality is projected will have a direct impact on an organization's ability to fundraise.

6   *User*   Many brands also convey a sense of the nature of the user. Charity brands can suggest the kind of individual who will either donate to the cause, benefit from the work it undertakes, or some combination of the two. Age Concern, for example, has built a brand that is regarded as responding to the needs of the elderly, tackling the issues that are of concern to this group and attracting funding both from this age category, but also from caregivers in the preceding generation, who will be facing these issues themselves in 10 to 20 years' time. Similarly the charity ENABLE uses its brand to good effect. It is the largest membership organization in Scotland for people with learning disabilities and family caregivers. It was formed in 1954 by a small group of parents because many families with a child with learning disabilities felt alone and isolated. They wanted better services for their sons and daughters and better support for parents. The brand they have now built over the years conveys a strong sense of what the group is really looking for from supporters. The message is not one of sympathy or pity, but rather that the organization seeks to empower its beneficiaries to make a real change in their lives. The brand conveys to donors that this is what they are 'buying' by making a donation.

Of course there is more to branding than the mere selection of an appropriate name. All the communications the organization creates, both in character and style, should reinforce the brand image that the nonprofit is trying to project. The focus should thus be not only on what is said, but how it is said, and this should pervade all the communication channels employed. Thus all direct mail, press, TV, radio, Internet and outdoor advertising should reflect the brand, but so too should the manner in which the organization responds to telephone enquiries, interacts with all its beneficiary groups and even presents required statutory data such as annual accounts.

WHY BRAND?

There are a number of reasons why an organization should consider branding. Organizations that develop brands are simply more successful at fundraising than those that do not. Frumkin and Kim (2001) found that nonprofit organizations that spent more marketing themselves and branding their organization to the general public did better at raising contributed income. Regardless of the field that nonprofit organizations serve in, positioning around mission and using this to drive the brand positively influenced the flow of contributions. Why should this be?

First, brands are an aid to learning. If branding has been used as a tool to educate members of the public over time there is then no need for a fundraiser to begin from a 'zero base' in his/her fundraising communications. There will be a baseline of understanding about the work the organization undertakes and its values in the minds of potential supporters. This makes the fundraising task a lot easier. Harvey (1990), for example, identified that the most familiar nonprofits tended to generate greater levels of both help and giving, reinforcing the notion that branding may play a key role in 'drip-feeding' potential donors with a knowledge of various facets of the organization's role, values and work. This is highly significant since as Bendapudi and Singh (1996) note that where a knowledge of the charity's image is lacking donors may either ignore a communications message or 'distort' it to excuse themselves from making a gift.

Branding is also of relevance since the learning imparted to potential donors through the brand can serve to reduce the risk to them in offering a donation. Agency theory is relevant here, since in making donations donors are in effect requiring nonprofits to act as their agents in disbursing funds. The brand image of a nonprofit will provide numerous clues as to how well a particular nonprofit will perform in this capacity. This is particularly the case in impersonal forms of fundraising such as direct mail, press or radio advertising where the donor may be entirely reliant on their *perception* of the organization in deciding to offer a donation. On a related theme Tapp (1996) argues that brands can serve to enhance trust between a nonprofit and its donors/potential donors. Brands provide assurance that an organization is worthy of trust and that funds donated will be used in a manner consistent with standards that have been established over time (Ritchie and Swami 1998).

A further key benefit that branding can offer is differentiation (i.e. making it clear how an organization differs from the competitors). It conveys what is distinctive about the range of activities undertaken, or the manner in which these are approached. It is absolutely essential that the concept of differentiation is fully understood and integrated into brand strategy, or a nonprofit's communication budget may actually benefit other organizations in the sector which the donor may support in the mistaken belief that they are supporting the focal organization. Research has consistently shown that organizations with similar brand names, values or personalities can quickly become confused in the minds of donors to the point where a regular payment is offered to one organization, While the donor believes they are supporting another (Sargeant and Jay 2004).

It is also worth noting that the sheer number of nonprofit organizations that are presently seeking funds can easily confuse even the most diligent of donors. Branding can help reduce this clutter, make it clear why a particular organization is deserving and thus make it easier to raise funds (Hankinson 2000).

Successful branding can also have a dramatic impact on the bottom line by opening up opportunities to offer the brand to appropriate third parties, as is the case with Cause Related Marketing (see Chapter 11). In the USA a number of large charities have even introduced their own branded products, earning substantial sums of revenue as a consequence. The Children's Television Workshop has been highly successful in its licensing arrangements for some 1,600 Sesame Street products, ranging from a Big Bird battery-operated toothbrush to a Cookie Monster Bulldozer, to 30 companies, including J.C. Penny and Hasbro (Meyers 1985). Commercial endeavours of the Children's Television Workshop with its brands were estimated to generate $70.3 million in 1995. Other examples include Girl Scout Cookies, a first-aid kit developed by the Red Cross, and the best-selling software in American schools by the Bank Street College of Education in New York.

Branding can also offer a form of reputation insurance to a nonprofit. Having built up a consistent image over time that becomes trusted and increasingly well understood by donors and other stakeholders, short-term crises can be survived. The Aramony scandal rocked the United Way in the USA when the chief executive was accused of wasting donated funds by building up expenses such as unnecessary flights on Concorde. This had a dramatic impact on donations in the short term; however, the reputation of the organization was such that in the medium term the organization was able to regain its share of gifts and relative position in the market. Thus While one would hope that scandals as acrimonious as the Aramony affair would be relatively rare, nonprofits will inevitably find that on occasion they will make mistakes. A strong brand makes it considerably more likely that such mistakes will be forgiven or even overlooked.

Finally, branding is an aid to loyalty, particularly where the benefits we discussed above accrue in part to the donor. As donors are rewarded for their association with the brand and begin to learn more about the activities it undertakes, the brand begins to serve as a tool for building a closer relationship with the donor. Polonsky and Macdonald (2000) thus argue that organizations with an established brand can leverage this to build donor loyalty and protect themselves from competitive pressures. Indeed there is empirical support for this proposition provided by Sargeant et al. (2001).

BRAND STRATEGY

Having discussed the concept of branding and how it can be of relevance to nonprofits, we will move on in this section to consider how a brand strategy is developed.

Brand relationships

Thus far in the text we have implicitly assumed that it is only the nonprofit as a whole that will be branded. This need not be the case. While the nonprofit's name may constitute one level of branding it is quite possible that distinct fundraising products could be branded, or even discrete components of the service the organization provides to beneficiaries. A number of approaches are thus possible:

1   *Corporate umbrella brand*   Where the organization itself is branded. There are numerous examples of this as it is by far the most common nonprofit practice. The United Way, Red Cross, UNICEF and the World Wildlife Fund all have strong and in some cases international corporate brands.
2   *Family brand*   Nonprofits may elect to have separate brands for their fundraising and service provision products. Schemes such as Adopt a Dog, or Sponsor a Granny have been branded by their respective nonprofits as distinctive fundraising vehicles. These may well be subdivided to send a different message to distinct donor segments. Similarly, there may be branded components of service provision such as Talking Books or Lifeline, which could in turn have sub-brands for specific categories of service user.
3   *Individual branding*   An organization can simply brand aspects of its service provision or fundraising with separate and entirely unrelated brands. Such a strategy may be appropriate where the donor or service user population is diverse and/or where service provision is complex with many different components. In such circumstances it is unlikely that a family or umbrella brand could be coherently developed.

In taking such decisions it is important to bear in mind that there can be risks in relying too heavily on just one brand. While we have noted that a strong brand can help mitigate the risk of unfavourable publicity should something go wrong, weaker brands may not weather the storm and any ill-performance or dissatisfaction can be directly reflected on the organization. When an organization develops multiple brands this risk is mitigated since if the public trust in one is damaged there are one or more opportunities to regain this through the work of the other brands in the portfolio. By developing multiple brands and a leadership in multiple target markets, the organization increases its chances of survival (Kotler and Andreason 1996).

Of course, no brand strategy is carved in stone and multiple brands must be managed in exactly the same way as multiple products. Gallagher and Weinberg (1991), for example, suggest employing the matrix depicted in Figure 13.1. Here each brand is evaluated for its contribution to the mission and contribution to the economic viability of the organization. As with other models of portfolio, those brands falling in the lower right-hand corner of the matrix would be clear candidates for divestment, while those in the top left-hand corner would be clear candidates for investment. Those in the diagonal would require further evaluation to determine an appropriate strategy to adopt.

Differentiation

Whatever approach is ultimately adopted, each brand must be carefully differentiated from those of the competition. We discussed in Chapter 4 the concept of positioning and it is positioning that forms the basis for shaping an appropriately differentiated approach.

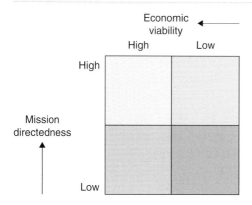

Figure 13.1 Brand portfolio analysis

To achieve this an organization must undertake a detailed analysis of the other provision in the market and identify in particular those organizations with similar names, brands, values, activities and stakeholder groups. In the case of each brand the organization should look at how it compares with the nature of other provision and what, if anything, is genuinely distinctive about it.

In seeking to achieve this, organizations frequently employ a model such as that depicted in Figure 13.2. There are notable similarities between this and Aaker's six categories of meaning discussed earlier. It is simply a further way of conceptualizing a brand and thus seeking to identify components that either are, or could be, genuinely distinctive. It also draws a helpful distinction between the rational components of a brand, where perhaps the donor is consciously aware of

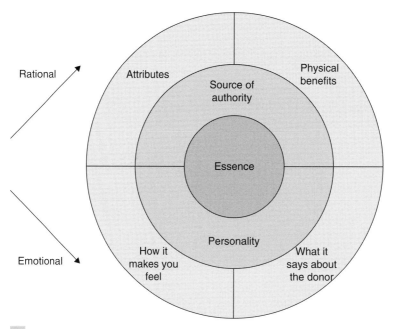

Figure 13.2 A model of brand

the rationale for their support, and the emotional aspects of a brand, which may impact at a more subconscious level. It comprises:

1   *Brand essence*   The core of what the brand will stand for.
2   *Source of authority and support*   The brand may be differentiated on the basis of the quality of the organization's authority (i.e. those whose views are expressed). A number of the large cancer research charities, for example, can draw on the authority of the medical staff and researchers they represent.
3   *Attributes.*
4   *Physical benefits*   To the donor or beneficiary.
5   *Personality*   The human attributes of the brand.
6   *How it makes the donor feel*   Does the brand offer any emotional benefits to the donor as a reward for their support?
7   *What it says about the donor*   Does the brand convey an identity to the donor by virtue of their support?

Brands may be differentiated by one or more of these components. The strongest brands tend to be those that can offer a strong sense of differentiation on all seven components, but on a very practical level this is often very difficult to achieve.

Brand partnerships

The majority of the largest nonprofit organizations in both the USA and the UK have developed strong brands, either by the conscious evolution of strategy, or by default where, whether the organization likes it or not, a brand has evolved by virtue of the organization's presence in a given market.

Other brands have been built through collaboration with for-profit commercial organizations. There are numerous examples of small nonprofits that have been helped to become household names by virtue of their association with a large corporate partner. American Express, in particular, has been very helpful to a number of fledgling nonprofits.

Equally many nonprofits will elect to develop brand partnerships with companies in return for a fee or some form of cause-related marketing agreement. In such circumstances the nonprofit brand is very much a partner in the agreement and may indeed have more to offer the corporate by way of meaning and values than could ever be offered in return. The following advantages and disadvantages might come into play:

Advantages

■   The relationship can generate considerable income for little financial or human cost on the part of the nonprofit.
■   The positive brand images of the for-profit can be transferred, at least in part, to the nonprofit.

Disadvantages

■   A nonprofit organization will probably have little say in how the branding process will evolve since the branding strategies will typically be developed by the commercial partner to ensure that their specific objectives are met.
■   There are very real risks that image of the nonprofit could be damaged if the commercial partner is later found to be behaving inappropriately in some aspect of its operations. This can be particularly damaging where these activities are at odds with the mission of the nonprofit.

EXPLORING BRAND VALUES

Given that many nonprofit brands pertain to the organization as a whole and that the values they project are a key component, it is worth exploring for a moment what is meant by the term 'organizational value' and how this can be reflected in a charity brand.

Dose (1997:227–228) defines organizational values as: 'evaluative standards relating to work or the work environment by which individuals discern what is "right" or assess the importance of preferences'. Similarly, Van Rekom (1997) refers to an organization's 'central value orientations' as pervading all its behaviour and Collins and Porras (1996:66) regard values as a set of 'timeless guiding principles' which require no external justification. This latter point is expanded by Saviour and Scott (1997) who argue that while values are highly important in explaining the behaviour of individuals and groups within organizations, they are often unperceived, unspoken and taken for granted. Organizational values are 'common sense' and thus require no explanation.

Academic interest in organizational values has frequently focused on the relationship between specific values, or forms of values, and organizational performance. Authors such as Deal and Kennedy (1982) and Collins and Porras (1996), for example, have identified a link between 'strong' organizational values and corporate success. The authors argue that the difference between good and visionary companies is that the latter have a stronger sense of their core values. Companies that enjoy enduring success have a set of core values that are not compromised by the vagaries of the marketplace but remain fixed, and many of these values have a 'likeable' or 'humanist' dimension. This point is particularly key for nonprofits, many of whose brands reflect these very dimensions. The lesson is that successful brands convey a consistent and strongly differentiated message over time.

Practitioners in the nonprofit sector often claim that being value[s] based is one of the features that distinguishes their organizations from those in the public or private sectors (Aiken 2001). The distinctive way in which nonprofits manage and organize themselves is viewed as due in part to organizational values, and writers such as Batsleer et al. (1991) argue that without these values some nonprofits would simply not exist. Although it is recognized that charity values are difficult to identify, their maintenance and development is seen as being crucial to the distinctive identity of the sector and important for the wider health of society as a whole (Putman and Feldstein 2003; Korten 1998).

Charity values appear not only to drive the organization, but also to have an ethical or moral dimension. Hankinson (2000) argues that a charity's symbolic values relate to its beliefs, for example being passionate, caring and innovative. This is supported by Malloy and Agarwal (2001) who argue that the dominant climate in nonprofits is based on an individual caring or 'feminine' model. Saxton (2002) deepens our understanding by suggesting 46 distinctive values that may be associated with British charities. These are depicted in Exhibit 13.1

CAMPAIGN INTEGRATION

While we have stressed on numerous occasions throughout this chapter the need for all communications to reflect the nature of the brand, we have as yet not focused on the increasingly important topic of campaign integration. The brand has a key role to play in this, since all forms of nonprofit communication should be true to the brand or brands it adopts. Too many nonprofits assume that they are dealing with discrete groups of stakeholders who will not have access to other communications that the organization might generate for other stakeholder groups. They do not as a consequence see the need to be consistent from one form of communication to another. To be successful, however, the whole organization has to 'live the brand' and to reflect its various dimensions in literally every form of communication that leaves the organization.

EXHIBIT 13.1   BRITISH CHARITY BRAND VALUES

■ Accountable	■ Effective	■ Inspiring
■ Ambitious	■ Engaging	■ Outspoken
■ Approachable	■ Established	■ Passionate
■ Authoritative	■ Exciting	■ Practical
■ Bold	■ Exclusive	■ Professional
■ Boring	■ Fair	■ Reputable
■ Caring	■ Focused	■ Responsive
■ Cautious	■ Friendly	■ Rich
■ Challenging	■ Generous	■ Supportive
■ Complacent	■ Greedy	■ Sympathetic
■ Compassionate	■ Helpful	■ Traditional
■ Conservative	■ Heroic	■ Trustworthy
■ Determined	■ Inclusive	■ Visionary
■ Dedicated	■ Independent	■ Welcoming
■ Direct	■ Informative	
■ Dynamic	■ Innovative	

Source: Saxton (2002).

Many nonprofits produce 'style guides' that stipulate how letterhead, compliments slips and other communications will be laid out. Others focus on the use of the logo, its colours, where it should be positioned on a page and the variants that are acceptable. It must be realized that this is only a small part of brand management and should not be regarded as a satisfactory approach in isolation.

It is rather more important to manage the tone of communication, both written and verbal, to ensure that this reflects the brand values and personality. It is all too easy to be regarded as uncaring and arrogant when a fundraiser fashions a hurried reply to a donor enquiry, or provides faulty information to an enquiring journalist.

Of course achieving consistency in approach is not easy and some organizations have taken steps to produce a brand book that stipulates not only the details of the logo and presentation, but also how the organization should convey its core values. This sort of publication specifies in great detail the content of the brand and how an appropriate style of communication may be fostered. It also provides information as to where individual members of staff can turn for advice if they are unsure how to implement any aspect of the guidelines.

MANAGING MULTIPLE COMMUNICATIONS

Of course there is more to campaign integration than just consistency of brand message. A non-profit organization will be involved in sending many different communication messages over the course of a typical year, almost certainly involving a variety of media. The difficulty here is that many different departments will also be involved. Fundraisers, trading staff, service providers and corporate branders will all be striving to convey often very disparate messages over the course of the year.

In many cases this diversity in communication may not matter, particularly if they are strongly branded and directed to very distinct stakeholder groups. More often than not, however, an individual may be subject to a variety of different communications and in the case of donors (with whom we are primarily concerned here) it will be important to ensure that the overall pattern of what they receive is appropriate and timely. To achieve this it is absolutely essential that all departments and functions with responsibility for external communications meet at regular intervals to plan the nature of the communications that will be dispatched. It is also essential that this is done by looking at distinct categories of donor (e.g. legacy pledger, direct mail donor, major donor, trust donor).

A view should be taken on the volume of communication that any one individual should receive, to ensure that they are not bombarded by the organization. Care should also be taken to ensure that the order in which these communications are received is appropriate, and that in aggregate the communications paint a consistent picture of a relationship with the donor evolving over time.

Many nonprofits achieve this by a high degree of interactive planning between departments and then control the process by including the address of a staff member in each segment of the fundraising database. This individual then takes responsibility for recording everything that they receive which can in turn be fed back to planners to ensure that any inconsistencies identified are in the future avoided. From our own experience this can be something of an eye-opener. While a fundraiser may assume that the only communications a donor receives are the quarterly appeals they dispatch, they may also be being asked for planned gifts, legacy gifts, to buy goods from a catalogue, to engage in proactive campaigning on behalf of the organization and to volunteer to assist in local service provision. They may also receive an annual report and a regular service provision newsletter. Of course, some of this overlap may be appropriate, but for some segments of donors it will be inappropriate for the organization to initiate all these categories of communication.

SUMMARY

In this chapter we have examined the contribution that successful branding can make to fundraising practice. We have outlined a number of key benefits the development of a branding strategy can offer and discussed a number of key branding decisions currently facing nonprofits.

In doing so we have perhaps painted a rather rosy picture of what branding can offer, but it is important to understand that, despite the advantages, some constituencies, including donors, may be antagonistic towards the organization spending monies on branding. Indeed, a number of major charities have recently been openly criticized in the press for spending on this rather than on service activities per se. While this may just be a matter of reassuring the public of the benefits, there are a number of legitimate criticisms of branding expenditure that can be raised.

Spruill (2001) argues that branding can create barriers that prevent nonprofits from creating collaborative partnerships with each other for either service delivery or fundraising. Managers are understandably reticent about diluting their brand and thus unwilling to develop partnerships as a consequence. Spruill also argues that branding can develop a spirit of 'unhealthy competition' for visibility, prompting others to undertake similar expenditure, none of which will directly benefit beneficiaries. There can also be a sense that the voice of smaller causes is buried under the noise created by high-profile 'names'. Meyers (1985) notes that such concerns prompted Planned Parenthood to drop the idea of licensing condoms, which could have earned about $300,000 a year in royalties.

Of course such objections assume that it is possible for a nonprofit not to brand. As we noted earlier, nonprofits have brands whether they choose to call them that or not, and the development of effective brand management is a matter that deserves serious management attention. In an era when consumers and hence donors are becoming increasingly sophisticated, their expectations of nonprofits are becoming similarly enhanced. Modern fundraising and nonprofit marketing practice needs to reflect this change.

DISSCUSSION QUESTIONS

1   Your nonprofit is considering a change of name. What impact might this have on fundraising?
2   Select a well-known nonprofit and illustrate the components of its brand diagrammatically.
3   As a fundraising director, you have been responsible for creating a committed giving product that is now better known than your organization's name. Prepare a presentation for your CEO explaining how and why this has happened, what the impact might be and what actions you would recommend the organization to take.
4   Select a recent high-profile nonprofit campaign and evaluate critically the extent to which the various aspects of the campaign were integrated. Suggest how this might have been improved.

REFERENCES

Aaker, J.L. (1997) 'Dimensions of Brand Personality', *Journal of Marketing Research*, August: 347–356.

Aaker, D.A. (1995) *Building Strong Brands*, Free Press, New York.

Aiken, M. (2001) *Keeping Close to Your Values: Lessons From a Study Examining How Voluntary and Co-operative Organizations Reproduce their Organizational Values*, Open University, Milton Keynes.

Batsleer, J., Cornforth, C. and Paton, R. (1991) *Issues in Voluntary and Non-profit Management*, Addison Wesley, Wokingham.

Bendapudi, N. and Singh, S.N. (1996) 'Enhancing Helping Behavior: An Integrative Framework for Promotion Planning', *Journal of Marketing*, 60(3): 33–54.

Collins, J.C. and Porras, J.I. (1996) 'Building Your Company's Vision', *Harvard Business Review*, (September–October): 65–77.

Deal, T.E. and Kennedy, A.A. (1982) *Corporate Cultures*, Penguin Books, Harmondsworth.

Denney, F. (1998) 'Not-For-Profit Marketing in the Real World: An Evaluation of Barnardo's 1995 Promotional Campaign', *International Journal of Nonprofit and Voluntary Sector Marketing*, 4(2): 153–162.

Dixon, M. (1996) 'Small and Medium Sized Charities Need a Strong Brand Too: Crisis' Experience', *Journal of Nonprofit and Voluntary Sector Marketing*, 2(1): 52–57.

Dose, J.J. (1997) 'Work Values: An Integrative Framework and Illustrative Application to Organizational Socialisation', *Journal of Occupational and Organizational Psychology*, 70(3): 219–240.

Finegan, J.E. (2000) 'The Impact of Person and Organizational Values on Organizational Commitment', *Journal of Occupational and Organizational Psychology*, 73(2): 149–169.

Frumkin, P. and Kim, M.T. (2001) 'Strategic Positioning and the Financing of Nonprofit Organizations: Is Efficiency Rewarded in the Contributions Marketplace?' *Public Administration Review*, 61 (May/June): 266–275.

Gallagher, K. and Weinberg, C.B. (1991) 'Coping With Success: New Challenges For Nonprofit Marketing', *Sloan Management Review*, 33 (Fall): 27–42.

Grounds, J. and Harkness, J. (1998) 'Developing a Brand From Within: Involving Employees and Volunteers When Developing a New Brand Position', *Journal of Nonprofit and Voluntary Sector Marketing*, 3(2): 179–184.

Hankinson, P. (2000) 'Brand Orientation in Charity Organizations: Qualitative Research into key Charity Sectors', *International Journal of Nonprofit and Voluntary Sector Marketing*, 5: 207–219.

Hankinson, P. (2001a) 'Brand Orientation in the Charity Sector: A Framework for Discussion and Research', *International Journal of Nonprofit and Voluntary Sector Marketing*, 6(3): 231–242.

Hankinson, P. (2001b) 'The Impact of Brand Orientation on Managerial Practice: A Quantitative Study of the UK's Top 500 Fundraising Managers', *International Journal of Nonprofit and Voluntary Sector Marketing*, 7(1): 30–44.

Harvey, J. (1990) 'Benefit Segmentation for Fundraisers', *Journal of the Academy of Marketing Science*, 18(1): 77–86.

Kennedy, S. (1998) 'The Power of Positioning: A Case History from the Children's Society', *Journal of Nonprofit and Voluntary Sector Marketing*, 3(3): 224–230.

Korten, D.C. (1998) *Globalizing Civil Society: Reclaiming Our Right to Power*, Seven Stories Press, New York.

Kotler, P. and Andreasen, A. (1996), *Strategic Marketing For Nonprofit Organizations* 5th edn, Prentice Hall, Englewood Cliffs, NJ.

Malloy, D.C. and Agarwal, J. (2001) 'Ethical Climate in Nonprofit Organizations: Propositions and Implications', *Nonprofit Management and Leadership*, 12(1): 39–54.

Meyers, W. (1985) 'The Nonprofits Drop the "Non"', *New York Times*, 24 November.

Polonsky, M.J. and Macdonald, E.N. (2000) 'Exploring the Link between Cause-related Marketing and Brand Building', *International Journal of Nonprofit and Voluntary Sector Marketing*, 5(1): 46–57.

Patnam, R.D. and Feldstein, L. (2003) *Better Together: Restoring the American Community*, Sinon and Schuster, New York.

Ritchie, R.J.B. and Swami, S. (1998) 'A brand new world', *International Journal of Nonprofit and Voluntary Sector Marketing*, 4: 26–42.

Roberts Wray, B. (1994) 'Branding, Product Development and Positioning the Charity', *Journal of Brand Management*, 1(6): 350–370.

Sargeant, A. and Jay, E. (2004) 'Reasons for Lapse: The Case of Face-to-face Donors', *International Journal of Nonprofit and Voluntary Sector Marketing*, 9(2): 171–182.

Sargeant, A, West, D.C. and Ford, J.B. (2001) 'The Role of Perceptions in Predicting Donor Value', *Journal of Marketing Management*, 17: 407–428.

Saviour, L.N. and Scott, J.V.J. (1997) 'The Influence of Corporate Culture on Managerial Ethical Judgments', *Journal of Business Ethics*, 16(8): 757–776.

Saxton, J. (1995) 'A Strong Charity Brand Comes from Strong Beliefs and Values', *Journal of Brand Management*, 2(4): 211–220.

Saxton, J. (2002) *Polishing the Diamond*, Future Foundation, London.

Spruill, V. (2001) 'Build Brand Identity for Causes, Not Groups', *Chronicle of Philanthropy*, 13 (June): 45.

Sternberg, P. (1998) 'The Third Way: The Repositioning of the Voluntary Sector', *Journal of Nonprofit and Voluntary Sector Marketing*, 3(3): 209–217.

Tapp, A. (1996) 'Charity Brands: A Qualitative Study of Current Practice', *Journal of Nonprofit and Voluntary Sector Marketing*, 1: 327–336.

Van Rekom, J. (1997) 'Deriving an Operational Measure of Corporate Identity', *European Journal of Marketing*, 31(5): 410–422.

Part IV

Critical issues in fundraising

Chapter 14

The rise of new electronic channels

OBJECTIVES

By the end of this chapter you should be able to:

- Understand the significance of the Internet as part of an integrated fundraising mix.
- Develop a strategy for website development.
- Develop an e-fundraising mix.
- Explain how site design can facilitate relationship fundraising.
- Explain the factors that drive success in Internet fundraising.
- Describe the fundraising opportunities offered by interactive television.
- Describe the fundraising opportunities offered by SMS text messaging.

INTRODUCTION

No text on fundraising would be complete without a consideration of the opportunities offered by the Internet. Since its introduction in 1991, the use of the Internet has grown faster than any other electronic medium, including, historically, the telegraph. In 1993 when the first web browser became available, only 140 websites existed and only 1 per cent of these were commercial (or '. com') sites. At the time of writing the number of organisations with an online presence stands at 168 million, with new domain registrations up 22 per cent on the previous year (2007). Of course these growth rates are not sustainable. It seems likely that the growth currently being recorded will reach a plateau within the next decade as the numbers of consumers and organisations likely to benefit from a web presence begin to reach the optimum. Indeed it seems likely that the most significant growth over the next few years will occur in Asia where countries such as China are investing heavily in broadband technology.

In respect of the number of users, the research agency Nielsen conducts a regular survey of the number of active Internet home users (i.e. individuals who have logged on in the past month). Table 14.1 contains a summary of their data. Some 29 million people are active users of the Internet in the UK, with 153 million being active in the United States. As Table 14.1 also indicates, these numbers are continuing to grow.

Despite the scale of the opportunity the nonprofit sector has been fairly slow to capitalize on the new technology on both sides of the Atlantic. Based on data from a variety of sources we

Table 14.1 *Worldwide Internet home users, August 2008*

Country	July 2008	August 2008	Growth (%)	Difference
Australia	11,452,652	11,169,844	−2.47	−282,808
Brazil	23,715,159	24,331,212	2.60	616,054
France	26,151,352	26,984,002	3.18	832,649
Germany	36,773,740	37,795,221	2.78	1,021,481
Italy	19,561,913	20,646,132	5.54	1,084,220
Japan	49,049,579	50,128,725	2.20	1,079,146
Spain	15,782,617	15,707,229	−0.48	−75,388
Switzerland	3,762,984	3,771,663	0.23	8,679
U.K.	28,112,820	28,751,970	2.27	639,151
U.S.	152,690,056	153,144,180	0.30	454,124

Source: Nielsen Online, 2008: Reproduced with kind permission.

estimate that at present less than 2 per cent of giving is accounted for by online donations. The sector has a long way to go before it achieves the same degree of success as other sectors of the economy. In comparison, 41 per cent of computers, 21 per cent of books and 8 per cent of all clothing is now bought online.

That said, examples of good and creative practice do exist and the Internet is now being used effectively by a number of nonprofits for the purposes of fundraising, communication, information provision, branding, advocacy, selling products and building relationships. In the UK, the most frequently quoted online success story is Comic Relief (www.comicrelief.com) which received £1.75 million in six hours in one of their Telethon nights, representing 8 per cent of the total for their appeal. The National Society for the Prevention of Cruelty to Children (www. nspcc.org.uk) claim considerable success from offering password protected access to regular donors who can enter a privileged section of the NSPCC website and alter their mailing preferences, view their giving history, change their address details and make a donation (see Plate 14.1). UNICEF UK (www.unicef.org.uk) offer a similar service for major donors, and ActionAid (www.actionaid.org) has pioneered a number of special sites in their youth marketing and child sponsorship campaigns.

Campaigning groups such as Greenpeace (www.greenpeace.org.uk) and Amnesty International have also been notable in using e-mail alerts in their lobbying campaigns, and employ their websites extensively in supporter communication. In the USA the World Wildlife Fund offer a much-cited interactive site (www.panda.org) where users can collect 'stamps' for their 'Panda Passport' as they engage in a variety of activities (including campaigning and offering funds) to support the organisation. The Environmental Defense Fund (www.edf.org) offers a highly interactive site (www.scorecard.org) which allows users to identify the companies that are polluting the air, land and water in their specific zipcode, and e-mail or fax them to complain (see Plate 14.2).

In this chapter it is our intention to explore how fundraising over the Web and other emerging media is best conducted and to learn from both academic research and examples of best practice.

Plate 14.1 *NSPCC website*

Source: © NSPCC. Reproduced with kind permission.

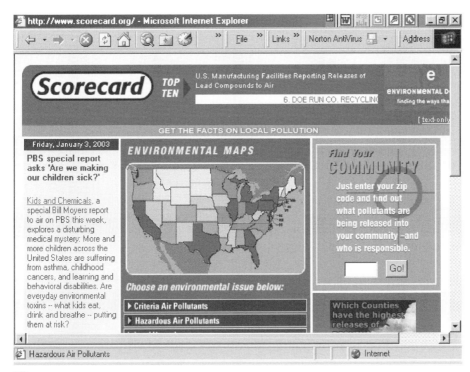

Plate 14.2 *EDF Scorecard website*

Source: © EDF (www.scorecard.org). Reproduced with kind permission.

SITE DESIGN

The costs of setting up a website for the first time can vary considerably. Such costs are clearly a function of the complexity of the site, the number of pages, the amount of information that will be posted and the degree of interaction that will be offered to visitors. Costs can also be a function of the quality of design undertaken and the degree of integration that will take place with other existing computer systems such as the donor database and financial management systems.

Smaller nonprofits can find the costs of start-up considerably lower, with a number of Internet service providers (ISPs) now offering flexible design and hosting packages for only a few hundred pounds. For most nonprofits, however, the costs associated with establishing an Internet operation for the first time can be very considerable. It is therefore important that the design be carefully thought through to achieve its stated objectives.

In designing a site the following points should be considered:

Determine precise goals

The organisation should be clear from the outset what the specific goals of the website will be. Is it designed to raise funds, provide information, coordinate volunteers, provide nonprofit services, or more likely some combination of the same? Whatever the purpose, this needs to be agreed up-front since the cost of 'bolting-on' additional functionality at a later date is likely to be very considerable.

If the purpose is to raise funds it is important to bear in mind that very few organisations are able to generate acceptable returns from their presence on the Web. Only those with high-quality content that attracts traffic from the major search engines are at present raising money successfully. For those organisations whose cause makes it difficult to provide attractive/informative site content, there may still be good reasons for going online, but the organisation needs to be clear from the outset what these might be and be realistic in respect of the fundraising goals (if any).

Keep the site simple

While it might be tempting to adopt the most modern up-to-date graphic presentations and offer users complex levels of interaction and routes through the site, the most successful sites are undoubtedly those that are simple and easy to use. Many consumers who access a site for the first time will leave the site again after only a few seconds if it is not immediately apparent that the site will both meet their needs and be easy to navigate. If it takes an age to download complex graphics, potential visitors may be deterred and simply move on to the next site before the process is completed. Similarly, if a complex path must be navigated to find the pages that are of most interest, many users will lose interest before reaching their desired target. For this reason many homepages contain a simple navigation guide. Plate 14.3 provides an example – the American Cancer Society homepage. The right-hand side of the screen contains a menu offering each class of user their own unique gateway into the site.

Striving for simplicity in use should therefore be an overriding design specification and it would not be unusual for site designers to develop a series of flow charts that illustrate the route it is proposed that various classes of users will take through the site. These can subsequently be edited to ensure that navigation is as smooth, direct and simple as possible.

Develop content that is both beneficial and pertinent to visitors

Great care should be taken to ensure that the needs of various stakeholders are reflected in the site. Of particular relevance here would be a consideration of the specific benefits that will be

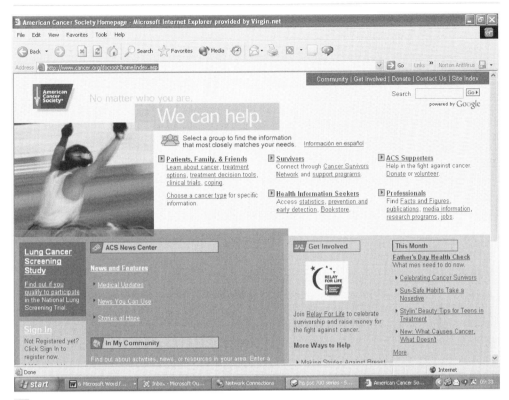

Plate 14.3 *American Cancer Society website*

Source: © American Cancer Society. Reproduced with kind permission.

sought by each category of potential users. In designing the site it will be important to seek the views of each key grouping and to ensure that not only is pertinent material provided, but that anything not of direct relevance is dropped. Peripheral information (particularly if it contains graphics) serves only to lengthen download times and slow down access to the site. At a simple level one should therefore be asking, 'What information do potential users really need?'

Use caution in developing links to other sites

There are two primary reasons for offering this caveat. First, organisations can find themselves in considerable legal difficulty if they suggest to those visiting their site that the site is in some way endorsed by a third party. Establishing links from a host site to another organisation is therefore something that should be undertaken with considerable care. Indeed it is good practice to seek the permission of any organisation to which it is proposed to forge a link.

Aside from the legal difficulties that might be encountered in including links, a second major concern is the degree of encouragement that might be offered users to exit. Internet research has consistently shown that there are two major types of readers inhabiting the Web: browsers and seekers. Seekers are those that have a specific information need in mind and work their way methodically through sites to achieve their goal. Browsers, by contrast, are using the Web almost as one might drive a car for recreational purposes. They move from place to place looking for the next exciting experience or tranche of useful information. They keep one hand on the virtual doorknob (Johnston 1999).

In attempting to retain this second category of user it is therefore somewhat ironic that many organisations are intent on providing as many possible exits as they can on a given screen. Clearly one would wish to provide as friendly and useful an environment as possible for users, but providing higher numbers of links merely increases the likelihood that someone will be tempted away even before they have glanced at the content of the host organisation's site.

Keep contact information in front of the visitor at all times

At any stage in visiting a website or perusing the data available, visitors may identify a need for further information. Users may also decide part-way through visiting a site that they wish to make a donation, or request further information. Not all users of a site will wish to do this online and it is thus good practice to ensure that the contact information for an organisation is available at all times, perhaps following a convention such as providing it at the bottom of each page.

Ask for a donation on every page

Allied to the above, if one of the purposes of the site is to raise funds, the site should ask for a gift on every page. It is not enough for a nonprofit to assume that a potential donor will navigate their way through the site to find the requisite donation page. Many gifts are made on impulse and it should be made as easy as possible to make a donation. An 'ask' or a link to the fundraising section of the website must therefore be provided on every page. Indeed, if an organisation derives a large percentage of its income from legacies, there may even be an argument for including a link to legacy information on every page too.

Fulfil promises in a timely manner

When a donation has been made, any promises that have been made in respect of recognition for that gift need to be honoured as quickly as possible. Similarly, requests for literature, further information, or contact with specific individuals should be met in a timely manner. As was explained in Chapter 7 the quality of service provided will be a key determinant of how well an organisation can retain its donors.

Publicize your site in every medium possible

Designing an attractive and user-friendly site will not in itself guarantee success. Potential customers and users still need to be made aware of the online presence. The launch and ongoing operation of a website should therefore be reflected in other forms of marketing communication an organisation might generate. Business cards, letterhead, advertising and other forms of direct marketing communications should all feature the web address and seek to make it available at times when potential customers might require it for access.

Develop and adhere to a privacy policy

Despite the almost exponential growth in the number of consumers going online, fewer than 40 per cent of web users are estimated to have actually made a purchase online and fewer than 1 per cent a donation. Key barriers to online purchasing and donations would appear to be concerns over the security of credit cards, privacy issues and the perceived problem of returning defective or inappropriate merchandise. Consumer concerns in respect of security, in particular, have received considerable publicity in recent years, although the incidence of actual credit card theft over the Internet is estimated to be minimal and many times smaller than would occur in a traditional retail environment. As always, however, it is the perception that matters and many sites now go to great lengths to offer consumers secure connections, in some cases achieving accreditation by organisations such as Verisign, TRUSTe or BBBOnline.

Another major concern is privacy. Many consumers worry that if they share information with a site they will as a consequence receive a high volume of unsolicited mail or e-mail (Hart et al. 2008). They also worry that their personal data might be shared with other organisations without their consent being sought. For many individuals the issue of privacy is thus a major concern and sites are increasingly compelled to offer some reassurance in this regard, by posting an easily accessible privacy statement which maps out exactly how personal information will be used (if at all).

Central to the issue of privacy is the cookie. A cookie is a small, encrypted data string that website servers write to the hard drive of a user's computer. It contains the user's unique ID for the website. It can be accessed on subsequent visits to a site by the host computer and interrogated to eliminate the need for a user to log in. In effect the cookie allows a site to recognize a returning visitor and if appropriate tailor the environment to suit their needs. Cookies can thus be used to deliver web content specific to visitor interests, keep track of orders and control access to premium content. Cookies cannot be used to access or otherwise compromise the data on a user's hard drive.

Many users object to sites storing data on their hard drive and consider the practice an invasion of their privacy. The use of such mechanisms can therefore deter many potential visitors from returning once they discover the practice is in operation. For this reason many privacy statements make it clear whether cookies will be used and their purpose. The American Cancer Society, for example, includes the planned use of cookies in its privacy statement.

Test and measure results

Once operational it is essential that an organisation reviews the performance of its site. There are a variety of different measures that can be employed for this purpose and an equal variety of measurement tools each with slightly different outputs and modus operandi. Some of the more common measurements undertaken are provided below:

- *Ad views (or impressions)*   The number of times a www ad banner is downloaded by visitors.
- *Reach*   The total number of users that a vehicle reaches - calculated by deriving the number of persistent, unique cookies present in a site's log files over a period of time.
- *Frequency*   A measure of how often a unique user interacts with a site over a period of time – calculated as a series of requests by a unique visitor without 30 consecutive minutes of inactivity.
- *Visit*   User's interaction with a site within a specified time period. The visit includes all the pages seen on the same site during one session. It is now common practice to consider a visit terminated when new pages are not consulted for more than 15–30 minutes, depending on the country in which the website is located.
- *Visit duration*   The period over which a visit is undertaken. Most measurement software provides a range of data on this variable including mean, median and modal durations.
- *Visitors*   The number of individuals consulting the same site in a given period. The total number of visitors thus takes account of visit duplication. It should be noted that some systems refer to visitors as users.

Measurement software is also capable of tracking movement through a particular site. By tagging each web page with a unique identification number it is possible to trace the typical way in which visitors, or specific segments of visitors, interact with the material presented. It can also track the typical duration that visitors spend viewing each individual page. Clearly all this data can be used to great effect in refining ineffectual aspects of the site and improving the quality of a visitor's experience.

Finally, it is important to note that many organisations will simply assess the performance of the website by the trading income it has been able to generate and/or the fundraising income that can be attributed to it. At the time of writing average gifts through the Internet are impressive and compare very favourably with those from other direct marketing media. It is not uncommon for average gifts to be twice those achieved in the off-line environment (Hart et al. 2005).

WRITING ONLINE

Before a web page can be satisfactorily created a number of issues must be considered.

Flow chart/site map

When organisations prepare off-the-page advertising, or put together a fundraising appeal mailing, information is laid out in a linear format. Each paragraph of the text leads logically to another. In essence the designers have provided a logical sequence that guides the reader through each section of the information presented.

When writing for the Web, however, a complex non-linear format replaces this simplistic framework. Websites generally consist of a maze of interlocking decisions and directions. For larger sites the easiest way of opening up access for visitors to the site is to consider offering a flow chart or site map which makes it very clear how the material within the site will be divided.

A map such as the one in Plate 14.4 performs a number of functions; it:

- gives the users the freedom to create their own experience rather than be guided through pages that the organisation feels might be appropriate;
- can highlight those aspects of the site that are most important and likely to be visited regularly;
- provides a useful pictorial overview of the information that the site contains.

Inclusion of links

Links move the user to a new web page. In most versions of browser the cursor is pointing at a link when the arrow changes to a pointing finger. Pretty much any object can be designed as a link, but the five more common kinds are described here.

Text-based links – hypertext links

These are usually very easy to identify as they appear in a different colour from the rest of the text and are often underlined. The web page illustrated has a number of these links and they helpfully change colour after a visit to remind the user that they have already explored that link.

Most common browsers can also be set to remember pages that the users have visited. Microsoft Explorer, for example, allows users to set the colours of visited and unvisited links by

Plate 14.4 *Greenpeace site map*
Source: © Greenpeace. Reproduced with kind permission.

accessing the View menu and clicking on Options. They then click the General tab and on the right of the screen will view a box illustrating the colour of visited and unvisited links. A colour palette allows the user to choose the colour they prefer in each case.

Images

Links can also be also be created by graphics, icons or photographs. As is usual with a link, the cursor will change to a hand and pointed finger when directed at such an image. Clicking on the image will transfer the user to the new site or page.

Image maps

Some of the more complex sites on the Web have a number of different links embedded in a single picture or map. Such maps can be a very powerful way of illustrating the design and layout of the site. The links are usually obvious and users will see the cursor change into a hand as they move over various aspects of the map. A glance at the bottom of the browser will confirm that the destination URL changes as each part of the image is run over with the mouse. Clicking on any one item will move the user to that part of the site.

Long versus short copy

When writing for the Web many writers feel that long copy should be avoided. As direct marketers know all too well from their experience with direct mail this is not necessarily the case. The test is always whether the text is relevant and whether all the key information and arguments are included. If extraneous information is provided, the text is too long; if it covers the key essentials it is probably about right.

It should be remembered that many visitors will have 'self-selected' their visit. They will have determined that the site has relevance to their needs and will not necessarily be put off by longer copy. The key in writing text for the Web, however, lies in breaking it up into manageable chunks. Copy should not fill one long page. If individuals have to continue scrolling down one page to reach the desired information they are considerably more likely to tire of the experience and leave.

Instead web authors can compact the text by using a series of hypertext links. This allows the user to skip those sections of the text that are of no relevance and to jump immediately to those that are. Her Majesty's Stationery Office (hmso.govt.uk), for example, makes many statutes such as the Data Protection Act available online. Rather than present the whole document as an extended page, the table of contents is offered as a menu and users can jump through a hypertext link to those sections of the Act that are of most interest.

Bullets

While few organisations would choose to make extensive use of bullet points in most of their corporate communications, bullet points and the Internet are a match made in heaven. Not only are they a convenient means of summarizing information, but bullet points can also be authored as hypertext links steering users from one section of the site to another. Bullet points can also be made an attractive feature of a given page.

The power of words

In designing copy for a web page many of the same rules apply as would be the case in direct mail, direct response press advertising, or indeed any other direct marketing media.

Use short sentences and vary the length

In writing copy nothing matters except the meaning. Short sentences are OK. Verbs are not necessarily required. Not really. Nor is it necessary to create long verbose sentences that simply demonstrate one's dexterity in the use of punctuation. To quote George Smith (1996:87)

> A (sentence) need not be long, need not defer to the Johnsonian tradition of the periodic sentence that ran to perhaps 200 words complete with subclauses and the full complement of colons and semi-colons to separate the various constructs; a tradition that continues to this day in the hands of writers such as Bernard Levin a journalist who rarely deploys 20 words when 200 can fulfil his sense of personal grandeur, a quality that some may admire but which most would resist on the basis that there are only so many hours a day in which one can read a newspaper.

As Smith later notes – hands up those who fell asleep during that last sentence!

Use short paragraphs and vary the length

Paragraphs can consist of only one sentence.
There is nothing wrong with that.
But if a writer consistently engages that technique it can become boring.

Far better to group the ideas and ensure that the length of paragraphs is varied. This will not only look more visually appealing, the text should also be easier to read.

Use 'I' and 'you' not 'we' and 'one'

The difficulty in using words such as 'we' is that text can very quickly appear very pompous. A phrase such as 'we at Routledge' conveys a certain arrogance, where the use of 'I' makes the text more intimate, personal and unassuming.

It is also good practice in the context of trading to allow potential buyers to 'rehearse' the benefits of ownership through the text. Phrases such as 'you will experience' put the buyer in the position of already owning the product and suggests to them how they will feel thereafter.

Avoid clichés

While the Internet is still comparatively new there are already words that are suffering from overuse. Words or phrases such as

Cutting edge
Check it out
Cool
Hot

are not particularly helpful and will only serve to irritate the reader. Sites with original language stimulate the eye and gain additional attention.

Avoid polysyllables

Long words are rarely more impressive than short ones. They create the impression of a bureaucratic, inhuman organisation that is distant from the needs of its customers. Smith (1996:89) uses the following examples to make the point:

Approximately	About
Participate	Take Part
Establish	Set up
Utilize	Use

FUNDRAISING ONLINE

We have previously examined the use of traditional media for donor recruitment. In this section we will focus on digital media and in particular examine how new audiences may be attracted to nonprofits online. In this environment a range of different tools is available, as shown in Figure 14.1

Search engine marketing

Search engines such as Google, Ask and Altavista allow users to search for materials online by typing in key words or phrases. A list of the matching web content is then provided by the engine. The task for the marketer is to ensure that their organisation's website nears the top of the list when relevant searches are conducted. Two approaches are possible here, since many search engines generate both natural search listings and paid for or pay-per-click listings.

In respect of the former, natural or organic listings emerge 'naturally' from the results of the search the user has conducted. Results are listed in order of the relevance of the match between the content of the web page and the keyword or phrase typed in. They appear on the left in Google, Yahoo and MSN Search. To improve their position in these listings marketers must engage in Search Engine Optimization to take account of the way in which search engines typically collate their listings. In particular marketers need to:

■ Match the key words on the organisation's website with the words most likely to be used by potential customers searching for the work the organisation does. Particular attention should be given to the frequency with which these words appear in the site (keyword density) and the title tags given to each page.

■ Consider the links that drive traffic into each page. In deciding on its rankings, Google will count each inward link to a site as a 'vote'. Sites with lots of inbound links will therefore perform well. Equally, some algorithms take into account the quality of those links so, for

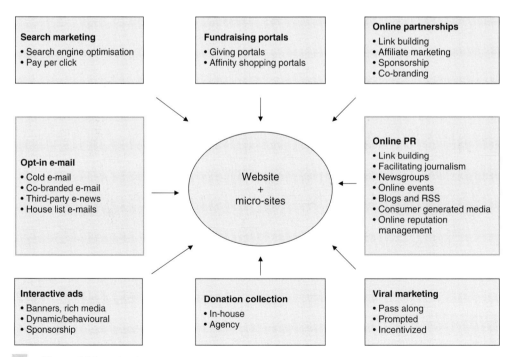

Figure 14.1 *E-fundraising mix*

example, a site linked to by the British Museum is likely to get a better ranking than one linked to by an individual's personal website. The presumption would be that if high-quality sites link to the site, then the content must be reliable and worthwhile.

Pay-per-click listings, by contrast, function rather like traditional advertising. To get a high listing here it is necessary to be willing to pay a higher fee than one's competitors. The highest bidder for a particular keyword or phrase will usually be listed at the top of the page, although the Google algorithm does factor in the number of click-throughs that a given ad is able to achieve. Those with a higher click-through rate will tend to appear nearer the top of the list.

Of course with pay per click, as the name suggests, the fundraiser must pay for each click-through to their site from the search engine. It is therefore not just a matter of achieving the highest rate of click-through possible. A good deal of money can be wasted driving traffic to the site that has absolutely no interest in the content or cause on offer. The key to successful pay per click advertising lies in writing the best possible copy for the text box that will appear in the listing so that users can judge the relevance for themselves and only genuinely good prospects will follow the link. Fundraisers using pay-per-click also have to consider the appropriate amounts to bid for each listing and manage their budgets accordingly.

Online public relations

There are seven core activities of online PR of interest to fundraisers.

Link building

The goal of online PR is to maximize the number of favourable mentions of the brand, organisation or the work being conducted on third-party websites. Third-party endorsements are as useful in the online environment as they are in the off-line. Such mentions are also useful because they often contain links back to the organisation's website and thus aid in search engine optimization. A useful way of identifying who is currently linking to your organisation is to visit the Google website and in the search box enter 'link: www.(your domain name)'. A list of the websites linking in to that site will be generated.

Communicating with journalists online

E-mail and websites can be used to pass on information to journalists who might be interested in featuring the work of the organisation in an upcoming article or comment. Some organisations go so far as to establish dedicated press rooms on their site where an archive of press releases and other information is provided that journalists may use. It is also possible to submit genuinely newsworthy material to the media through news feeds (such as www.prweb,com or www. prnewswire.com).

Newsgroups

Equally, there may be occasions when it is more helpful for the organisation to contact potential supporters itself. One way this might be achieved is through the use of Internet newsgroups. There are many thousands of these, each of which is focused on a specific issue or topic. Online press releases can be targeted at any news groups it is felt might have an interest in the subject matter of the item. Infinite Ink offers a useful service for locating news groups on specific issues: http://www.ii.com/Internet/messaging/newsgroups/

Online events

A further good way of marketing a site and generating interest in its content is to consider hosting an event online. Those nonprofits with access to celebrities or individuals with distinctive expertise or knowledge could consider running an online event. Typically this might comprise an online discussion of a cause-related issue, a 'surgery' session where individuals could ask advice or even an auction of donated goods or services.

Blogs and RSS

Web logs or 'blogs' are an increasingly popular way of publishing news and event listings online. Many arts organisations have now established blogs to demonstrate the credibility of the organisation and engage with their audiences (e.g. http://www.artinliverpool.com/blog/). As an aside, readers with a particular interest in interactive marketing will find the digital marketing guru Dave Chaffey's blog worth following (www.davechaffey.com).

Really Simple Syndication (RSS) allows users to sign up for regular news on topics of interest. Blogs, video and news of any type is sent directly to an individual's computer where it is read by specialist reader software such as FeedDemon. News feeds also allow the user to see when new website content has been added and to view all the latest headlines and video in one place, as soon as its published, without having to visit the original website. Since users can specify the kinds of information they are specifically interested in, marketing in this way can be highly effective.

Online reputation management

There are two types of reputational management of interest. In the first the organisation takes a proactive approach to seeding positive content about itself on popular sites. As an example, YouTube's 2007/2008 Clinton Global Initiative commitment enables nonprofit organisations that register for the program to receive a free nonprofit-specific YouTube channel where they can upload footage of their work, public service announcements, calls to action and more. The channel also allows them to collect donations with no processing costs using Google Checkout for Non-Profits. YouTube's global platform thus enables nonprofits to deliver their message, showcase their impact and needs, and encourage supporters to take action.

The second facet of online reputation management concerns managing unfavourable coverage and responding where appropriate to criticism. A key facet of online PR is therefore monitoring how an organisation is being covered by third-party websites. Services such as Googlealert (www.googlealert.com) and Google alerts (www.google.com/alerts) can be used to alert you to when any new pages are published that include mention of your organisation. As an aside, these tools can also be a valuable way of checking on the online promotions undertaken by competitors or similar organisations in other parts of the country. They may well have good ideas that can be borrowed or adapted for your own use.

Consumer-generated media

'Consumer-generated media' (CGM) encompasses the millions of consumer-generated comments, opinions and personal experiences posted in publicly available online sources on a wide range of issues, topics, products and brands. CGM is also referred to as 'online consumer word of mouth' or 'online consumer buzz'. CGM originates from:

- blogs
- message boards and forums

- public discussions (Usenet newsgroups)
- discussions and forums on large e-mail portals (Yahoo, AOL, MSN)
- online opinion/review sites and services
- online feedback/complaint sites.

Online discussion forums, membership groups, boards and Usenet newsgroups represented the first CGM wave, while blogs and online videos represent the latest. CGM is important because consumers place far more trust in their fellow consumers than they do in traditional marketers and advertisers. For any fundraiser trying to be heard or break through the clutter, understanding and managing this CGM is critical for success. Figure 14.2 illustrates this point.

CGM data are easy to find on search engines, so fundraisers and advertisers no longer control the message or the medium. When a consumer types an organisation's name, brand or activities into a search engine, it is almost certain that some of the first results – good or bad – will be posted and created by other consumers. In addition, the media, analysts, competitors and other stakeholders encounter this readily available CGM 'reference material' when they are researching issues, topics and trends online.

While it may be difficult for organisations to stay on top of this material themselves, there are many agencies that will track this activity on behalf of clients. Nielsen Buzzmetrics, for example, will locate and analyse CGM activity providing data for their clients that can then be actioned appropriately, perhaps by correcting misinformation and/or by posting comments of their own. From a fundraiser's perspective, the more positive buzz one can develop, the greater the traffic that can be generated to the organisation's website and, ultimately, the greater the number of visitors who may consider offering a gift.

Online partnerships

Online partnerships may take one of four forms.

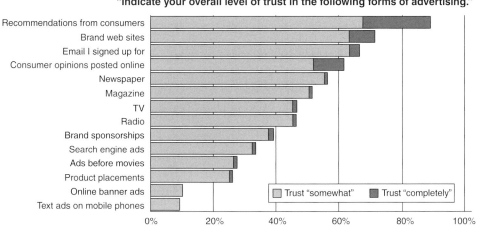

"Indicate your overall level of trust in the following forms of advertising."

Base: 470 responses recruited from PlanetFeedback.com members.
Source: Forrester Research, Inc. and Intelliseek.

Figure 14.2 *Trust in forms of advertising*

Source: Forrester Research, Inc. and Intelliseek. Reproduced with kind permission.

Links

The significance of developing a good network of links has already been highlighted and nonprofits should exploit potential partnerships where they can encourage reciprocal links (i.e. where two-way links are agreed between each site). The specialist site Linking Matters (www.linkingmatters.com) provides considerable guidance on how best to maximize this opportunity.

Affiliate marketing

It may be appropriate for some organisations to consider establishing a network of affiliates who earn a commission for the sales or leads they generate. Membership organisations in particular may derive benefit from these arrangements. In the for-profit context, Amazon.com has an active network of affiliates who each earn a commission on the purchases made by every visitor they direct to the Amazon website. A commission-based system lowers the risk for the organisation as it only need pay for results, but on the downside affiliates can ultimately become competitors for search engine optimization and pay-per-click advertising, thereby pushing up the costs. The non-profit also loses some control over how the brand is presented and if the affiliate is involved in a wide range of activities there may even be reputational risk involved in operating in this way.

More usually in the context of fundraising, affiliate schemes are set up as the converse, i.e. where the nonprofit earns income from a relationship with a for-profit vendor such as Amazon. Books linked in some way to the cause can be promoted on the site with links through to Amazon which then pays commission on any sales that are generated.

Online sponsorship

Online sponsorship involves a sponsoring organisation linking its name with that of the nonprofit for the purpose of strengthening its brand. It is more than the provision of a simple banner or other form of advertising and typically takes the form of a genuine involvement with what the nonprofit is trying to achieve online, perhaps by sponsoring specific forms of content, or engagement with specific stakeholder groups. Nonprofits in the UK seeking to publicize their sponsorship opportunities may wish to consider placing a listing in the UK sponsorship database (http://www.uksponsorship.com/).

Co-branding

Co-branding takes online sponsorship one stage further. It is an opportunity for partnership rather than mere sponsorship, so the difference is one of degree. In co-branding, both partners work together to further the goals of both. An arts organisation might therefore work with a corporate partner to co-brand a password-protected part of its website for high-value donors. The corporate partner has exposure to potential high-value clients, while the arts organisation gains an additional facility it might not otherwise be able to afford.

A further example would be the co-branding of a particular campaign where the sponsor's name is clearly associated with this activity on the nonprofit's website and the campaign is also highlighted on the site of the corporate partner. In the case of the latter, detailed information about the work, the impact on beneficiaries and so on would be embedded in the corporatesite. Plate 14.5 provides one such example. Here Microsoft is celebrating their involvement with the NSPCC and the difference the two organisations have made to ending child cruelty and enhancing the safety of children online. The corporate partner has been able to lend its considerable

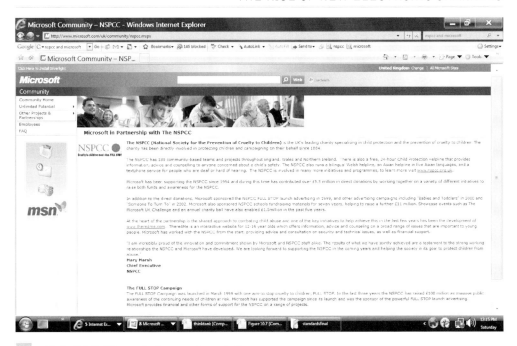

Plate 14.5 *Microsoft Community website*

Source: © 2009 Microsoft Corporation. Reproduced with kind permission.

expertise to assist the NSPCC in the design of its programs, while the NSPCC offers Microsoft the opportunity to demonstrate in a very practical way the corporate values of the organisation.

Interactive advertising

The term interactive advertising refers to all advertising through the Web, e-mail, wireless technologies and interactive television. Internet advertising commonly takes the form of banner ads, skyscrapers and underlay or overlays.

Banner ads are the most common and can appear in several different locations on a webpage. Skyscrapers are also common and these vary, as their name suggests, by the nature of their shape. They tend to be long and skinny and run along one side of the page. Web pages can be viewed in many different resolutions (typically set by the user in their browser) and the selected resolution refers to the dots or pixels per inch (dpi or ppi). The term 'resolution' can also refer to how many pixels are set to fit horizontally (across) and vertically (down) a monitor. Essentially, 800 × 600 and 1024 × 768 are currently the most common resolutions, and the normal width of a skyscraper ad is 120 pixels. Some people prefer a slightly wider building, however, or perhaps one that expands when a mouse passes over it.

The term 'overlay' is also quite intuitive and refers to an ad that is served over the page being viewed by the user. The video-sharing website YouTube has many clips featuring discussions of how overlays can be used to good effect and the range of effects that can be achieved using different technologies. A search on 'overlay ads' on www.youtube.com will bring up these materials. Underlays, by contrast are ads that appear under the page being viewed and which therefore become visible only when the relevant browser window is closed.

Each time an ad is served an *ad impression* is created. The number of ad impressions is thus a key metric in this environment, although many users may view the same ad on a number of occasions, so the *advertising reach* is also key. This refers to the number of unique individuals who view the advertisement.

The four most common ways online ads are purchased are CPM, PPC CPA and CPC.

- *CPM (cost per impression)*   Where advertisers pay for exposure of their ad to a particular audience. CPM costs are the cost to serve a thousand impressions. The use of the M in the acronym is a little confusing, but it refers to the Roman numeral for one thousand.
- *PPC (pay per click) or CPC (cost per click)*   In this scenario advertisers pay each time a user clicks on their listing and is directed to their website. They do not pay for the listing itself and pay only when the listing is clicked on. As discussed earlier, under the pay-per-click system, advertisers bid for the right to be listed under a series of target-rich words that direct relevant traffic to their website. They only pay when someone clicks on that listing.
- *CPA (cost per action) or cost per acquisition*   With this method payment is made on the basis of performance. It is typical of the remuneration method employed for affiliates. Here, the publisher carries all the risk of running the ad and the advertiser pays only for those consumers who actually complete a desired action, usually a purchase. CPL (cost per lead) is also common with publishers being remunerated when users complete a registration form or 'sign-up' to something that is core to the nonprofit's mission. For the sake of completeness, CPO (cost per order) may also be encountered where, as the name suggests, a fee is payable every time an order is placed.
- *CPC cost per conversion.*   This is simply the cost of acquiring a customer and is typically calculated by dividing the total cost of a campaign by the number of conversions. What constitutes a 'conversion' will vary depending on the purpose of the campaign. It might be a donation, but it may also be taking action or registering an interest in some aspect of the nonprofit's work.

Nonprofits seeking to evaluate between the various advertising alternatives open to them will typically need the following information.

- The CPM or cost per thousand ad servings.
- The click-through rate (the percentage of ad servings that result in an individual clicking the ad).
- The conversion rate (the percentage of customers clicking through that will make a purchase or take the desired action).

Consider the following fictitious example for an ad on Yahoo.

CPM = $1.50
Click-through rate = 0.1 per cent
Conversion rate = 2 per cent

What will it cost to generate one impression?
This is simply the CPM rate ÷ 1,000
So $1.50 ÷ 1,000 = $0.0015

How many impressions will it take to generate one click?
This is simply 100 ÷ click-through rate
So 100 ÷ 0.1 = 1,000

How much will one click cost?
This is calculated as:
cost per impression $\times$ how many impressions to generate one click
So $0.0015 \times 1,000 = $1.50

How many clicks are needed to generate a sale/donation?
This is calculated as:
$100 \div$ conversion rate
So $100 \div 2 = 50$

How much will one sale/donation cost?
This is calculated as:
the number of clicks needed to generate a sale/donation $\times$ the cost of each click
So $1.50 \times 50 = $75

With experience, as ads with different publishers are trialled, nonprofits can use these calculations to compare between the various advertising options open to them and optimize their online communications mix. They may for example develop a table comparing the costs of generating a sale/donation by advertising on each of the major search engines and allocate their budget accordingly.

Opt-in e-mail

Opt-in e-mail is critical to the successful development of online relationships. The key to success lies in the 'opt-in' and in many countries this is now a legal requirement. When users visit a site and have the opportunity to sign up for e-mail newsletters or alerts, they should specifically tick a check box to indicate their consent. Ideally they should also be able to specify the frequency and content of the information they will receive.

Most opt-in e-mail is *warm* in the sense that a visitor to a site, or a customer, has explicitly signed up to receive communications from the organisation. Such house list campaigns can be very effective and organisations should think through carefully the pattern of communications each segment of individuals will receive. Over time the efficacy of the timing and content of this can be evaluated and changes made to strategy accordingly.

Cold e-mail is often conducted too, perhaps where an organisation rents a list from a provider such as Experian (www.prospectlocator.com) which consists of the contact details of individuals who have given permission to be approached by specific categories of organisation. Given the hostility that many people feel towards unsolicited e-mail it is important when renting lists to include a statement of origin indicating how the communication was initiated to differentiate it from spam.

In the fundraising context, it may also be appropriate to consider the use of co-branded e-mail and work jointly with other nonprofits or corporate partners, designing communications that will be of interest to their stakeholders/customers and jointly communicating with shared lists. Although this is technically still cold e-mail, because a relationship already exists with one of the partners it is likely to generate a higher response.

Viral marketing

Viral marketing or 'word of mouse' uses the power of the Web for rapid and personal communication. It is a mechanism whereby an organisation's donors (or other stakeholder groups) are encouraged to pass along a message to their friends and associates promoting the organisation. This message may be a video clip, cartoon, political message or news item. It could be sent as a link, a Flash e-mail, a jpeg or a text message over the Web or SMS networks. Whatever its form, the key to successful viral marketing is that the content should be compelling enough for people to *want* to pass it along.

A number of nonprofits have now made use of the medium, most notably Barnardo's in the UK, which created an 'e-baby' which was dispatched to all members of staff, who were in turn encouraged to share it with their own friends and relatives. The e-mail contained a program for an e-baby which the recipient would have to look after – or when not available leave with an e-crèche. When tired of the baby it could be returned to Barnardo's when the individual would be invited to make a donation.

Kirby (2003) argues that three components should be considered in a viral campaign:

1 *The viral agent*   Creative material, message or offer and how it is spread (text, image, video).
2 *Seeding*   Identifying websites, blogs or people to send your e-mail to, to start the virus spreading.
3 *Tracking*   To monitor the effect, to assess the return on the cost of developing the agent and seeding.

Smith and Chaffey (2005) identify five categories of viral e-mail:

1 *Pass along e-mail*   In this case the e-mail itself is the only mechanism involved in spreading the message. The viral message may be contained in an attachment or it may perhaps contain a link to a video clip or game. The aim here is to ask recipients to pass the message along to their friends and acquaintances.
2 *Web facilitated viral (e-mail prompt)*   Where the e-mail contains a button labelled 'e-mail a friend' or 'tell someone else about our work'. When users click through they open a form which requests the address to which the e-mail should be forwarded and there is also (typically) an opportunity to send an accompanying message to the friend. An example of this approach from WWF is depicted in Plate 14.6. In this case users are invited to pass along access to an interactive game, 'The Seagull Strikes Back', where the aim is to target seagull poo at politicians who are screwing up the environment. Points are awarded for each successful hit and on completion of the game further involvement with WWF is solicited.
3 *Web-facilitated viral (web prompt)*   In this case a web page on an organisation's site will be set up to contain the link 'tell a friend'. In the arts context this may, for example, appear on a page promoting a new season or special event. Users can be given the opportunity to spread the word to family and friends they know will be interested.
4 *Incentivized viral*   Here the contact details are not freely given. Instead the organisation encourages an individual to part with the contact information by offering some form of incentive, perhaps entry into a draw. Each time a set of details is passed on a new entry can be made in the draw. Such incentives can be offered on the organisation's web page or through an e-mail communication. Please note, however, that before undertaking a campaign of this nature it will be important to consider the privacy rules that apply in your home country. Since the recipient has not given their consent to be contacted it can be illegal in some jurisdictions. Gaming rules may also be an issue.
5 *Web-link viral*   This final category refers to links that are seeded in newsletters, articles, discussion group listings or blogs. These may be communications the organisation itself has

Plate 14.6 *The Seagull Strikes Back*

Source: WWF 2008. Reproduced with kind permission.

initiated or they may be seeded in third-party communications. The key here will be to use online PR to get as much coverage for the viral agent as possible.

Fundraising portals

There are five types of portal that are of relevance to fundraising, namely:

1 *Giving portals*   such as helping.org supported by the AOL Time Warner Foundation. These organisations allow nonprofits to be added to their list of supported organisations and donors visiting the site can elect to make a donation to their chosen causes. Helping.org was reported to have raised £3 million for good causes in early 2001 and donations for all categories of cause are supported. In the UK the Charities Aid Foundation have launched 'Givenow' in partnership with AOL which performs a similar function allowing individuals to send donations to a wide range of nonprofit organisations. It is important to recognize that While these general sites exist, some have a more limited geographic focus or are limited to just one category of organisation. Some for example focus on animal rights only (e.g. animalfunds.org). It is usually free for a nonprofit to register with these portals and some, including helping.org, will provide software for the nonprofit to provide a branded click-through link on their website.

2 *Affinity shopping portals*   There are a number of virtual shopping malls online that support the nonprofit community. In such cases the mall charges commission to the stores that populate it and then shares a percentage of this commission with nonprofits. In many cases nonprofits need only register for shoppers to have them as an option of designated recipient charity.

3   *Online charity auctions*   A number of commercial organisations such as eBay or specialized organisations such as allstarcharity.com auction items donated by celebrities and donate the funds generated to good causes. In the UK organisations such as Oxfam GB (www.oxfam.org.uk) and Breast Cancer Care (www.breastcancercare.org.uk) have also run their own very successful fundraising auctions online.

To work with eBay nonprofits must first sign up with missionfish (www.missionfish.org). eBay sellers can then pick the nonprofit and a percentage of their proceeds to share on each sale. Once the item is listed bidding begins on eBay in the normal way (although nonprofits do reserve the right to cancel items listed on their behalf). If the item sells, the seller gets paid by the buyer and ships the item in exactly the same way as they would normally. Missionfish collects the donation from the seller, pays the nonprofit and provides a tax receipt.

4   *Sponsorship portals*   Sites such as www.justgiving.org have revolutionized the way in which sponsored events are now operated. In the old days, if one were looking to raise funds for an organisation, perhaps by taking part in a sponsored run or challenge event, it would be necessary to obtain a commitment on paper from every potential sponsor. With justgiving. org supporters can create an online fundraising page with the charity's name and logo, and e-mail it to everyone they know. Friends, family and colleagues can donate by credit or debit card and justgiving then automatically reclaims the Gift Aid (plus a government supplement) before forwarding the total (less a 5 per cent transaction fee and VAT) to the beneficiary charity. Charities receive almost £12 for every £10 donation. A helpful video explaining the process is available at http://www.justgiving.com/statements/about_us/fee.asp

5   *Charity search engines*   A number of search engines are set up to donate funds to nonprofits. GoodSearch for example donates 50 per cent of its revenue to charities and schools designated by its users. GoodSearch is used exactly as one would any other search engine and because it is powered by Yahoo! it generates excellent results. Rectifi is a similar UK-based example. In this case the search engine donates 100 per cent of its profits from advertising to good causes. Searchgive.com operates in a slightly different way. On average, searches generate about $0.01 per search and the organisation sends the user's chosen charity a cheque when their account reaches $25.00.

Donation collection

A further key issue for fundraisers to address online is how their donations will be handled. There are a number of ways of arranging for donations to be processed electronically. The first and most common is to use a payment service provider (PSP) facility, where the nonprofit website connects through when someone wants to make a payment. The money goes to the PSP's account, with the nonprofit typically receiving payment some days or weeks later. Nonprofits using this option typically gather the donor's information on their own site before routing the individual off for the payment to be processed. In this way they can respond in a timely way with a thank you. These services typically operate on a set-up fee, plus a percentage (or flat fee) per transaction.

The second option, for larger nonprofits, is to create a secure server within their website which allows them to collect the details of credit/debit cards. These details can then be fed into their normal card-processing arrangements.

Finally there is the option of real online card processing through a facility such as Barclays ePDQ, PayPal or WorldPay. When a donor elects to make a payment, they are directed to a secure payment environment, where they can pay by debit or credit card. The facility automates and completes the transaction. Again there may be a set-up charge, monthly fee and/or transaction charge depending on the provider.

Volresource (2008) lists a wide range of payment services available to nonprofits including:

- www.Bmycharity.com offers various online fundraising/donation services.
- www.CharityChoice.co.uk is an online directory, currently working with the Cooperative Bank to provide a free online donation facility for registered charities.
- Charity Technology Trust (www.ctt.org) offers various card-processing technology, on and off line.
- Committed Giving (www.committedgiving.net) provides a secure system to take and verify direct debit donations.
- Direct Debits Online provides an online fundraising system from www.Baigent.net which enables online credit card, debit card and direct debit donations.
- Fused Technologies (www.fused-technologies.co.uk) offers a range of facilities such as digital direct debit.
- JustGiving (www.justgiving.com) offers online giving, plus paper-free Gift Aid reclaims, either through their site or as a technology within a charity's own website.

RELATIONSHIP MARKETING ON THE WEB

Writers such as diGrazia et al. (2000) advocate that good websites should treat different constituents differently. They suggest that websites should identify, differentiate, interact and customize if they are to successfully build relationships with visitors. Each of the facets they suggest is briefly described below:

Identify

Websites should capture information in respect of users. This involves much more than simply gathering the name and address of visitors, but rather gathering information about their habits, preferences and interests. Of course, there is a trade-off here. Web users are increasingly being asked for their details when they visit specific sites. The most effective way to encourage completion appears to be in tying it to specific benefits such as a tailored environment or home page, or specific promotional offers.

Some sites have recognized user reticence to supply information and have adopted a 'build' policy in the sense that only a few details are recorded each time a user visits a site. Over time a detailed profile is built up, yet users perceive that the data collection process is minimal and inoffensive. The method is known as 'drip irrigation' dialogue.

Differentiate

To build a relationship strategy on the Web one needs to understand the relative worth of each user. In some circumstances it can thereafter be appropriate to tailor the content to reflect relative worth. At its most simple level this may involve prioritizing the effort of designers to offer the greatest utility to higher value donors.

It is also possible to differentiate content by the needs of particular users, using a technique known as 'collaborative filtering'. This involves comparing the interests of a specific user with those of a larger cohort of visitors with a similar profile. In essence the organisation can demonstrate to a user they know what he/she might be interested in and offer a list of pertinent suggestions for reading and/or support. Aside from engendering a feeling of relationship this technique can also provide substantial added value, by suggesting resources that the user might not otherwise have been aware of.

Interact

The most effective websites engage the potential donor in a dialogue and add value by being seen to interact with the user. Examples of successful interaction abound. The Dana Farber Cancer Center (www.danafarber.org) for example has almost 600 easily searchable articles on cancer that may also be downloaded. The Virtual Wall created by the Vietnam Veterans Memorial Foundation (www.thevirtualwall.org) provides a database of 58,000 soldiers who were killed in action and users can post messages, create remembrances for individual soldiers and participate in chats. The Moratorium Campaign also has a highly interactive site (www.moratoriumcampaign.org) where users who want to end the death penalty can provide their 'signature' on a virtual petition.

Customize

The final aspect of implementing a relationship strategy lies in customizing some aspect of the service based on a particular user's needs. Many of the newer sites allow users to visit a site and to tailor the site to their own specific requirements. In many ways, this fourth dimension follows from the first. Having gathered information about users it is important that the organisation then uses that knowledge to add value for consumers, by customizing the offering as a result. The World Wildlife Fund, for example, sends out regular updates on specific issues that it knows a number of visitors to the site will find of interest.

In using the Internet as a relationship-building tool, therefore, organisations should pay particular attention to these four dimensions and perhaps appraise their performance against the best performing sites on the Web. They may also find it instructive to conduct an analysis of the performance of related sites (perhaps those of similar causes) to develop a benchmark for their own performance and delineate scope for potential improvement.

RELATIONSHIP MARKETING AND FUNDRAISING EFFECTIVENESS

Recent work by Sargeant et al. (2007) suggests that a more detailed framework may offer enhanced utility for fundraisers. The authors examine the impact of eight characteristics drawn from the domain of relationship marketing on the ability of sites both to recruit new donors and to secure donations at various levels. The eight characteristics the authors identify are listed as follows:

1   *Accessibility*   The extent to which the site makes it easy to offer support. Ideally sites should make it easy to donate, with links from every page to the fundraising section of the site. This dimension measures how easy it is for an individual to navigate to the donation page.
2   *Case for support*   This factor relates to the extent to which the site clearly articulates why the organisation warrants support.
3   *Respect*   The extent to which the organisation communicates with the donor in a courteous and appropriate manner. Are they treated as a donor, with an appropriate acknowledgement or timely thank you when they make a donation?
4   *Accountability*   The extent to which the site indicates it is accountable to supporters for the way in which it uses resources such as donated funds and personal data.

5   *Interaction*   The extent to which the site offers users the ability to interact with the organisation in a variety of ways, perhaps by signing up for a newsletter, allowing the user to pose questions of an expert, posing short Cosmo-style or 'rate yourself' quizzes, providing downloadable materials/content, etc.

6   *Education*   The extent to which the site provides appropriate content and/or facilities for the donor to deepen their understanding about the cause.

7   *Customization*   The extent to which the donor may tailor the site content and/or the communications received to reflect his or her own interests or needs.

8   *Empowerment*   The extent to which the site allows donors to take action or to feel that they have had an impact on the cause.

The researchers were able to rate a series of nonprofit websites on each of these dimensions and explore the correlation between these ratings and variables such as the number of new donors recruited in the past year, the level of online donations achieved and the level of the average donation. Their results are depicted in Table 14.2 where the correlations are indicated. One asterisk indicates a significant correlation, while two indicates a highly significant correlation.

It is not unusual for studies such as this to find few relationships between site variables and the actual amounts that individuals donate. This will always be driven in the main by demographics. What is interesting from Table 14.2 is the high number of significant correlations obtained between the site characteristics and the number of new donors the site is able to attract. Only three of the eight are insignificant. Respect and customization are not significantly correlated with the number of new donors attracted, but in a sense one would not expect to see these correlated as these are typically addressed *after* a donation has been made (i.e. when a thank you is necessary and when information has been exchanged that could form the basis of customization). We believe that these factors are still important to address in site design, but they are more likely to impact on retention than recruitment.

Perhaps the most interesting 'insignificant' result is the lack of a correlation between the strength of the case for support and any of the performance measures in the table. We believe that this merely reflects the reality of online giving. Individuals rarely surf the Web thinking 'Who shall I give to today?' Instead they surf the Web looking for information on cancer because their

Table 14.2 Correlation between relational constructs and site performance

Construct	Online donations in past year (£s)	Donations via mail (£s)	Average donations (£s)	Number of new donors
Accessibility	.30*	−.20	.12	.32*
Case for support	−.07	−.17	.08	.08
Accountability	.36*	.01	.27	.45**
Respect	−.22	−.01	.25	−.02
Education	.29*	.03	.16	.61**
Interaction	.01	.24	.13	.33*
Customization	−.10	.25	.17	.15
Empowerment	.27	.12	.30*	.58**

*Significant at the 0.05 level. **Significant at the 0.01 level.
Source: Sargeant et al. (2007). Reproduced by kind permission.

life has just been touched by the disease. Similarly they may surf the Web looking for information on solvent abuse, because their life has been touched by that issue for the first time. As a consequence, when they arrive on a nonprofit website, most visitors have arrived there deliberately and already know why cancer or solvent abuse is an issue. They do not need to be convinced of it in the same way that a direct mail or DRTV donor might have to be. Instead they need only to be facilitated to make a donation at the point during their visit when they are motivated to do so.

INTERACTIVE TELEVISION

Interactive television has been offered since 1999 in the UK and for a similar period of time in selected pilots in the US. It represents the first real attempt to engage viewers equipped with modern digital technology in a two-way conversation with advertisers and/or programme makers. Interactive TV (iTV) links the digital decoder (which unscrambles satellite or cable broadcasts) to the subscriber's own telephone line to create a return path to the supplier's organisation. This return path can then be used to indicate when a subscriber wishes to make a purchase/donation, request additional information or access an interactive service, such as banking or e-mail.

Most early systems allowed the viewer to enter the interactive section of their channel package, by selecting it just as they would any of the traditional viewing channels. They were then faced by a menu very similar to that they might encounter on the Internet. By highlighting and clicking on a range of icons, the user could very quickly enter and play a range of computer games, or look to make a number of purchases from one of a number of online stores. In these early pilots, however, the interactive component was held largely separate from the 'normal' television environment and the opportunity to directly interact with specific broadcasts was very limited.

More recent versions permit more integration with broadcast content so that viewers can interact, albeit in a fairly basic way, with programming. Only a small number of nonprofits has as yet elected to make use of the medium and the full potential has yet to be realized. As the technology continues to improve and begins to offer full integration with normal television viewing, the opportunities for effective fundraising will increase exponentially. As an example, viewers of a news broadcast showing pictures of an unfolding natural disaster could be facilitated to learn more about the work of the various relief agencies by pressing a button on their remote control and being transferred to the relevant website. From there, they could be facilitated to offer an online donation. All from the comfort of their armchair!

SMS TEXT MESSAGING

At the time of writing in 2008 Britons are sending more than one billion text messages per week according to Mobile Data Association. This figure is 25 per cent higher than in 2007 and is the same number as the total sent during the whole of 1999. This impressive growth has yet to be matched by levels of interest in the medium on the part of fundraisers.

Appeals have typically taken one of two forms.

1   Donors are recruited in partnership with other media by encouraging them to text their donation. The cost of the text is set to cover the donation including whatever fee the mobile company wishes to charge. These donations via premium SMS then appear on customers' monthly bills or are debited from prepaid cell phone account balances. A number of charities have used this form of text messaging in partnership with ticket media. The back of each

(train/theatre/airline) ticket can contain a number that the user can text to make a donation and/or to keep in touch with the work of the charity. Plate 14.7 depicts a highly creative campaign from Meir Panim (a network of soup kitchens in Israel). It consisted of a series of interactive banner ads asking individuals to 'SMS for lunch'. On their website a boy was featured facing an empty plate. The site encouraged donations and once the system received an SMS the banner changed (for a while!) to show a full plate of food with the boy smiling.

In America, the most visible and widely publicized campaigns have been for victims of the Asian tsunami and more recently a fundraiser for Katrina victims and those of the California wildfires. Mobile customers of participating mobile carriers could send a text message to the short code '2HELP' (24357) containing the keyword 'Help' to make a tax-deductible donation to the American Red Cross relief efforts. Amnesty International and UNICEF have experimented with PayPal mobile as a new form of payment mechanism. Donors simply text the word 'AMNESTY' or 'WATER' to a short code to receive a link to donate $10 to their chosen organisation. However, a potential donor needs a PayPal account to make for a smooth and quick transaction and even then there is a multi-step process that may deter potential donors.

2   Donors are invited to text in to support a campaign and are then called back by the charity to sign them up to a direct debit. The economics of this two-stage process are still unclear with charities reporting mixed results, but it seems fair to say that as with other media the performance of a campaign will be a complex function of the cause, the campaign and the nature of the target audience. In the United States the Edwards' presidential campaign sent everyone on its mobile list (those individuals that had opted-in to receive text messages by signing up at events or on the Edwards website) an SMS asking participants to listen to a

Plate 14.7 *SMS for lunch*

Source: Meir Panim. Reproduced with kind permission.

SPORT RELIEF

Sport Relief, a joint venture between BBC Sport and the charity Comic Relief, was among the first organisations in the UK to employ SMS text messaging for fundraising. In a campaign timed to coincide with the soccer World Cup there were three opportunities to give, highlighted on air on BBC Sport television programmes. Viewers could enter the Total Ticket sports quiz, guess the year of TV tennis footage shown during Wimbledon and receive updates on the soccer World Cup. To take part viewers had to text in to the BBC. Each text message cost £1 of which 60p was donated to Sport Relief. Over £100,000 was raised.

special message from Elizabeth Edwards. Those that made the call (15 per cent of recipients on the mobile opt-in list) were then directed – after Elizabeth's appeal – to press 1 to be connected to an operator to make a donation. About 10 per cent of those 15 per cent did – with an average donation of $120.

Despite the massive growth in texting we allude to above, the charity sector has been reluctant to embrace its potential. To illustrate why this might be Mason (2006) cites the case of an appeal by CLIC Sargent for its 'Home from home' campaign. Poster ads invited callers to 'Text "BRICK" to 88100. 94p of every £1.50 goes to CLIC Sargent'. This is a pretty standard rate for premium-rate text donations – though each different campaign has lots of variable cost elements; usually around 35 to 40 per cent of a donation is siphoned off by the other parties to the transaction.

And there is no shortage of parties waiting to take their cut. The taxman gets his share – HMRC used to take VAT on the whole amount but now only charges it on the cost of servicing the donation. The mobile marketing agencies that run the campaigns – think Incentivated, Flytxt, justgiving, Charity Technology Trust, txt-appeal – will generally reap up to 6 per cent. Then there are the aggregators, the middlemen who rent the short code (88100 in CLIC Sargent's case) from the mobile networks and then rent it on to the charity – their fee can also be up to 6 per cent. And if the donor uses a pay-as-you-go mobile, even the newsagent that sold the card figures in the calculation.

But while all these pennies add up, even their combined total doesn't begin to snap at the heels of the proportion that the mobile networks take. It's very difficult to ascertain exactly how much they reap, as it's not a figure they openly broadcast, but the Institute of Fundraising states they keep 15 to 19 per cent of any donation – even though the cost of processing the message is just 3p. They also make another 10p from the standard message charge donors pay for sending the text.

(Mason 2006)

At the time of writing Joe Saxton, the outgoing Chair of the Institute of Fundraising is campaigning to achieve a reduction in these fees.

Many charities find the current charges made by phone providers - simply for collecting donations via SMS - prohibitive. HMRC has thankfully been re-examining the broader VAT issue on charity phone bills. We now invite the telecoms industry itself to address its charge structures, specifically in relation to text-donations. The fundraising potential could well be substantial, not least amongst the young. By striking the right balance, mobile phone operators, charities and donors can *all* benefit.

(nfpSynergy 2008)

Of course text messages can be used for a variety of other purposes not immediately related to fundraising. There are many campaigning uses, where individuals can be sent updates on the progress of a campaign or subscribe to alerts to be kept appraised of any emerging issues, such as a natural disaster in the Third World. Texts can also be used to inform supporters of forthcoming events and link to an ability to purchase tickets or get involved. Oxfam GB, for example, used text messaging as part of their 'maketradefair' campaign.

SUMMARY

In this chapter we have briefly reviewed a number of the new e-media that can be employed for the purposes of marketing and fundraising. In particular we have examined the role of the Internet, the opportunities created by the medium and a number of the key facets of raising funds in this arena. We have also introduced an extended e-fundraising mix and suggested numerous ways in which fundraisers can maximize their potential to raise funds successfully online.

It seems clear that the use of electronic channels for fundraising will continue to grow over the next decade. The pace of technological change makes it essential that organisations continue to appraise themselves of the opportunities available and to plan innovative ways of developing the level of interaction and customization they offer to customers as a consequence.

DISCUSSION QUESTIONS

1 You are the fundraising manager of Breakthrough Breast Cancer. Suggest how the Internet could be used by the organisation to raise funds.

2 How might a small nonprofit organisation setting up a web presence for the first time publicize the existence of its site?

3 You work for a large animal rights charity. Your CEO believes that interactive TV might offer your nonprofit a new and exciting channel for acquiring donations. She has asked you for some guidance in a report outlining what you consider to be the key advantages and disadvantages of the medium.

4 Using your understanding of the e-fundraising mix, suggest how a small hospice might seek to drive traffic to its fundraising website.

5 In your role as the fundraising manager of a large national charity you are preparing a presentation to a visiting group of students about recent developments in e-media. Outline the points that you would cover in this presentation.

REFERENCES

DiGrazia, C., Dahlen, J. and Reale, T. (2000) *How Charities Can Profit on the Web*, Peppers and Rogers Group, Stamford, CT.

Hart, T., Greenfield, J.M. and Johnston, M. (2005) *Nonprofit Internet Strategies*, Wiley, San Francisco, CA.

Hart, T., Greenfield, J.M. and Haji, S.D. (2008) *People to People Fundraising: Social Networking and Web 2.0 for Charities*, John Wiley, San Francisco, CA.

Johnston, M. (1999) *The Fund Raisers Guide to the Internet*, NSFRE/Wiley, New York.

Kirby, J. (2003) 'Online Viral Marketing: Next Big Thing or Yesterday's Fling?' http://www.nmk.co.uk/article/2003/4/2/online-viral-marketing (accessed 1 January 2009).

Mason, T. (2006) 'The GR8 TXT Robbery', http://www.professionalfundraising.co.uk/home/content.php?id=1310&pg=4&cat=30 (accessed 27 October 2008).

nfpSynergy (2008) 'Institute of Fundraising Asks Joe Saxton to Forge a Campaign Coalition', http://www.nfpsynergy.net/downloads/SMSCampaignCoalitionRevized per cent20_2_.pdf?PHPSESSID =e8c093e51863845e76d14caee173d0e5 (accessed 27 October 2008).

Sargeant, A., West, D.C. and Jay, E. (2007) 'The Relational Determinants of Nonprofit Web Site Fundraising Effectiveness: An Exploratory Study', *Nonprofit Management and Leadership*, 18(2): 141–156.

Smith, G. (1996) *Asking Properly: The Art of Creative Fundraising*, White Lion Press, London.

Smith, P.R. and Chaffey, D. (2005) *E-Marketing Excellence: At the Heart of E-business*, 2nd edn, Butterworth Heinemann, Oxford.

Volresource (2008) 'Online Income Services', http://www.volresource.org.uk/services/inconline.htm (accessed 27 October 2008).

Chapter 15

Benchmarking fundraising performance

OBJECTIVES

By the end of this chapter you should be able to:

- Explain the need for effective benchmarking of fundraising performance.
- Understand the drawbacks of using published accounts for the purposes of comparing the performance of two or more organizations.
- Describe a process by which the benchmarking of fundraising costs may be accomplished.
- Explain typical patterns of performance experienced in modern fundraising practice.

INTRODUCTION

The issue of cost has long been a subject of concern to charity managers, not only so that individual managers can ensure the most appropriate use is made of their organization's resources, but also to ensure that this is seen to be the case by those who support the organization. Non-charitable expenditures are unpopular with the majority of donors, and it is now not unusual for charities to be criticized by either the media or the general public for what are seen as 'wasteful' expenditures.

As a consequence Hind (1995) notes that a certain 'paranoia' has gripped the management of many charities, characterized by an anxiety to avoid such 'unnecessary' expenditures. Nonprofit managers are now keen to use every means at their disposal to present their performance in the most positive light possible and in some cases have undoubtedly reapportioned cost accordingly.

Putting aside the public interest in fundraising cost and the need for fair and accurate reporting, the need for effective benchmarking to guide organizational management should not be underestimated. Every nonprofit, no matter how large or small, should be aware of its performance and how this might compare to other, similar organizations in the sector. Only by conducting this form of analysis can nonprofits ensure that they continue to provide value for money to donors and are operating within acceptable boundaries of efficiency.

In this chapter it is our intention to review what is known about the behaviour of charity and fundraising costs, illustrating typical patterns of performance for each form of fundraising undertaken. We will also examine how benchmarking should be undertaken and explore current issues that must be tackled to ensure that the process is as accurate as possible.

NONPROFIT PERFORMANCE

A nonprofit organization is in essence one that is barred from distributing its net earnings to those who exert control over it, including, for example, shareholders, members, governors, directors and so on (Hansmann 1980). It therefore exists with the sole purpose of satisfying one or more identified societal needs. The generation of profit by such enterprises is, however, not banned per se. Some nonprofits can and do earn a healthy operating surplus; it is only the distribution of this surplus that is limited. Indeed it must be retained and reinvested in the production/supply of ever-greater amounts of the goods/services the nonprofit was originally constituted to provide. In the case of most nonprofits this process is not problematic since demand usually far exceeds supply.

As Hansmann (1980) points out, however, the nonprofit is far from being an ideal organizational form. The removal of the profit incentive can give rise to a number of potential problems. Nonprofits could, for example, be slow to respond to the demands made of them and there is perhaps a greater potential for nonprofits to be wasteful of valuable resource than their for-profit counterparts. Less scrupulous organizations might also find ways of distributing their operating surplus in the form of enhanced staff salaries, or other perks and benefits. Hence, as Henke (1972:51) notes, 'as (nonprofits) increase in size and influence, it becomes increasingly important (to find some way) to measure their performance'.

Regrettably there has been a number of well-publicized instances where this would appear to be a genuine cause for concern. Baily and Millar (1992) cite the example of the United Way and the damage that was done to the organization by revelations about the unnecessary expenditures (such as flights on Concorde) incurred by its incumbent CEO. In a further example Cutlip (1990) reports that the National Kids Day Foundation raised $4 million between 1948 and 1963 and managed to spend the entire amount on fundraising and administration costs. In response to the inevitable criticism, the organization attempted to argue that their aim was to promote the idea of aiding needy children rather than actually providing services.

Historically the accountancy profession has always been more concerned with the measurement and control of for-profit enterprise. As Henke (1972:51) notes, 'the profession has never really faced up to the problem of trying to convey to the constituent groups of (nonprofit) organizations the data which would disclose the operational stewardship of the management of these entities'. This is partly due to the fact that there is seldom any real measure of operational efficiency for these organizations. While in the for-profit sector, loss-making organizations are soon forced out of existence, in the case of nonprofits, an operating deficit could easily indicate to donors an organization worthy of additional support. Inefficient organizations can potentially survive as the donor has no way of distinguishing those that are efficiently meeting the needs of their recipient group(s) from those that expend needless sums of money on administration and management. Inevitably because of their ease of calculation simple financial ratios have been used to discern between these two groups.

Of course it is not entirely legitimate to use ratios to draw direct comparisons between one charity and another, particularly where this comparison is based on published accounts (Rooney 1999). This is simply because the manner in which these accounts are prepared does not lend itself to this purpose.

PUBLIC REPORTING OF PERFORMANCE

Registered charities in the UK must file detailed annual accounts with the Charity Commission. These accounts are prepared in accordance with the most recent accounting SORP (Statement of Recommended Practice) and the data are now made available on an annual basis through the

Plate 15.1 *Guidestar UK website*

Source: Guidestar UK 2009. Reproduced with kind permission.

Guidestar UK website (www.guidestar.org.uk). Members of the public or other interested parties can visit the site and download not only the accounts, but supplementary data that the charities themselves are encouraged to contribute (see Plate 15.1).

Despite the fact such data are now readily available, published accounts should not be used as the basis to compare the fundraising performance of various charities. There are a number of reasons why this is the case.

1   The manner in which charity accounts are presented. Unlike business organizations the accounts are compiled following the principles of 'fund accounting' (i.e. one organization may comprise a number of funds) making the application of a standard ratio analysis problematic (Palmer and Randall 2002).
2   There are also issues of variation in accounting policies and the definitions of key categories. As Pharoah (1997) notes, accounting practices can vary substantially from one organization to another and what may be classified as fundraising expenditure for one organization may be classified as charitable expenditure by another. 'Feasibility work (for example), carried out as part of the preparation for bids for large capital grants can sometimes be considered as direct charitable expenditure and not as a fundraising cost' (Pharoah 1997:168).
3   Similarly, many organizations have a mission which requires them to involve themselves not only in benefiting the members of a certain target group, but also in educating the general public about the needs of this group or the issues at stake. Thus a charity such as the Terrence Higgins Trust will not only endeavour to alleviate the suffering of those with HIV infection or AIDS, it will also seek to raise the public awareness of AIDS and to eliminate many of the common misconceptions associated with the illness. Similarly the Royal National Institute of Blind People (RNIB) works to aid individuals who have suffered sight loss or deterioration. It also campaigns, raising awareness of the wider issues facing

this section of the community. Those organizations that feel it important to develop such a role face a dilemma in accounting terms over the manner in which they report the costs of awareness generation or educational activity. Since there are often substantial benefits to be gained by combining these activities with those specifically designed to raise funds it often becomes impossible to distinguish between them. Is an ad a fundraising ad, or is it part of a wider campaigning effort? In these circumstances charities must decide quite arbitrarily whether to show the costs against fundraising or as direct charitable expenditure, a decision that will obviously have profound implications for the subsequent appearance of their fundraising ratios.

4   To deal with this issue, many charities now adopt the practice of 'awareness recharging' where a proportion of the cost of fundraising (typically 10–20 per cent) is taken out of fundraising and shown as a direct charitable expenditure. Organisations engaging in this practice argue that one of the central purposes of fundraising communications is to raise an awareness of the cause. This, they would argue, is a legitimate goal of the organization and hence it is appropriate to make this adjustment. Equally, there are also nonprofits who take quite a different perspective, arguing instead that fundraising benefits from the awareness-raising activities of the organization. They therefore charge the fundraising budget a percentage of what they spend on building the brand of the organization. Both these practices are quite legitimate and both represent an open and honest attempt to clearly report on the work of the organization. Unfortunately both can lead to potentially very different figures being reported in the annual accounts.

5   The structure of an organization's funding can also have a dramatic impact on these figures. Those organizations that are fortunate enough to receive a small number of grants on an annual basis and derive the lion's share of their funding from these, will have a significantly better cost structure than those organizations involved in soliciting funds from the general public. Not only will greater numbers of staff be required to administer fundraising from the general public, but the costs of communicating with an often diverse population of donors can be substantially higher (Sargeant and Kaehler 1998). Moreover the sheer volume of transactions can add quite significantly to IT, data processing and even banking costs (Hind 1995).

6   Using fundraising ratios to compare between organizations could also be criticized on the grounds that such figures (unless averaged over a three- to five-year period) will fail to take account of large one-off contributions such as a particularly large grant or legacy income. A charity that might otherwise exhibit rather poor patterns of performance can thus overnight be transformed into one of the most efficient in the sector.

The combination of these difficulties makes it impossible to attempt to compare the performance of two or more charities based solely on their published accounts.

FACE, ACE AND FUNDRAISING RATIOS

Despite these difficulties a number of writers have used financial reports to calculate a series of key ratios to compare the performance of nonprofits. The ratio of fundraising and administration costs to total expenditure (FACE) is frequently used as a benchmark to measure the efficiency of charities. As Hind (1995) notes, there is a general perception that a FACE ratio of more than 20 per cent is unacceptable (i.e. a charity should spend at least 80 per cent of every £1 donated on the cause). There would appear, however, to be little empirical evidence to suggest that 20 per cent is actually an appropriate benchmark to adopt. Hind argues that a low FACE ratio can be counter-productive, maintaining that the charity is neither investing sufficiently in an administrative

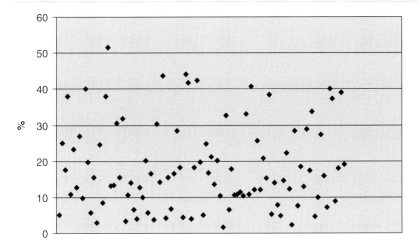

Figure 15.1 *Scatterplot of FACE ratio*

infrastructure to support its charitable work, nor making an adequate investment in fundraising to safeguard the charity's future if the FACE ratio is below 10 per cent. As a rough guide Hind thus recommends that in other than exceptional cases, FACE ratios should lie somewhere within the range 10–30 per cent. Again, it is important to remember that there is no justification for the numerical value of these limits, it is simply a matter of opinion.

Work by Sargeant et al. (2008a) involving a survey of the top 500 fundraising charities identified that charities were spending a mean of 18.6 per cent of their total expenditure on fundraising and administration. The median expenditure was found to be 15.48 per cent. A scatterplot of their data is presented in Figure 15.1 and demonstrates very vividly the wide variation in reported performance. It is important to note that the data analysed in this study is not based on published accounts but rather on data drawn from the management accounts of the reporting charities. It is therefore considerably more valid.

Further insights can often be provided by splitting non-charitable expenditures into administration and fundraising costs. The percentage of administration costs to total expenditures is known as the ACE ratio and in work by Sargeant et al. (2008a) charities were found to be spending a mean of 4.32 per cent of their total expenditure on administration. Figure 15.2 contains a scatterplot of their data which provides a sense of the variability in performance achieved. While most charities appear to be clustered around the 5 per cent mark a significant number appear to spend considerably higher percentages. Against this backdrop recent data from nfpSynergy (2008) tell us that the public believes charities spend 40 per cent of their income on administration. This is clearly far from the truth and suggests that the sector has a long way to go in educating the public about the realities of such costs.

For the purpose of benchmarking it makes most sense to express the costs of fundraising in terms of the cost of raising £1. While on the face of it, this might seem like a fairly straightforward calculation, this is far from the case. Should legacies be included? Should trading income be included? Should government contracts for services be included? Equally, what costs are actually fundraising costs? The costs of goods sold through a trading catalogue? The costs of administering foundation grants when received?

To provide a solid basis for examining this issue Sargeant et al. (2008a) were very prescriptive about the figures that were to be included in the responses to their survey. Exhibit 15.1 contains the details.

319

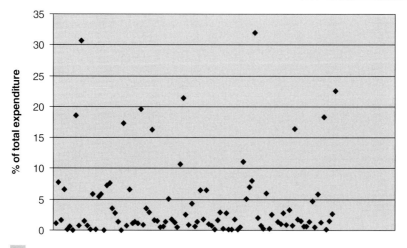

Figure 15.2 *Scatterplot of ACE ratio*

EXHIBIT 15.1   CALCULATING THE RETURNS FROM FUNDRAISING

To calculate the returns accruing from fundraising, respondents were asked to report all the income received from all of their fundraising activities (i.e. individuals, trusts and corporates). The questionnaire specified that this was to include:

(a)   All income achieved from solicited and unsolicited donations and the monetary value of any gifts in kind.

(b)   All income received in the form of tax refunds from the Inland Revenue for gifts made in a tax-efficient manner (e.g. through Gift Aid).

(c)   All income from Grant Making Trusts where the fundraising department was deemed responsible for the solicitation of the grant.

(d)   Any income in the form of grant aid or payments for contracted services undertaken by the charity on behalf of central or local government, where the responsibility for raising this income is held within the fundraising function of the charity and the costs of doing so are allocated back to the fundraising division.

(e)   All fundraised income from companies (i.e. donations, gifts in kind, sponsorship income, income from corporate trust funds and income raised through joint promotions and cause-related marketing). Where elements of income from companies were accounted for in an associated trading company for legal or tax purposes, respondents were asked to include the gross income from these.

(f)   The gross income from sales made in charity shops. If the activity was undertaken through an associated trading company, respondents were again asked to allocate the income across from this source.

Against this, respondents were asked to indicate the direct costs associated with their fundraising. This was also to include:

(a) Any expenditure incurred in fundraising activities with individuals.
(b) Any expenditure incurred from receipt of unsolicited donations and gifts in kind.
(c) Any expenditure incurred in the promotion and administration of gifts made in a tax-efficient manner.
(d) All fundraising expenditure associated with trust fundraising, where the fundraising department was deemed responsible for the solicitation of the grant.
(e) All expenditure associated with securing grant aid or payments for contracted services undertaken by the charity on behalf of central or local government where the responsibility for raising this income was held in the fundraising division of the charity and the costs for so doing were allocated back to the fundraising division.
(f) All expenditure associated with fundraising from companies (i.e. donations, gifts in kind, sponsorship income, income from corporate trust funds and income raised through joint promotions and cause-related marketing). Where elements of expenditure associated with income from companies were accounted for in an associated trading company for legal or tax purposes, respondents were asked to include the relevant gross expenditure.
(g) The gross expenditure incurred in association with sales made in charity shops. If the activity was undertaken through an associated trading company, respondents were asked to allocate the expenditure across from this source.

The aim of defining voluntary income and its associated expenditure in this manner was to reflect public perceptions of what might be regarded as fundraising and to ensure that the costs and revenues associated with these activities were included in the analysis. The aim was to provide a fair reflection of the performance of the 'typical' fundraising function.

Sargeant et al. (2008a) in an examination of the direct costs (only) of fundraising find that charities spend a median of 16p and a mean of 20p to raise £1. The distribution is highly skewed with a standard deviation of 15.4p. What this means is that although the 'usual' pattern of performance is around 15–16p there are a few organizations that distort the mean by virtue of their unusually high costs. This idea is illustrated in Figure 15.3. When results are skewed in this way the mean figure would be driven upwards by the extremes of performance in the sample. In such circumstances the median (or middle) value is a better indicator of the 'typical' performance attained.

Their study also captured data on the overhead costs associated with fundraising (e.g. rent, heating, light, telephone and in some cases a share of the salaries of senior staff, where these staff had some involvement in fundraising). It is interesting to note that 61.5 per cent of respondents to the survey indicated that they had no such costs. Since this seems unlikely the response undoubtedly reflects that fact that many organizations presently have no mechanism for analysing their costs in this way. These costs quite obviously exist, but they are allocated to a different category of organizational expenditure. As a consequence, adding in the overhead costs associated with fundraising (where reported) has only a marginal impact on the aggregate pattern of performance reported. The cost per £1 raised climbs to a median of 17p and a mean of 21p.

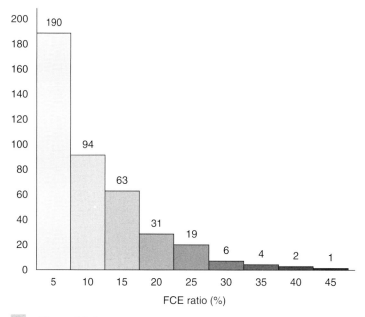

Figure 15.3 *Frequency distribution of fundraising costs to total expenditures (FCE) in 410 charities, 1992–1996*

Source: © Charities Aid Foundation. Reproduced with kind permission.

The reported cost of fundraising has been shown in previous studies to be a function of:

- *The size of the organization*   There seem to be economies of scale in fundraising activity that make it cheaper for larger organizations to raise funds than smaller ones. This is certainly true within the larger charities, although there is now some evidence to suggest that very small nonprofits may also achieve higher levels of performance, presumably because much of the time necessary to raise funds in smaller organizations is 'donated' by volunteers.
- *The nature of the cause*   Work by Sargeant and Kaehler in 1999 and Sargeant and Lee (2003) has consistently shown that some categories of cause find it more difficult to raise funds than others. It would thus be unfair to compare the performance of a UK disability charity with that of an overseas aid organization. The former would tend to find it more difficult to raise funds than the latter, reflecting nothing more than the level of public interest in these causes in the UK.
- *Age/experience*   Those nonprofits that are new to fundraising, or new to the use of certain techniques, will find that it takes times to establish a reasonable pattern of performance. Many techniques require investment over a period of many years before an adequate return on investment can be reported. Thus the move by a nonprofit into the use of a new media or method of fundraising may adversely affect its aggregate fund ratios in the short to medium term.

There are of course many other factors that can influence the cost of fundraising, but these tend to have less marked effects on the ratio reported. Many of these are dealt with below.

BENCHMARKING SPECIFIC FORMS OF FUNDRAISING

All the figures in the previous section are based on an examination of fundraising in aggregate. While this can yield some insights' the returns accruing from various forms of fundraising are actually very different. It therefore makes a lot more sense to look at the returns accruing to specific forms of fundraising activity. The returns accruing from work with major donors, trust/foundations and companies are, for example, considerably higher than those accruing from direct marketing activity.

Trust/corporate fundraising

Organisations fortunate enough to derive a large proportion of their income from grants will tend to report significantly lower costs of fundraising. *Fundratios*, currently the UK's only detailed analysis of fundraising performance, reports that it currently costs around 10p to raise £1 from trusts (Centre for Inter-Firm Comparisons 2008). Costs in this domain consist largely of the staff time necessary to research and prepare proposals; although it can cost a substantial sum to hire a high-quality grant-writer, these costs pale into insignificance alongside the monies they are able to bring in.

Corporate fundraising is a complicated activity to benchmark. Costs are a function again of the staff time necessary to stimulate this category of giving, but soliciting successful partnerships can often take a period of years to accomplish. Calculating the return here is further complicated by the great diversity in categories of gift that may be offered (e.g. gifts in kind, staff secondments and of course cash donations). It is difficult to place a monetary value on many of these forms of giving and hence the performance reported by *Fundratios* and authors such as Sargeant and Kaehler (1998) (typically indicating that it costs 20p to raise £1 in this domain) must be interpreted with great care.

Major donors

The very nature of work with major givers makes the development of benchmarks for this type of fundraising problematic. It can take many years of cultivation before a sizeable donation may be offered and for a charity new to this form of fundraising it may be two to five years before the activity becomes profitable. From work by Sargeant et al. (2008a) it appears that at present it costs charities engaging in this activity around 17p to raise £1. This mean figure probably understates the value of major gift fundraising to UK charities however, since the solicitation of major gifts is a relatively new phenomenon in this country. While a few charities have been engaged in this form of fundraising very successfully for a great many years, most have not. We therefore suspect that the typical returns accruing from this form of fundraising will climb steeply over the next decade as charities begin to gain experience in this domain. Table 15.1 provides additional data on the current performance of major gift fundraising in the UK. Drawn from Sargeant et al. (2008a) it provides some insight into the salaries of major gift officers and a sense of the income that each member of staff is able to generate. The highest and lowest patterns of performance in their sample of organizations are depicted alongside the median.

Direct marketing: donor recruitment

A common mistake in attempting to benchmark direct marketing activity is to assume that all such activity is alike and to bundle all the costs and revenues associated with these activities together to calculate a single overall ratio. This approach is fundamentally flawed because it fails to draw a distinction between donor recruitment activity, where most charities lose money, and donor development activity, where significant returns accrue over time.

Table 15.1 *Programme productivity: major gift fundraising*

	High	Median	Low
Income per head of staff	£1,800,000	£315,500	£11,666
Income per full time equivalent staff member, including volunteers	£1,117,695	£386,829	£8,750
Number of major donor staff	3.00	1.00	0.33
Staff cost per head of staff	£46,768	£39,876	£14,538

There are two other complexities unique to the UK where, as we discussed in Chapter 6, donors may be either committed (regular) or uncommitted (cash) givers. The latter offer only a series of occasional gifts in response to direct marketing solicitations, whereas the former are recruited to a regular monthly or yearly gift, which is deducted directly from their bank accounts. The pattern of giving and the performance of these two types of fundraising differ.

Cash giving

Work by Sargeant et al. (2008b) conducted in the United Kingdom examined the use of direct marketing in fundraising in some detail. In this study we began by examining the returns accruing from donor recruitment activity, focusing first on the media used to recruit 'cash' givers (i.e. individuals sending donations by cheque, not giving regularly through a mechanism such as direct debit). Table 15.2 contains a comparison of the performance of the five media typically employed to recruit this category of donor. It is important to note that we report here only the direct costs associated with conducting each activity.

Viewed in aggregate the results suggest a very similar pattern of performance across the various media. It is clear that the majority of recruitment media are loss-making. The notable exception to this is reciprocal direct mail, where charities swap lists of their supporters with other organisations. This will sometimes happen directly, but it typically takes place through a third-party database. It is important to note that although the recruitment costs are lower in this medium, donors recruited through reciprocals tend to be lower value (since charities only swap their lower value supporters) and when donors are exchanged in this way their lifetime value to the initiating organisation falls by between 10 and 15 per cent. These results should therefore

Table 15.2 *Performance of recruitment media – cash donations*

Media	Cost per donor (£)		Average response rate		Return per £1 of investment	
	Mean	Median	Mean	Median	Mean	Median
Cold direct mail	30.59	35.29	1.00	0.90	0.40	0.38
Reciprocal direct mail	15.29	13.78	2.98	2.67	1.24	0.98
Unaddressed mail	27.81	25.34	n/a	n/a	0.65	0.55
Direct response press advertising	99.21	56.12	n/a	n/a	0.40	0.32
Inserts	19.56	21.56	n/a	n/a	1.33	0.87

not be interpreted as suggesting that the performance of reciprocal mailings is necessarily superior to that of the other recruitment media.

The performance of direct response press advertising is also noteworthy and in particular the greatly skewed pattern of performance achieved (as indicated by the large difference between the mean and median costs). In the context of fundraising, press advertising generally performs very badly, with most charities achieving an unacceptable pattern of performance. Emergency appeals appear to be the exception because of the heightened public awareness and supportive copy elsewhere in the publication. It can also be very successful in the context of high-value fundraising products like child sponsorship schemes. Response rates are still poor, but the high value of the product makes the investment worthwhile.

Regular giving

Turning next to the issue of recruitment into regular giving, Table 15.3 contains the detail of this analysis. Since it would make little sense to examine the immediate return accruing from the recruitment of a regular giver (i.e. perhaps giving only £2 per month), for the purposes of comparison we have instead examined the returns accruing from the investment in this activity over the first year of the donor relationship. A total of five commonly employed media were examined. As previously, we report only the direct costs of conducting each form of fundraising.

The results indicate a broadly comparable set of costs across each media, with substantial variation in performance between individual charities in the case of inserts. A number of charities in the sample reported very poor results with this activity in the period in question. Overall it is clear that recruitment into committed giving is a very costly activity that will only generate a return on its investment in the medium term, typically the second year of a donor relationship. Since regular givers exhibit a higher degree of loyalty than cash donors, often 'upgrade' their giving level during their relationship with a charity, and require fewer communications this situation is unproblematic (see below).

The performance of direct dialogue or face-to-face fundraising is noteworthy. This technique involves teams of (usually) agency recruiters soliciting donors on the High Street or at a public event into a regular donation by direct debit. While this medium attracts a high degree of media interest, the returns it is able to generate are actually very respectable when compared with the range of alternatives. When one considers that many charities have also negotiated clawback guarantees (where the costs of recruitment will be refunded if a donor lapses within a specified period) it would appear to perform well.

Table 15.3 *Performance of recruitment media – regular giving*

Media	Cost per donor (£)		Average response rate		Return per £1 of investment	
	Mean	Median	Mean	Median	Mean	Median
Cold direct mail	131.73	146.00	0.16	0.15	0.19	0.17
Unaddressed mail	119.87	100.45	n/a	n/a	0.87	0.76
Inserts	116.32	195.35	n/a	n/a	0.70	0.28
Direct response television	156.12	146.03	n/a	n/a	0.66	0.27
Direct dialogue	117.53	96.98	n/a	n/a	0.75	0.71

325

Aggregate recruitment performance

The next step in the analysis was to calculate the aggregate performance of donor recruitment activity. To do this we combined the recruitment costs and revenues reported by our participating charities and added in any previously unallocated indirect costs in each case. We were then able to calculate the typical return accruing to an organisation's donor recruitment function. We find that the mean return accruing from £1 of investment in recruitment activity is 63p with a standard deviation of 52p. The median was found to be 48p. These results indicate a somewhat skewed pattern of performance with a small number of organisations reporting break-even or better. The norm, however, as indicated by the median in this case, was for the activity to be conducted at a loss. It was not uncommon for charities to fail to recoup at least 50 per cent of their investment in the short term.

Direct marketing: donor development

We then gathered data in respect of donor development (i.e. communicating with donors following their initial recruitment). As previously, we draw a distinction between the development of cash donors and the development of regular donors. We also focus initially on the direct costs in each case.

Cash donors

Table 15.4 contains a summary of the data gathered. Donors were typically receiving six communications from the charity each year yielding a return of around £5 for every £1 of investment. As expected, response rates are much higher in the domain of donor development with rates of circa 9 per cent common across the sector. Data were also gathered in respect of the average lifetime of a cash giver. In this case the mean lifetime was found to be 4.92 years with a median of 5.5.

Regular donors

In Table 15.5 a similar analysis is presented for regular givers. As expected, regular donors receive fewer communications than their cash counterparts and the ongoing return from these

Table 15.4 *Donor development mailings – cash donations*

Measure	Mean	Standard deviation	Median
Number of mailings received	5.55	1.94	6.00
Return on investment (£)	5.67	5.13	5.00
Response rate (%)	9.2	4.3	8.6

Table 15.5 *Donor development mailings – regular givers*

Measure	Mean	Std dev	Median
Number of mailings received	4.67	2.23	4.00
Return on investment (£)	11.37	15.87	2.63

individuals is high. It is important to stress that in calculating the ROI in this case, we have examined only the costs of ongoing communications. The reader will recall that the costs of recruitment are relatively high for this form of giver and this would need to be taken into consideration when calculating lifetime returns on investment. We are unable to provide such figures here. The mean lifetime of a regular giver was found to be 6.34 years, with the median 5.9 supporting the findings of previous studies that regular givers exhibit higher degrees of loyalty towards the organisations they support (Sargeant and McKenzie 1998).

The benchmarking of telemarketing in fundraising activity is notoriously difficult because nonprofits tend to use the medium in a variety of different ways and some organisations use their own teams, while others employ agencies for this purpose. In our survey we therefore confined ourselves to the calculation of two key metrics. In the first we examined the use of telemarketing to encourage upgrades from cash to regular donations. We found that a mean of 38.8 per cent of individuals called increased the value of their gift. The median was 30 per cent.

We were also able to examine the use of the activity to solicit additional donations. In this case for every £1 of investment, a mean return of £1.39 was achieved (standard deviation £0.39). The median was found to be £1.32.

Aggregate development performance

In the preceding analysis of development activity we have examined only the direct costs associated with the activity. Factoring in any previously unallocated indirect costs, we find that for every £1 of investment in this activity, organizations are achieving a mean return of £3.73 with a standard deviation of £1.91. The median return was found to be £3.03.

Direct marketing: aggregate performance

As a final step we examined the total costs and revenues accruing from all forms of direct marketing undertaken by our respondents. In this case we find that for every £1 of investment in direct marketing, organizations are achieving a mean return of £2.21 (standard deviation £1.35). The median return was found to be £1.65.

ENHANCING THE PUBLIC TRUST

As we highlighted in the introduction to the text, nonprofits will be drawn to benchmarking as an issue for one of two reasons. First, they will be concerned about how their performance is perceived by donors or other stakeholders and, second, they will wish to assess the quality of their performance with respect to others in the sector, usually for the purposes of managing the fundraising function.

The first of these two motives for involvement in benchmarking activity can drive the nonprofit to present their performance in the best possible light, taking full advantage of the latitude that reporting conventions will allow. In essence fundraisers need to ensure that they understand the 'rules of the game' at least as well as their counterparts in other organizations and can manipulate these to good effect. After all, if fundraisers in one organization adopt the practice of awareness recharging there would seem to be no good reason why others with a similar justification should not do likewise.

Of course, this kind of practice does the donor no favours. He/she will have a legitimate and genuine interest in what performance is actually being attained and increasingly how much it costs a particular organization to raise a dollar/pound. While there may be an understandable temptation to downplay costs, fundraising continues to represent an excellent investment achieving returns well above that which would be offered by any stock market. All too often the profession forgets this and becomes almost apologetic to donors about the need to spend money in this way. It is the difference between saying to a £100 donor 'we spent £90 of your gift on programmes and managed to keep fundraising expenditure down to £10' and saying instead 'we spent £90 of your gift on programmes and guess what – with the other £10 we went out and got another £100'. Fundraisers, their trade associations, government and sector umbrella bodies have a key role to play in facilitating this change in emphasis and in ensuring transparent and honest reporting of all the *actual* costs of fundraising.

It is interesting to note that the public grossly overestimate the sector's costs. The UK public currently believes that it costs twice as much to raise a pound as is actually the case. This misconception has undoubtedly prompted many of the calls for greater regulation and controls over the activities of fundraisers. The sector is now awash with regulation when in reality all that was probably needed was greater effort in relation to education. Two key initiatives have recently been launched by the sector in an attempt to deal with these misconceptions and to bolster wider public trust and confidence in the sector.

The ImpACT Coalition

The ImpACT Coalition (Improving Accountability, Clarity, and Transparency) is an initiative of a group of over 130 UK charities and trade bodies, including Shelter, Cancer Research UK, Oxfam, UNICEF, NSPCC, RNID, WWF-UK, the British Red Cross, the Institute of Fundraising, the National Council for Voluntary Organisations, the Association of Chief Executives of Voluntary Organisations and the Charity Finance Directors Group. Members of the coalition agree to regularly promote six key themes in their communication.

Theme 1 Charities are effective and do a great job.
Theme 2 To raise (more) money, charities have to spend money.
Theme 3 Charities use donations carefully and wisely.
Theme 4 Charities are highly regulated and adhere to a range of strict standards.
Theme 5 Charities work together.
Theme 6 Charities need the public's donations because they really do make a difference.

The coalition is committed to promoting openness and transparency on the part of its membership and across the wider voluntary sector.

CharityFacts

CharityFacts (www.charityfacts.org) (see Plate 15.2) is a web-based initiative designed to improve public trust and confidence in the profession of fundraising. Its aim is to educate members of the public about the realities of fundraising costs and to explain how the process of fundraising works in different media.

Unique on the Web, it provides donors with advice and information on issues such as the costs of fundraising in each media, the percentage of their income charities spend on administration costs and what donors should expect of the charities they give to. CharityFacts was founded by the authors of this text and the RSPCA, NSPCC, Cancer Research UK and the British Red Cross.

The information on the site is drawn from a periodic survey of UK charities conducted by Professor Adrian Sargeant and Professor Stephen Lee (Director of the Centre for Voluntary Sector Management at Henley Business School).

Plate 15.2 *CharityFacts website*

Source: CharityFacts 2009. Reproduced with kind permission.

All UK charities are encouraged to link to the site as part of a commitment to openness and transparency. Indeed, the new National Occupational Standards for Fundraising explicitly require fundraisers looking to demonstrate competency in this domain to link their organisation's website to CharityFacts (UK Workforce Hub 2008).

OBTAINING BENCHMARKING DATA

For fundraisers seeking benchmarking data for the purposes of comparison there are a number of institutions and studies that can assist in this process. In the UK, charities can approach the Centre for Inter-Firm Comparisons (who produce the *Fundratios* study) or the research team at the National Council for Voluntary Organisations. Data can also be downloaded from the www. charityfacts.org website. There are also a number of academics conducting work in this field, including staff at the Centre for Voluntary Sector Management at Henley Business School and the Indiana University Center on Philanthropy.

Uniquely, however, the sector has a strong history of collaboration between organizations and it may be possible for fundraisers to exploit their contacts with peers to determine how other organizations are performing in respect of certain categories of fundraising. The Institute of Fundraising has established a number of special interest groups or SIGs to allow fundraisers interested in particular aspects of fundraising to network and share information. While the data gleaned from colleagues will undoubtedly be of immense value it should be remembered that different organizations will have different approaches to accounting for fundraising and thus fundraisers need to ensure that they are genuinely comparing like with like.

Whatever approach is eventually adopted we would recommend the process depicted in Figure 15.4. It begins with the fundraiser deciding what he/she intends to benchmark and why. We refer to this in Figure 15.4 as the rationale for the benchmarking exercise, since it will drive what follows. The use to which the benchmarking data will be put will drive the choice of

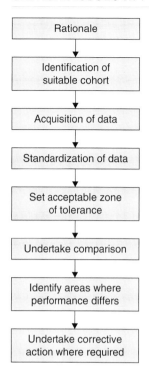

Figure 15.4 *Benchmarking process*

organization's that the fundraiser will want to compare their organization's performance against. It may be that they are interested in organizations of a similar size, working with a similar category of cause or simply undertaking a similar pattern of fundraising activity. There is no one right approach here; the choice will be driven by the rationale for the exercise.

Having selected the cohort of organizations that will be included in the exercise it will then be necessary to gather the comparative data. These may be obtained from published sources (although be wary of the caveats we expressed above) or it may be obtained directly from the organizations themselves and either taken from their annual published accounts or internal management accounting data. Peer networks can be utilized for this purpose.

The next step is to examine how the data collected were assembled and to ensure as far as possible that the data across the whole cohort are standardized and hence reported in the same way. This will be particularly difficult in the case of published sources, but a telephone call to the nonprofit can often clarify their policies on practices such as an awareness recharging and so on. The researcher should also be sensitive to atypical dimensions to the results for particular organizations, such as the receipt of an unusually large legacy that can greatly distort reported performance. These would normally be omitted from the analysis.

When the data have been standardized the nonprofit can then proceed to undertake the comparison and to examine its own performance against the cohort of other nonprofits. In doing so it should be aware of the presence of any outliers in the sample and beware of skewed distributions as highlighted earlier. Comparison against the mean may produce misleading results if the distribution is skewed and the median may well be a better measure of central tendency.

If the number of organizations contained in the cohort is high then there are a number of statistical tests that could potentially be employed to determine whether the performance of the organization relative to others is good, typical or poor. If the number of organizations is small (and in most cases with this kind of work it will be) then considerable care in interpretation is necessary.

All too often nonprofits can conclude that their performance is considerably poorer than other players in the sector, when, in reality, although performance does differ, the difference is negligible and certainly unworthy of serious management attention. For this reason some nonprofits establish a 'zone of tolerance' where for a particular activity they agree that they will ignore variations of, say, plus or minus 10 per cent of the mean. Only when reported performance falls outside of that boundary do they look to identify why this might be the case.

Clearly, fundraisers can look at those aspects of their operations where they seem to be performing less well than the competition and seek to take corrective action. Equally, even where their performance is typical (or good), the analysis might highlight other nonprofits that seem to perform very well in certain respects. A further investigation of why this might be so can be of considerable value, since there may be aspects of the professional practice of other organizations that could be copied or adapted for use. If, for example, a charity is found to be performing exceptionally well in the development of major donors, it may be that lessons can be learned from how they identify prospects, structure their approach, involve donors in the organization and ultimately make the ask. To obtain some of this information it may be possible to examine the trade press for reports on the actions undertaken, but more usually it will again be necessary to leverage the peer network that many professional fundraisers share, to truly understand the reasons for particular performance.

FUNDRAISING PERFORMANCE AND BUDGETING

Before closing this chapter it is important to highlight one other use to which benchmarking data may be put and that is to informing fundraising budgets. Organisations with many years of experience with different forms of fundraising will know what returns to expect from each media or activity. When examining how they are going to achieve the coming year's fundraising total they can therefore work back from that to determine what they need to spend in each media to achieve this goal. Of course, they can also work this in the opposite way by calculating what is attainable from a given level of fundraising spend. Historic data will always provide a fair indication of the likely future performance of each form of fundraising undertaken and many spreadsheets are set up on the basis of the broad rules of thumb such analyses provide.

For those charities new to the use of a media or category of fundraising, the data we have presented in this chapter can be used in concert with peer discussions and internal information to provide an estimate of the performance that is likely to be achieved. Clearly, such forecasting will have a wide margin of error, but in the absence of hard data on past performance, it can at least provide fundraising managers with a broad sense of what to expect and guide their budgeting accordingly.

SUMMARY

In this chapter we have examined the critical issue of benchmarking and highlighted a number of ways in which nonprofits can look to compare their performance with others in the sector. We have reviewed the drawbacks of using published accounts as the basis for comparison. We have also examined differences in reporting conventions and policies that can serve to distort benchmarking results.

There are a number of factors that can drive reported fundraising performance, including the size of the charity, the nature of its cause, its past experience with particular techniques, the categories of funding sought and so on. Thus to be in a position to accurately compare the performance of particular nonprofits it is essential that the fundraiser ensures that he/she is comparing like with like.

We have also reviewed the extant studies of fundraising costs and reported typical levels of performance, particularly within the context of the UK. While the chapter contains useful benchmarking data it must be appreciated that the returns we illustrate should be used only as a guide to the performance that may be expected by each media. In many cases the experience of the charities participating in the study varied widely, making the establishment of industry benchmarks problematic.

We concluded by suggesting a process that nonprofits could adopt to undertake their own benchmarking exercise and would recommend that the performance of the fundraising function is regularly compared against that of other similar organizations. This will ensure that the nonprofit maintains a consistent pattern of performance and does not miss any opportunities to improve the quality of its professional practice.

DISCUSSION QUESTIONS

1   What factors can influence the FACE ratio?
2   What is meant by the term 'skewness'? Why is it important to understand this term in relation to benchmarking activity?
3   A member of your Board has written to you complaining that it seems to cost your organization 5p more in the pound to raise funds than other nonprofits in the locality. How might you respond?
4   In your role as the head of development at a UK university, prepare a presentation to the Board explaining how the university might seek to benchmark its fundraising performance against other nonprofits.
5   A donor has written to you complaining that you spend too much on mailing him newsletters and other campaign materials. He feels that you should spend the money on raising money from trusts/foundations and corporates. How might you respond?
6   You have been contacted by a journalist from a national newspaper who claims to have 'discovered' that you are losing money from your direct mail programme. What might be the likely causes of this and how would you handle the interview?

REFERENCES

Baily, A.L. and Millar, B. (1992), 'United Way: The Fallout After the Fall', *Chronicle of Philanthropy*, March, p. 1

Centre for Inter-Firm Comparisons (2008) *Fundratios 2008: Charity Fundraising Comparison*, Centre for Inter-Firm Comparisons, Winchester, Hampshire.

Cutlip, S.M. (1990) *Fundraising in the United States: Its Role in America's Philanthropy*, Transaction Publishers, New Brunswick, NJ.

Hansmann, H.B. (1980) 'The Role of the Nonprofit Enterprise', *Yale Law Journal*, 89: 835–898.

Henke, E.O. (1972) 'Performance Evaluation for Not-For-Profit Organizations', *Journal of Accountancy*, 133: 51–55.

Hind, A. (1995) *The Governance and Management of Charities*, Voluntary Sector Press, London.

nfpSynergy (2008) 'Public Believe 40% of Charity Income Goes on Admin Costs', http://www.nfpsynergy.net/mdia_coverage/nfpsynergy_in_the_news/public_believes_40_of_charity_income_goes_on_admin_costs.aspx (accessed 30 October 2008).

Palmer, P. and Randall, A. (2002) *Financial Management in the Voluntary Sector*, Routledge, London.

Pharoah, C. (1997) *Managing Finance in the Voluntary Sector – A Delicate Balance,* Charities Aid Foundation, Tonbridge.

Rooney, P. (1999) 'A Better Methodology for Analyzing the Costs and Benefits of Fund Raising at Universities', *Nonprofit Management and Leadership,* 10(1): 39–56.

Sargeant, A. and Kaehler, J. (1998) *Benchmarking Charity Costs,* Charities Aid Foundation, London.

Sargeant, A. and Mckenzie, J. (1998) *A Lifetime of Giving: An Analysis of Donor Lifetime Value,* Charities Aid Foundation, West Malling.

Sargeant, A. and Kaehler, J. (1999) 'Returns on Fundraising Expenditures in the Voluntary Sector', *Nonprofit Management and Leadership,* 10(1): 5–19.

Sargeant, A. and Lee, S. (2003) 'Benchmarking Fundraising Practice', Institute of Fundraising Annual Conference, Birmingham, July.

Sargeant, A., Jay, E. and Lee, S. (2008a) *Fundraising Benchmarking Study* 2008, Henley Management College, Henley-on-Thames, Oxon.

Sargeant, A., Jay, E. and Lee, S. (2008b) 'The True Cost of Fundraising: Should Donor's Care?' *Journal of Direct, Data and Digital Marketing Practice,* 9(4): 340–353.

UK Workforce Hub (2008) *National Occupational Standards for Fundraising,* UK Workforce Hub, London.

Chapter 16

Managing fundraising teams

OBJECTIVES

By the end of this chapter you should be able to:

■ Understand the principles underpinning best practice in relation to staff and volunteer recruitment.

■ Describe the main reasons for volunteer/staff turnover and develop appropriate retention strategies to deal with each.

■ Describe key theories of workplace motivation and explore the implications for your personal approach to management.

■ Conduct a performance appraisal and feedback interview.

■ Understand the circumstances under which an employment contract may be fairly and lawfully terminated.

INTRODUCTION

In this chapter we consider a number of the key issues associated with the management of successful fundraising teams. While much of the content here falls in the domains of either human resource management or organizational behaviour, our goal in this chapter is to provide an overview of the most significant of these issues and to set them firmly in the context of fundraising. The principles underpinning good management practice are shared across all sectors, whether organizations are 'for-profit' or 'not-for-profit' but there are a number of nuances to take account of when working in the voluntary sector context. Best practice in relation to the management of volunteers, for example, does have a lot in common with the management of employees, but there are also significant differences that a voluntary sector manager needs to be aware of. The motivation of volunteers can be very different from that of employees and organizations may have to use a variety of different channels to communicate the need to individuals who might be interested in supporting them in this way.

The chapter will consider how to recruit, retain and manage both categories of fundraising teams.

RECRUITMENT

The first stage in the recruitment process lies in determining whether a vacancy actually exists. An individual may have left or be planning to leave the organization, or a case may have been made by a team leader for additional resources to be assigned to his/her area of operations. In both cases a degree of investigation is required to be sure that recruiting a new member of staff, or volunteer, is warranted. A plea for additional assistance may sometimes be only a plea for additional recognition, so care needs to be taken to ensure that the need is real. Equally, even where there is the case, as Torrington et al. (2008) note, there are many alternatives to recruiting.

- Re-organising the work to distribute tasks to other team members.
- Using overtime to accomplish the tasks.
- Simplifying or mechanizing the work.
- Staggering the hours to make it possible for other team members to take on the role.
- Subcontracting the work to a third party or agency. Nonprofits employing direct marketing media, for example, have routinely had to identify how much of the work they wish to conduct in house or leave to their communications agency or third-party contractors such as fulfilment houses.

If the decision is taken to recruit, the next step in the process involves defining what the role will consist of. This process is known as *job analysis* or *work analysis* (Sanchez and Levine 1999) and may involve interviews with team members, the completion of questionnaires gathering data on the role and even a degree of observation, so that the nature of the role can be clearly defined. Organisations also need to consider which aspects of the role require particular expertise, since it is these dimensions that will specify the skills/knowledge required by the ideal candidate for the position. It will be similarly important for the organization to be aware of what aspects of the role will appeal to prospective candidates and what the 'ideal' candidate will probably need to know about the position to want to apply. This knowledge can then guide both the recruitment message and the content of any information/application pack provided.

Similarly, the starting point for many organizations in the recruitment of volunteers lies in determining the tasks that these individuals might perform. As a consequence they can begin by asking 'What can volunteers do around here?' This approach is misguided and Jackson (2001) highlights three major weaknesses of adopting this perspective:

- An organization can screen out potential options based on staff's own beliefs about volunteer competence. Sadly, research has consistently shown that staff often undervalue volunteer input and perceive significantly lower levels of competence than is the case (Fisher and Cole 1993).
- An organization can run the risk of inventing work for volunteers, so that there is something to give them to do, rather than because it genuinely requires such input.
- Volunteers can be used as a vehicle for offloading the most burdensome or mundane tasks the organization must carry out, resulting in poor motivation and a high post-recruitment attrition (or turnover) rate.

Instead the author recommends that the following process be adopted:

- Staff and volunteers should be asked to list the things they do in their job, or in a specific area of their job. It is important that this process be as precise as possible (i.e. answering the phone, filing, etc., rather than simply saying 'admin.').

- Using this list as a backdrop, staff and volunteers should then be asked to indicate which of their tasks they like doing, which they dislike doing, and which they should be doing. They should also be asked why they hold these views.
- Staff and existing volunteers should then be asked to create a 'wish list' of things that they would ideally like to be able to achieve, and that they wish the nonprofit could achieve if it/they had the time, skills, money and so on.

Jackson (2001) argues that these data provide fertile ground in which to evaluate the need for volunteers and to ensure, where such new roles are created, that a genuinely meaningful post, with a number of potentially enjoyable tasks, can be developed. The involvement of existing volunteers in this process is key because it furnishes management with a detailed insight into what presently motivates them and what might motivate them in the future. Using these data to define a potentially satisfying role is critical.

Job descriptions and person specifications

Having identified the nature of the role to be created, a nonprofit will then be in a position to develop a job description. At a minimum such job descriptions typically comprise the following elements:

- *Title*   If the role is a volunteer position, organizations should avoid the term 'volunteer' and use the nature of the role as the basis for an appropriate job title.
- *Overall purpose*   What the purpose of the role is, how it relates to other roles in the organization, and the contribution that it will make to the achievement of the mission.
- *Activities and key outputs*   This section of the job description maps out the tasks that the individual will fulfil and the measures of success that will be used to gauge their performance. Some organizations map out a range of suggested activities to achieve the outputs rather than being prescriptive. This allows for some flexibility and respects the fact that individuals can often bring a substantial amount of personal and subject expertise to their role.
- *Line management / team structure*   The individual or individuals to whom the individual will report and the team within which they will work. In some cases this might be a supervisor in the functional part of the organization in which they are working, or in the case of a volunteer it may be a specialized volunteer service coordinator (VSC). While the use of a VSC can assist in certain circumstances because such individuals have a good understanding of the nature of volunteering, it can often be better for volunteers to be supervised directly by the line manager in whose department they are working. The reason for this is simply that the volunteer can then feel an integral part of the team rather than an outsider, donating their time.
- *Benefits*   In the case of paid staff, the details of their salary, bonuses and benefit package will be described here. For volunteers the job description should outline the benefits that will accrue as a result of the individual volunteering their time. In the USA, these benefits can have considerable value, with volunteers being remunerated by vouchers (for use in local stores) or some form of allowance. In the UK, where the legal definition of a volunteer is a little different, direct remuneration is avoided as a contract of employment can thereby be created and conditions such as the national minimum wage would then apply. Formal benefits in the UK are rare and where they are available they are typically tied to the cause. Volunteers to a heritage charity, for example, may qualify for free or reduced entry to sites for themselves and members of their family.

- *Timeframe and location*   The job description will contain the details of where the individual will work, the hours it is expected that they will contribute and for how long (in the case of a fixed-term contract) they will continue to work in this capacity. Some volunteer posts can involve an open-ended commitment, but many organizations are realizing that modern lifestyles no longer permit this level of engagement and that an open-ended need might actually dissuade potential volunteers. There may thus be circumstances where a specific timeframe is included in the job description so that both parties know from the outset how long the arrangement will last.
- *Arrangements for reimbursement of out-of-pocket expenses*   A good volunteer job description will also contain a summary of the categories of expenses that will be reimbursed (e.g. travel) and the typical length of time it will take the organization to reimburse the individual. This is considered good practice because a clear statement from the outset can prevent any future misunderstandings (Fisher and Cole 1993).
- *Equal opportunities statement*   Finally, every job description should contain an equal opportunities statement, which spells out the organization's stance on recruiting individuals with disabilities or from minority groups. It is important to note that this should be more than a simple statement of policy from the trustees of the organization; it should also be backed up with training to staff, to ensure that the reality of recruitment is firmly grounded in this statement.

These are the basic components of a job description. From a marketing perspective, it is important to recognize that this document will play a critical role in persuading appropriate individuals to apply (or not!). The best job descriptions therefore move beyond these basics and are written in such a way as to reflect the marketing role many of these undoubtedly play. At its simplest level, this means that job descriptions should move beyond a simple list of uninspiring tasks. Jackson (2001) argues that job descriptions should explain how the tasks the individual must perform fit into the larger picture of what the organization does and in particular how the responsibilities of the post will assist in the achievement of the mission. He also advocates focusing on results rather than tasks, so that where appropriate the individual can have some control over how his/her role is performed.

Of course, the job description is only half of the recruitment equation. It is now common practice to develop a person specification which translates the role that will be performed into a series of skills and abilities that will be necessary to satisfactorily complete that role. Person specifications thus address the likely profile of the volunteer, their skills and abilities, their availability, and any motivational needs they might have. Person specifications normally distinguish desirable characteristics from essential characteristics. As we shall see later, this distinction can be enormously helpful in performing an initial screen of completed applications.

In the UK when designing a person specification it is essential that the organization does not seek to discriminate between applicants on the basis of key characteristics such as age, gender, race, religion, marital status, sexual orientation or disability. This is true in the case of both volunteers and paid employees. The law allows for only a very few exceptions when it is essential to the role that an individual possess certain personal characteristics (e.g. advertising for a female lavatory attendant for the ladies washroom). The authors can think of no circumstances where this exemption might be relevant to a fundraising role, so great care must be taken not to discriminate on these grounds either *directly* or *indirectly*.

Direct discrimination is straightforward. It occurs when an employer treats one or more of the groups we mention above unfavourably. Examples include advertising for a man to fill a vacancy or specifying an age range for applicants. Where an employer has been found to have directly discriminated, there is no defence. Once a tribunal makes that determination the proceedings will summarily end with a victory for the applicant.

Indirect discrimination is more subtle. It occurs where an employer creates a provision, criterion or practice that makes it more difficult for one of these groups to apply than others. Advertising for individuals who are taller than 5'11" would, for example, make it more difficult for women to apply than men. In one case an employer stipulated that applicants should live within five miles of the headquarters of an organization which happened to be based in a predominantly white area of an otherwise multicultural city. This had the effect of making it more difficult for individuals from ethnic minorities to apply and was found to be indirect racial discrimination. Where indirect discrimination has occurred an employer is permitted the defence that the requirements they have set have been set for justifiable reasons (e.g. including a test of strength for individuals who will have to lift heavy loads as part of their duties; the fact that more men could pass the test than women would not render the discrimination unlawful if the requirement were wholly genuine). The test for a tribunal is to decide whether the 'provision, criterion or practice' constitutes a proportionate means of achieving a legitimate aim. As a technical note, the position in respect of disability discrimination is different. In this case the law restricts protection to direct discrimination and victimization in the workplace (Torrington et al. 2008).

The penalties for breaching the law can be substantial, but the resulting bad publicity can be even more costly for a voluntary organization as its reputation will be tarnished as a consequence.

Recruitment channels

Having developed the job description and person specification, the organization can then proceed to communicate the vacancy to prospective applicants. There are a number of different channels that might be used for this purpose, as Table 16.1 makes clear. Voluntary sector organizations appear to make extensive use of advertisements in the local/national press and specialist sector magazines, such as *Professional Fundraising*, *Charity Times* and *Third Sector*. The majority of organizations also make use of the Internet, posting job opportunities on their website. This figure has increased markedly over the past five years.

The final point worthy of note from Table 16.1 is the incidence of word of mouth, with around a third of organisations encouraging this form of promotion. The data in the table relate only to paid employment, but it seems likely that in the context of volunteering the incidence of word of mouth would be much higher. Organisations need to utilize the network of contacts they already have when looking to fill these positions. The 1997 National Survey of Volunteering in England showed that 50 per cent of the people who volunteered did so because they were asked, and similar percentages have been reported in the USA. All staff and existing volunteers may thus have a part to play in identifying appropriate individuals who might be able to assist the organization.

If utilizing this network of contacts is impractical, or existing links have already been exhausted, Wymer and Starnes (2001a) argue that volunteer recruitment can then be achieved either directly or indirectly. Direct recruitment consists of a nonprofit reaching out directly to potential volunteers through activities such as advertising, direct marketing, publicity, events and public speaking engagements.

Indirect recruitment occurs when other institutions are used as intermediaries to assist in the process of recruitment. Many communities now have volunteer referral centres which act as a focal point for individuals who are interested in giving up their time. These referral centres promote community volunteering and keep a wealth of up-to-date information about the opportunities available (Ellis 1989).

Table 16.1 *Usage of various methods of recruitment by voluntary community and not-for-profit organizations in 2008*

Method	% Indicating
Local newspaper advertisements	86
Own corporate website	82
Recruitment agencies	71
Specialist journals and trade press	60
National newspaper advertisements	60
Jobcentre plus	50
Secondments	45
Encouraging speculative applications/word of mouth	35
Educational liaison	29
Employee referral scheme	20
Apprentices	13
Physical posters/billboards/vehicles	11
Radio or TV advertisements	7
Other	14

Source: CIPD (2008) Recruitment, Retention and Turnover: Annual Survey Report, CIPD, London. Reproduced with kind permission.

In the search for volunteers it is important that a nonprofit exploits all the opportunities that may exist for indirect recruitment through third parties. The rationale here is simply that scarce resources need not be wasted on an activity that can be better accomplished by another organiza-tion. In the UK there is a network of volunteer bureaux that provide this function and Councils for Voluntary Service (CVS). There is also Timebank, a national charity that aims to get more people volunteering across the country. Timebank works with a number of partners to achieve this goal, including the BBC and 'Do-It' the national volunteering database (found online at www.do-it.org.uk). Do-It offers a postcode-searchable database featuring over 850,000 volun-teering opportunities from major charities such as the National Trust and Oxfam and local voluntary and public sector organizations. This is illustrated in Figure 16.1

Shortlisting

When a pool of applications is received it will be necessary to review the data supplied by the candidates to determine who to invite for interview, or other form of selection process. There are three broad ways of developing a shortlist.

The first involves assembling a panel of managers or team members who will conduct the initial sort. They typically proceed as follows (developed from Torrington et al. 2008:163):

1   Using data from the job description and person specification, they agree between them the criteria that will be employed to decide who to place on the shortlist.
2   Using these criteria each member of the panel then reviews the applications and individu-ally produces a list of say 8–10 candidates. The key at this stage is to focus on reasons for including people rather than excluding them so that a deliberate attempt is made to identify the strengths of the applicant pool.

339

Figure 16.1 *Do-It.Org homepage*

Source: Do-It.Org 2008. Reproduced with kind permission.

3   Selectors then reveal their lists and look for consensus. If the preceding two stages have been conducted well, the degree of consensus may already be high enough to develop a shortlist for interview. If not, the team needs to proceed to stage 4.

4   At this point it will be necessary to discuss candidates preferred by some but not all in order to clarify and reduce the areas of disagreement. A possible tactic here is to classify candidates as strong, possible or weak.

5   Selectors produce a shortlist by discussion, guarding against including compromise candidates, not strong but offensive to no one.

Some organizations have developed formal scoring systems so that candidates can be assessed on a range of relevant criteria. In such cases the assessors look for evidence of the criteria in each application and score the candidate accordingly. They might thus receive an A (high degree of evidence), B (some degree of evidence) or C (no evidence provided). Applications with two or more C scores might thus be discarded. Some organizations now employ software packages to enable them to process applications online. This requires a tightly constructed application form which, when completed, can be automatically reviewed and, if appropriate, forwarded for consideration.

Selection methods

Shortlisted candidates can then be invited to participate in the selection process. A variety of selection methods may be employed.

Interviewing

The most widely employed method is undoubtedly the interview. However, this is also the most subjective method and in studies examining the relationship between the performance of different selection methods and subsequent on-the-job performance, it performs very badly. Interview performance is generally not a good indicator of how someone will perform in a role. Interviewers tend to insert their own prejudices into the selection decision and fail to ask appropriate questions (Pynes 2003). To minimize such difficulties Dixon et al. (2002) propose the following steps:

- Develop interview questions based on a job analysis.
- Ask effective questions, probing each key facet of the role and the skills needed to undertake it.
- Ask each candidate the same set of questions.
- Use detailed rating scales to record candidate performance and note relevant examples and illustrations that support the grade assigned.
- Train interviewers.
- Use interview panels so that more than one person conducts the interview. Campion et al. (1988) demonstrate that this reduces the impact of personal biases in the selection process.
- Take notes during the interview which can be referred to later. This will aid the selection process but it can also help in justifying a decision should it later be challenged.
- Evaluate selection decisions based on subsequent employee performance (a point we shall return to later in this chapter).

Testing

There are a variety of different forms of tests that may be administered as part of the selection process. These include:

- *Intelligence tests*   An ability to score highly on such tests does correlate with the capacity to retain new knowledge, to pass examinations and to succeed at work. However such tests need to be carefully validated in the context of the specific job a candidate is applying for. Ceci and Williams (2000) identified that intelligence is determined, at least in part, by context, so a candidate's score may not translate into an ability to act intelligently in a specific context.
- *Special aptitude tests*   These are designed to measure specific abilities such as perceptual abilities, verbal abilities, numerical ability and critical reasoning. An example of a question drawn from a critical reasoning test is provided in the box.

During the past week, 120 RamTech Corporation employees have reported symptoms of a strain of food poisoning known as disporella, but only eight of these employees have tested positive for the strain. A RamTech spokesperson claims that the apparent outbreak of disporella can be attributed to contaminated food served two weeks ago at the company's annual employee picnic.

Which of the following, if true, would most support the claim made by the RamTech spokesperson above?

- ○ (A)   Disporella symptoms generally last only a few days.
- ○ (B)   RamTech's cafeteria facilities provide lunch to RamTech employees during every workday.
- ○ (C)   People with disporella do not generally test positive for disporella until at least one week after disporella symptoms begin to occur.
- ◉ (D)   People with disporella often do not exhibit disporella symptoms until more than a week after contracting disporella.
- ○ (E)   A person can test positive for disporella without exhibiting symptoms of disporella.

Source: http://www.west.net/~stewart/gmat/qmcriti.htm (accessed 20 December 2008).

- *Attainment tests*   Many employers will use simple tests to measure the level of skill an employee might have in a dimension necessary for the role. In appointing an database analyst, for example, they might test proficiency in using Excel or an analytical package such as SPSS or SNAP.
- *Personality tests*   These are designed to assess a person's typical behavioural traits and characteristics by measuring dimensions such as dominance, sociability and self-control. Commonly employed tests are the Minnesota Multiphasic Personality Inventory and the Edwards Personal Preference Schedule. Considerable debate rages over the appropriateness of such testing as personality can be context-dependent and can change over time (Iles and Salamon 2005). Such tests are also open to faking (Heggestad et al. (2006).
- *Group methods*   Some roles require a considerable amount of group work and the ability to function successfully in a team can therefore be a critical aspect of someone's suitability for employment. As a consequence some employers set applicants a group task to complete and assess through observation how well each individual performs in this context.
- *Assessment centres*   These typically employ a range of selection methods to evaluate candidates. Candidates attend the assessment for an extended period of time (typically a half or full day) to complete a variety of tasks. The results from assessment centres, because of the variety of tasks completed, are highly correlated with subsequent on-the-job performance.

Final decision-making

In assessing the performance of individual candidates, care should be taken to assess the individual against the person specification, not against the other candidates. This is typically achieved by employing a matrix such as that in Figure 16.2

In the authors' experience few, if any, applicants meet all of the desirable characteristics outlined in the person specification, but the organization should find a few that do meet all of the essential criteria they outlined and exhibit one or more of the desirable characteristics. References from the applicant/s selected as most suitable may then be applied for and criminal record checks conducted if appropriate. If the references are satisfactory the individual/s will then be put through an induction/training programme and, if appropriate, placed on probation for a specific period of time after which their appointment can be confirmed.

Necessary Criteria	Applicant 1	Applicant 2	Applicant 3	Applicant 4
1				
2				
3				
Etc				
Desirable Criteria				
1				
2				
3				
Etc.				

Figure 16.2 *Selection matrix*

Induction

Induction is a critical part of the recruitment process as it allows the organization to brief the volunteer/employee on its history, mission and the nature of the role they will perform. It is important as it serves to explain how the role the individual will perform forms part of the organization as a whole. It also provides them with all the necessary information and skills they might need to satisfactorily carry out their role.

Despite the benefits a formal induction process can offer, volunteers are often neglected. As Ratje (2003:17) notes: 'nonprofit organizations often rely on volunteers as a vital component of their interaction with clients and potential donors. Yet selection, training and motivation for volunteers can be poor or non-existent'.

The omission of a formal induction can lead to poor performance and give rise to a great deal of dissatisfaction on the part of the volunteer, who might ultimately decide to quit. A lack of formal training can also place the organization in breach of legal requirements since for example, there may be health and safety procedures the individual should be aware of.

From a fundraising perspective, the failure to induct the volunteer presents further problems. To quote Ratje (2003:17) once more: 'imagine a potential donor for a homeless shelter who walks in the door with a checkbook in hand, but then speaks with a volunteer who knows little about the mission, the tax deductability of the donation or just has a bad attitude'. The impact on the organization's brand image and ability to fundraise would obviously be profound, and yet successive studies have found that a lack of training or induction is one of the most-cited problem areas by volunteers (Wymer and Starnes 2001b). It would thus appear that the nonprofit sector has much to do to improve these aspects of volunteer management. For a detailed consideration of induction/training issues, the reader is advised to consult a specialist text such as Fisher and Cole (1993) or Doyle (2002).

Control and evaluation

The final stage of the recruitment process will involve conducting a periodic review of its success. Wright and Storey (1994:209) suggest that an organization should review:

- The number of initial enquiries received which resulted in completed application forms.
- The number of candidates at various stages in the recruitment and selection process, especially those shortlisted.
- The number of candidates recruited.
- The number of candidates retained in the organization after six months.

To this list we would add monitoring the success of the various selection methods employed at predicting subsequent on-the-job performance. We would also encourage employers to conduct periodic surveys of the individuals exposed to the process to determine whether there may be any scope for improvement. Finally, and perhaps most crucially, it will be necessary to monitor that the recruitment and selection process is fair and that no groups are unfairly discriminated against at each stage in the selection process. If an imbalance is perceived remedial action must be initiated.

RETAINING VOLUNTEERS

Volunteer turnover

Many organizations struggle to retain volunteers. Turnover rates in excess of 100 per cent have been reported by some in the course of a typical year. To calculate the rate of turnover, the following formula is typically used. It was developed by the USA Department of Labor for the purposes of measuring staff turnover rates in the private sector, but it is equally applicable to a nonprofit context (Mathis and Jackson 1982).

$$\frac{[\text{Number of volunteer separations during the year}]}{[\text{Total number of volunteers at midyear}]} \times 100$$

There are also more subtle problems created by high turnover rates. High turnover occurs for a reason and a high turnover can suggest that there is something wrong with the role the volunteer is being asked to perform or the circumstances in which it is being conducted. The environment could be over-challenging (or, at the other extreme, very dull) or it may be unfriendly or unsupportive. All these things can come back to haunt an organization as a dissatisfied volunteer will likely tell many of their friends about their poor experience. In short, a high turnover rate can impact negatively on an organization's brand or reputation.

Interestingly, research tells us that volunteers are most likely to quit after three months, six months and twelve months of volunteering (Fischer and Schaffer 1993). The authors tell us that this occurs because volunteers begin their work in a honeymoon stage of euphoria, but regress to 'post-honeymoon blues' after gaining some experience. After longer periods of time, they are likely to quit because they were not able to accomplish what they had hoped or because the organization does not represent the values they thought it did on joining.

We also know that some categories of volunteers are more likely to experience turnover than others. Heidrich (1988) identified that fraternal service organizations, veterans' organizations and cooperatives had a lower turnover than most groups, while youth-serving organizations had a higher turnover.

Sources of dissatisfaction

We have already alluded to a number of sources of volunteer dissatisfaction, but it is worth elaborating for a moment on what the literature suggests are the key reasons volunteers quit working for nonprofit organizations. Wymer and Starnes (2001b) provide a helpful summary of the available research and suggest that the following factors are common causes of turnover.

- *Unreal expectations*   The volunteer may find that the work she has been asked to do does not meet her initial expectations. This could clearly be the fault of either the nonprofit or the individual herself. The individual could have approached the work with an overly optimistic view of what could be accomplished, or the nonprofit could have painted too glowing a picture of the time commitment, type of work or probable impact on the cause.
- *Lack of appreciative feedback*   There is evidence that many volunteers feel undervalued by either the nonprofit or its team.
- *Lack of appropriate training and supervision*   A number of volunteers quit because they feel unsupported by the organization or ill-equipped to perform the duties they have been requested to undertake. Problems can also arise with supervision since, as we noted earlier, organizations must make tough decisions about whether to supervise the volunteer as a volunteer, or whether to have them supervised by the line manager in the service department in which they are working. The balance of evidence is that volunteers prefer the latter, so that they can feel part of a team, but the real lesson from the literature is that 'it depends' and as a consequence the issue must be approached with some sensitivity (Leviton et al. 2006).

■ *Excessive demands on time*   Some volunteers find that longer hours are required than they had originally envisaged, or that the work they are undertaking encroaches on their home life and eats into the time available for other leisure pursuits.

■ *Lack of personal accomplishment*   Equally, some volunteers discover that the post is not as personally rewarding as they had originally thought. Perhaps there is less opportunity to learn new skills, or they are simply unable to make the difference they had hoped for (Kaufman et al. 2004).

■ *Burnout/emotional exhaustion*   Some volunteers find themselves physically and psychologically exhausted by their role. Others find that the role evokes excessive anxiety, which impacts on their home life.

■ *Feelings of second-class status with respect to full-time staff*   A common issue raised by dissatisfied volunteers is their relationship with paid staff. Many report being treated as in some sense inferior to paid staff, despite the fact that their time was being volunteered, rather than paid for.

This latter point warrants some elaboration as the interface between staff and volunteers can be a particular source of conflict. Staff are often critical of the attitude of volunteers, who can appear to be:

■ short-term members of the team and therefore not likely to assume responsibility for the long-term repercussions of their activity;

■ insufficiently aware of the workings and ethics of the organization and thus likely to make mistakes when representing it;

■ unwilling to take direction or guidance.

The attitude of management with regard to volunteers is therefore key. By setting an example in the way that they treat volunteers, they can assist in maintaining good relations between paid and unpaid staff. The optimum attitude is to treat volunteers entirely straightforwardly and as much like paid staff as possible. This should encompass opportunities for training, development and advancement, and the setting and monitoring of targets, benchmarks and goals. This 'professionalization' of volunteering is challenging for nonprofits, and carries significant costs, but experienced organizations maintain that it brings results and greatly reduces turnover.

Retention strategies

Given the range of issues highlighted above, nonprofits need to give adequate consideration to the problems that might arise in all the volunteer roles they are creating and seek to minimize the opportunity for things to go wrong. While the list is not exhaustive, the volunteer management literature suggests that the following points are worthy of consideration.

■ *Screening*   The process of screening applicants for volunteer posts should be rigorous. Every effort must be made to filter out individuals who are not physically or psychologically suited to the role that has been created. Individuals can also be screened out who have unrealistic expectations, or whose motivation seems unsuited to the role.

■ *Matching*   Every effort must be taken to match volunteers with particular roles. As we noted earlier, every role should contain some pleasant tasks alongside the boring and mundane. Variety should be created, and this should be matched to the needs of specific individuals wherever possible.

■ *Tenure*   This is a simple point, but surprisingly effective if actioned. Stittleburg (1994) notes that volunteers are significantly less likely to quit a project where a specific end-date has been supplied (i.e. they are significantly more likely to work out their contract). It appears that a fixed-term obligation is more likely to be honoured than an open-ended commitment.

■ *Support*   Throughout this chapter the opportunities to provide greater support to volunteers have been highlighted. The literature suggests that the following points are among the most critical to address.

   ■ *Communication*   Applebaum (1992) tells us that volunteers suffer from difficulty contacting staff, a lack of feedback from case workers, concerns about value of written reports, a misunderstanding of policies or procedures and not being briefed properly by staff. It is essential that volunteers, irrespective of the hours that they work (which can often be why such problems occur–since they may not be on site when staff briefings take place), are party to the same internal communications as paid staff.

   ■ *Inclusion in decision making*   Volunteers should be invited to participate in any staff consultations the organization may undertake–and be invited to offer suggestions for service improvements in the same way as paid staff.

   ■ *Supervision*   Irrespective of the line approach adopted, supervision must be friendly, accessible and supportive (Applebaum 1992).

   ■ *Recognition programmes*   Nonprofits may either create a formal recognition system or deal with recognition on a more ad hoc basis as the need arises. Simple communications, such as notes of thanks, a mention in a newsletter or internal paper, or an expression of gratitude to a spouse or employer have all be found to be effective forms of recognition. Other nonprofits have nominated volunteers for external awards or displayed positive client comments on noticeboards.

   ■ *Performance evaluation or appraisal*   Volunteers should be subjected to the same internal programme of evaluation as paid staff. Most commonly, this may be a periodic appraisal of their performance and, ideally, the organization's performance in assisting them to achieve their personal goals. An action plan for the coming period can be agreed upon and appropriate development opportunities actioned.

   ■ *Exit interviews*   Despite the best efforts at retention, volunteers will still leave. When they do, a lot can be learnt from an exit interview. This can be an excellent way of identifying areas in which the organization might improve the quality of support and opportunities it offers to its volunteer base. While some turnover will be due to unavoidable factors, such as relocation, or a change in the individual's lifestyle, there will undoubtedly be some volunteer turnover that proves to be due to one or more of the factors we discussed earlier and on which the organization can take action to improve.

EMPLOYEE RETENTION AND MOTIVATION

As one might expect employees can become dissatisfied and leave for very similar reasons to volunteers. Branham (2005) for example reports that employees quit because:

1   The job or workplace does not live up to expectations
2   There is a mismatch between the person and job
3   Too little coaching and feedback are offered
4   There are too few growth and advancement opportunities
5   They feel devalued and/or unrecognized

6   They suffer stress from overwork and a poor work life balance
7   They suffer a loss of trust and confidence in senior leaders

To deal with these issues Torrington et al. (2008) outline five broad measures that have been demonstrated to have a positive impact on retention.

Pay

There is considerable debate over the nature of the relationship between pay and staff retention. Some researchers have emphasized the correlation between the value of the reward package and lower attrition rates (Cappelli 2000), while others have pointed to questionnaire-based studies that suggest that pay is less important than other factors that influence a decision to quit. Note the absence of pay/remuneration in Branham's list above. A more detailed consideration of the factors impacting motivation is therefore required and this is a subject we will return to in detail below.

Managing expectations

Just as volunteers will leave if the role does not match up to their expectations, so too will employees. A major cause of turnover is the discovery that the role is not as challenging or enjoyable as once thought. There is therefore a need to strike a balance at the recruitment stage between sending out positive messages that encourage individuals to apply, while also sending out realistic messages about what to expect when the role begins (Hom and Griffeth 1995).

Induction

As we noted above, induction plays a critical role in reducing attrition.

■   It allows individuals to adjust emotionally and practically to the workplace, acquainting them with how their role fits into the wider picture and where to source information and/or resources they might need.
■   It provides a forum for communicating information about the mission and goals of the organization. It also provides an opportunity to communicate critical information about policies and procedures, notably relating to health and safety issues.
■   It provides an opportunity to communicate the values and culture of the nonprofit – in effect the way in which the organization chooses to operate. These will inevitably be learned over time, but it is good practice to explore these in an induction process to prevent misunderstandings that can ultimately lead to dissatisfaction.

Family–friendly HR practices

In the UK the Working Time Regulations 1998, Employment Relations Act 1999, the Employment Act 2002 and the Work and Families Act 2006 have furnished employees with a number of new rights including:

■   Paid maternity leave of 26 weeks for all paid employees irrespective of their length of service.
■   Additional maternity leave for women who have completed 26 weeks' continuous employment with their employer by the beginning of the 14th week before their expected date of birth. Additional maternity leave starts immediately after ordinary maternity leave and continues for a further 26 weeks. Additional maternity leave is usually unpaid.

347

- Reasonable time off to attend prenatal clinics.
- Four weeks paid holiday in addition to bank holidays.
- Reasonable unpaid time off for employees to deal with family emergencies such as the sickness of a child or the death of a relative.
- The right of carers and parents of young children to request flexible working.
- The right to up to two weeks paternity leave for new fathers.

Many employers choose to go beyond these statutory minimums, taking a variety of steps to make it easier for employees to manage the home work balance. Such packages offer real value to staff and can significantly boost retention.

Improving the quality of line management

This is a further factor which impacts on both volunteers and paid staff. Too often people are promoted into supervisory positions with inadequate training and support. As a consequence many managers cope poorly with the interpersonal aspects of their role finding it difficult to motivate their team, provide balanced feedback and/or to take account of the views of others in their decisions. Dissatisfaction with line management is a major cause of attrition and, while it may be a truism, people tend to leave managers, not organizations.

The solution is for organizations to assess carefully the management skills of their staff and promote only those individuals suitable to the position. It may also be appropriate to provide supervisory training and to ensure that all line managers have their skills in this area regularly appraised.

Encouraging diversity in the workplace

To Torrington et al's (2008) original list we would add the dimension of encouraging diversity. Recognizing and valuing diversity in the workplace is central to good people management practice and it will certainly impact on retention. Managers play a critical role in creating inclusive workplaces where everyone feels valued and able to contribute to the success of the organization. This involves an organization moving beyond the basic requirements of anti-discrimination laws and establishing best practice.

To address diversity issues organizations need to consider two key questions. What policies, practices and ways of thinking have differential impact on different groups? What organizational changes should be made to meet the needs of a diverse workforce as well as to maximize the potential of all workers?

Encouraging and celebrating diversity is not as straightforward as it may at first sound. Many people believe in the proverb 'treat others as you want to be treated', but the implicit assumption here is that 'how you want to be treated' is how others want to be treated. But when you look at this statement through a diversity lens, you begin to ask what respect looks like and whether it looks the same for everyone.

The answer of course depends on the individual. We may share similar values, such as respect or a need for recognition, but how we show those values through behaviour may be different for different cultures. Rather than treating others as they would expect to be treated, managers need to consider treating others as *they* want to be treated. Moving the frame of reference from an ethnocentric view ('our way is the best way') to a culturally relative perspective ('let's take the best of a variety of ways') will assist managers to help the organisation to manage more effectively in an increasingly diverse work environment.

Ignoring diversity issues is costly in terms of time, money and efficiency (Daniels and MacDonald 2005). Some of these consequences can include: unhealthy tensions between people of differing gender, race, ethnicity, age, abilities and so on; loss of productivity because of increased conflict; inability to attract and retain talented people of all kinds; complaints and legal actions; an inability to retain some societal groups, resulting in considerable lost investment in recruitment and training.

At a minimum senior managers should thus consider (Chartered Institute of Personnel and Development 2008):

■ How to build diversity concepts and practices into management and other training and team-building programmes to increase awareness of the need to handle different views, perceptions and ideas in positive ways.
■ Introducing awareness-raising programmes about diversity and skills training to help people work together better in a diverse environment.
■ Including diversity issues in induction programmes so that all new employees know about the organisation's values and policies.
■ Training line managers about diversity, aiming to help them understand the issues and drive them into organisational and operational policies and practices.

MOTIVATION AT WORK

Thus far in this chapter we have focused on how to minimize the attrition of both staff and volunteers. In this section we move on to consider how managers might motivate individuals to deliver optimal levels of performance. Three key perspectives on workplace motivation will be outlined.

Two-factor theory

Two-factor theory was developed by Fred Herzberg who in collaboration with his colleagues conducted a series of interviews with employees in the Pittsburgh area of the United States. Interviewees were asked to recall two separate job-related events in which their satisfaction at work either improved or declined. The authors concluded that the factors that led to dissatisfaction were different from those that led to satisfaction (Herzberg et al. 1959). The idea is depicted graphically in Figure 16.3.

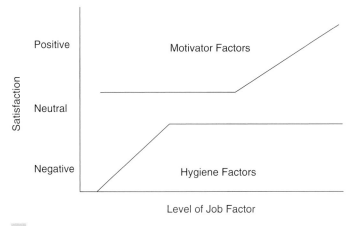

Figure 16.3 *Relationship between level of job factors and level of employee satisfaction*

Satisfiers usually related to the content of the job, such as feelings of accomplishment, recognition, career advancement and a sense of responsibility. While these factors had the capacity to make people feel good about their work, their absence would not make an employee unhappy. By contrast hygiene factors, which include job security, company policies, interpersonal relations and working conditions, can generate considerable discontent when absent. Improving these factors can reduce this discontent, but it will not provide an incentive for them to strive for superior performance.

There remains a debate over whether the relationships between these factors and worker satisfaction are actually as depicted in Figure 16.3. Some researchers have found support for these relationships while others maintain that both sets of factors have the ability to enhance satisfaction to a greater or lesser degree (Schneider and Locke 1971).

Expectancy theory

An alternative perspective on motivation is offered by Victor Vroom (1964). While Herzberg focused on the motivation to secure two categories of need (or outcomes), Vroom separates the effort (which arises from motivation) from performance and outcomes. He argues that, in order for a person to be motivated, effort, performance and motivation must be linked and proposes three variables to account for this, which he calls Valence, Expectancy and Instrumentality. The idea is illustrated graphically in Figure 16.4.

Expectancy is the belief that increased effort will lead to increased performance. This might typically be affected by factors such as:

1   Having the right resources to increase performance (e.g. raw materials, time)
2   Having the right skills to increase performance
3   Having the necessary support to get the job done (e.g. appropriate supervisory support, or guidance).

Instrumentality is the belief that if an individual achieves superior performance that a valued outcome or reward will be received. This could be affected by factors such as:

1   Having a clear understanding of the relationship between performance and outcomes (i.e. understanding the rules of the reward 'game')
2   Developing trust in the people who will take the reward decisions
3   There being transparency in the process that determines the allocation of rewards.

Valence is the attractiveness of the expected outcome. This will almost certainly vary from one individual to another. Some may find the existence of merit pay a motivating factor while others might be motivated by offers of additional time off or the chance of promotion.

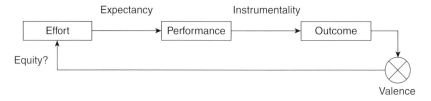

Figure 16.4 Expectancy theory

Vroom (1964) posits that effort will thus be a function of the extent to which an individual believes that the enhanced performance is possible, the extent to which they believe that that level of performance will lead to the reward (outcome) promised and the attractiveness of that reward. The theory is well supported by research (Vroom 2005), but its application would appear to have more relevance to settings where a conscious reward maximization decision-making process is operating. The idea that employees engage in a form of cognitive calculus before deciding whether or not to expend effort seems a little implausible; yet, despite this, expectancy theory remains a popular framework for examining motivation.

Equity theory

Equity theory was developed by John Stacy Adams (1965), a workplace and behavioural psychologist. His theory is based on the belief that individuals become demotivated, both in relation to their job and their employer, if they feel as though their inputs are greater than the outputs they receive. Table 16.2 summarizes what Adams regarded as typical inputs and outputs.

Adams argued that individuals would estimate their personal ratio of outcomes to inputs and would become demotivated if they perceived an inequity. Adams also argued that each person will calculate a similar ratio for someone they believe to be in a similar position. This individual is known as a *comparison other*. Adams predicts that an individual will be relatively satisfied if his/her own ratio of outcomes to inputs is equivalent to the comparison other. In other words individuals will be satisfied where:

$$\frac{\text{Outcomes A}}{\text{Inputs A}} = \frac{\text{Outcomes B}}{\text{Inputs B}}$$

If person A perceives they are undercompensated in relation to person B the following will be true:

$$\frac{\text{Outcomes A}}{\text{Inputs A}} < \frac{\text{Outcomes B}}{\text{Inputs B}}$$

Table 16.2 *Examples of inputs and outputs in Adams's equity theory*

Inputs	Outputs
Effort	Financial rewards (salary, benefits, perks, etc.)
Loyalty	Recognition
Hard Work	Reputation
Commitment	Responsibility
Skill	Sense of Achievement
Ability	Praise
Adaptability	Stimulus
Flexibility	Sense of Advancement/Growth
Determinaton	Job security
Support of Colleagues	
Ethusiasm	
Trust in superiors	

In this case feelings of inequity will result that will require reduction. This might be achieved by:

- asking for a raise to increase outcomes;
- decreasing inputs by becoming less productive;
- person A might also try to increase B's inputs by forcing them to work harder.

The converse is true, where:

$$\frac{\text{Outcomes A}}{\text{Inputs A}} > \frac{\text{Outcomes B}}{\text{Inputs B}}$$

In these circumstances equity theory predicts that person A will experience guilt and will attempt to restore equity by altering one of the four dimensions. They might thus:

- convince themselves that their own inputs are higher (or their outputs lower) than they are in reality;
- leave the employment or apply for a transfer;
- choose a different individual as a comparison other, someone who provides a more comfortable contrast.

The predictions of equity theory are also well supported by research, but interestingly it is particularly valuable in predicting the behaviour of individuals who score highly on the dimension 'altruism'. It appears as though equity theory may provide a better description of the behaviour of 'principled individuals', while expectancy theory may offer more utility for the balance of the working population (Campbell and Pritchard 1976).

PERFORMANCE EVALUATION

Why evaluate?

A key task for most fundraising managers will be the regular review of the performance of members of their team. Many organizations, for example, have a formal annual performance evaluation process, or appraisal system, so that each individual member of staff can receive regular feedback on their work. Cascio (1998) highlights four key roles performed by this process:

1 Determining promotions, transfers, terminations and training requirements
2 Providing feedback to employees to enable them to improve their performance
3 Validating the recruitment and selection programme
4 Deciding on the package of rewards an employee might receive (e.g. merit pay).

Who should evaluate?

Most organizations use their line management to conduct the appraisal process, since they are likely to be responsible for the individual's output and to have the clearest perception of their overall performance. Increasingly, however, it has become apparent that others may be better placed to conduct this analysis than the immediate line supervisor. Organizations are now making considerable use of self-managed teams, home working and other mechanisms that create distance between the employee and their line manager. In such circumstances it may be more appropriate to give peers and/or subordinates input to the process.

It is also common practice for employees to have input to the process themselves. Armour (2003) reports that around half of executives and 53 per cent of employees now have input to their performance evaluation. There are of course difficulties in permitting this to take place. Employee evaluations of their own performance tend to be inflated and often out of line with managerial assessments (Atkins and Wood 2002), an issue that can potentially give rise to conflict. Robbins and Judge (2007: 620) conclude that 'because of these drawbacks, self evaluations are probably better suited to developmental than evaluative purposes and should be combined with other sources of information to avoid rating errors'.

An alternative approach to performance evaluation is depicted in Figure 16.5. A 360 degree evaluation allows for feedback from the full range of individuals who might have contact with an employee's work. The rationale here is that people tend to behave differently in different contexts, so 360 degree evaluation provides a more rounded perspective than just relying on one or two evaluations. Organisations using this technique typically gather five to ten per employee.

The evidence on the effectiveness of this technique remains mixed (Atkins and Wood 2002) although many of the difficulties may arise from problems operationalizing the technique rather than the approach per se. In some cases organizations fail to provide proper training to assessors, while others lack a mechanism for reconciling disagreements between the various assessors.

Methods of performance evaluation

These might typically include:

- *Written essays*   The most straightforward form of evaluation is undoubtedly a narrative essay detailing the employee's strengths and weaknesses. Whether the appraisal is worthwhile, however, will probably be a function of the degree of writing skill possessed by the assessor.
- *Critical incidents*   Assessors using this technique write down anecdotes that illustrate examples of effective and ineffective behaviour on the part of the employee. These can then be discussed at the appraisal interview. The advantage of this approach is that the focus is on real behaviours rather than poorly defined traits.
- *Graphic rating scales*   One of the most widely used assessment methods because they are relatively easy to construct and complete. They require the assessor (or nonprofit) to create a list of factors that drive good performance and then to rate the employee (perhaps from 1 to 5) on each dimension, as in the following example.

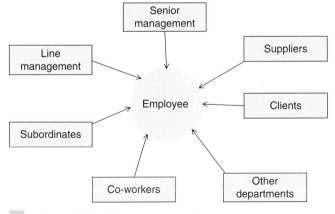

Figure 16.5 *360 degree evaluations*

Uncooperative	1	2	3	4	5	Cooperative
Tardy	1	2	3	4	5	Punctual
Lazy	1	2	3	4	5	Industrious

Although they do not provide the depth of information that the previous methods can, they have the merit of being cheap and easy to administer. On the downside, a reliance on a simple list of factors only indirectly related to performance may provide no more than a format for a supervisor to express their liking or disliking of an employee (Vecchio 1991). Each scale item then receives a very similar score.

■ *Behaviorally anchored rating scales (BARs)*   This approach combines the critical incident and graphic rating scale approaches. Statements that describe competent, average and incompetent behaviour are gathered from employees and supervisors. These are then categorized as performance dimensions, such as interpersonal skills, technical knowledge and so on. Anything regarded as ambiguous is disgarded. A group of judges is then asked to rate each incident on a five point scale in terms of whether the incident represents outstanding (5), average (3) or poor (1) performance. Specific incidents are then selected to act as anchors or benchmarks to be input on the final scale. An example for use in a 360° appraisal of the 'accessibility' of a line manager is provided here.

My supervisor is available when needed.

5   My supervisor is easily accessible and stays in contact with me throughout the year.
4   My supervisor is easily accessible and provides me with guidance at the proper time.
3   My supervisor is usually accessible.
2   It is sometimes hard to reach my supervisor in person.
1   My supervisor is extremely hard to get hold of.

BARs have a number of advantages over other methods of assessment. First, as they are written in job relevant terminology, the ratings provide more meaningful information than attempting to assess personality traits. They are also helpful in that they define the strengths and weaknesses of the individual and can thus form the basis of discussion in the appraisal interview. The use of BARs does however involve the organization in considerable effort in construction and since they are by definition job specific, it can prove very costly to develop these for every organizational role.

■ *Behavioural observation scales (BOS)*   Latham and Wexley (1981) developed a further behavioural approach to assessment. BOS differ from BARS in that BOS require the evaluator to indicate the frequency of exhibition whereas BARs require the evaluator to specify only the nature of the behaviour exhibited. An example of a BOS rating scale for a direct dialogue fundraiser is provided here.

1   Does not block the path of pedestrians on the street:
    Almost never 1 2 3 4 5 Almost always

2   Provides the required declaration of the nature of their remuneration:
    Almost never 1 2 3 4 5 Almost always

3   Closes the conversation by saying thank you to the donor:
    Almost never 1 2 3 4 5 Almost always

The feedback interview

Irrespective of the method employed to conduct the review, the results must then be constructively fed back to the individual employee. This is typically achieved through the vehicle of an appraisal interview, the goal of which is to create an atmosphere where a genuine discussion can take place of an individual's strengths, weaknesses, training/development needs, future interests, career goals and so on. Offering feedback and, where necessary, constructive criticism, is a task that many managers find makes them uncomfortable. This feeling is frequently shared by subordinates because they disagree with the ratings and/or opinions of their supervisor (Heneman 1974). As we noted earlier, people tend to view their own performance as superior. In a study of 249 managers, for example, Carrol and Schneier (1982) found that 67 per cent rated themselves as delivering above average performance. Given these difficulties, training for assessors is regarded as essential.

Conducting a feedback review

In conducting the review it is important that any observations are supported by facts. The reviewer must therefore review the appraisal documentation and gather any relevant information that might be needed to support the conclusions drawn. This might, for example, be data on the quality/quantity of output or data on absenteeism. An outline should also be prepared of the key points that will be discussed. This will later serve as a guide to the interview discussion.

In the interests of fairness employees need to be given advance notice of the meeting and its objectives (e.g. to determine merit pay). This gives the individual the opportunity to prepare their own thoughts and a list of issues that they too might like to raise. It is also good practice to ask the reviewee to assess their own performance in advance of that meeting. The greater the opportunity they have to express themselves during the process the more satisfied they are likely to be as a consequence (Greller 1975).

In conducting the interview itself the appraiser should focus on issues rather than personalities. Thus, rather than using phrases such as 'you have been late too often' the appraiser might say 'you have been late eight times, can you suggest ways in which we might improve this performance?' If personal criticism should be necessary this should be stated without hostility and be accompanied by an explanation of why the behaviour in question cannot be allowed to continue. A discussion can then be initiated of what actions could be taken to improve the situation, with the appraiser taking the time to listen with an open mind to the views of the appraisee.

Most appraisers like to take a sandwich approach to providing criticism and praise. To create a comfortable and relaxed atmosphere at the beginning of a session, appraisers typically focus on a number of the individual's strengths and the impact these might have had on the organization. They can then focus on any problem areas before closing with a discussion of the individual's remaining strengths so that the interview ends on a positive note.

In closing, the appraiser should review any steps that might have been agreed to move things forward. This might include any required changes in behaviour but it may also involve actions on the supervisor's part such as arranging access to training, changing the nature of the job role or allowing more flexible working. The appraiser should always offer their assistance to the appraisee to bring about any changes that might be required. Such offers need to be both specific and genuine, thus changing the role of the appraiser from one of judge to one of coach.

Finally, all appraisers should be aware of their legal obligations to treat all employees fairly and impartially. Care must be taken to ensure that any personal biases they might have are not reflected in either the conduct or outcome of the performance evaluation process.

ENDING THE CONTRACT OF EMPLOYMENT

Fundraising managers will inevitably have to deal with the termination of a contract of employment at some point during their careers. This may come as a consequence of a post being made redundant or it may occur where the performance of the incumbent is in some way unsatisfactory. It is beyond the scope of this text to provide coverage of all the legal issues that may be encountered should this step prove necessary and managers are thus advised to seek specialist legal advice as appropriate.

In the UK there are many circumstances when the termination of an employment contract will be unlawful. These include:

- Dismissal for a reason relating to pregnancy or maternity.
- Dismissal for a health and safety reason (e.g. someone refusing to work in unsafe conditions).
- Dismissal because of a spent conviction.
- Dismissal for refusing to work on a Sunday (retail and betting workers only).
- Dismissal for a trade union reason (e.g. someone electing to join a trade union).
- Dismissal for taking official industrial action (during the first 12 weeks of the action).
- Dismissal in contravention of the part-time workers or fixed-term employees regulations.
- Dismissal for undertaking specific forms of public service (e.g. jury service).
- Dismissal for asserting a statutory right (e.g. requesting flexible working).
- Dismissals that take place before the completion of the disciplinary and dismissal procedures (DDPs) required by the Dispute Resolution Regulations 2004 (where one year's continuous service has been completed).

Potentially fair reasons for dismissal might include:

- *Lack of capability or qualifications.*
- *Misconduct* This may be either gross or ordinary.
  - *Gross misconduct* occurs where an employee behaves in a manner that would be intolerable for any reasonable employer and commits an express breach of either their contract of employment or the common law duties owed by an employee to their employer. In such circumstances it may be necessary and appropriate to summarily dismiss the employee.
  - *Ordinary misconduct* involves lesser transgressions such as breaching some rules in the workplace, or not following the instructions of a supervisor. In most cases of ordinary misconduct it would be considered unfair to summarily dismiss an employee and a warning should instead be given on at least one occasion.
- *Redundancy* This occurs where a particular job ceases or is expected to cease to exist. An employee who is dismissed shall be taken to be dismissed by reason of redundancy when the dismissal is wholly or mainly attributable to:

The fact that his employer has ceased, or intends to cease, to carry on the business for the purpose of which the employee was employed by him, or has ceased or intends to cease, to carry on that business in the place where the employee is employed.
Or
The fact that the requirements of that business for employees to carry out work of a particular kind or for employees to carry out work of a particular kind in the place where he was so employed, have ceased or are expected to cease or diminish.

(Employment Rights Act 1996, s 139(1))

- *A statutory bar*   In some cases there may be a legal bar to employment such as the expiration of a work permit, or someone employed as a driver losing their driving licence.
- *Dismissal due to industrial action*   After the dispute has continued for more than 12 weeks.
- *Mandatory retirements*   Following the procedures in the Employment Equality (Age) Regulations 2006.
- *Some other substantial reason*.

The final point warrants some elaboration. Employers can, for example, terminate the contracts of employees who refuse to adopt changes in working practices or their terms and conditions. To be considered a fair reason for dismissal an organization must merely demonstrate that the change in practice would deliver a clear organizational advantage.

As we stated from the outset, however, the law in relation to dismissal is highly complex and managers are advised to seek professional advice from either their personnel department or a specialist legal counsel to ensure that they treat their employees fairly and operate within the law. They may otherwise find themselves at the centre of an action for wrongful or unfair dismissal, involving their organization in considerable time and expense.

SUMMARY

In this chapter we have discussed a wide range of issues that fundraising managers or team leaders may need to deal with during the normal course of their work. We have outlined how both volunteers and staff may be recruited to an organization and examined the factors that will typically impact on their retention. We have also explored a number of theoretical frameworks that managers can use to think through how to motivate the members of their team, considering two-factor theory, expectancy theory and equity theory. We concluded by looking at the circumstances (in the UK) when a contract of employment may be legitimately terminated and where it would automatically be deemed unlawful. In the next chapter we will move on to consider other issues of relevance to fundraising management, namely group dynamics and leadership.

DISCUSSION QUESTIONS

1   What is meant by the phrase 'work analysis'? Why is this a critical component of the recruitment process?
2   How might an organization set up a performance appraisal system to minimize the risk of discriminating unfairly against a specific group of employees?
3   You have been invited to attend an interview for the post of director of fundraising at a large national charity. As part of the selection process you have been invited to give a presentation on how you would seek to motivate your team. What would you say?
4   What is the difference between direct and indirect discrimination? What are the implications of both for fundraising managers?
5   'Programmes designed to reduce work life conflicts discriminate against single employees.' To what extent do you agree or disagree with this statement? Why?
6   In what ways might the management of volunteers differ from the management of salaried employees?

REFERENCES

Adams, J.S. (1965) 'Inequity in Social Exchange', *Advances in Experimental Social Psychology*, 62: 335–343.

Applebaum, S. (1992) *Recruiting and Retaining Volunteers from Minority Communities: A Case Study*, UMI Dissertation Services, Ann Arbor, MI.

Armour, S. (2003) 'Job Reviews Take on Added Significance in Down Times', *USA Today*, 23 July: 4B.

Atkins, P.W.B. and Wood, R.E. (2002) 'Self Versus Others' Ratings as Predictors of Assessment Center Ratings: Validation Evidence for 360° Feedback Progams', *Personnel Psychology*, Winter: 871–904.

Branham, L. (2005) *The Seven Hidden Reasons Employees Leave*, American Management Association, New York.

Campbell, J.P. and Pritchard, R.D. (1976) 'Motivational Theory in Industrial and Organizational Psychology', in M. Dunnette (ed.) *Handbook of Industrial and Organizational Psychology*, Rand McNally, Chicago, IL.

Campion, M.A., Pursell, E.D. and Brown, B.K. (1988) 'Structured Interviewing: Raising the Psychometric Properties of the Employment Interview', *Personnel Psychology*, 41: 25–42.

Cappelli, P. (2000) 'A Market Driven Approach to Retaining Talent', *Harvard Business Review*, January/February: 103–111.

Carrol, S.J. and Schneier, C.E. (1982) *Performance Appraisal and Review Systems*, Scott Foresman, Glenview, IL.

Cascio, W.F. (1998) *Applied Psychology in Human Resource Management,* 5 edn, Prentice-Hall, Upper Saddle River, NJ.

Ceci, S. and Williams, W. (2000) 'Smart Bomb', *People Management*, 24 August: 32–36.

Chartered Institute of Personnel and Development (CIPD) (2008) Diversity: An Overview, http://www.cipd.co.uk/subjects/dvsequl/general/divover.htm. (accessed 21st December 2008).

Daniels, K. and MacDonald, L.A.C. (2005) *Equality, Diversity and Discrimination*, Chartered Institute of Personnel and Development, London.

Dixon, M., Wang, S., Calvin, J., Dineen, B. and Tomlinson, E. (2002) 'The Panel Interview: A Review of Empirical Research and Guidelines for Practice', *Public Personnel Management*, 31(3): 397–428.

Doyle, D. (2002) *Volunteers in Hospice and Palliative Care*, Oxford University Press, Oxford.

Ellis, S.J. (1989) *Volunteer Centers: Gearing up for the 1990s*, United Way of America, Alexandria, VA.

Fisher, J.C. and Cole, K.M. (1993) *Leadership and Management of Volunteer Programs*, Jossey Bass, San Francisco, CA.

Fischer, L.R. and Schaffer, K.B. (1993) *Older Volunteers: A Guide For Research and Practice*, Sage Publications, Newbury Park, CA.

Greller, M.M. (1975) 'Subordinate Perception and Reaction to the Appraisal Interview', *Journal of Applied Psychology*, 60: 544–549.

Heggestad, E., Morrison, M., Reeve, C. and McCloy, R.A. (2006) 'Forced Choice Assessments of Personality for Selection: Evaluating Issues of Normative Assessment and Faking Resistance', *Journal of Applied Psychology*, 91(1): 9–24.

Heidrich, K.W. (1988) '*Lifestyles of Volunteers: A Marketing Segmentation Study*', PhD dissertation, University of Illinois at Urbana-Champaign.

Heneman, H.G. (1974) 'Comparisons of Self and Superior Ratings of Managerial Performance', *Journal of Applied Psychology*, 59: 638–642.

Herzberg, F., Mausner, B. and Synderman, B. (1959) *The Motivation to Work*, Wiley, New York.

Hom, P. and Griffeth, R. (1995) *Employee Turnover*, South Western College Publishing, Cincinatti, OH.

Iles, P. and Salamon, G. (2005) 'Recruitment, Selection and Assessment', in J. Storey (ed.) *Human Resource Management: A Critical Text*, Routledge, London.

Jackson, R. (2001) 'How to Recruit and Retain the Right Volunteers', Proceedings, *Recruiting, Retaining and Training Volunteers*, Henry Stewart Conferences, London, October.

Kaufman, R., Mirsky, J. and Avgar, A. (2004) 'A Brigade Model for the Management of Service Volunteers: Lessons from the Soviet Union', *International Journal of Nonprofit and Voluntary Sector Marketing*, 9(1): 57–68.

Latham, G.P. and Wexley, K.N. (1981) *Increasing Productivity Through Performance Appraisal*, Addison Wesley, Reading, MA.

Leviton, L.C., Herrera, C., Pepper, S.K., Fishman, N. and Racine, D.P. (2006) 'Faith in Action: Capacity and Sustainability of Volunteer Organizations', *Evaluation and Program Planning*, 29(2): 201–307.

Mathus, R.L. and Jackson, J.H. (1982) *Personnel: Contemporary Perspectives and Applications*, 3rd edn, West Publishing, St Paul, MN.

Pynes, J.E. (2003) 'Strategic Human Resources Management', in S.W. Hays and R.C. Kearney (eds) *Public Personnel Administration: Problems and Prospects*, 4th edn, Prentice Hall, Upper Saddle River, NJ.

Ratje, J.M. (2003) 'Well Prepared Volunteers Help the Brand Image', *Marketing News*, 14 April: 17.

Robbins, S.P. and Judge, T.A. (2007) *Organizational Behavior*, Prentice Hall, Upper Saddle River, NJ.

Sanchez, J.L. and Levine, E.L. (1999) 'Is Job Analysis Dead, Misunderstood or Both? New Forms of Work Analysis and Design', in A.I. Kraut and A.K. Korman (eds) *Evolving Practices in Human Resource Management*, Jossey Bass, San Francisco, CA.

Schneider, J. and Locke, E.A. (1971) 'A Critique of Herzberg's Classification System and a Suggested Revision', *Organizational Behavior and Human Performance*, 12: 441–458.

Stittleburg, P.C. (1994) 'Recoruiting and Retaining Volunteers', *NFPA (National Fire Protection Association) Journal*, 88(2): 1175–1192.

Torrington, D., Hall, L. and Taylor, S. (2008) *Human Resource Management*, 7th edn, Financial Times – Prentice Hall, London.

Vecchio, R.P. (1991) *Organizational Behavior*, 2nd edn, Dryden Press, Orlando, FL.

Vroom, V.H. (1964) *Work and Motivation*, John Wiley, New York.

Vroom, V.H. (2005) 'On the Origins of Expectancy Theory', in K. Smith, and M. Hitt, (eds) *Great Minds in Management: The Process of Theory Development*, Oxford University Press, Oxford.

Wright, M. and Storey, J. (1994) 'Recruitment', in I. Beardwell and L. Holden (eds) *Human Resource Management*, Pitman, London.

Wymer, W.W. and Starnes, B.J. (2001a) 'Conceptual Foundations and Practical Guidelines for Recruiting Volunteers to Serve in Local Nonprofit Organizations: Part 1', *Journal of Nonprofit and Public Sector Marketing*, 9(1): 63–96.

Wymer, W.W. and Starnes, B.J. (2001b) 'Conceptual Foundations and Practical Guidelines for Retaining Volunteers Who Serve in Local Nonprofit Organizations: Part 1', *Journal of Nonprofit and Public Sector Marketing*, 9(1): 97–118.

Chapter 17

Group dynamics and leadership

OBJECTIVES

By the end of this chapter you should be able to:

- Distinguish between a work group and team.
- Understand the stages of team development.
- Understand the factors that drive team performance and the implications for fundraising management.
- Select team members appropriate to a given task.
- Describe key perspectives on leadership.
- Critically evaluate your own approach to leadership.
- Lead a successful fundraising team.

INTRODUCTION

An understanding of group dynamics is a critical component of successful fundraising management. Teams are commonplace in fundraising and a manager may be responsible for managing a work group that could include both employees and volunteers. These individuals may be based out of one office, or there may be subgroups working from different locations around the country. He/she may even have responsibility for virtual groups as many charities now switch to home working to cut down on overhead costs, particularly when a 'local' presence is required in many disparate areas of the country. To add to this complexity there will also be occasions when supporters are actively involved in the fundraising process and may even become part of a team working to encourage others to give to the organisation. Many larger charities, for example, have major gift committees that might include donors, board members and community leaders, and a fundraiser may therefore have responsibility for maximizing the performance and the satisfaction of this highly diverse group.

In this chapter we will therefore examine the issue of group dynamics and study how people interact in group/team contexts. We will look at what motivates people to participate in groups and the factors that drive their performance. We will also examine the characteristics of effective groups and how fundraisers might lead these to improve their impact on the organisation. A number of different perspectives on leadership will be presented. We begin, however, by discussing the nature of groups.

THE NATURE OF GROUPS

Robbins and Judge (2007:300) define a group as 'two or more individuals, interacting and interdependent, who have come together to achieve particular objectives'. According to these authors, groups may be:

- *Formal*   Where the nature and role of the group is defined by an organisation's structure and/or work assignments. The activities of these groups are guided by the mission and objectives of the organization. A group of regional fundraisers coming together to plan a fundraising event would be a common example of a formal group.
- *Informal*   Where the nature and composition of the group is not formally defined by the organisation. Typically informal groups are formed by employees to enhance their own satisfaction and enjoyment. Individuals may come together to have lunch, or to socialize either inside or outside of the work environment. They can often generate significant social bonds and thus if the goals of the group are congruent with the goals of the organisation they can be a significant force for good. Where this is not the case they can be a significant barrier to change, posing challenges to the organisation's management whenever this is proposed. Because of the status and social benefits such groups confer, members can be highly resistant to change or management moves to disband them.

    On balance though informal groups tend to be a force for good. They can be key to motivation in the work environment as they satisfy a number of the social needs of both employees and volunteers. From previous chapters the reader will appreciate how significant these needs can be, particularly for volunteers, where the social interaction may even be the primary reason for their involvement. It is therefore important for managers to recognize the significance of informal groups and to encourage their development where appropriate. Consideration may thus be given to designing patterns of work, or even the design of the workplace itself, to foster this interaction.

Sayles (1957) further subdivides groups as follows:

1   *Command groups*   Are determined by the relevant section of the organizational chart indicating the individuals who report to a particular manager. These individuals are referred to as their command group.
2   *Task groups*   Are again organizationally determined. Task groups comprise all those individuals necessary to complete a given task. The membership may be drawn from a command group but it can also stretch into other (related) areas of work. A task group to promote legacies, for example, may involve individuals working in the realm of campaigning, service provision and branding.
3   *Interest groups*   Are not organizationally defined. Such groups consist of individuals who band together to achieve a specific objective such as a change in the working environment, working conditions or to support a peer with a grievance against the organisation.
4   *Friendship groups*   Comprise individuals who elect to come together for their own satisfaction and enjoyment. Typically these are individuals who share common characteristics or interests, such as football, music and so on. They therefore extend beyond the work environment.

Other authors view the distinction between command and task groups as the difference between a group and a team. Robbins and Judge (2007), for example, see work groups as individuals who interact to share information and make decisions that assist each group member in performing their role. They do not engage in collective work, or expend joint effort, so the performance of the group is merely the sum of the performance of all its members.

Teams, by contrast, are groups of individuals who come together to solve a particular problem or complete a particular task. They are thus highly dependent on each other for success and expend considerable coordinated effort to complete their work. As a consequence there can be a good deal of synergy created, with the result that the output from the team is much greater than would have been the sum of the individual efforts of all its members. It is this synergy that has driven recent management interest in team working and many organizations now create teams of fundraisers that have responsibility for their own field of operations. There can thus be a legacy team, a direct marketing team, an events team, and so on.

TYPES OF TEAMS

There are four key categories of work team of interest in fundraising

1   *Problem-solving teams*   These typically comprise groups of 5-12 individuals brought together by the organization to look for ways of, for example, improving the efficiency and effectiveness of its fundraising, improving worker/volunteer satisfaction and so on.
2   *Self-managed work teams*   The defining characteristic of these teams is the fact that they take responsibility for their own supervision, including the planning and execution of their work, problem solving as required and liaising with key suppliers. Again, they might typically comprise 5-10 members working on one form of fundraising or income generation.
3   *Cross-functional teams*   In this case membership comprises individuals of the same hierarchical level or 'rank' within the organisation. They are drawn from different functional areas to work on a specific task. A charity designing or redesigning its web presence may thus assemble individuals from fundraising, campaigning, service provision and IT to plan and develop the site and associated communications.
4   *Virtual teams*   The increasing technological sophistication of many voluntary organizations and the desire to facilitate home working has led to an increased use of virtual work teams. Here individuals work together on specific tasks, on either a temporary or permanent basis, but meet only rarely (if at all) face to face. Instead they meet through media such as Skype, video/tele-conferencing and e-mail.

The structure of each team is illustrated in Figure 17.1

STAGES OF TEAM DEVELOPMENT

Anyone who has been part of a team, either at work or as part of their education, will be aware that the dynamics of that team can change over time. While initially the members may be cautious in expressing themselves, as the team members get to know one another they begin to lose some inhibitions and become more vocal. This can lead to conflict between two or more members and may take time to resolve before the team can function effectively as a unit. These various stages of development are well documented; Tuckman (1965) identified that groups as typically passing through five stages of development.

1   *Forming*   As the members come together for the first time there may be uncertainty about the purpose of the group, what it is designed to achieve and by when. There may also be some ambiguity about how it will be structured and who will lead and be responsible for

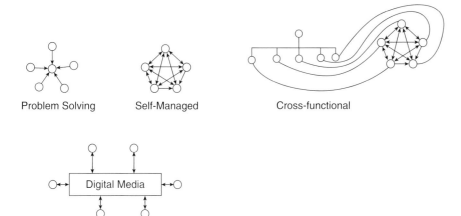

Figure 17.1 *Types of team*

its output. At this stage members learn how to interact with their peers and test what responses and behaviours are acceptable. As this becomes clearer, team members will conclude this phase by identifying themselves as a member of the group.

2 *Storming*   In this stage participants accept the existence of the group but begin to rail against the constraints it imposes. There may also be clashes of will as one or more members argue about who should lead the group and how it will be organized. When this phase is complete a hierarchy will emerge and the pattern of organisation will be clear.

3 *Norming*   In this stage members of the team will assimilate a common set of expectations about how the group will behave. Close relationships between group members will begin to develop and team members will experience a group identity and a degree of camaraderie. This stage closes when the norms of behaviour are fully assimilated.

4 *Performing*   As the name suggests groups in this phase are fully functional. Members are fully accepting of the structure and the roles they must fulfil. The focus is now firmly on task completion rather than getting to know one another.

5 *Adjourning*   Some work teams are set up for a short-term purpose such as arranging an event or conducting a particular campaign or appeal. When these tasks draw to a close the emphasis switches to concluding the activities and preparing for disbandment. Some group members may feel a high degree of satisfaction that the task is accomplished, while others may experience a sense of loss as the social interaction and camaraderie is lost.

The model appears to hold true for many different types of teams in a multitude of different situations, but there is some disagreement about when groups are at their most effective. It is generally accepted that groups become more effective as they progress through each of the first four stages, but not all groups follow this model. In some circumstances a degree of conflict can actually aid performance so some groups may be most effective at the storming phase (McGrew et al. 1999). This might be the case where a group has been formed to generate new fundraising ideas or think of new approaches. More progress may be made where people are still prepared to express honest opinions rather than adhere to group norms. Equally, some research has indicated that it is possible for groups to engage in multiple steps simultaneously and even to regress to a previous stage (George and Jessop 1997). Finally, the model has been criticized because it takes little account of context. Ginnett (1990) cites the example of flight crews who may meet only minutes before a departure and yet must immediately progress to the performing stage.

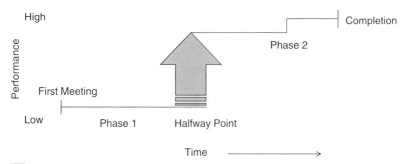

Figure 17.2 *The punctuated equilibrium model*

After all, most passengers would not be comfortable with the notion of their flight crews storming at around 30,000 feet! For most fundraising contexts, however, the model does provide a useful framework for managers and team leaders to reflect on the normal development of their teams.

That said, one of the more interesting strands of research on group dynamics has shown that certain types of teams can behave very differently (Gersick 1988). In the fundraising context some teams are formed for specific periods of time, perhaps to plan for an event or to develop a specific campaign. Temporary groups working to deadlines tend to conform to the 'punctuated equilibrium model' which is depicted in Figure 17.2. In this case, during their first meeting, the team will develop a framework of behavioural patterns and assumptions that defines how the problem or issues will be approached. These rules then guide the group for the first half of its life and are typically pretty rigidly interpreted. In other words, the group has a 'set' way of approaching the issue. A period of inertia follows when the group pursues this approach, even in the face of contradictory evidence suggesting that it may not be working. What is fascinating about Gersick's work is that teams exhibit a transition at the halfway point during their life and seemingly always at this point. It appears to make no difference that some teams come together for a matter of hours, while others may work together for months. It is as though teams working to deadlines experience a form of mid-life crisis, realizing that they are halfway through the allotted time, and then regroup and radically reshape their approach. The transition is thus characterized by a burst of changes and the adoption of new perspectives. In Phase 2 a new equilibrium emerges followed by a new period of inertia when the new approach is implemented. The group's last meeting is characterized by a final burst of activity to complete the activity or task. As we noted earlier, Seers and Woodruff (1997) stress that this model is limited to temporary task groups working under time constraints only.

IMPACT OF TEAM PROPERTIES ON PERFORMANCE

In arranging for a task to be completed (or a problem to be addressed) the first decision a fundraising manager may have to take is whether to leave responsibility for its completion to an individual or whether to create a group for this purpose. In situations where a breadth of expertise or problem-solving skill is required there may be little option but to assemble a group, but equally there are many situations where a genuine choice does exist. Many tasks can either be broken down into their component parts and handled by individuals *or* they can be tackled holistically by a group. In reaching this decision the evidence from research is that the very presence of other people can actually facilitate individual performance (Zajonc 1965). This is known as the *social facilitation effect* and arises in contexts where tasks are relatively straightforward and well rehearsed. Having other people around seems to act as a motivating factor. It is interesting to note that this social facilitation is pervasive across species. Even chickens and cockroaches appear to perform simple tasks better in the presence of others of their species (Vecchio 1991). By contrast, where tasks are complex and require a good deal of concentration, the presence of others can be a detriment. This is known as the *social inhibition effect*. Managers must therefore consider the nature of the work that must be accomplished and take their team versus individual decisions accordingly. Where teams are required a number of factors will drive their performance.

Group size

Groups of five to seven are commonly found in the workplace and it is argued that groups of this size can work well because there is enough scope to bring in a breadth of relevant expertise while avoiding some of the difficulties inherent in larger group sizes. Research tells us that larger groups can be cumbersome with more formalized 'rules' necessary to control the volume of participants and their contributions. These rules can slow down decision-making, lead to the isolation of some group members, or even lead to the creation of subgroups, some of which may not be fully committed to the task. Satisfaction can also be lower in larger groups as communication is less personal, social bonds are weaker and there are fewer opportunities to participate.

Composition

As we alluded to above, the composition of the group will also be an issue. Managers need to reflect on the skills a team will require and match the right individuals with the right skills to the appropriate team. Groups with a diverse range of skills tend to outperform teams that lack such diversity, at least in problem-solving situations (Shaw 1981). The key though is that all the selected skills, however diverse they might be, should be relevant to the task.

Roles

Managers must also consider the role(s) that each individual will be expected to play in the group/team situation. The word 'role' is used in this context to define the differentiated set of activities each participant will perform. Three categories of role exist

1   *Expected role*   This is the formal role as defined by managers, peers or current incumbents.
2   *Perceived role*   The set of activities the individual believes he/she is expected to perform, which may or may not conform to the 'expected' role.
3   *Enacted role*   The actual set of activities the individual performs.

Figure 17.3 presents the relationships between these concepts. The process begins with the setting of standards by managers and, if appropriate, peers and subordinates. These standards are then communicated to the individual. If the process of communication is imperfect, the individual will form a perception of their role that may differ from the expected standards. This can happen as a consequence of the individual receiving incomplete or partial information giving rise to *role ambiguity*. They can also receive conflicting messages from different managers or peers making it impossible for the post-holder to reconcile all the demands placed on them. This can lead to *role conflict*. Finally, as the role is enacted, the individual may have difficulty in fulfilling their perceived role if insufficient time and resources are available to complete the task.

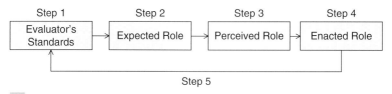

Figure 17.3 *A role episode*

Source: Adapted from Katz and Kahn (1978).
Reproduced with kind permission.

Evaluators will observe the enacted role and draw conclusions about the extent to which it meets the standards they have set. One iteration through the model is known as a role episode.

Opinions differ on the extent to which role ambiguity and role conflict should be regarded as undesirable and to be avoided. Robbins (1974) determined that moderate degrees of conflict and ambiguity can actually have positive effects. Jobs that lack these dimensions can be regarded as being bland and uninspiring. In the team context, managers or team leaders must therefore reflect on the level of guidance or rules that will be imposed. Some conflict may actually aid creativity and problem-solving and allow individuals to draw on strengths that may otherwise be constrained.

Team roles

We have thus far focused on individual expertise and the functional roles this might play in a team. These are all legitimate factors in deciding on team membership, but there are other considerations too. Notable here is the concept of a team role. While everyone brings work experience and expertise to the table, people also bring their favoured ways of behaving in a team setting. Some may like to take charge, while others focus on the completion of the task. Others will want to question the approach and look outside the team for further information and counsel. There will also be individuals who tend to be good at generating ideas, while perhaps being less competent at sifting the good from the bad, or seeing them through to completion. All these different roles are team roles.

A key researcher in this field, Dr Meredith Belbin, conducted numerous studies at Henley Management College in the UK over a period of nine years. His team studied the behaviour of managers from all over the world in a variety of team situations (Belbin 1981, 2003). Those participating in the study completed a battery of psychometric tests and were then placed in teams of varying composition to take part in a complex management exercise. Participants' core personality traits, intellectual styles and behaviours were assessed during the simulation. As the research progressed, different clusters of behaviour were identified. These were the team roles we refer to above. A summary of the roles identified by Belbin is provided in Exhibit 17.1. Individuals typically have a dominant team role that they 'prefer' to perform, with a secondary role that they could perform if called on to do so.

Belbin's work is highly significant since it tells us that the most effective teams tend to be those that comprise a mix of different team personalities. There is no such thing as a 'bad' or even a 'good' team personality. The strength lies in creating a balance. In seeking to optimize team performance, managers might thus decide membership on the basis of both the work and team roles an individual may be able to perform. There is a variety of different team personality assessment tools available but the Belbin team personalities have been developed with considerable rigour and shown to be good predictors of overall team performance (they can be found online at www.belbin.com).

EXHIBIT 17.1 BELBIN TEAM ROLES

Team-Role Descriptions

Team Role	Contribution	Allowable Weakness
Plant	Creative, imaginative, unorthodox. Solves difficult problems.	Ignores incidentals. Too pre-occupied to communicate effectively.
Resource Investigator	Extrovert, enthusiastic, communicative. Explores opportunities. Develops contacts.	Over-optimistic. Loses interest once initial enthusiasm has passed.
Co-ordinator	Mature, confident, a good chairperson. Clarifies goals, promotes decision-making, delegates well.	Can be seen as manipulative. Offloads personal work.
Shaper	Challenging, dynamic, thrives on pressure. The drive and courage to overcome obstacles.	Prone to provocation. Offends people's feelings.
Monitor Evaluator	Sober, strategic and discerning. Sees all options. Judges accurately.	Lacks drive and ability to inspire others.
Teamworker	Co-operative, mild, perceptive and diplomatic. Listens, builds, averts friction.	Indecisive in crunch situations.
Implementer	Disciplined, reliable, conservative and efficient. Turns ideas into practical actions.	Somewhat inflexible. Slow to respond to new possibilities.
Completer Finisher	Painstaking, conscientious, anxious. Searches out errors and omissions. Delivers on time.	Inclined to worry unduly. Reluctant to delegate.
Specialist	Single-minded, self-starting, dedicated. Provides knowledge and skills in rare supply.	Contributes on only a narrow front. Dwells on technicalities.

www.belbin.com © e-interplace, Belbin Associates, UK. 2001

This BELBIN® handout is the property of Belbin Associates, UK and protected by copyright, database, trademark and other intellectual property rights. You must retain all copyright and other proprietary notices contained on this original and on any copy you make. You may not sell or modify this handout. The use of this handout on any other Web site is prohibited. You agree not to adapt, translate, modify, decompile, disassemble, or reverse engineer the handout. 'BELBIN' is a registered trademark of BELBIN ASSOCIATES, UK.

Source: www.belbin.com © 2009 Reproduced by kind permission.

Cohesiveness

Cohesiveness is a key concept in team performance. It is defined as the degree to which members are attracted to each other and are motivated to stay in the group (Keyton and Springston 1990). Generally the greater the degree of cohesion the greater will be the performance of the team (Mullen and Cooper 1994) but the strength of this relationship depends on the performance

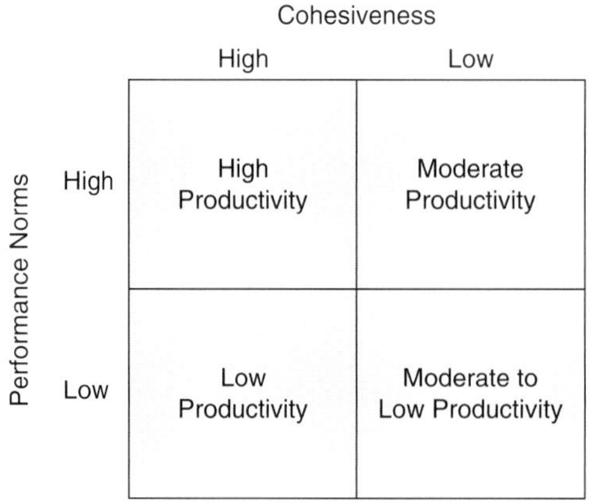

Figure 17.4 *Relationship between group cohesiveness, performance norms and productivity*

Source: Robbins and Judge (2007).
Reproduced with kind permission.

norms established by the group. Where norms are high a highly cohesive group will outperform a non-cohesive group, but where performance norms are low and cohesiveness high, productivity will be low. If the performance norms are low all participants will tend to follow this lead. These relationships are depicted in Figure 17.4

The capacity for enhanced productivity aside, cohesiveness confers other benefits:

- Members of cohesive teams tend to experience higher levels of satisfaction than teams that lack cohesion. Members gain value from the strength of their mutual bonds.
- Cohesive groups can generate a strong sense of shared identity or 'we-ness'. While this can be desirable it can also lead to hostility to other groups who may be in competition for resources. Cohesive groups can come to believe that they are in some sense 'superior'.
- Cohesion can also prove a significant barrier to change. It may be necessary for the group membership (or for the way it approaches its work) to change. This can be threatening as both can offer considerable utility to group members. As a consequence change can often be strongly resisted.

The link between performance and cohesion can outweigh many of these potential disadvantages. For this reason it is typically viewed as a desirable quality in teams. For managers seeking to build it, Gibson et al. (1994) suggest:

- *Making the group size smaller*   We have already talked about the optimum size of team for many tasks being around 5–7 individuals. For teams above this size a reduction in membership would make it easier for social bonds and communication to develop which in turn build cohesiveness.
- *Encouraging agreement on goals*   When individuals 'buy-in' to the desirability of achieving team goals they are likely to expend greater effort in making the team function. This too facilitates cohesion.
- *Increasing the time the team spends together*   This may seem a little obvious, but allowing the individuals space to foster interpersonal relationships is frequently a viable option.
- *Increasing the status of the team*   This has the impact of making membership more desirable. In the fundraising context this might be achieved by empowering the team to take more of its own decisions or enhancing the package of benefits available to participants.
- *Offering group rather than individual rewards*   This has the effect of increasing reliance on other group members for the attainment of desired outcomes, such as bonuses for the

achievement of a target. Increasing the inter-reliance of team members increases cohesion. People make more of an effort to work together because it is in their best interest to do so.

■ *Physically isolating the team*   Maximizing the amount of social contact the individual has with other members of their team and minimizing the amount of contact they may have with others will increase cohesion. For this reason (and to minimize distractions) many organizations plan 'retreats' into the schedule for specific teams, where they can meet outside of the normal work environment and bond as a team.

GROUP DECISION-MAKING

Individual versus group

As we have already highlighted, the quality of decision-making by groups can be superior to that of individuals. Involving a greater number of people in decision-making makes it possible to draw on more complete information and knowledge. A wider and more diverse range of possible solutions will be considered and the very act of involving individuals can often achieve a much higher degree of 'buy-in' to the conclusions drawn.

There are of course some negatives too. Groups take time to assemble and while these individuals are working as a group there is an opportunity cost as they will not be engaged in completing their usual roles and responsibilities. Some groups can be dominated by one or two strong personalities who control and shape the discussion, making it difficult for everyone to express a view, particularly dissent. It may also not be clear who has ultimate responsibility for the consequences of the group's actions or decisions which can in turn drive greater risk-taking behaviour because of the loss of accountability.

Whether to opt for individual or group decision-making is therefore a tough issue for managers to address. On balance, the right choice probably depends on the management objectives. If he/she is looking for accuracy then a group decision is probably superior because of the wider range of views that will be taken into consideration. Gigone and Hastie (1997) caution, however, that while the team decision may generally be more accurate it will be less accurate than the view of the most accurate group member. If speed is a primary consideration individual decision-making will be preferred, while if creativity or securing 'buy-in' are more significant issues, then opting for a group decision is a better way to go (Swap 1984).

Groupthink

Where groups are selected to take decisions, management need to be aware of the capacity for groups to develop what Janis (1972) referred to as *groupthink*. It arises as a consequence of the norms of behaviour that are generated as the group dynamic evolves. These norms can create a degree of pressure for conformity which can hinder or even deter the consideration of unusual or conflicting views. Janis identified eight symptoms of groupthink:

1 *An illusion of invulnerability*   The group can come to view itself as having greater control over the consequences of its actions than is actually the case. This enhanced level of confidence can drive groups to make much riskier decisions than individual managers.
2 *Rationalization*   The group's norms can become so powerful that members tend to discredit any information or evidence that conflicts with the consensus view of the group. The focus shifts to deliberately seeking information that reinforces this view and ignoring any alternative data or signals.

3 *Negative stereotyping*   Flows from (2) above. Groups can begin to view others who threaten their views in a stereotypical way ('They don't agree with us, but that's because they are in competition with us for resources. We'd expect them to say that, wouldn't we?').

4 *Assumption of morality*   Groups can come to view themselves as highly ethical while they see others as inherently immoral. In groupthink situations groups can be led to morally questionable decisions which they justify by reference to a higher moral ideal (e.g. 'We must take this approach so we can meet all the needs of our beneficiaries').

5 *Pressure to conform*   The group exerts a powerful influence on its membership to conform to the consensus view. It becomes increasingly difficult, even for those members who may have concerns, to express a dissenting opinion. Rather than create conflict they accede to the dominant view.

6 *Self-censorship*   Allied to the above, each member may carefully begin to monitor their own contributions, checking them against the consensus view and filtering out anything that might be regarded as 'disloyal' or 'inappropriate'.

7 *An illusion of unanimity*   The strength of the behavioural norms is such that any reservations members might have are stifled. This creates the impression of unanimous endorsement of the group approach or decisions when in reality a number of individuals may disagree.

8 *Mindguards*   These can be thought of as the mental equivalent of bodyguards. Instead of guarding the person, individuals acting as mindguards protect the group leadership from dissenting perspectives. They act to deflect objections or to bury information that might challenge the current perspective.

Groupthink therefore poses a significant challenge to management, particularly in the case of groups where there is a high degree of cohesion. In a sense cohesion can breed groupthink, so steps need to be taken to minimize the risk of this phenomenon developing. Team leaders need to take steps such as deliberately encouraging dissenting views, actively assigning individuals to seek out challenging perspectives and allowing relevant experts from outside the team to sit in and offer their input. There are also procedural safeguards that might be put in place, such as creating a formal 'space' when a last chance to raise any doubts can be given to all participants.

Group decision-making techniques

Robbins and Judge (2007) identify four approaches to group decision-making:

1 *Interacting groups*   These are by far the most common. Groups of various sizes come together face to face and engage in verbal and non-verbal communication as they work to reach a decision. While commonplace these groups can often be subject to groupthink and can censor creative or radical alternatives as a consequence.

2 *Brainstorming*   Here the group leader states a problem and then participants are invited to contribute any and all solutions they can see. No criticism is permitted at this stage and all the alternatives are recorded, perhaps on a whiteboard or flipchart for later discussion. When every contribution has been secured the group then works down through the suggestions, evaluating the alternatives and discussing them until a consensus view is achieved.

3 *Nominal group technique*   This similarities to brainstorming but restricts discussion during the decision-making process, hence the term nominal. When these groups meet each member writes down their ideas on the problem. After this silent period each group

member presents one idea to the group. There is still no discussion but as previously the ideas are recorded. When all the ideas have been presented the group discusses each idea and evaluates them. Each group member then silently rank-orders all the ideas they have heard. The idea that emerges with the highest ranking is the final decision. Research has indicated that groups of this nature tend to outperform brainstorming groups (Faure 2004).

4   *Electronic meeting*   These are proving increasingly popular as organizations continue to embrace modern technology. In this case the group sits around in a horseshoe shape facing a screen and are equipped with a PC or laptop. As the issues are presented participants are invited to enter their views via their keyboard. They appear on screen but are anonymized so that no one is aware of the original author. Proponents of the method argue that this leads to greater levels of honesty in response as even unpopular views can be articulated. It is also argued that the method can speed up decision-making as there is no opportunity for the social loafing that might otherwise take place in groups. Studies, however, have shown that electronic meetings may actually be less effective, take up more time and result in reduced participant satisfaction (Baltes et al. 2002).

LEADERSHIP

In this section of the text we move on to consider the issue of leadership. Fundraisers at all levels within an organization, whether they be salaried or working as volunteers, will encounter a variety of group situations and may be called on to manage one as part of their role. It is therefore imperative that they reflect on their individual strengths and weaknesses as a leader and on what behaviours or characteristics might make them more effective in this role. To this end we will consider a wide range of different perspectives on leadership, beginning as always with a definition.

For us, leadership is a process by which an individual guides others towards the achievement of an objective. It is therefore best thought of as an influencing process. While in some circumstances a leader may have to resort to coercion, successful leaders avoid this, exerting incremental influence beyond the formal authority bestowed on them by the organisation. Over the past century many thousands of studies have been conducted into what constitutes leadership and the factors that drive success in this role. A useful summary of this work is provided by Bass (1990a:19).

> The earlier definitions identified leadership as a focus of group process and movement, personality in action. The next type considered it as the art of inducing compliance. The more recent definitions conceive leadership in terms of influence relationships, power differentials, persuasion, influence on goal achievement, role differentiation, reinforcement, initiation of structure and perceived attributions of behaviour that are consistent with what the perceivers believe leadership to be. Leadership may involve all these things.

The balance of this chapter will consider each of these perspectives in turn, beginning with trait theory.

Trait theory

In the early half of the twentieth century researchers sought to understand leadership by comparing the characteristics or traits of effective leaders with ineffective leaders. This seemed a legitimate approach as it is quite intuitive that leaders would share common characteristics that

Table 17.1 *Commonly identified attributes of successful leaders*

Traits	Skills
■ Adaptable to situations	■ Clever (intelligent)
■ Alert to social environment	■ Conceptually skilled
■ Ambitious and achievement-orientated	■ Creative
■ Assertive	■ Diplomatic and tactful
■ Cooperative	■ Fluent in speaking
■ Decisive	■ Knowledgeable about group task
■ Dependable	■ Organized (administrative ability)
■ Dominant (desire to influence others)	■ Persuasive
■ Energetic (high activity level)	■ Socially skilled
■ Persistent	
■ Self-confident	
■ Tolerant of stress	
■ Willing to assume responsibility	

would make them perform well in this role. It followed that if other people could also be found with these traits, then they, too, could also become great leaders. Ralph Stogdill (1948) published a now seminal review of this material. What was fascinating in his review and devastating for the scientific community at the time was that the numerous studies he examined failed to paint a consistent picture and their findings were frequently at odds with one another. Thirty years of research had actually achieved very little.

That said, the work on traits should not be entirely discounted. In a later review Stogdill (1975) was able to outline a number of traits that seemed to emerge more frequently from the literature. These are illustrated in Table 17.1. In interpreting these results though, it is important to realize that the desirability of many of these characteristics may actually depend on the context.

More recently McCall and Lombardo (1983) have examined instances of success and failure and identified four primary traits by which leaders could succeed or 'derail':

1 *Emotional stability and composure*   Calm, confident and predictable, particularly when under stress.
2 *Admitting error*   Owning up to mistakes, rather than putting energy into covering up.
3 *Good interpersonal skills*   Able to communicate and persuade others without resort to negative or coercive tactics.
4 *Intellectual breadth*   Able to understand a wide range of areas, rather than having a narrow (and narrow-minded) area of expertise.

Behavioural theories

The failure of trait theory in the 1940s to explain variation in leadership performance led researchers to focus on a different facet of leadership, namely the behaviours exhibited by successful leaders. There was considerable interest in this field in the 1960s because if appropriate behaviours could be identified this suggested that instead of identifying individuals with the right traits to become managers, organisations could actually train the individuals they wanted to promote to provide them with the requisite skills.

An example of the behavioural approach is depicted in Figure 17.5. It is developed from work conducted at the University of Michigan's Survey Research Center. The team there came up with

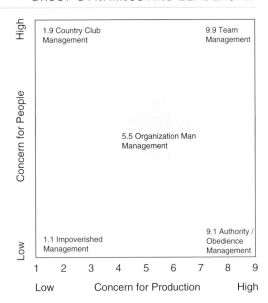

Figure 17.5
The managerial grid

Source: Blake and Mouton (1978:11).
Reproduced with kind permission.

two dimensions of leadership behaviour that appeared key in predicting performance: employee oriented and production oriented. The former tend to emphasize the importance of interpersonal relationships in achieving the tasks of the organization, while the latter focus on the technical nature of the tasks and task completion itself. Blake and Mouton (1978) developed this idea into the managerial grid. They depicted nine positions on two axes which together create 81 different positions in which a particular leader's style may fall.

- *Impoverished management* Minimum effort to get the work done. A basically lazy approach that avoids as much work as possible.
- *Authority compliance* Strong focus on task, but with little concern for people. Focus on efficiency, including the elimination of people wherever possible.
- *Country Club management* Care and concern for the people, with a comfortable and friendly environment and collegial style. But a low focus on task may obtain questionable results.
- *Man management* A weak balance of focus on both people and the work. Doing enough to get things done, but not pushing the boundaries of what may be possible.
- *Team management* Paying strong attention to both dimensions. As a consequence people are committed to the task and the leader is committed to her people (as well as the task).

The authors regarded the 9.9 team management approach as the optimal for a leader to adopt. While this is a clear advance on trait theory, to modern eyes this too seems overly simplistic. The focus on just two dimensions is difficult to justify and the prescriptions take no account of the environment in which the leader is operating.

Contingency theory

Contingency theory offers a more plausible perspective on leadership. As the name suggests it posits that the desirable approach that a leader might have will vary by context. Thus under condition A, style Y might be appropriate, while in condition B, style X would be more appropriate.

A consequence of this is that leaders who are very effective at one place and time may become unsuccessful either when transplanted to another situation or when the factors around them change. This helps to explain how some leaders who seem highly successful for a while then appear to go off the boil and make very unsuccessful decisions.

Fred Fiedler (1967) was the first author to develop a comprehensive contingency model for leadership. His approach was to generate a 'least preferred co-worker' (LPC) score for leaders by asking them to think of a person they have worked with, that they would least like to work with again, and then to score that person on a scale of one to eight for each of a set of 16 contrasting adjectives, for example:

Pleasant 8 7 6 5 4 3 2 1 Unpleasant
Helpful 8 7 6 5 4 3 2 1 Unhelpful
Warm 8 7 6 5 4 3 2 1 Cold

Fiedler believes that based on the pattern of responses an individual gives he can determine their basic leadership styles. If the least preferred co-worker is defined in relatively positive terms (a high LPC score) then the individual is interested in pursuing good personal relations with co-workers. In other words, if you were to describe your least favoured co-worker in favourable terms, Fieldler would regard you as 'relationship-oriented'. By contrast, if your least preferred co-worker was described in relatively unfavourable terms, you would be deemed to be most interested in productivity and labelled 'task-oriented'. As a technical note, Shiflett (1981) identified that around 16 per cent of individuals will score somewhere in the middle range and thus not be classifiable. The discussion below thus pertains to the remaining 84 per cent who can be identified as being either high or low.

The next step in adopting the Fiedler model is to evaluate the situation in which the leader will be operating. There are three contingency dimensions that Fiedler believes adequately define the leadership context

1 *Leader-member relations* The extent to which the leader is accepted and generates positive emotional reactions from their subordinates. A situation in which leader member relations are relatively good is potentially much easier to manage than a situation in which such relations are strained.
2 *Task structure* The extent to which the tasks can be clearly specified. In a situation with a high degree of task structure this will be evident in job descriptions, policies, etc. In addition goals will be clear and performance measures easily understood. Multiple solutions are unlikely to exist. In situations with low task structure the converse will be true.
3 *Leader's position-power* The extent to which the leader has authority to assess follower performance and give reward or punishment. Other things being equal, situations in which a leader has position-power will be easier to manage than situations where such power is lacking.

Combining these situational variables generates the eight possible combinations, or octants, depicted in Figure 17.6. Fielder predicts that in a category 1, 2, 3, 7 or 8 situation task-oriented leaders will perform better. Relationship-oriented leaders will perform in moderately favourable situations: categories 4 to 6.

So do these ideas help us think through voluntary sector management? In short, yes. The model suggests that we could appraise the leadership context and then select a leader with the style most

#	Leader–member relations	Task structure	Leader's position-power	Most effective leader
1	Good	Structured	Strong	Task oriented
2	Good	Structured	Weak	Task oriented
3	Good	Unstructured	Strong	Task oriented
4	Good	Unstructured	Weak	Relationship oriented
5	Poor	Structured	Strong	Relationship oriented
6	Poor	Structured	Weak	Relationship oriented
7	Poor	Unstructured	Strong	Task oriented
8	Poor	Unstructured	Weak	Task oriented

Figure 17.6 *Conclusions from the Fielder model*

appropriate to that context. Equally, we could take the alternative approach, identifying the orientation of the leader and adapting the context to maximize their impact (e.g. by introducing more or less structure to the tasks).

Another approach has been proposed by Paul Hersey and Ken Blanchard (1974, 2001). In contrast to Fiedler's contingency leadership model and its underlying assumption that leadership style is hard to change, the Hersey-Blanchard situational leadership model suggests that successful leaders can and do adjust their styles to fit the needs of their subordinates or 'followers'. For Hersey and Blanchard the key issue in making these adjustments is follower 'maturity' or their 'readiness' to perform in a given situation. Readiness is in turn based on two major factors – follower ability and follower confidence. These ideas are depicted in Figure 17.7.

As we have previously indicated, the model is based on the assumption that managers can change the emphasis in their approach between a focus on relationships and a focus on tasks. These variations will allow the leader to cope with different levels of follower maturity by adopting one of four management styles.

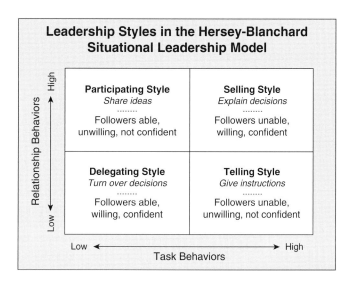

Figure 17.7 *Leadership styles in the Hersey–Blanchard situational leadership model*

1   *Delegating style*   Allowing the group to take responsibility for task decisions. This is a low-task, low-relationship style and is most appropriate where followers are able, willing and competent to perform their roles. The style is one of turning over decisions to followers who have high task readiness based on abilities, willingness and confidence about task accomplishment.

2   *Participating style*   Emphasizes the sharing of ideas and engagement in participative decision-making. This is a low-task, high-relationship style and will be most effective where followers are able but not confident. As you might expect, this participation style with its emphasis on relationships is supposed to help followers share ideas and thus draw forth understanding and task confidence.

3   *Selling style*   Explaining task directions in a supportive and persuasive way. This is a high-task, high-relationship style and is most appropriate where followers lack capability but are willing or confident about the task. In this case, the selling style and its emphasis on task guidance is designed to facilitate performance through persuasive explanation.

4   *Telling style*   Giving specific task directions and closely supervising work. This is a high-task, low-relationship style and will be appropriate to situations where followers are unable, unwilling and not confident of their ability to complete the task. It works by giving instructions and bringing structure to a situation thus enhancing confidence.

Hersey and Blanchard believe that leaders should be flexible and adjust their styles as followers and situations change over time. The model also implies that if the correct styles are used in lower-readiness situations, followers will mature and grow in their abilities and confidence. This willingness to understand follower development and respond with flexibility allows the leader to become less directive as followers mature.

The Hersey-Blanchard situational leadership model is intuitively appealing and has been widely used in management development programmes. Even though empirical research support has been limited, the conclusion seems to be that the basic ideas of the model have merit. Leaders would do well to consider altering styles to achieve the best fits with followers and situations, reviewing these as circumstances change over time. Also, the model reminds leaders that the skill levels and task confidence of followers should be given continuing attention through training and development efforts (Graeff 1983; Yukl 2006).

CONTEMPORARY LEADERSHIP THEORIES

Charismatic leadership

During the 1980s the focus in leadership shifted to the topics of charisma and how organizations achieve global competitiveness. In the original Greek charisma means a divinely inspired gift such as being able to foretell the future or perform a miracle. Its meaning in the context of leadership is rather more mundane and refers to a form of social influence based on how followers see a leader. Conger and Kanungo (1998) identify four characteristics of charismatic leaders.

1   *Vision and articulation*   They have a vision or idealized goal for the future and can communicate this vision in a way that others can easily understand and buy-in to.

2   *Personal risk*   Charismatic leaders are willing to take on a high level of personal risk. They are willing to put their reputation on the line to achieve their goals and will be seen to be an active player in the team.

3   *Sensitivity to follower needs*   They are highly perceptive individuals with an ability to sense the needs of others and respond to them with genuine sensitivity.
4   *Unconventional behaviour*   Charismatic behaviours are viewed by their followers as behaving in some way out of the ordinary.

There can be little doubt that fortunate individuals can inherit charisma and thus an ability to lead. Thankfully there is also evidence that individuals can be trained to project an aura of charisma by using passion to engender enthusiasm in others, communicating with their whole body, working hard on their relationships with others and reflecting on the aspirational and emotional needs of others. In a fascinating experiment Howell and Frost (1989) were able to train undergraduate business students to appear charismatic to their peers. We can thus conclude that while not everyone may be born with natural charisma, leadership training can and does have an impact.

Research generally supports the notion that charismatic leadership has a positive impact on an organization, particularly where the work environment involves a high degree of stress and uncertainty (House 1977). Individuals working for a charismatic leader tend to exert more effort in the completion of their tasks because they like the leader and want to see him or her succeed. They are also likely to experience higher levels of personal job satisfaction (House 1996).

There are dangers, however, and charismatic leadership can become problematic when the boundaries between the individual and the organization begin to blur. Self-interest and personal goals can begin to override what is actually in the best interests of the organization. A high level of charisma can also give rise to a reluctance to express dissenting views in the workplace. Followers are actively motivated not to appear disloyal, either to the leader or to their peers.

Transformational leadership

The final strand of leadership research that we will examine in this text concerns what is known as transformational leadership. The previous models we have outlined have concerned what might be termed *transactional leaders*, in other words individuals who focus on motivating their followers to achieve the necessary tasks and in so doing achieve their own personal goals, salary, bonuses, recognition and so on. By contrast, transformational leaders inspire their followers to look beyond their own self-interests for the greater good of the organization. This category of leader is therefore capable of having a profound effect on organizational performance. The differences between transactional and transformational leadership are summarized in Figure 17.8.

In interpreting the figure it is important not to see the two approaches as mutually exclusive. Bass's idea is that the most high-performing managers will exhibit the characteristics of both and should thus be capable of both transactional and transformational approaches. Bass (1990a) proposed a framework for analysing these leadership perspectives (see Figure 17.9). This is depicted in Figure 17.9 and is known as the full range of leadership model. Managers become progressively more effective as they work their way up the hierarchy. This differs from Figure 17.8 only in so much as Bass is recognizing here that some leaders can be completely ineffective by virtue of failing to intervene where necessary and taking responsibility for the actions of their followers. The initial step on the ladder is thus a failure in management. Good leaders avoid these errors, accomplish the managerial functions of structuring the work environment as efficiently as possible (sometimes by delegation in senior positions) and spend as much time as possible on the transformational aspects of their role.

Transactional Leader

Contingent Reward: Contracts exchange of rewards for effort, promises rewards for good performance, recognizes accomplishments.

Management by Exception (active): Watches and searches for deviations from rules and standards, takes correct action.

Management by Exception (passive): Intervenes only if standards are not met.

Laissez-Faire: Abdicates responsibilities, avoids making decisions.

Transformational Leader

Idealized Influence: Provides vision and sense of mission, instills pride, gains respect and trust.

Inspirational Motivation: Communicates high expectations, uses symbols to focus efforts, expresses important purposes in simple ways.

Intellectual Stimulation: Promotes intelligence, rationality, and careful problem solving.

Individualized Consideration: Gives personal attention, treats each employee individually, coaches, advises.

Figure 17.8 *Transactional vs. transformational leaders*

Source: From Bass (1990b: 22). Reprinted by permission of the publisher, American Management Association, New York.

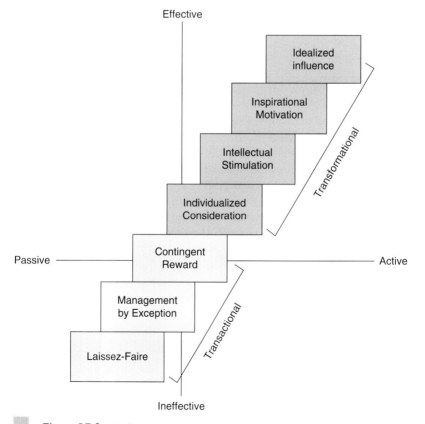

Figure 17.9 *The full range of leadership model*

SUMMARY

In this chapter we have examined the nature of teams and explored when and how teams should be constructed. We have also looked at how the performance of teams can be optimized, by considering issues such as group size, work roles, team roles and group cohesiveness. We have also looked at some of the pitfalls to avoid in group decision-making, notably the concept of groupthink. All these issues are relevant to fundraisers managing or taking part in work teams. Readers should now be in a position to critique the current approach adopted by their organizations and to suggest relevant improvements.

We have also examined the topic of leadership, providing an overview of key theoretical frameworks and ideas. As the reader will by now appreciate there are many perspectives on what constitutes effective leadership and the factors that lead to this success. While we have no easy solutions for someone wishing to improve their leadership skills and as a result the performance of their teams, we can offer some hope in that leadership skills, like many other aspects of management, can be effectively developed through training. They can also benefit from personal reflection on the level of fit between the approach currently being adopted and the circumstances faced by the team. Contingency theory and Bass's full range of leadership model, in particular, provide much food for thought. In common with Bass we adhere to the belief that individuals are capable of adapting their style to fit the situation and the academic literature is therefore helpful because it suggests what changes, in particular circumstances, would be likely to enhance performance.

DISCUSSION QUESTIONS

1   You have been asked to put together a team to originate and manage a capital campaign for your organization. How would you proceed to assemble your team? Who would comprise it? Why would you select these individuals?
2   What is groupthink? Have there been circumstances where you have witnessed this behaviour in a team? What actions might have been taken to avoid this?
3   'Good leaders are born not made.' Using your knowledge of leadership theory, critically evaluate this statement.
4   Pick an individual that you consider to be an outstanding leader. What is it about this individual that you believe makes this individual so successful? How does this gel with the theories presented in this chapter.
5   How might you operationalize the Fieldler model in the context of your fundraising team?
6   Critically evaluate your own approach to leadership. In the light of your reading, how might you adapt your style to better suit the context faced by your team?

REFERENCES

Baltes, B.B., Dickson, M.W., Sherman, M.P., Bauer, C.C. and LaGanke, J. (2002) 'Computer Mediated Communication and Group Decision Making: A Meta Analysis', *Organizational Behavior and Human Decision Processes*, January: 156–179.

Bass, B.M. (1990a) *Bass and Stogdill's Handbook of Leadership*: *Theory, Research and Managerial Applications*, 3rd edn, Free Press, New York.

Bass, B.M. (1990b) 'From Transactional to Transformational Leadership: Learning to Share the Vision', *Organizational Dynamics*, Winter: 22.

Bass, B.M. (1993) 'Transformational Leadership: A Response to Critiques', in M.M. Chemers and R. Ayman (eds) *Leadership Theory and Research*: *Perspectives and Directions*, Academic Press, San Diego, CA.

Belbin, M. (1981) *Management Teams*: *Why They Succeed or Fail*, Butterworth Heinemann, London.

Belbin, M. (2003) *Management Teams*: *Why They Succeed or Fail*, 2nd edn, Butterworth Heinemann, London.

Blake, R.R. and Mouton, J.S. (1961) *Group Dynamics – Key to Decision Making*, Gulf Publishing, Houston, TX.

Blake, R.R. and Mouton, J.S. (1978) *The New Managerial Grid*, Gulf Publishing, Houston, TX.

Conger, J.A. and Kanungo, R.N. (1998) *Charismatic Leadership in Organizations*, Sage, Thousand Oaks, CA.

Faure, C. (2004) 'Beyond Brainstorming: Effects of Different Group Procedures on Selection Ideas and Satisfaction with the Process', *Journal of Creative Behavior*, 38: 13–34.

Fiedler, F.E. (1967) *A Theory of Leadership Effectiveness*, McGraw-Hill, New York.

George, J.F. and Jessup, L.M. (1997) 'Groups Over Time: What Are We Really Studying?' *International Journal of Human-Computer Studies*, 47(3): 497–511.

Gersick, C.J.G. (1988) 'Time and Transition in Work Teams: Toward A New Model of Group Development', *Academy of Management Journal*, March: 9–41.

Gibson, J.L., Ivancevich, J.M. and Donnelly, J.H. (1994) *Organizations*, 8th edn, Irwin, Burr Ridge, IL.

Gigone, D. and Hastie, R. (1997) 'Proper Analysis of the Accuracy of Group Judgements', *Psychological Bulletin*, January: 149–167.

Ginnett, R.C. (1990) 'The Airline Cockpit Crew', in J.R. Hackman (ed.) *Groups That Work (and Those That Don't)*, Jossey Bass, San Francisco, CA.

Graeff, C.L. (1983) 'The Situational Leadership Theory: A Critical View', *Academy of Management Review*, 8: 285–291.

Hersey, P. and Blanchard, K.H. (1974) 'So You Want to Know Your Leadership Style?' *Training and Development Journal*, February: 1–15.

Hersey, P. and Blanchard, K.H (2001) *Management of Organizational Behavior: Leading Human Resources*, 8th edn, Prentice Hall, Upper Saddle River, NJ.

House, R.J. (1977) 'A 1976 Theory of Charismatic Leadership', in J.G. Hunt and L.L. Larson (eds) *Leadership*: *The Cutting Edge*, Southern Illinois University Press, Carbondale, IL.

House, R.J. (1996) 'Path Goal Theory of Leadership: Lessons, Legacy and a Reformulated Theory', *Leadership Quarterly*, 7(3): 323–352.

Howell, J.M. and Frost, P.J. (1989) 'A Laboratory Study of Charismatic Leadership', *Organizational Behavior and Organizational Decision Processes*, April: 243–269.

Janis, I.L. (1972) *Groupthink*, Houghton Mifflin, Boston, MA.

Katz, D. and Kahn, R. (1978) *The Social Psychology of Organizations*, Wiley, New York.

Keyton, J. and Springston, J. (1990) 'Redefining Cohesiveness in Groups', *Small Group Research*, May: 234–254.

McCall, M.W. Jr. and Lombardo, M.M. (1983) *Off the Track*: *Why and How Successful Executives Get Derailed*, Centre for Creative Leadership, Greenboro, NC.

McGrew, J.F., Bilotta, J.G. and Deeney, J.M. (1999) 'Software Team Formation and Decay: Extending the Standard Model for Small Groups', *Small Group Research*, 30(2): 209–234.

Mullen, B. and Cooper, C. (1994) 'The Relation Between Group Cohesiveness and Performance: An Integration', *Psychological Bulletin*, March: 210–227.

Robbins, S.P. (1974) *Managing Organizational Conflict*, Prentice Hall, Englewood Cliffs, NJ.

Robbins, S.P. and Judge, T.A. (2007) *Organizational Behavior*, Prentice Hall, Upper Saddle River, NJ.

Sayles, L.R. (1957) 'Work Group Behavior and the Larger Organization', in C. Arensburg (ed.) *Research in Industrial Relations*, Harper and Row, New York.

Seers, A. and Woodruff, S. (1997) 'Temporal Pacing in Task Forces: Group Development or Deadline Pressure', *Journal of Management*, 23(2): 169–187.

Shaw, M.E. (1981) *Group Dynamics*, 3rd edn, McGraw Hill, New York.

Shiflett, S. (1981) 'Is There a Problem with the LPC Score in LEADER MATCH?' *Personnel Psychology*, Winter: 765–769.

Stogdill, R.M. (1948) 'Personal Factors Associated With Leadership: A Survey of the Literature', *Journal of Psychology*, 25: 35–71.

Stogdill, R.M. (1975) *Handbook of Leadership: A Survey of the Literature*, Free Press, New York.

Swap, W. (1984) *Group Decision Making*, Sage, Newbury Park, CA.

Tuckman, B.W. (1965) 'Developmental Sequences in Small Groups', *Psychological Bulletin*, June: 384–399.

Vecchio, R.P. (1991) *Organizational Behavior*, 2nd edn, Dryden Press, Orlando, FL.

Yukl, G. (2006) *Leadership in Organizations*, 6th edn, Pearson, Upper Saddle River, NJ.

Zajonc, R.B. (1965) 'Social Facilitation', *Science*, 149: 269–274.

Chapter 18

Legal and ethical aspects of fundraising management

OBJECTIVES

By the end of this chapter you should be able to:

- Understand the legislative framework that impacts on fundraising.
- Describe the principles of data protection.
- Describe the requirements for legal/ethical charity advertising.
- Describe other aspects of legislation pertinent to the UK.
- Understand key ethical issues associated with fundraising practice.
- Understand the rationale for codes of ethics and professional practice developed by professional fundraising bodies.

INTRODUCTION

Pick up a copy of any leading voluntary sector journal and you will inevitably find references to nonprofits that have been felt to have acted inappropriately. Sometimes these actions may have been taken in violation of some legal requirement, but more frequently organizations are accused of behaving unethically, perhaps taking funds from a corporate donor with ties to dubious business practices in the Third World, or producing fundraising communications that are felt to be overtly shocking or even downright offensive.

Of course journalists writing for these media have a vested interest in highlighting what they perceive to be breaches of professional ethics or even fundraising law, since intense levels of public interest and concern mean that such 'bad' news makes great copy that sells the journal or newspaper. While the voluntary sector contributes only a small proportion of GDP, it commands a high moral profile leading to a disproportionate amount of media scrutiny and coverage.

Of course this is not necessarily a bad thing, since the agency role that nonprofits play in dispersing funds donated by one group of individuals for the benefit of another requires that there be a high degree of public trust. Donors, who typically have no direct way of assessing how their funds are being used, must rely on their trust in the organization to reflect their wishes and to honour their obligations.

Managing public perceptions of the sector should thus be of immense concern to professional fundraisers. While they may exert little influence on the activities of other organizations they can at least ensure that their own professional practice reflects the highest possible legal and ethical standards.

In this final chapter we review these obligations and discuss the key facets of legislation that fundraisers in the UK should be aware of. This legislation in effect sets the minimum standards that should be achieved in fundraising, but in no sense should be seen as reflecting desirable standards in each case. The law frequently says nothing about what most individuals would regard as a good professional standard likely to engender genuine levels of trust in voluntary organizations. It is this grey area between the minimum and desirable standards that is the domain of fundraising ethics and we deal with a number of key ethical issues, together with professional codes of conduct, later in this chapter.

One final word of warning. This is not a textbook on the law, it is a fundraising textbook. In the space of one chapter it is impossible to do justice to the full range of legislation that can impact on fundraisers. Instead we highlight a number of the key legal issues fundraisers should take account of, providing an overview in each case. There are many nuances in this complex domain and regulations change on a regular basis. Readers faced with a particular issue are strongly advised to conduct follow-up reading (perhaps using some of the sources we mention) and/or to seek professional advice and guidance.

It must also be recognized that the law varies greatly from country to country. Even within the UK there are often different rules for the different countries that comprise the union. In this chapter we shall focus on the law of England and Wales, noting that in most cases similar rules will apply to Scotland and Northern Ireland. The Institute of Fundraising *Codes of Fundraising Practice* are an excellent source of information on the law in each country. They should be regarded as the primary source of information in this domain.

For readers of this text outside the UK, approaches to the regulation of fundraising will obviously vary greatly, but this chapter should still add value as many of the issues we discuss here have resonance across the globe. Data protection and consumer privacy, the extent to which charities may trade, and the management of professional fundraisers are of general interest and concern.

DATA PROTECTION AND PRIVACY ISSUES

One of the most pressing and topical issues in fundraising is the question of donor privacy. The ever-reducing costs associated with owning and managing computing and data-processing power have brought database technology within the affordable price range of even the smallest nonprofits. In the early years, much of what one could store on a database and the uses to which this might be put were unregulated. There have been numerous instances where personal data have been collected, stored and passed to third parties, resulting over time in some individuals being deluged with marketing and fundraising communications. This has impacted severely on the public trust and many charities have been criticized for failing to take account of legitimate demands for privacy in their various campaigns. Consumers and hence donors are no longer happy for organizations to store and manipulate personal information and utilize this for the purposes of marketing and fundraising.

Of course, it is very often commercial organizations and not nonprofits that are the worst offenders. The overwhelming majority of nonprofits have always acted responsibly and in a manner consistent with their overall ethos and mission. Nevertheless some commercial enterprises have given the whole direct marketing industry a bad name, by sending out high-volume poorly targeted communications which simply irritate consumers and by refusing to accede to legitimate demands to curtail their activities. It is interesting to note that at the time of writing this is particularly the case for so called Spam e-mails which now account for over 50 per cent of the communications traffic initiated over the Internet and are a cause of enormous consumer indignation.

Inevitably, when faced with what they regard as industry malpractice, politicians and legislators feel the need for intervention and will ultimately take steps to compel offenders to act in a more responsible way. What this means in practice is that many nonprofits find themselves faced with new swathes of legislation designed to protect the public from sharp commercial practices. Nonprofits get caught up in the backlash against certain forms of marketing activity.

Data protection

In the European Union the community of nations has recently enacted data protection legislation that offers new rights to consumers irrespective of the country in which they live. These rights and hence the law have been interpreted slightly differently from one European nation to another, but the rules share a range of common features.

The Data Protection Act 1988 was designed to bring the UK's regulatory framework into line with that now required by European regulations. It applies much more stringent controls over the use of personal data than was previously the case. Under the new Act all personal data (i.e. held about a particular individual) are now caught under the legislation. All organizations holding such data must register under the Act with the Data Commissioner and ensure that they follow the letter of the law in dealing with such personal data. Interestingly the new Act contains provisions for both data stored on a computer in electronic format *and* data stored in other hard copy formats which would include paper files, notebooks and so on. Thus fundraisers involved in the solicitation of major gifts will, for example, find that the notes they make about each donor or prospect will now be caught under the Act. This is highly significant since under the Act anyone who has their personal data stored by a third party (a nonprofit) now has a number of specific rights

- They may request the data controller (i.e. the individual managing the data in a nonprofit) to supply a brief description of the personal data held, the purposes for which they are being held and the recipients to whom they are or may be disclosed.
- They may also request a copy of the personal data held and any information that might be available to the data controller in respect of how those data were acquired. This applies to all personal data irrespective of format and hence fundraisers must be aware that donors could conceivably request all the data the organization holds on them. This has the potential to be embarrassing if records are not strictly controlled, since in the authors' experience, fundraisers often record their own views on the individual, which may on occasion be unflattering!
- They may opt out of receiving further communications (see below) and charities must then 'delete' the individual from their records. In practice the individual's name and contact details will actually still be held on file to ensure that this obligation is met. Nonprofits will need to ensure that should his/her name appear on any cold recruitment lists the organization might purchase that this is recognized and that the individual's wish not to receive further communication is still respected. This could not happen if the whole record was deleted since the nonprofit would have no way of knowing that the individual had requested no further contact.
- Where the data are being processed to evaluate matters which relate to him/her directly, such as a credit check or an analysis of their performance at work, they also have the right to be informed of the logic involved in the decision-making process.

To control the potential for a trivial series of requests for information the Act provides that the data controller is not obliged to provide any of this information unless a request is made in writing and a fee is paid. The Act allows data controllers to charge a reasonable fee for providing copies of any data held but controls the maximum amount that organizations are permitted to charge for this purpose.

The Act also provides an individual with the right to apply in writing to a data controller to prevent their information being processed for the purposes of direct marketing. This is also a significant new right and data controllers will need to ensure that subjects availing themselves do not have their data processed in this way.

The Act further creates a new category of personal data – namely sensitive personal data. This information consists of:

- The racial or ethnic origin of the data subject
- His/her political opinions
- His/her religious beliefs
- Whether he/she is a member of a trade union
- His/her physical or mental condition
- The subject's sexual orientation
- The commission or alleged commission of any offence
- The proceedings for any offence committed or alleged to have been committed by him/her, the disposal of such proceedings or the sentence of any court in such proceedings.

The same rules as for personal data apply, but in addition a number of other restrictions are imposed on organizations holding or planning to hold one of these categories of data. One of the key restrictions is that data controllers must (with a few exceptions) seek the permission of the data subject for this information to be stored. Consent must now be given for the organization to hold the data. While one might think that the need for a nonprofit to store such information is rare, many medical research charities hold information about an individual's health or medical circumstances. While this may largely be used for the purposes of service provision it can also prove invaluable in fundraising. Sensitive nonprofits take care not to send fundraising messages stressing the plight of the victims of a particular disease to those that they know are already sufferers. Some messages can be distressing and responsible organizations thus take considerable care to segment their audience. Under the new Act this will be made more problematic since they must now seek permission to hold this data.

From a fundraiser's perspective the Act has had two major impacts. The first is the requirement on nonprofits to allow individuals to opt out of receiving further communications either from them, or from third parties that their data may be shared with. As a consequence fundraising communications now afford the donor the opportunity to decline further communication (see Plate 18.1) through what is known as an 'opt-out'. There is presently a debate raging around this issue since in some European countries practitioners have adopted a more stringent interpretation of the European Union legislation and compelled organizations to ask respondents to 'opt-in' to future communications.

This may sound like a small change, but individuals rarely take the time to read text in detail and only a small percentage will ever tick option boxes. What this means is that countries in which an opt-out clause is adopted, the majority of donors can be legitimately contacted again, since few will avail themselves of an opt-out. In countries where opt-in is adopted the reverse is true and fundraising by mail can frequently become uneconomic since specific permission must be secured before subsequent communications can be initiated. In effect nonprofits will have to write for permission to write!

The other key implication that arises from the Act is the extent to which it is legitimate for a nonprofit to hold information for extended periods of time. The Act notes that data can only be

A donation from you could help us do so much more.

Title: Mr ☐ Mrs ☐ Miss ☐ Ms ☐ Other ☐

Name

Address

Postcode

Telephone

Please enter your name and address above as it helps us to reduce our administration costs.

I enclose a cheque, made payable to 'British Red Cross', for: £18 ☐ Your choice £ _____

OR,

please debit my Visa/MasterCard/Amex/Diners Club/CAF Charity Card/Switch Card with the amount specified.

Card Number ☐☐☐☐ ☐☐☐☐ ☐☐☐☐ ☐☐☐☐ ☐☐☐☐ ☐☐

Expiry date ☐ / ☐   Switch Issue Number/Start Date (if applicable) ☐ / ☐

Signature _____   Date _____

I am a UK Tax Payer and I would like the British Red Cross to treat all donations I make as Gift Aid donations. ☐ Yes ☐ No

Registered Charity No. 220949

☐ Please tick this box if you do not wish to receive mail from other reputable charities.

☐ Please tick this box if you do not wish to receive further communications from the British Red Cross.

When returning your donation form, please place it in the envelope provided with the FREEPOST address showing clearly through the window.

JUN01/13392

Plate 18.1 *Example of an opt-out*

Source: © British Red Cross. Reproduced with kind permission.

held for a reasonable period without further consent being sought from the data subject. Sadly the Act is not definitive about what constitutes a reasonable period and only successive case law will clarify the true position. If a fundraiser secures a donation from a donor this year he/she is effectively granting permission to be contacted again, unless they specifically opt out of receiving further communication. Their consent may legitimately be implied by the fact that they have supported the organization. However, if over the coming 12 months the fundraiser tries in vain to secure a further donation, at what point does the donor's consent to be contacted expire? Would this occur after a further two, three, four or more mailings? The position is actually unclear, but it seems reasonable to speculate that this would take place after 18 months to two years of further communications, since most nonprofits would describe the donor as being lapsed after this period. Writing to them thereafter would very likely be a criminal offence unless successive opportunities to opt out were offered in the communications they received. As the reader will appreciate, this is a technically complex and fast-moving area of legislation and professional fundraisers are well advised to seek periodic reviews of their practice from their legal team to ensure that their obligations under the Act are being met.

Privacy issues

As we noted above, the Data Protection Act offers wide-ranging protection to consumers. In addition to this consumers may also elect not to receive either unsolicited direct mail or telemarketing calls by registering their contact details with either the mail or telephone preference service respectively (www.mpsonline.org.uk and www.tpsonline.org.uk). At the time of writing it is a legal requirement to abide by the telephone preference service stop list, while the equivalent mail list is good practice but not legally mandatory. That said, this is an issue currently under debate. New regulations – the Consumer Protection from Unfair Trading Regulations (CPUT) which came into effect in May 2008 – prohibit 'making persistent and unwanted solicitations by telephone, fax, email or other remote media except in circumstances and to the extent justified to enforce a contractual obligation' (p.15). The issue is whether the term 'remote media' includes direct mail, but the Direct Marketing Association believes that it does and has advised its members accordingly. These new regulations have teeth so fundraisers must ensure that they adhere to the new rules by carefully de-duplicating any lists they are proposing to use against the national stop list or face a prison sentence or fine of up to £5K. Fundraisers as well as the charity itself are deemed responsible under CPUT regulations (Direct Marketing Association 2008).

The other interesting nuance that CPUT has introduced is the need for fundraisers to be completely open and transparent about how consumer data will be used. If it is their intention to sell the names and addresses of their donors through a list swop or reciprocal programme, CPUT suggests that they will have to be explicit about this, allowing individuals who wish to, to opt out. This is a rather different form of opt-out than the sector has been used to in the past. If it is the intention to sell data to third parties, the charity will be obligated to say so (e.g. it is our intention to sell your data at a profit to third parties, do you wish to opt out?). Indeed, the best advice we can offer at this point is that charities need to think through and develop a privacy policy which reflects all the uses to which personal data will be put and makes all this detail crystal clear to supporters.

MAINTAINING COMMUNICATION STANDARDS

The appropriate management of personal data is not the only issue fundraisers must address. A further critical concern is maintaining an appropriate professional standard in the communications that an organization generates. In the UK a series of voluntary controls have been in existence for over 40 years. At the core of these controls is the British Code of Advertising Practice currently policed by the Advertising Standards Authority (ASA).

This body is funded by a levy on advertising expenditures (i.e. the industry itself) and exists to pressurize advertisers that contravene the Code of Advertising Practice into withdrawing offending ads. The system for broadcast media is more robust, requiring pre-vetting of advertising materials before they are actually broadcast. This is not the case for non-broadcast media such as press advertising where the system operates retrospectively. That said, advertisers can ask that their material be vetted in advance of publication, but this does not guarantee that any subsequent complaints that may be received by the regulator would not be upheld.

Taking the example of a press ad, if a member of the public suspects that an ad has contravened the code he/she may complain to the ASA who are then obligated to investigate the complaint and issue a ruling. If the ASA finds in favour of the complainant it issues a media notice ordering the offending ad to be withdrawn or, in the case of a direct marketing programme, to be terminated. Given that most suppliers of advertising space or materials are members of a trade association, the issue of a media notice is usually enough to ensure compliance. In the handful of cases where unscrupulous operators continue with activities that contravene the code, the government may now intervene under the Control of Misleading Advertisements Regulations (1988) and issue an injunction preventing the activity from continuing.

In addition to responding to public complaints the ASA also conducts an ongoing programme of monitoring and currently scrutinizes more than 15,000 advertisements per annum. While the code contains a number of specific guidelines for product categories (such as alcohol or tobacco), the general rule is that all advertising must be:

- legal
- decent
- honest
- truthful.

But how does one define each of these terms? The first is quite straightforward since the advertising of consumer credit, food, drugs and medicaments for example requires that certain information be

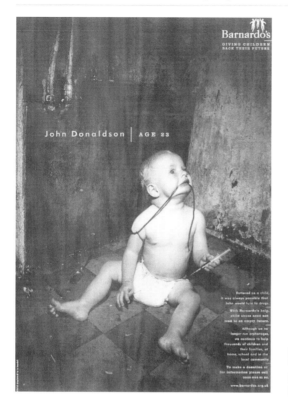

Plate 18.2 *Barnardo's advertisement*
Source: © Barnardo's. Reproduced with kind permission.

provided in the communication if it is to be legal. The terms decent, honest and truthful are less easy to interpret, particularly given that a certain amount of advertising 'puffery' is allowed by the code.

The advantage of self-regulation is that bodies such as the ASA can look at each individual ad and form a view of whether it meets these criteria, given the nature of the organization, the intended audience and what specifically the ad is intended to achieve.

In Plate 18.2 we reproduce an ad that appeared in a number of major national newspapers for a children's charity. It featured a baby sitting alone in squalid surroundings. Dirt covered the floor and walls; in his teeth the baby held a cord, which was tightened round his right arm to make a tourniquet; in his left hand he held a syringe as if to inject heroin. The headline stated 'John Donaldson Age 23'; the body copy stated, 'Battered as a child, it was always possible that John would turn to drugs. With Barnardo's help, child abuse need not lead to an empty future. Although we no longer run orphanages, we continue to help thousands of children and their families at home, school and in the local community.' The complainants objected that the advertisement was shocking and offensive.

In this case the ASA decided not to uphold the complaint. In reaching the judgement the ASA filed the following report:

> The advertisers believed the advertisement complied with the Codes. They said it was part of a campaign to raise awareness of their preventative work with children and young people; the campaign was designed to make people reconsider their opinions about Barnardo's work and the subjects depicted in each advertisement. The advertisers argued that they had not intended merely to shock. They said they had taken the precaution of researching the

388

campaign twice among their target audience of ABC1 adults aged 35 to 55 and their supporters, staff and service users; they submitted the research findings, which they believed
showed most people understood the advertisement's message and found its approach effective in changing opinions about Barnardo's work. The advertisers maintained that, because
the consequences of drug addiction were potentially devastating, the stark image was justified as a means of raising public awareness of the potential dangers for disadvantaged
children; they believed it was an effective way of making the point that Barnardo's could
help keep them safe. Their consumer research acknowledged that some people found images
of alcoholism or drug abuse upsetting. They nevertheless maintained that an image based on
the innocence of a child and potential pain in adult life communicated the message that
Barnardo's was a contemporary charity with modern perspectives on child development.
The advertisers submitted extracts from published research, which showed that disadvantaged and abused children were particularly vulnerable to emotional and behavioural problems in later life; they provided recent survey results that showed that parents and children
found drugs worrying and frightening. They asserted that the child depicted had not been
put at risk and that the advertisement was made with full parental awareness and consent.
The advertisers said they had monitored public responses to their advertisement; they had
received more supportive responses than complaints. *The Independent* (newspaper) said they
had received less than five complaints and considered that the advertisement would not
cause serious or widespread offence to their readers. *The Guardian* (newspaper) said they
believed their readers would understand the advertiser's message and they had received no
complaints. The *Scotland on Sunday* (newspaper) said they regarded drugs very seriously and
considered that Barnardo's advertisement was compelling and justified. They said they had
received no complaints. *The Times*, *The Scotsman*, the *Independent on Sunday* and *The Observer*
did not respond. The Authority noted the advertisement had offended or distressed some
readers. It nevertheless acknowledged that the advertisers had intended to convey a serious
and important message. The Authority considered that they had acted responsibly by conducting research among their target audience to ensure the message was understood and
unlikely to shock or offend. The Authority noted the picture of drug abuse was directly
related to the advertiser's preventative work with children and considered that the target
audience was likely to interpret the image in the context of the accompanying text. The
Authority accepted the advertiser's argument that they had not intended merely to shock.
It considered that, because the advertiser had used the image to raise public awareness of
the seriousness of drug abuse and the action that could be taken to prevent it, the advertisement was unlikely to cause either serious or widespread offence or undue distress and was
acceptable.

Plate 18.3 contains an example of an ad that ran for the baby charity Tommy's headlined 'Your
50p will keep a premature baby alive for 1.8 seconds. Please give generously'. It featured a cartoon drawing of a zebra in a hospital bed. Text at the bottom of the poster stated '£15 will help
Tommy's put an end to miscarriage, premature birth and stillbirth'. The complainants, who
interestingly comprised both members of the public and a competing charity BLISS, the National
Charity for the Newborn, believed the advertisement misleadingly implied contributions would
be spent keeping babies alive.

In this case the ASA upheld the complaint and in their report noted the following:

The advertiser said the poster would not be used again because they had used all the poster
space they could. They said the advertisement's message was that it was expensive to run a
premature baby unit. They believed that by putting money into research to find a cause and

Plate 18.3 *Tommy's advertisement*
Source: © Tommy's Campaign. Reproduced with kind permission.

prevent premature birth happening the NHS would be saved from the expense of supporting premature babies. The advertisers said the strapline '£15 will help Tommy's put an end to miscarriage, premature birth and stillbirth' made clear that donations funded their research into stopping premature birth. They provided a copy of their Memorandum of Association, which explained their funds had been directed at the prevention of premature birth. They maintained the topic of the advertisement was consistent with their dedication to raising awareness of the subject. They said that when readers called the number in the advertisement they were told at the start of the call that the donation helped provide funds for medical research into miscarriage, premature birth and stillbirth. The advertisers said they had received a lot of feedback about the advertisement but had received no complaints. They were surprised that readers had interpreted the advertisement in a way different from that intended.

The Authority considered that the claim misleadingly implied that donations would go towards the costs of supporting a premature baby. Because they did not, the Authority asked the advertisers to amend the advertisement and to take more care in future to make clear how donations would be used.

Almost all forms of marketing communications are now overseen by the Advertising Standards Authority, except:

■ Claims on websites, where misleading claims must be reported to the local trading standards department.
■ The sponsorship of broadcast programmes, where Ofcom (www.ofcom.org.uk) has responsibility for oversight.
■ Shop window displays or in-store advertising, which again are matters for the local trading standards department.

■ *Political advertising* All complaints of political bias in TV or radio advertising are made to Ofcom (www.ofcom.org.uk). Complaints about non-broadcast ads, where the purpose of the ad is to persuade voters in a local or general election or referendum are matters for the Electoral Commission (www.electoralcommission.org.uk).

FUNDRAISING STANDARDS BOARD

To the above list we might also add 'fundraising', at least in some cases. The Fundraising Standards Board (FRSB), launched in 2007, is the self-regulatory body for fundraising in the UK (www.frsb.org.uk). It exists to deal with public concerns and complaints about fundraising activity and to help the public to give with confidence. It is, however, entirely voluntary for charities to sign up to the scheme and at the time of writing only 800 UK charities have chosen to do so. Charities that join the scheme agree to:

■ Adhere to the Institute of Fundraising's *Codes of Fundraising Practice* and the Board's own Fundraising Promise (see Exhibit 18.1).
■ Have procedures in place to deal with public complaints. They should also offer a complaints 'safety net', so members of the public know they can contact the FRSB if they are not satisfied with the charity's response.
■ Demonstrate their membership of the FRSB scheme by displaying their 'tick' on fundraising materials.

EXHIBIT 18.1 THE FUNDRAISING PROMISE

We are members of the Fundraising Standards Board self-regulatory scheme. The Fundraising Standards Board works to ensure that organisations raising money from the public do so honestly and properly. As members of the scheme, we follow the Institute of Fundraising's Codes of Fundraising Practice and comply with the key principles embodied in the Codes and in this Promise.

We are committed to high standards

We do all we can to ensure that fundraisers, volunteers and fundraising contractors working with us to raise funds comply with the Codes and with this Promise. We comply with the law including those that apply to data protection, health and safety and the environment.

We are honest and open

We tell the truth and do not exaggerate. We do what we say we are going to do. We answer all reasonable questions about our fundraising activities and costs. Please contact us, visit our website or see our Annual Report if you require further details.

We are clear

We are clear about who we are, what we do and how your gift is used. Where we have a promotional agreement with a commercial company, we make clear how much of the purchase price we receive. We give a clear explanation of how you can make a gift and amend a regular commitment.

We are respectful

We respect the rights, dignities and privacy of our supporters and beneficiaries. We will not put undue pressure on you to make a gift and if you do not want to give or wish to cease giving, we will respect your decision. If you tell us that you don't want us to contact you in a particular way we will not do so.

We are fair and reasonable

We take care not to use any images or words that cause unjustifiable distress or offence. We take care not to cause unreasonable nuisance or disruption.

We are accountable

If you are unhappy with anything we've done while fundraising, you can contact us to make a complaint. We have a complaints procedure, a copy of which is available on request. If we cannot resolve your complaint, we accept the authority of the Fundraising Standards Board to make a final adjudication.

FundRaising
Standards Board

Source: FRSB 2009. Reproduced with kind permission.

The FRSB encourages members of the public to complain to the charity in the first instance. If they are not satisfied with the response FRSB staff will work with the complainant and the charity to try to resolve the issue. If this fails the matter will then be referred to the Board of the FRSB who will make adjudication. FRSB adjudications are judged against the Institute of Fundraising's *Codes of Fundraising Practice* and/or the Fundraising Promise. Charities can have their membership of the FRSB withdrawn if a serious breach of these codes is found to have taken place. The process is illustrated in Figure 18.1. At the time of writing the FRSB Board has been asked to make only one adjudication.

OTHER FUNDRAISING LAW

In the UK there are a number of other components of legislation that fundraisers need to be aware of in their professional practice. The most notable of these include:

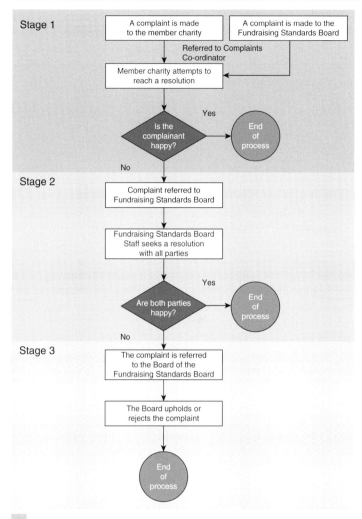

Figure 18.1 *FRSB complaints procedure*
Source: FRSB 2009. Reproduced with kind permission.

Communication of registered status

The Charities Act 1992 requires that all registered charities must make their status clear in all communications. As the Act states:

> The fact that it is a registered charity shall be stated in English in legible characters –
> (a) in all notices, advertisements and other documents issued by or on behalf of the charity and soliciting money or other property for the benefit of the charity;
> (b) in all bills of exchange, promissory notes, endorsements, cheques and orders for money or goods purporting to be signed on behalf of the charity; and in all bills rendered by it and in all its invoices, receipts and letters of credit.
>
> (Charities Act 1992:1–3–1)

From a fundraising perspective this means that all forms of fundraising communications and receipts must contain details of the charity registration number. Failure to include this information is an offence and it is likely that the Act would treat each separate instance as a separate offence, implying that, for example, a charity not printing its registration number on a mailshot comprising 10,000 units, could be guilty of 10,000 separate offences.

Lotteries and raffles

There are three types of lottery under current law (Institute of Fundraising, 2007).

1 *Small lotteries* Small lotteries can be run during fundraising events (such as pub quizzes, garden fêtes or dinners) to raise additional monies for the organisation. The law says that no more than £250 may be spent on purchased prizes, but the value of donated prizes carries no limit. None of the prizes can be cash prizes, although vouchers are deemed acceptable. The draw must take place at the event and tickets can only be sold at the event.
2 *Private lotteries* These can only be offered to people who live or work in the same premises or who belong to the same membership organisation. All proceeds must be split between prizes and the membership organisation. Tickets can be printed, but a sweepstake is also permitted.
3 *Society lotteries* For tickets to be sold over a period of time, charities must run a registered society lottery. If the sale of tickets will not exceed £20,000 for a single lottery or £250,000 in one calendar year, the local council will have responsibility for licensing the activity. If the sums involved are likely to be greater than this then the lottery must be registered with the Gaming Commission.

For society lotteries there is a small initial registration fee (typically £35) payable to the local council and then, to remain registered, each society is required to pay an annual fee thereafter. Once registered, societies have to submit a return after each lottery showing the amounts collected, the amount spent on prizes and any expenses concerned with conducting the lottery. These returns are held for 18 months and are available for public inspection.

Tickets sold as part of a registered society lottery must be properly printed and carry:

- the details of the name of the society
- the name and address of the promoter
- the date of the lottery draw
- the price of the ticket (which must not exceed £2)
- the name of the printer
- the name of the local council that the society is registered with (or the Gambling Commission if appropriate), and
- the registered charity's number (if applicable).

Tickets should not be bought or sold by young people under the age of 16. An example of a lottery ticket is provided in Plate 18.4

It should be noted that at the time of writing, the rules in this area are changing. The Gambling Act 2005 which came fully into force on 1 September 2007 will change some of the rules for lotteries. The Gambling Commission will be responsible for regulating the gambling industry including society lotteries and is currently consulting on how it will regulate the sector including issuing licences and producing codes of practice. Charities and other organisations should check

Plate 18.4 *Specimen raffle ticket*
Source: © National Eczema Society. Reproduced with kind permission.

the Gambling Commission's website www.gamblingcommission.gov.uk for changes to the rules, or consult the latest Institute of Fundraising Code of Practice for lotteries.

Street and house-to-house collections

In the UK it is not uncommon to see charity collections taking place on the High Street of any major town or city. In many ways this is one of the most visible forms of fundraising many charities will undertake. Historically, charity fundraisers have also sought permission to call at the homes of individuals living in particular areas. Both these forms of fundraising require a licence and this is granted by the requisite local authority. There is typically no fee for this, but a formal application must be made if the activity is to be legal.

In England house-to-house collections are caught under the House To House Collections Act 1939 and the House To House Collections Regulations 1947/1963. The law requires that charities wishing to undertake this form of fundraising are licensed and that each promoter of a collection should exercise due diligence to ensure that all persons acting as collectors are 'proper and fit'. No person is permitted to act as a collector unless they have a 'Certificate of Authority', a prescribed badge and, if money is to be collected, a marked collection box or a receipt book (with receipts and counterfoils or duplicates consecutively numbered). The amount donated, an indication of the purpose of the collection and a distinguishing number must be provided on the receipt. The law also:

- prevents anyone under 16 from acting as a collector;
- requires collectors not to annoy householders and to leave the property if requested to do so;
- requires the charity to furnish an account of the collection to the licensing authority.

Street collections are governed by the Local Government Act 1972 and the Police, Factories ETC (Miscellaneous Provisions) Act 1916. Once again the law requires collectors to obtain a permit. Collections may only take place on the day/time stipulated in this permit. Collections are required to take place in a manner that is not likely to annoy or inconvenience any person. In addition, collectors must:

- remain stationary;
- ensure that if he/she is working with others that they should not be closer together than 25 metres;

- carry a collecting box (which must be numbered consecutively and sealed in such a way as to prevent them from being opened without a seal being broken);
- place all collected monies in this collecting box and deliver this box unopened to the charity on completion of the collection;
- be unpaid. No payments may be made to collectors.

Those charities administering street collections must also provide an account of the collection to the licensing authority which must include a summary of the monies raised, the expenses incurred in connection with the collection, a list of collectors and a list of the amounts contained in each collecting box. The law also requires that the financial statement be certified both by the charity and a qualified accountant.

Face-to-face fundraising

Fundraisers conducting face-to-face or direct dialogue solicitations must now make a formal statement to potential donors specifying:

- the institution or institutions for which they are raising funds;
- if there is more than one institution, the proportions in which they are to benefit; and
- if they are professional fundraisers, the method by which their remuneration is determined and the 'notifiable amount' of that remuneration (this will be the remuneration of the professional fundraising organisation if the fundraiser is employed by such an organisation); or
- if they are paid officers, employees or trustees of the institution acting as collectors in a public charitable collection, the fact that they hold those positions and that they are receiving remuneration. A public charitable collection is a charitable appeal which is made in any public place or by means of visits to houses or business premises (or both).

The notifiable amount is the actual amount if known at the time or the estimated amount calculated as accurately as possible. Further information and guidance is available from the Office of the Third Sector website where a series of model statements are provided. The law (the Charities Act 1992) requires that a statement must be made at the time of the solicitation and so, in practice, before a donor has authorized an agreement to donate. Similar rules apply in Scotland and Northern Ireland.

TRADING AND FUNDRAISING

Fundraisers can frequently be involved in forms of trading to raise funds for their organization. It is therefore important to have some knowledge of how the law regards such activities and what a charity can and cannot do.

What constitutes trading?

The starting point in this area of the law is to determine what does or does not constitute trading. Whether an activity constitutes trading depends on a number of factors including:

- the number and frequency of transactions
- the nature of the goods or services being sold

- the intention of the charity in acquiring the goods which are to be sold
- whether the goods are capable of being used and enjoyed by the charity selling them
- the nature and mechanics of the sales, and
- the presence or absence of a profit motive.

Trading would therefore include the sale of Christmas cards, the sale of goods through a catalogue and the selling of books, reports and other items online. It would also include the sale of souvenirs such as those routinely offered by many arts and cultural organizations.

Charity law allows charities to trade provided that the trading falls into one of the following categories:

- primary purpose trading
- ancillary trading, or
- non-primary purpose trading that does not involve significant risk to the resources of the charity.

Primary purpose trading is trading which contributes directly to one or more of the objects of a charity as set out in its governing document. It includes trading in which the work in connection with the trading is mainly carried out by beneficiaries of the charity, as that will normally be primary purpose trading. Examples (Charity Commission, 2007) include the:

- provision of educational services by a charitable school or college in return for course fee;
- sale of goods manufactured by disabled people who are beneficiaries of a charity for the disabled;
- holding of an art exhibition by a charitable art gallery or museum in return for admission fees;
- provision of residential accommodation by a residential care charity in return for payment;
- sale of tickets for a theatrical production staged by a theatre charity;
- sale of certain educational goods by a charitable art gallery or museum.

The profits from primary purpose trading are exempt from corporation tax (or income tax in the case of charitable trusts). This exemption from tax is only available if the profits are applied solely to the purposes of the charity. However the sales which have given rise to those profits will be regarded as a business activity for the purposes of determining liability to VAT.

'Ancillary trading' contributes indirectly to the successful furtherance of the purposes of the charity. This is treated as part of 'primary purpose trading' for both charity law and tax purposes. An example of ancillary trading is the sale of food and drink in a restaurant or bar by a theatre charity to members of an audience. The level of annual turnover in trading which is said to be ancillary may have a bearing on the question of whether the trading really is ancillary, but there is currently no specific level of annual turnover beyond which trading will definitely not be regarded as ancillary.

Non-primary purpose trading

Charity law permits charities to carry on non-primary purpose trading in order to raise funds, provided that the trading involves no significant risk to the assets of the charity. Examples include the sale of items through a catalogue and the sale of purchased merchandise (i.e. as opposed to donated goods).

The significant risk to be avoided here is that the turnover is insufficient to meet the costs of carrying on the trade, and the difference has to be financed out of the assets of the charity. This is an issue because in a business situation creditors would normally have the right to take court action to seize an organisation's assets if their bills remained unpaid. In the charity context it will have been donors who supplied those assets and donors who had a reasonable right to expect that those assets would be applied for the benefit of the community and not to pay trading debts. The purpose of denying charities the right to take 'significant risk' in trading is therefore to protect the assets of the charity.

Whether or not the risk of non-primary purpose trading is 'significant' depends on a number of factors, including:

- the size of the charity
- the nature of the business
- the expected outgoings
- turnover projections, and
- the sensitivity of business profitability to the ups and downs of the market.

As the reader will appreciate the assessment of risk is something of a judgement call and one typically for the trustees and their advisers. A safe approach to this issue is probably to conduct only trading which qualifies for the 'small-scale exemption' (detailed in the following section). Any trading likely to exceed this level can still be conducted but if risk is involved it must be conducted through a trading subsidiary (see below).

The small-scale exemption

The small-scale exemption is an exemption from corporation tax (or income tax in the case of charitable trusts) on the profits from small-scale non-primary purpose trading and the income from some other business activities carried on by charities. It applies only where all the relevant profits or income are applied for the charity's purposes.

In order to qualify for the small-scale exemption within a given period, either

- the annual turnover of the relevant non-primary purpose trading of the charity must not exceed the 'relevant threshold' during the chargeable period, or
- if it does exceed the 'relevant threshold', the charity must have had a reasonable expectation at the start of the chargeable period that it would not do so.

The position can be complicated by certain forms of miscellaneous income the charity earns during the period, but ignoring this complexity for the purposes of illustration, the relevant threshold is presently calculated as indicated in the table.

Total of all incoming resources in a particular chargeable period of the charity	Maximum permitted annual turnover of the relevant trading in that chargeable period
Under £20,000	£5,000
£20,000 to £200,000	25% of charity's total incoming resources
Over £200,000	£50,000

There is no statutory definition of the term 'all incoming resources'. However HM Revenue and Customs regard this as the total receipts of the charity for the chargeable period from all sources (e.g. grants, donations, investment income, trading receipts, etc.). If the turnover of the relevant trading exceeds the maximum level (as indicated in the right-hand column in the table) the small-scale exemption does not apply unless the charity had a reasonable expectation at the start of the chargeable period that it would not exceed that level.

A trading turnover within the scope of the small-scale exemption is unlikely to contravene the charity law restrictions on carrying on non-primary purpose trading. The low maximum permitted level of trading turnover means that any risk to the charity's resources from the trading is likely to be small. Therefore, unless prohibited by its governing document, any charity can carry on small-scale, non-primary purpose trading, and be exempt from corporation tax (or income tax in the case of charitable trusts) on the profits, provided that the profits are applied for the purposes of the charity (Charity Commission 2007).

Trading and tax

A charity's trading profits are, in certain circumstances, exempt from tax. This includes profits from primary purpose trading, ancillary trading and profits made from lotteries and from certain types of fundraising event. Exemption is subject to the proceeds being applied to the charitable purposes of the organisation.

There is no general exemption from corporation tax (or income tax in the case of charitable trusts) on the profits of non-primary purpose trading carried on by a charity, even where the profits are all applied for the charity's purposes. However, some exemptions do apply, for example for lotteries or in the case of the small-scale trading we describe above. If an exemption does not apply, tax will be payable on the profits generated.

Income received by a charity from the sale of goods that have been donated to it is not generally regarded as trading profits and is not taxable (Charity Commission 2007).

Trading subsidiaries

Where trading (other than trading in pursuit of its charitable objects) involves significant risk to a charity's assets, it must be undertaken by a trading subsidiary. But even where it is not essential for the trading to be undertaken by a trading subsidiary, the use of trading subsidiaries may produce benefits, for example in reducing tax liabilities. In particular, trading subsidiaries may make donations to their parent charity as Gift Aid, so reducing or eliminating the profits of the subsidiary which are liable to tax. Of course there are downsides to trading subsidiaries too. In establishing one a charity will need to ensure that it is effectively managed, a requirement that will doubtless necessitate additional expenditure on salaries and administration.

Trustees of charities with one or more trading subsidiaries need to be aware of their responsibilities. In particular they need to remember, in all decisions made in regard to a trading subsidiary, that the interests of the charity are paramount. The interests of a trading subsidiary, its directors, creditors or employees, must all be secondary to those of the charity. This is because the purpose of using a trading subsidiary is to benefit the charity in some way, for example to protect the charity's assets from the risks of trading, or to increase the level of financial return to the charity by saving tax. If the charity's assets are employed or put at risk for the benefit of the subsidiary, or its directors, creditors or employees, then that purpose is frustrated. In such cases, the trustees of the charity may be personally liable for any loss of, or decline in value of, the charity's assets (Charity Commission 2007).

CODES OF FUNDRAISING PRACTICE

As we noted in our introduction, the law impacting on fundraising is subject to regular change. To assist fundraisers in keeping their knowledge up to date the Institute of Fundraising produces a series of very helpful *Codes of Fundraising Practice*. These provide a guide to the law and best practice in relation to fundraising activity throughout the United Kingdom. The codes cover a wide range of activities. Existing codes are updated on a regular basis and new codes are developed where a need for them has been identified.

The codes provide a guide to the law, but they also specify the activities that fundraisers *should* engage in and thus straddle the divide between legal and ethical practice. It is for this reason that the codes form the backbone of the work of the Fundraising Standards Board. Members of the FRSB must ensure that their fundraising is fully compliant with the codes.

We strongly recommend the codes to all students of fundraising. They are neat and concise guides to best practice and cover domains such as direct mail, lotteries and gaming, fundraising through electronic media, face-to-face activity and, most recently, accountability and transparency.

ETHICS IN FUNDRAISING

The study of ethics is essentially involved in determining right from wrong. Such decisions will be driven by an individual's own beliefs and values and those of the wider society in which they live. In Judeo-Christian society, for example, these values may be derived from respect and compassion for the individual and a wider concern for the impact of one's actions on others. Ethics operate at a different level from the laws of a particular society since as we have noted these laws frequently provide only for minimum standards of behaviour. They deal with the worst excesses of a society and with aspects of that society that are of wider interest and concern. They also reflect the prevailing view of the government, which one hopes in a democracy would in turn reflect the views of the majority of the members of that society.

Ethics by contrast operate at a 'higher' level. While a particular action may not be illegal, it may nevertheless be regarded by a given individual as wrong because it indirectly harms others, or is not in the best interests of the organization that employs them. It is this grey area beyond the realms of the law that is the domain of ethical judgements and where the fundraising profession has invested considerable time and effort to determine what does and does not constitute appropriate behaviour.

In our discussion of ethics it is not our intention to review the contribution of a procession of different philosophers. Rather, it is our intention to adopt a pragmatic approach and to introduce a range of common ethical dilemmas for fundraisers and two codes of conduct that have been established by the fundraising profession to provide guidance across the sector.

In reading what follows, it is important to bear in mind that there are no right or wrong answers in the domain of ethics. Some answers may be 'righter' than others, but ultimately professional fundraisers must make their own decisions about what is appropriate guided by the standards established by the bodies that represent the profession as a whole. In the United States, this is the Association of Fundraising Professionals (www.afpnet.org) and in the United Kingdom, the Institute of Fundraising (www.institute-of-fundraising.org.).

Current ethical dilemmas are discussed here.

Remuneration

This debate concerns what constitutes appropriate remuneration for fundraising activity. Particularly at issue is whether fundraisers should be paid by salary or receive a commission for every donation they successfully solicit. Indeed, should this remuneration vary depending on the value of a particular gift? The payment of commission or bonuses has long been a practice of for-profit managers looking to retain and motivate their staff. Most managers do not have an ethical dilemma over whether to initiate a payment system of this type since the need to achieve sales and hence profit for the business is paramount and bonuses can be a very effective motivational tool. However, in the context of fundraising, the payment of bonuses is felt to be problematic since it could lead to undue pressure being exerted on donors to give. Fundraisers remunerated by commission would have a vested interest in persuading as many people as possible to give, even where it was clearly inappropriate for them to do so, or where their needs would be better served by giving to another organization in perhaps a very different way. This occurs because the fundraiser has to make a living and if they are paid on commission the only way they can achieve this is to 'sell' ever more donors on making a gift. The security of a salary effectively removes this pressure and makes it less likely that fundraisers will be driven to ignore the needs and wishes of the prospects they meet. They can, in effect, afford to take a longer term and more selfless view of the solicitation process.

Personal gifts

Many fundraisers become personally acquainted with their high-value donors and in some cases develop genuine and enduring friendships as a consequence. It is not uncommon under these circumstances for fundraisers to be presented by donors with often quite valuable gifts. The ethical dilemma here is whether such gifts should be accepted and whether the value should be retained by the individual or ceded to the nonprofit. Again this is a complex area, because fundraisers should not seek to benefit from the relationships that they have with their donors. The integrity of the relationship with the nonprofit should be the first priority and it should always be maintained. That said, small gifts or tokens of affection may be acceptable, but of course the dilemma then becomes a decision over the point at which the value of such gifts begins to make them unacceptable. There are no right answers here and the safest solution is almost certainly to decline any personal gifts from donors, no matter how small they may be.

Privacy

Some fundraising techniques are regarded as more intrusive than others. However, many of these techniques can also be highly effective forms of fundraising. Organizations and hence fundraising teams must therefore decide which techniques they believe it is legitimate to pursue. There are those that would argue that nonprofits should not adopt any techniques that are in some way intrusive, but this is a gross simplification and only generates the further question - Who decides whether something is intrusive and how many people must hold the view before it is discontinued? In the USA the use of telemarketing agencies by nonprofits to raise funds has generated considerable debate. Calling people in their own home at times that may not be convenient is a highly intrusive activity. While individuals have come to expect this practice of business organizations, there is a sense that nonprofits should be more respectful of privacy issues. Again, though, this is not as straightforward as it might at first appear. If a school will cease to exist because of a lack of funds or local people are dying because of health or drug problems, there are few of us who would suggest that a nonprofit should not attempt to raise funds to resolve these issues in every way possible. If one accepts this as a proposition, one then has to decide which causes and how great a need would warrant the use of intrusive techniques. This is thus an insoluble conundrum.

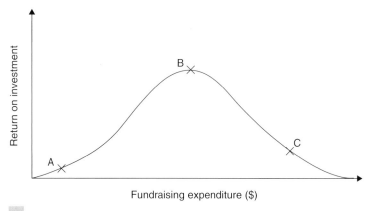

Figure 18.2 *Returns from fundraising expenditure*

Efficiency

A further dilemma arises around the issue of when one should stop fundraising. Figure 18.2 illustrates the returns that organizations generate from fundraising at different levels of expenditure. Clearly this is a gross simplification of reality but it serves to illustrate the general experience of most nonprofits. When expenditure is low on fundraising, organizations may not be investing enough to take advantage of economies of scale, or to achieve a significant enough media impact to overcome the clutter of other appeals. At this stage, point (A) in the figure, £1 of investment may achieve only break-even returns or slightly above. As expenditure rises the nonprofit reaches a point where it achieves its maximum possible return on investment as economies of scale are eventually realized. Let's say for the sake of argument that the nonprofit achieves a return here of £5 for every £1 of investment (Point (B) in the figure).

If the expenditure is increased still further the returns for each incremental pound of expenditure then begin to fall. There are many reasons for this, but it often occurs because at a certain point it will become progressively more difficult for an organization to find additional new donors. It is still very cost-effective to raise funds, but the return begins to drop away to £3:1, then £2:1 and so on. This is represented as point (C) in Figure 18.2. The difficult ethical issue is that in pure economic terms the nonprofit would be better off continuing to invest in fundraising to the point where marginal investment equals marginal revenue (i.e. to the point where an additional £1 raises exactly £1). This would maximize the income the organization was able to generate, but few donors would be happy with such a high percentage of their gift being spent on fundraising! Such a high level of fundraising expenditure, if adopted by all nonprofits, would be likely to cause great offence and widespread public concern as fundraising messages began to dominate the media. It is thus rather more likely that an organization will decide to cease expenditure on fundraising at a point where the return for the incremental pound is at a somewhat higher level. Of course, what this level should be is a matter for debate.

Appropriate corporate support

A number of nonprofits have faced criticism when they have accepted gifts from companies that can be thought to be unsuitable partners, or indeed that undertake practices that directly oppose the mission of the nonprofit. This issue is considered in detail in Chapter 11.

Distortion of mission

It is a fact that for most nonprofits certain elements of what they do will be more attractive to potential funders than others. It is also sadly true that some of the most difficult and ground-breaking work will also be that which challenges donors and is therefore most difficult to raise funds for. A number of ethical dilemmas then arise. First, the organization could be tempted to distort its mission to embrace other aspects of endeavour that are inherently more popular with donors. It might also be tempted to distort how the funds solicited are actually used. In other words a donor might be left with the impression that their gift will be used to support Project A, when in fact it will be used for the equally deserving, but less popular, Project B. Many within the fundraising profession would consider this to be unethical and the decision thus an easy one to resolve, but where projects share much in common and thus the distinction between them becomes blurred, it becomes a matter for judgement in respect of whether the donor is being substantially misled. This is frequently more of an issue in impersonal communications such as direct mail, where a mass audience is being addressed and hence campaigns may need to be generic.

ETHICAL CODES AND STANDARDS OF PROFESSIONAL PRACTICE

In the UK the Institute of Fundraising is the professional body that seeks to represent all fundraisers. The aim of the Institute is to develop the highest standards of professional practice among its membership and to invest in the development of these standards over time. A central component of their approach is the creation of the *Codes of Fundraising Practice* we described earlier. These codes serve to drive up professional standards in relation to each major form of fundraising.

While immensely valuable, these codes supply only half of the professional equation. While it is essential that we apply fundraising techniques in accordance with the law and prevailing ethical standards, the codes say little or nothing about the way that fundraisers should conduct themselves as professionals. The Institute, in common with other professional bodies worldwide, has therefore developed a separate Code of Conduct which it is expected that all members will adopt. Violation of this code can lead to disciplinary action being taken and, as a final sanction, expulsion from the Institute. The Code of Conduct is reproduced in Exhibit 18.2.

EXHIBIT 18.2 INSTITUTE OF FUNDRAISING CODE OF CONDUCT

All members of the Institute of Fundraising undertake to:

- conduct themselves at all times with complete integrity, honesty and trustfulness
- respect the dignity of their profession and ensure that their actions enhance the reputation of themselves and the Institute
- act according to the highest standards and visions of their organisation, profession and conscience
- advocate within their organisations adherence to all applicable laws and regulations
- avoid even the appearance of any criminal offence or professional misconduct

- bring credit to the fundraising profession by their public demeanour
- encourage colleagues to embrace and practise this Code of Conduct.

They shall:

- not misuse their authority or office for personal gain
- comply with the laws of the United Kingdom which relate to their professional activities, both in letter and spirit
- advocate within their organisations compliance with the laws of the United Kingdom which relate to their professional activities, both in letter and spirit
- not exploit any relationship with a donor, prospect, volunteer or employee for personal benefit
- not knowingly, recklessly or maliciously injure the professional reputation or practice of other members of this profession
- at all times act honestly and in such a manner that donors are not misled
- not knowingly or recklessly disseminate false or misleading information in the course of their professional duties, nor permit their subordinates to do so
- not represent conflicting or competing interests without consent of the parties concerned after full disclosure of the facts
- not knowingly act in a manner inconsistent with this Code, or knowingly cause or permit others to do so.

Professional competence

All members of the Institute are expected to:

- strive to attain and apply a high level of competence to the efficient conduct of the work entrusted to them
- improve their professional knowledge and skills in order that their performance will better serve others
- recognize their individual boundaries of competence and be forthcoming and truthful about their professional experience and qualifications
- seek to ensure that all who work with them have appropriate levels of competence for the effective discharge of their duties
- endeavour always to work in harmony with their colleagues and to encourage less experienced colleagues to attain and apply their own levels of acceptable professional competence.

Fundraising competence

Full and Certificated members are required to show competence in:

- establishing and communicating a case for support
- planning, organising and monitoring the allocation of resources
- research, analysis and strategy development
- coping with change and problem solving
- ability to work with colleagues, suppliers and others to achieve fundraising objectives.

Confidentiality

Members shall:

- not disclose (except as may be required by statute or law) or make use of information given or obtained in confidence
- from their employers or clients, the donating public or any other source without prior express consent
- adhere to the principle that all information created by, or on behalf of, an organization is the property of an organization and shall not be transferred or utilized except on behalf of that organization.

The Fundraising promise

Members will promote and support the principles of the Fundraising Promise in the course of their professional activities.

Source: Institute of Fundraising. Reproduced with kind permission.

All the documentation now provided in relation to standards and ethics is designed with the central aim in mind of enhancing donor trust in the sector. Trust lies at the very heart of voluntary organizations and without it the sector would find it impossible to secure funds. Donors must trust the nonprofits they support to behave appropriately and in a manner consistent with their mission. Only by adopting and following both the letter and the spirit of these codes will fundraisers provide donors with the reassurance that they need and begin to drive dubious professional practice out of the sector.

NATIONAL OCCUPATIONAL STANDARDS FOR FUNDRAISING

Finally, no chapter on standards would be complete without reference to the National Occupational Standards for Fundraising. These were developed by the UK Workforce Hub in collaboration with the Institute of Fundraising in early 2009 and can be found online at http://www.ukworkforcehub.org.uk/

The standards are important because they specify the standards of performance those raising funds and resources should be working to across the UK. They also describe the knowledge and skills fundraisers need in order to perform to the required standard. Fundraisers can use them to check that they are doing a good job and to identify any knowledge they need to acquire or skills they need to develop. Organizations can also use the standards to ensure that their fundraisers are competent and have the knowledge and skills to deliver on their strategy in an appropriate way. The fundraising standards are also employed by the Institute of Fundraising as the basis for their qualification programme.

The standards comprise three major groupings which reflect the typical roles that individuals might have: fundraising support, fundraising and fundraising management. This framework is depicted in Figure 18.3 and the detail for each unit can be readily downloaded from the UK Workforce Hub website.

Fundraising Support

✓	Unit Title	Ref
	Assist with fundraising planning	F1
	Assist with fundraising implementation	F2
	Contribute to the maintenance of relationships with supporters	F3
	Use your communication skills to support the work of fundraisers	F4
	Support the work of your team	F5
	Receive and process donations	F6
	Managing data to support fundraising	F7
	Assist with fundraising reporting	F8
	Ensure your own actions reduce risks to health and safety	X1

Fundraising

✓	Unit Title	Ref
	Develop and implement a plan for local/community fundraising	F9
	Develop and implement a plan for fundraising events	F10
	Develop and implement a plan for legacy fundraising	F11
	Develop and implement a plan for corporate fundraising activity	F12
	Develop and implement a plan for the generation of grant income	F13
	Develop and implement a plan for major gift fundraising	F14
	Develop and implement a plan for fundraising through electronic media	F15
	Develop and implement a plan for the recruitment of donors using direct marketing media	F16
	Monitor, enhance and sustain relationships with supporters	F17
	Ensure your own actions reduce risks to health and safety	X1
	Use information technology effectively in fundraising	X2
	Lead others in the achievement of fundraising work	X3
	Provide learning opportunities for colleagues	X4
	Recruit, select and retain colleagues	X5
	Brief and work with third party suppliers of marketing/marketing communications services	X6

Fundraising Management

✓	Unit Title	Ref
	Conduct a fundraising audit	F18
	Develop and implement an integrated fundraising plan	F19
	Manage supporter retention	F20
	Lead the monitoring and evaluation of fundraising performance	F21
	Manage fundraising resources effectively	F22
	Work collaboratively with other functions or organizations	F23
	Promote public trust and confidence in fundraising	F24
	Develop a customer-focused organization	F25
	Provide leadership in your area of responsibility	F26
	Represent fundraising to the Board	F27
	Ensure your own actions reduce risks to health and safety	X1
	Use information technology effectively in fundraising	X2
	Lead others in the achievement of fundraising work	X3
	Provide learning opportunities for colleagues	X4
	Recruit, select and retain colleagues	X5
	Brief and work with third party suppliers of marketing/marketing communications services	X6

The suite covers all the main functions involved in fundraising. To use them effectively you need to identify the units relevant to the work you do, want to do or manage. Use this matrix to help you to build up your role profile or the profile of the fundraising function in your organization. You are likely to find that you undertake activities in more than one cluster.

Key: "X" in a Unit Ref means the same unit is found in more than one cluster within the suite

Figure 18.3 *Fundraising National Occupational Standards*
Source: *www.ukworkforcehub. org © 2009 Reproduced by kind permission.*

SUMMARY

In this chapter we have provided an overview of the most topical legal and ethical issues that fundraisers need to address and take account of in their work. While it is impossible to provide a comprehensive review of pertinent legislation, the most critical legal requirements have been described.

It is interesting to reflect how, over the past ten years, much additional regulation has been created with the express aim of controlling the activities of fundraisers. Fundraising is now one of the most highly regulated forms of marketing communication in the UK, rivalling financial service marketing for the attention of legislators. Yet is the fundraising sector really on a par with the financial service sector in respect of its history of abusing the public's trust?

We believe not. Much of the government interest in our sector has been driven by ill-informed speculation about what the public actually wants. Research outlined elsewhere in this text tells us that what the public want from our organizations, the sector presently delivers. The difficulty has actually lain in getting this message across. The public believe we spend far more on fundraising and administration than we actually do and they fundamentally fail to grasp the economics of donor recruitment activity (where most charities lose money in the short term). The failure of the sector to address these issues with a programme of education has meant that these misconceptions continue to be prevalent and continue to be the spur for additional government interest and concern.

A further way that public trust and confidence can be bolstered is by ensuring that as a profession we continue to practice our art while adhering to the highest ethical and professional standards. This chapter has also addressed the Institute of Fundraising Code of Conduct and important new documents such as the Fundraising Promise. It has also provided an overview of the new National Occupational Standards for Fundraising which should now be informing practice across the sector.

DISCUSSION QUESTIONS

1   Visit the website of the Association of Fundraising Professionals, the USA equivalent of the UK Institute of Fundraising (http://www.afpnet.org/). Access their Donor Bill of Rights. How does this compare with our Fundraising Promise?

2   Why is it important for fundraisers to understand what percentage of their fundraising income a charity derives from trading?

3   What rights does the Data Protection Act give to donors? What actions do fundraisers need to take as a consequence?

4   Your Board has decided that, since fundraising income has fallen this year, it will 'borrow' funds donated by donors for another purpose to cover the day-to-day costs of running the organization. How should you respond?

5   In your role as a head of fundraising you have been approached by an independent professional fundraiser who has worked as an agent for your organization in the past. She has told you that she has a donor willing to write a large cheque for £50,000 to support your organization. The professional fundraiser has indicated, however, that she would require a £5,000 finder's fee for soliciting this donation. How would you respond?

6   Many of the media in the UK have claimed that face-to-face street fundraising is unethical and is merely a form of social mugging. Do you believe this form of fundraising is ethical? Justify your response.

7 What statement must face-to-face (direct dialogue) fundraisers now make to potential donors before signing them up for a donation?

8 What are the three types of lottery relevant to fundraisers? What is meant by a society lottery? What advice would you give to a fundraiser looking to run one of these for the first time?

REFERENCES

Charity Commission (2007) *CC35 Trustees, Trading and Tax*, Charity Commission, London.

Direct Marketing Association (2008) 'Companies Ignoring TPS Face Prison Warns DMA', http://www.dma.org.uk/content/Nws-Article.asp?id=4258 (accessed 11 November 2008).

Institute of Fundraising (2007) *Everything You Need To Know About Raffles, Lotteries and Competitions*, Institute of Fundraising, London.

Index

Note: Page numbers in *italics* denote tables, those in **bold** denote figures or illustration

eBooks – at www.eBookstore.tandf.co.uk

A library at your fingertips!

eBooks are electronic versions of printed books. You can store them on your PC/laptop or browse them online.

They have advantages for anyone needing rapid access to a wide variety of published, copyright information.

eBooks can help your research by enabling you to bookmark chapters, annotate text and use instant searches to find specific words or phrases. Several eBook files would fit on even a small laptop or PDA.

NEW: Save money by eSubscribing: cheap, online access to any eBook for as long as you need it.

Annual subscription packages

We now offer special low-cost bulk subscriptions to packages of eBooks in certain subject areas. These are available to libraries or to individuals.

For more information please contact webmaster.ebooks@tandf.co.uk

We're continually developing the eBook concept, so keep up to date by visiting the website.

www.eBookstore.tandf.co.uk